THE LANGUAGE CRYSTAL

THE COMPLETE SOLUTION TO CIVILIZATION'S OLDEST PUZZLE

GRAMMAR PUBLISHING

Library Cataloging Data

Lyons, Lawrence William
The Language Crystal

New Age, Linguistics, Health, Nutrition,
Revelation, Numerology, Politics, Religion,
Science, Emotional Centering, Ecology

Contains Index

Illustrations and cover design
by Dee Dee Beene

Library of Congress Catalogue Number 87-80516

ISBN 0-942121-18-X

Copyright © 1988 by Lawrence William Lyons

First Edition, October 1988

Grammar Publishing
P.O. Box 2333
New York, New York 10009

(212) 353-2127

Manufactured in the United States of America

9 8 7 6 5 4 3 2 1

CONTENTS

This book is dedicated to the tree that was felled to make these pages. May the spirit of that tree help us to replenish the cycles of life upon this Planet Earth.

A NECESSARY FOREWORD

AND SOME BRIEF ACKNOWLEDGEMENTS

Why was the name of RA, Egypt's sun-god, the same as RA, the Hebrew word for "evil"? And why was MALUS, the Latin for "evil," the same as MALUS, the Latin for "apple tree"?

Literally thousands of puzzle pieces make up the whole of the Language Crystal. And when they are together, we can see what Adam and Eve ate in the garden to drive humanity into the strange adventure that we now call "history."

Thank you, Jana Klenburg, for seeing me through my escape from madness when the pains of teaching children and the trials of learning from ancient spirits were tearing me apart. My schizophrenic self and mystic self began to hear each other's voices. And thank you, Dimitri Boss for that crucial moment of guidance.

The friends who edited this work did so without payment, except for the fact that I listened. I always listened.

Mark Braunstein, a radical philosopher, advised me to develop a plot. Save "the Crystal Code" for a later book, he said, Yet a story already existed in the Language Crystal that none of us could have known when the writing of this book first began.

Thank you, Bob Pinkus, for worrying about our little planet. The love of animals you taught me has drawn me closer to the monkey inside myself.

And thank you, John, for introducing me to the magic of dyslexia. Your fighting spirit literally turned my linguistic visions inside out.

I will not disclose John's last name. For when he was my student, John was labeled "emotionally disturbed." And though I now know that dys-lexia ("bad-word") is not an illness, I have no idea how much that label disrupted young John's life.

5

After "they" told me to physically restrain young John, I quit the public schools and devoted my time to meditation. So, thanks to Howard Sadofsky who gave me my first set of *japa beads*.

Howard's family name, fits mystically into the bio-techno dilemma that we now face on Earth — "sad-of-sky." Yet, the Language Crystal carries a workable solution. Why did the sun-god and apple tree each get labeled "evil" by the Romans and the Jews? The mystery runs deep. And yet, the time is ripe for its resolution.

After years of intense meditation, I saw a "Crystal" on the ceiling. And within months, it came inside my head. I felt its light emitting words: "ram, lam, mal, mar." You can feel the basics in the language of the Angles.

Five more years of research and meditation, and then a linguistic implosion showed me how John's dyslexia could be entirely decoded.

The Language Crystal (as a vision) is available to anyone who meditates. The Language Crystal (as a book) was written and re-written to suit those loving readers who asked so many insightful questions and helped in so many other ways.

Thank you, Jo Willard for the early comments, Sharon Vollmuth for the savvy, Alex Pissaladis for the contrast, Rudy DeZan for historic background, Michael Mackay for the technical assist, Rick Cooper for exactness, Alan Levy for honestly caring, Alan Breslow for the drama, Gary Krasner for the color, Helen Stayna for the overview, George Moberg for the magic, Hrana Janto for the rays of sunshine, Alan Goldman for the chemistry, and Molly Ellowis for the sacred thread.

Most especially, thank you Barbara Lee (Brucha Leah) for being a blessing in times of weariness. Thank you, Barbara Lee Feldman for becoming my true B.LeeF, for doing the editing that brought this work down to Earth, and for teaching me the very deepest mysteries of humanity — found in the love of womankind.

Also, thank you Risa Honest, Susan Rothman, and Barry Mesh for introducing me to a view of "disease" that puts "vitality" in its proper perspective.

How can we de-mystify our words? By accepting our own nature — in the flesh.

How can we know that our flesh is sacred? We have the answer — in our words.

And so, the cycles seem unending. Yet, humanity now faces a crisis. For the language that began at the dawn of history (the language of technology) is threatening to obliterate the language of biology from the face of the Planet Earth.

"The Word," however, brings sense and sensuality together, for "the Word" is a person among all people. Surely, you have spoken to your words and you have listened to them speak to you. Still, "the Word" is in quotation marks herein because "the Word" is not always expressed in words. "The Word" is a living spirit among us, the foundation of any true democracy.

But let's not get ahead of our story.

In this book about the Language Crystal are some unusual shifts in tense, as if the future has already passed. This flaw is not intentional so much as it has resulted from in-tension.

"The Word" can pre-tend what is pre-sent, which seems like pretending in the present. Yet a future is gained in this union of poetry and logic on both sides of the brain. So-called "dyslexic" ways of seeing (when decoded by the Crystal) will make this new perspective clear.

The laws of biology relate to technology, as instinct to reason and poetry to grammar. Still, a dying river filled with paper promises needs more than one can write about. A force foretold as the Second Coming is "the Word" itself. And its re-turning has crystallized. So, to gather up our new momentum on this re-bound from the rim and limits of the uni-verse, let us speak again biologically to the life in the spirit on this Earth.

Thank you, mother, for teaching me to pray.

And thank you, father, for giving your life so that I might live mine.

Above, in the spaces where four lines approach a common point, you can "see" circles. And in an illusion related to the shape of your eye, the more you stare, the more vivid the circles become.

How much of what you "see" and "hear" is real? Does your mind compound illusions that begin in your body? And what role does your spirit play?

The Language Crystal answers these questions. And as you begin to use its messages, when you read between the lines of everday interactions, you will in fact call forth the next phase of reality. For the shape that things are in today can be changed by that creative power eternally beginning in "the Word."

CHAPTER 1

THE ANSWER IS CLEAR

"I going make a cown," said John, a seven-year-old student. I should have stopped to correct him. But there weren't any other teachers near by. And besides, I figured, I knew what John meant.

But in truth, I didn't know. John was "dyslexic." So, his vision and speech were dead set against the language I was being paid to teach him.

When the specialists consulted with me, one whispered that John had "brain damage." The other added that "pills might help." What the hell could pills do for brain damage? I didn't ask. In my position, it wouldn't matter. For they were the ranking "professionals."

Still, John and I had good times together. Once when sprawled on the classroom floor, John was tending to a cut-out cardboard boy that I had traced around him with orange chalk.

"I going make a cown," he said. That's right, "a cown," a funny, sad, dyslexic *cown*. I didn't know then, but that was my first clue to many hidden "dyslexic" meanings.

Wherever he may be today, I want to tell John, it wasn't his fault. He wasn't impaired or retarded. His dyslexic speech was a gift. And according to patterns in ancient scriptures, our broken words were everybody's fault.

You see, the linguistic specialists (who continue to drug young children like John) are in for a surprise. For dyslexia holds the answer to an age-old mystery. And John was speaking with an innate knowledge of the Language Crystal Code.

He confused the sound of "R" with the sound of "L." He wrote some words and letters backwards. And these were the keys to New Je-R-usa-L-em in answer to the ancient puzzle of "IS-RA-EL."

The cardboard figure was a teaching device in Special Education classes. And I (the teacher) was to encourage John (the student) to decorate the make-believe boy.

John paused — serious, even worrisome. He drew a smiling green mouth and said the word "cown" again making red stripes on the white cardboard pants. He added a bright red nose. And we laughed. John colored the shirt with a broken blue crayon leaving awkward spaces for what he called "the stahs."

Thank heaven, I didn't try to correct him! I didn't spell out C-L-O-W-N or enunciate the L to give him a cue or a clue. I had become a student of John's dyslexic mystery.

You need not be religious or even believe in the Bible to use this metaphor. But one question answered by the Language Crystal is: *What "evil" did Adam and Eve eat in the garden?* In answering this question the Crystal tells us how a language that was once whole got broken into pieces. Obviously, other species (whales and dolphins are examples) have their own languages. And human primates also have one.

In English *imp, wimp, pimp, simp, gimp, shrimp, blimp, skrimp, crimp, and primp* suggest irregular aspects. Are there any one syllable "imp" words that do not? Do some sounds carry built-in meanings?

Not all words containing similar sounds have similar meanings. But our every science begins by following **meaningful** patterns that already exist.

Why did the name of RA the sun-god become the Hebrew word for "evil," RA?

Was the ancient battle between the God of the Jews (EL) and the God of the Egyptians (RA) the result of some devilish "dyslexic" con-fusion between the sounds of R and L?

The Mystery

In John's world, a word could hide its L's.

He took a scrap of cardboard and made a hat for the figure, saying "cown" again, working in yellow and orange. His delicate hands pressed the blunted sissors. He cut four angular peaks on the golden hat. In a flash of childish zen, John caught my eye. We knew that we knew.

He had a *crown* of cardboard to place upon his cardboard *clown*. And through my silence, I had gained entry to the magic of "dyslexia" where backward spellings and R's and L's would unlock preconscious mysteries.

I didn't know then that using John's Code could solve the farm crisis of the USA. I had no idea that his mystical message could turn the idea of "war" into something brilliantly new.

Only in English (language of the Angles) can this puzzle be resolved. This scrap of scribbled paper from my early notes might give you a hint of how the puzzle could have driven me mad if I had let it. At first, the pieces made little sense. Yet, in time, the code was clear.

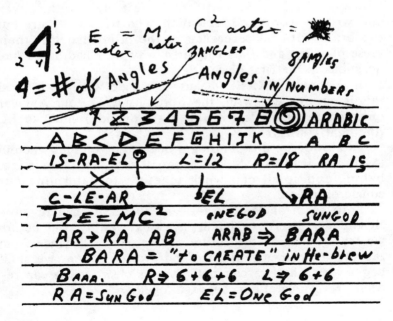

The R and L

The sounds of R and L are interchanged in Hebrew, Sanskrit, Egyptian, Oriental languages, and in Modern English. And only in written forms can the exchange of these sounds be codified.

So, John was brutalized by "teachers" and put on drugs by "specialists." Of course, the Celtic "Kathleen" was formed from the Greek "Katharine" by subtle R-L changes that took centuries. But the "specialists" ignored linguistic history.

In fact, we have gradations between the sounds we label R and L. But children who have less rigid ideas of how letters ought to be pronounced are often punished for their "con-fusion."

The symptoms of "R-L confusion" and "backward spelling" are not related to any diseases in the bio-, electro- or chemo-workings of the brain. These "symptoms" are natural patterns in sight and speech (as demonstrated in later chapters).

R-L confusions and reading backwards do more than link two functions in the brain. The right brain is credited with processing music and art, the left brain with spoken and written words. But scientists who tried to figure out the brain with no reference to the mind had lost their sense of spirit and thus forgotten why they had asked any questions in the first place.

In Hebrew, ISRAEL means "struggle with God." And this is our struggle with "the Word" itself. So, our Angular question becomes: Is RA (the light outside) equal to EL (the light within)?

To answer we are building a democracy of soul wherein logic and intuition have an equal vote, so knowledge, belief, and spirit can work together to determine our course of action.

Born again of Je-R-usa-L-em, the USA shall re-unite "Right" and "Left" to fulfill its global destiny. But before we try to imagine the future, let us gain a distance from the old historic meanings of our words. Then, we shall begin with what we commonly see as clear, so we can re-deem (re-evaluate) our language together.

CHAPTER 2

WHEN YOU WISH UPON . . .

NASA and CHERNOBYL are both prophetic words in the Bible, one from the Old Testament, one from the New. *NASA* is a Hebrew word that means "*to lift up*" נשׁא and "*to travel forth*" נסע . Both are transliterated as "NASA" — in English.

CHERNOBYL, in Ukranian means "*wormwood*." And in the Bible, "Wormwood" is the name of a star that poisons the waters of the Earth.

"And the third angel sounded, and there fell a great star from heaven, burning as it were a lamp [a power plant], and it fell upon a third part of the rivers, and upon the fountains of waters. And the name of the star was Wormwood [Chernobyl]: and the third part of the waters became wormwood. Many men died of the waters, because they were made bitter" (Rev. 8:10-11).

Why did NASA and Chernobyl falter around the same time? Was it President Reagan's Aquarian star sign? Or numerology? Or names? Or some power that would bring all these together?

CHERNO in Russian means "black." *BYL* is "a true story" or "the past." So, under Russian rule in the Ukraine, Cherno-byl meant "black past" as well as "wormwood." An unconscious mind-set had spelled disaster as invisible flames troubled our waters and we sought to fulfill the prophecies, "to lift up" and "to travel forth."

Let's add a few synchronous bits to our story. And remember that RA means "evil" in Hebrew while R equals 18 in the language of the Angles.

Just 18 days before Christmas 1987, Gorbachev came to the USA for nuclear reduction talks. At that 18th summit, it was agreed that no later than 18 months after the treaty went into effect, all shorter range missiles would be eliminated. And the number of warheads on each nation's deployed intermediate missiles would not exceed 180.

Christa, an astronaut with a symbolic name, died **18** miles down range from NASA's blast-off site. And Cherno-byl was enclosed by an **18**-mile safety zone. Also, Reagan sent **18** bombers to Tripoli in the raid that killed Qaddafi's **18**-month-old adopted daughter, Hana (*Time* 4/28/86). The same issue of *Time* that told of Qaddafi's daughter mentioned the **18** hostages held in Lebanon at that time. And Ronald Wilson Reagan (with 6 letters in each name) became a pivot of 18's as Je-R-usa-L-em went through its mystical transition.

Sounds heavy! But once the pattern is grasped, other "mystical" pieces begin to make sense.

These synchronous 18's fit an ancient cosmology of the kaballah. And kaballah is a Hebrew word for "to receive." For we are receiving the waves of wishes made in our ancient biological language, before the shame of Adam, before the murder of Abel, and before the fall of the tower of Babel.

Remember, it matters not if you "believe" in the Bible. The puzzle will work itself out for you even when you see it only as metaphor.

It is written that Jesus began teaching at the age of 12, spent **18** years in esoteric study, went back to public life at 30, died at 33, to arise on the 3rd day. And these numbers link Jesus to the crystallizing patterns of kabbalah.

On Friday, **18** minutes before sundown, candles are lit in a Jewish home. And the entire process of making matzoth takes **18** minutes to place the sacrificial unlevened bread on a kosher table. So, **18** gives that bread a mystical meaning.

What do lighting candles and baking bread have to do with nuclear explosions and missions in space? This question is answered at the core of the Language Crystal.

The numbers "eight" (*cha*) and "ten" (*i*) in Hebrew are also letters that spell the word for "life" (*chai*).

$$18 \quad = \quad \Pi^{,} \quad = \quad \text{life}$$

Why is the number **18** (life) connected to unleavened bread? Why was the bread of Hebrew tradition made a centerpiece of Christianity? Why in the Koran's **18**th sura does Muhammad deny the divinity of Jesus? And what does this have to do with Adam's curse or with nuclear disarmament?

Since 6 + 6 + 6 equals 18 and the Anti-Christ (666) is a division of "life" (18 in He-brew), the sacrifice of bread had mystically become "a host of eternal life." And if eternal life seems a long way from John's clown in its golden crown, bear in mind that our metaphor is continuous.

The Language Crystal is a reflection of our own biological reality. So it actually tells us what we need to know for our own future evolution.

The human animal is different from all other Earthly biology in that we have control of fire. And fire gives the Language Crystal its eternal light. So, the words "technology" and "techno" as used herein, refer to human use of fire (in any application), not to the power of other animals to technically change their environment. This is a most important distinction.

With fire, we have access to outer space. But with fire, we also have become irrational animals. For we needed the "un-conscious mind" to store our biological fear of the flame.

THE PLAN OF THIS BOOK

This book documents a miracle. Our personal names and names we give to places are abstractions. The numbers we use are also abstract. And the miracle is that these abstractions have encoded an ancient anatomical, biological law.

Face to face with the meanings of our words, we can re-deem our environment. And when we deem the change worthwhile, we can pass through the seam of our spiritual differences. Values that divide us can be re-valued. For when we wish, we can re-cycle our very own souls.

In our old view of the universe, the parts seemed parted by spaces. We thought of an atom as mostly space; within were particles. Between one atom and the next was space. And the spaces between atoms were joined to the space within all atoms.

This atomy picture also applies to spirit. For our most recent view is one in which force fields interact. The parts are not parted or trapped. They are fluid. And still they obey the law of the uni-verse, as we shall see.

Your personal anatomy (meaning "not-atomy") is not centered in its atoms. Your "center" joins the physical to the meta-physical. And forces of the physical work within powers of the meta-physical to determine the course of your an-atomy.

Not only is this true for humans (the animals capable of space travel), it applies to groups of humans who give names to their group spirits. The USA, Je-R-usa-L-em, and IS-RA-EL are more than physical entities. The Crystal tells us that we have invested spirit forces in the names that we have chosen for our groups.

But I did not set out to build these themes, I simply discovered them in the words.

In 1986, (when Chernobyl and NASA had their disasters) Moammar Qaddafi was in a "Holy War." **QADDAFI** in Arabic means "warrior." **MOAMMAR** means "long live." Had the bombs that killed his **18**-month-old child scattered the spirit of "Long Live the Warrior" into endless space?

Like the many rays of light that go to make up a holographic picture, our words can be refracted or refocused. Thus, an image can be changed.

The importance for us in being able to re-deem (re-consider) history is that redemptive thinking will help us re-shape our own biology. We can heal ourselves through our ability to communicate. And our feeling for words can re-create our an-atomy when our center is living in "the Word."

At this moment, thought waves we send forth are already shaping the symbols of the future.

How can we re-think our words?

My young friend John was, in fact, "emotionally disturbed." By this I mean that he was bothered by retarded teachers. To be true to himself, John had to live his poetry even though its logic was not true to school bells, clocks, overstuffed lunches, and "remedial" classrooms with locked doors.

John had *dyslexia*, meaning "bad-word" from the Greek (dys) and Latin (lex). He confused the sound of R with that of L, as dyslexics tend to do. But we shall see that in the R-L pattern is a "good-word," a message that is necessary to our survival on the Planet Earth.

John's way of seeing from the center outward led me to the mystic gateway of the Crystal City called "New Jerusalem." And here is where the 18 (life), fire in the bread, the concept of an-atomy (not atomy), and the rest of our Je-R-usa-L-em mystery fit together.

The word **Jeru-salem** literally means "possession of peace." And Je-R-usa-L-em shall crystallize for you in our Angular language (English) as soon the Code is clearly reflected in our new mind-set.

The R and L re-present 18 and 12 respectively in the English alphabet. And this is the base of our mystery. For the Crystal City of New Jerusalem can be envisioned only when Je-R-usa-L-em comes together organically in "life."

Imagine the wishes of every culture sent out to the stars. In every language, hopes are bounced off the ionosphere. Imagine all the languages that encode our desires forming into one crystallized thought, "possession of peace" (Jerusalem).

When you wish upon a star, not every wave that encodes your thought gets through. Some waves are bound to rebound off the ionosphere. And thought waves (electronic waves) that escape will travel on forever (merging into other waves). So, most important is the wish bouncing off the rim of the universe. And in this Space Age, "the Word" is, at long last, coming home.

For clarity sake, no hyphens in this text break a word for typographic convenience. Hyphens are ONLY at meaningful junctures. Also, no paragraphs run from one page to the next. And each page has a new heading.

The grammar goes beyond "he/she" constructs so that "he" and "she" are clearly distinguished. And "we," "us," and "our" refer either to all humanity, all spirits, or all biology, not to any nations, political groups, or so-called "races."

The word "earth" means dirt or sod while "Earth" refers to the planet. And other uses of capitalization are also meaningful.

Also, although pages may differ in length, no empty or half-empty pages are included with the text. Many layers of meaning are squeezed together — poetic and factual — so that their logic and poetry may be seen as one.

WARNING

Several of these introductory chapters may appear to be in an irrational juxtaposition, one to the other. And it may seem to the first-time reader that they need not be read in order. Yet, as you continue to read, the middle chapters depend on the ideas explored along the way. And a certain "feeling" will begin to emerge.

Once you have finished the book, you will still be living in your own metaphor, in your own space within the universe, and yet your feeling for all other spaces will have changed.

Since *meta* can mean "beyond" or "between," this metaphor between us is also beyond us. And since *phor* means "to carry," this metaphor of uni-verse is actually our "space-vehicle" in the spirit.

Meta-physically, words that de-scribe science must be born of con-science, the essence of balanced consciousness. The goal is control of fire-technology. And you will have the power to cast this magic "spell" — when you wish.

CHAPTER 3

THE METAPHOR OF ARMAGEDDON

Reagan, in English with Latin roots, meant "to rule." Reagan was President of the USA.

Regan (same roots) also meant "to rule." And Regan was White House chief of staff during the Iran-Contra affair. But Reagan (to rule) and Regan (to rule) came into conflict. And Regan ridiculed Reagan's astrology.

Shultz, German for "overseer," oversaw the State Department during the Iran-Contra scandal.

Hasenfus, "rabbit's foot" in German, was a good luck charm. But "Mr. Ruler" lost his "Mr. Rabbit's Foot" in Nicaragua while "Mr. Overseer" looked the other way. And in trying to re-deem his words, the "ruler" let his secret spells unravel.

Poindexter meant "a painer," the *poiner* who tortured people for the king, plus *dexter*, meaning "right." He was Mr. Ruler's National Security Adviser whose political bent multiplied pains in Iraq, Iran, Nicaragua, El Salvador, and in other nations, to guard against "the Left."

The Reagan-Regan rule was split; Howard *Baker* and James *Baker* were shifted to fill the gaps; and the Armageddon gang began to stumble. Jim *Bakker* of "Praise The Lord" (PTL) quit under pressure, having sinned with a woman from *Babylon* (NY), Jessica Hahn. And **Hahn** was a German name that meant "one who lives at the sign of the cock," symbolic of her escapade with Bakker, involving sex and drugged wine.

Yet bread and wine (foods of sacrifice) did not grow in the garden — a clue to the **18**'s as the pieces in our puzzle came together.

Dukakis meant "to lead," different from "to rule." But the 1988 decision is discussed in our final chapter where it is clear that "the President" was merely the present id of the People, turned inside out.

Israel in Hebrew means "struggle with God." **Palestine** means "migration." And **America** means "industrious" in Teutonic. So, this is our cosmic quest — migration among the stars — the real struggle of "going to Heaven."

Iraq has unclear roots; yet in Arabic **iraq** ("sweat") names an alcoholic drink. **Iran** ("upper class" in Sanskrit) has its root in "Aryan." And "White-Supremist" Aryans of the USA were ironically caught up in the karma of Iran. **El Salvador** means "the Savior." And *Nicaragua* (Old Nick in Agua) took on an Aquarian meaning in the time of Armageddon.

Bread and wine in sacrifice, class-struggles of history, the sweat of labor turned sour, a taste of vinegar on the cross — this puzzle of Je-R-usa-L-em where democracy is still in its infancy is solved within the Crystal.

David **Stockman**, keeper of White House *stocks*, resigned when the Budget crumbled. Larry **Speakes**, White House *Spokesman*, quit when Reagan's word was broken. And **Armacost** was Reagan's "point man on Iran," when trying to free the hostages. *Arm-a-cost* created an illusion of debate. Arms for hostages? "Never," said a Reagan-Regan rule.

CIA chief **Casey**'s name is from an Old English word meaning "watchful." But a brain tumor in the crisis cost him control of his *right* side. And as he wandered through the metaphor, Mr. Watchful never got a chance to testify. For he died on the first day of the Iran-Contra hearings (5/5/87).

George **Bush**'s name was "the sign of the wine merchant." He accepted the nomination for President on August 18th, 1988 when James **Baker** officially became his campaign manager. The signs of "bread and wine" were set. Yet, Dan **Quayle** was chosen as Bush's running mate. *Quayle* in Old English is a past tense of "to quench," (to decrease) for he immediately decreased the power of Bush. But let's not get ahead of our story.

Gary Hart twice quit the 1988 presidential race. And in combination with Donna Rice, he lived up to his name. **Rice** in Welsh meant "ardor, a burning passion." **Donna** meant "mistress" or "lady." And **Hart** was Old English for "a stag." So Hart went stag with the mistress of his burning passion.

"Mr. Stag" was photographed on a yacht named "Monkey Business" with "Ms. Burning Passion" on his knee. His family was back home in "Troublesome Gulch." These were real names of real places.

Hart applied for Federal matching funds on May **18**th, but filed too late (*NY Times* 7/3/87).

The Jim "Bakker" sex scandal with "Ms. Sign of the Cock" of "Babylon" would seem trite if not for his political support for Reagan. Bakker's name is a key in our sacrificial drama.

Armageddonists fueled not only covert actions directed by the President but also overt policy. And in the 7th year, after their mission faltered, Ronald (6) Wilson (6) Reagan (6) with six letters in each name began to talk peace (18 days before Christmas) with his reflective "Evil Empire."

Upheld by "Bakker," from being Governor in "the Sacrament" (Sacramento) to 666's reign at "Ranch in the Sky" (Rancho Del Cielo), Reagan had all the images of a bread sacrifice in our Christmas-to-Easter metaphor.

The ancient He-brew story of "something we ate in the garden" was pressing into our visions. We were about to re-solve the flesh-and-blood human sacrifice on the cross in our metaphor.

Less than one year after Bakker's follies were revealed, Jimmy Swaggart (who had swaggered forth to finger Bakker) caused the Armageddon gang to stagger again under the Whore, who was at another level the queen of 666's fiscal policies.

These codes from the language of angels spoke to the beast in everyman to drown his soul in the one crystal universe. Re-deemed in the Goddess unveiled, with children at her breast, we are no longer in competition with beastly-childish men.

"I want to be in that number."

In 1980, Reagan was elected on a day that the number 666 won the lottery in the nation's capital. But Reagan is only one of many other men labeled "666" to appear in history. We will get to the details of 666 (as a symbolic person) in a later chapter.

The Iraq-Iran war was pushed to the background in the media as a related tale unfolded. The names and numbers told the story. We have met few of the players. Here are some others in the cast.

Secord (retired military man), behind the gun-running flights from *El Salvador* (the Savior) to *Nicaragua* (Old Nick), had a name that meant "hard victory." His identity had been turned around in Nam. Later, when the Reagan-Regan rule was broken, the victory sign became a lie. Bank accounts and tax returns pinned the karma of "hard victory" to the Wheel of Bureaucractic Karma.

Singlaub, fund raiser for the Contras, preached with fervor, distracting the press from the secret illegal movement of funds. *Glauben* in German means "to believe." And *Sin-glaub* is "belief in Sion." For "Sin" was the Biblical name for that spot in the desert where Israel's children got lost.

Meese, the Attorney General who was supposed to prosecute the case, had a name meaning "mouse" in Flemish. He was so mousey about investigating the White House that he himself was investigated.

And Mr. Mouse went to the house of Mr. Watchful to have a beer after Mr. Rabbit's Foot was shot down. But Mr. Watchful, according to Mr. Mouse, knew nothing of the diverted funds.

Had Mr. Rule (Regan) or Mr. Rule (Reagan) told Mr. Mouse and Mr. Watchful to play nice? Did the Armageddon players think gun-and-cocaine smuggling between the Savior and Old Nick were means to the end that would fulfill the prophecies?

Was Mr. Meese just mousey enough to get the job and clever enough to snatch the forbidden cheese without getting bloodied in the trap?

The deeper meanings of these names often told a more complex truth than any press releases.

Obviously, Mr. Hasenfus did not play the role of a lost rabbit's foot all the days of his life. Also, Mr. Meese was not always a mouse. And Poindexter was a pleasure rather than a painer to many of his friends and associates.

It was only in the crystallizing years toward the end of Armageddon that these meanings surged in the puzzle of Je-R-usa-L-em. We were living in a time equal to ancient Biblical days.

To fill out the puzzle, I took *Nic-ar-agua* (an Indian name) to be a sign of Old Nick (the devil) on one side, and Aquarius (agua) on the other.

Giving voice to both its body and spirit, this definition of Nic-ar-agua, I imagined, would join "the Right" to "the Left" of Je-R-usa-L-em once the bridge was crossed to the New Millennium.

The drama yet to unfold in the Americas will set the tone for the future organic democracy that shall bring fruit trees to deserts, globally.

This blending of names with symbolic events is not new. **Moses** means "to draw out." Being drawn out of a river, he drew the oppressed out of captivity. **Jesus** literally means "savior." And all the stories of the Bible fit the multi-religious metaphor in our global naming game.

Living up to one's name can be an honor. But then again, our Casting Director had some sleezy roles for us to play for which no understudies or stand-ins could be hired.

So, Mr. Carl **Channell** was a money funnel in the Iranian-Contra deals. And TV channels got pro-Contra ads paid for by Mr. Channell's tax-exempt Endowment for the Preservation of Liberty. Mr. Funnel (Channell) bet that most minds in the USA were up for sale via persuasive TV ads.

After tax-evasion charges, Mr. Mouse signed up for a fund raiser (3/18/87) that would benefit the funds of Mr. Funnel. For Mr. Funnel was a friend of Mr. Mouse. Also, the story went that Mr. **Dole**, Senate Republican leader, was the official most "on the dole" of Mr. Funnel's funding channels.

The story that arms were being traded for hostages is questionable since Israel was selling weapons to Iran at the behest of the USA for more than two years **before** any Iranian-backed terrorists held any citizens of the USA as hostages.

No more than blame the devil for having a tail, can we blame the USA, Israelis, terrorists, sleeze mongers, or money-grubbing arms merchants. Each group played its part in our cosmic drama.

The CIA agent tortured to death had a name to suit his role as the Iran-gate sacrament. **Buckley** is derived from "bullock," an animal of sacrifice. "Thou shalt give the priests a young bullock as a sin offering" (Eze. 43-19). And as if by some evil miracle, William Buckley of the CIA was offered up, after being tortured to death.

And an Anglican envoy named **Waite**, who helped spread the lie that the USA would wait while he dealt for hostages with Kuwait, was taken hostage. His game had run its course. But when the hostage issue was no longer a phony question, the weapons continued to roll, winked at by "authorities."

If this story is depressing you, remember that it's being told to help us understand the metaphor that leads to a "possession of peace."

Poverty among us tells of a lack of balance that can be corrected as one of the thousands of miracles guided by the Language Crystal.

"Old Nick" edged "the Savior" out of the news while government terrorists crucified Salvadorians with the blessings of 666. Drugs from Nicaragua sold by U.S. operatives financed weapons shipments. And the **Christic** Institute exposed evidence that cocaine was being smuggled into the USA on planes affiliated with the CIA of Mr. Watchful.

You may recall the Christic Institute's work for Three Mile Island victims. But *Christic* in this opposition to 666 uncovered the cocaine that was shipped with federal funds as a new sacrificial drug. As with the bread and wine of old, our real offering was our own human flesh and blood.

CHAPTER 4

THE COSMIC MANDALA

The miracle of words and numbers that we shall explore herein dates back to the origins of man.

Obviously, man was civilized by woman. But "the son of man" was a stranger in Earthly terms.

Language, as a civilizing tool, was developed between mother and child at the breast. "M" (as in mama) is man's initial sound. And I suppose we are called "human" because we hum — "mmmmmm."

The shape of fossil jaws indicates that we had no vowel other than "long A" 50,000 years ago. But the date is not crucial. The order of development, however, puts R in a pivotal position. In Asiatic, *mjr* meant "man." In Indo-European, *mer-io* meant "young man," root of the English verb "to marry." Mars endured as the god of war. And Mr. (mister) is now a common title among men.

Our alphabet solves mister's mystery; for M-R is 13-18, the chapter and verse in Revelation where 666 denotes the beast. He murders for a homeland; war is his excuse. He spends a soldier's pay on whores, and rots his gut with booze.

Yet, R can bring a BEAST unto the BREAST. And R can make a FIEND our FRIEND. For R is equal to 18, an abstract "life," common to all men.

So, what has this to do with the Law of "the New Millennium"? The next five pages of facts will help to lay the groundwork for breaking the Crystal Code that unravels "the New Law."

RA was both the Egyptian sun god and Hebrew word for "evil." Thus, R marked a choice between good and evil. Some people claim this choice was "a sexual act" by Adam and Eve. But was it?

Our double meaning for RA relates to the "evil" **eaten** in the garden of Eden. So, to uncover the mystery between the R and 18, let us return to our Armageddon metaphor.

We left off our modern prophetic tale as the names and numbers in current events were beginning to fit with ancient patterns of Sacred Scripture.

"Breaking an **18-day** silence on the accident," Gorbachev said the Chernobyl disaster was used in an anti-Soviet campaign.[1] The reactor's core was **180 tons** of which at least **1.8 tons** were released.[2] "How much worse if there was an accident with one of the **18,000 nuclear missiles** now in place," said the president of International Physicians for the Prevention of Nuclear War.[3] A later headline in *the Times* announced, "**18,000 Chernobyl Evacuees** Given Checkups at Hospitals."[4]

The dreams that had possessed my soul were in fact coming true. But our monkey selves (monkey in this context means "humanity before the use of fire") were scared.

Under the curse of wormwood, evacuation was **36 hours** after the explosion.[5] And 36 (two 18's) means "rebirth" in kaballah.

And even those who cursed "the occult" (which simply means "hidden") were shouting from their pulpits about the hidden meanings.

Falwell, Robertson, Bakker, and Swaggart in the Armageddon camp said they awaited a Second Coming of "the Word," but denied the roots of their own mystery by preaching against kaballah.

And Reagan was influenced by numerology, as we shall see clearly in later chapters.

The USA spent **$1.8 million** over an **18-month** period to kill surplus cattle.[6] Remember the CIA agent, Buckley, had a name that meant "bullock." And the author of *Secret Warriors* said on CBS's *Night Watch* (4/11/88) Buckley had been held as a hostage in a Lebanese sector of Syria in a house designated by "the number 18." And 18 Hawks were traded for his flesh in a deal that failed.

(1) NY Times 5/15/86, (2) NY Times 6/12/86, (3) NY Times 5/14/86, (4) NY Times 6/4/86, (5) The Economist 5/17/86, (6) ABC 4/6/86

Coincidence?

This struggle of 18's tells of "life" in two very different realms — biology and technology.

The first official Soviet word about Chernobyl to Congress in the USA was, "Medical assistance is administered to those affected, **18** of whom are in serious condition."

The USA sold **18 AWACS** airborne warning and control systems) to Saudi Arabia. Were **18 bombers** over Libya also sent to keep the peace?

U.S. News (5/12/86) noted the Israeli attack on Syria's **18 missile batteries**. After Qadaffi said he'd retaliate, the USA put **18 jets** on stand-by in England (8/27/86). Israel shipped **18 Hawks** to Iran in the hostage deal. And North said **18** just happened to fit into the cargo carrier.

Delta's disasterous lift-off at Canaveral was at **6:18 P.M.** and had "a haunting similarity with Challenger."[1] Between the Delta and Challenger mishaps was a Titan failure **April 18th**, the first in **18 years**.[2] The French Ariane space rocket then failed in its **18th launching**, leaving "the West" without a space program, starting mid-1986.[3]

After the Challenger disaster, two plans were put forth by NASA, one with "a 12-month stand-down," the other with "an 18-month delay."[4] But only on October 3rd 1988 did Discovery's 4-day manned sapce probe prove itself.

A Sandoz chemical plant exploded in a town of **180,000 people**.[5] Its chemicals poisoned a Germanic symbol, the *Rhine* (the Clear) river.

The USA's trade deficit spurted to **$18 billion**, a record. A trade balance was hoped for, due to an **18-month** fall in the dollar.[6] Still, FDIC bailout funds for banks reached **$18 billion** at that time.[7] Oddly, after more failures, **$18 billion** was still in that fund in 1987.[8] But the movement of global markets was building for the Wall Street crash.

(1) NY Times 5/5/86, (2) U.S. News 4/28/86, (3) NY Times 6/1/86, (4) NY Times 4/15/86, (5) NY Times 11/12/86, (6) NY Times 8/31/86, (7) Time 7/28/86, (8) NY Times 1/12/87

In 1986, OPEC set oil at **$18** a barrel.[1] The price held into 1987, through Reagan's **18-month** "secret initiative," and beyond. Israel got **$1.8 billion** in military aid.[2] Reagan blocked the **$18 billion** Clean Water Act.[3] And then he had trouble passing water due to pro-state trouble as his Armageddon agenda slowly fell under the spell of Aquarius.

In early 1987, an over-ride of his veto on the Highway Bill took **$18 billion** from the Treasury.[4] Next, the House proposed a tax increase of **$18 billion**.[5] And then, both parties in both chambers drafted "similar budgets with about **$18 billion** in spending cuts."[6]

R equals 18; 18 signifies "life." I-ra-n and Is-ra-el each saw I-ra-q as an "enemy." So many pieces fit abstractly. Let's put the puzzle together.

Iraq produced **1.8 million** barrels a day.[7] OPEC put demand at **18 million** barrels a day.[8] The price was officially **$18 per barrel**. But OPEC's oil glut built for **18 months** and prices dropped.[9]

The first sure quote on funds in the Iran-Contra scandal was in *the Times of London*: "**$18 million** in arms sales" paid to a Swiss account held by an account in the Cayman Islands.[10]

The Iran-Contra story is spread out among other themes in this book. But please do not skip ahead, even if some of the numbers seem tedious at first.

The cumulative effect is more than statistical. Some seem mystical while others are consciously controlled. A Reagan-Gorbachev pact removed more than **1800 warheads** from their combined arsenals.[11] But an **18-month** Soviet test moratorium had ended without response from the USA.[12] — A strange numeric poetry.

(1) NY Times 11/5/86, (2) NY Times 11/15/86, (3) NY Times 11/14/86, (4) NBC 4/5/87, (5) NY Times 4/10/87, (6) U.S. News 4/6/87, (7) NY Times 11/9/86, (8) NY Times 11/22/86, (9) NY Times 10/19/86, (10) NY Times 12/6/86, (11) Time 2/23/87, (12) NY Times 4/22/87

The **Challenger** was hurled to heaven and exploded. And "Challenger" suddenly fit our metaphor as the challenge of "666" drove "Christa" to her death.

The next blast-off was to be February **18**, 1988. But Mr. **Aldrich** (old-rule) of NASA told of a delay until April Fool's Day, 1988.[1] And that fool flight was also delayed.

Much energy went to develop Delta 180.[2] Star Wars director, Gen. **Abrahamson** (pronounced *Abram-son*) said it did not break the ABM treaty. Others said it did and also missed its targets.

Another puzzle piece joins the names Abram and Abraham in our metaphor. But it will take a few more chapters to fit the clues together.

Reagan said (3/16/86), that more U.S. aid went to the Sandinistas in the first *18 months* than went to any other country. And his contra-diction began June **18th**, 1985 when he said, "America will never make concessions to terrorists." He had surgery for colon cancer on July **18th**, as weapons moved out through the USA's back door.

October **18th**, 1986, he signed Contra aid into law. Surgery for his enlarged prostate was later performed at the time he had a "routine **18**-month exam following up his colon cancer surgery."[3]

Reagan confessed, "For **18** months now, we have had under way a secret diplomatic initiative to Iran." His next news conference (11/19/86) began, "**Eighteen** months ago, as I said last Thursday, this Administration began a secret initiative to the Islamic Republic of Iran." Later in that same speech he added this odd linguistic twist: "We started about 18 months ago, *really*."

When you hear "really" tacked into a sentence, that sentence may lack its own reality. The truth was, "Project Democracy" began in 1983. And those 18 AWACS to the Saudis paid for covert shifts of aid to the Contras while the Iran money-swap was only in its planning stages.

(1) Time 3/16/87, (2) U.S. News 3/16/87, (3) NY Times 12/21/86

These facts fit when we re-think the metaphor of "Armageddon." Reagan said Israel initiated his "Iran initiative." But Reagan meant "rule." Iran, "upper classes." Palestine, "migration." Hakim, "wise man." And Israel, "struggle with God."

Shamir ("to guard") visited 666 on February **18th**, to guard against Reagan's charges. And the "Three Wise Men" came from Persia; so the metaphor continues (as we shall see).

The Federal trial of 17 arms merchants dealing with Iran fizzled when the USA itself was named as the **18th** dealer.[1]

The *N. Y. Times* (11/3/86) said, "Freed After 18 Months as Beirut Captive." But Jacobsen's name got smaller print than "**18 months**." Rev. Jenco was freed after **18 months**.[2] And Reagan knew of Rev. Wier's release but waited a full four days until September **18th** to tell the press.[3] Why?

The Contras have **18,000 troops**, said *the Christian Science Monitor*.[4] 5,000 in Nicaragua and 13,000 in Honduras," said *Times* official sources.[5] And in 1988, Haynes Johnson (*Wash. Post*) told of "18,000 Contras" on TV's *Washington Week* (*PBS* 1/24/88). The magic number went unchanged.

As stock prices fell, Reagan asked $270 million in Contra-aid, based on a projection for **18** months at $**180** million per year. Before the 18th summit, Reagan dropped his request. And starting 1988, came a new call for $36 million in aid with $3.6 million for arms.[6] The Democrats defeated Reagan's bid and made up a new package of **$1.8 million** monthly in aid.[7] One might ask if these financial decisions were made religiously or logically. The answer lies in our un-conscious.

Humanity had mystified itself and murdered its children to feed "the war machine." Why?

(1) NY Times 11/28/86, (2) C.S. Monitor 11/7/86, (3) NY Times 12/6/86, (4) C.S. Monitor 11/5/86, (5) NY Times 12/8/86, (6) NY Times 1/27/88, (7) NY Times 2/18/88

CHAPTER 5

A SURROGATE CHRISTMAS STORY

This is the story of Mary and her little baby. She had her child by the way of a miracle. And the magic came to her after a visit by "Mr. Star." In fact, she was introduced to "Mr. Star" by a man named "Christmas." But her baby was sold for an oath and illusions of gold as the spirit of Je-R-usa-L-em was traded on Wall Street.

As I read the names in "the case of Baby M," I shivered at the signs that were edging into the spirit of our universal allegory.

On Easter Sunday, Baby M was taken from **Mary**, her mother. Mary was indeed the biological mother of the child, but the medical con-ception was a biological de-ception, as some people ("higher up") said Mary was not "the real mother."

Mr. Stern was the father of Baby M. But **Stern** in German meant "*Star*." And so, it seemed that a force beyond us had penetrated Mary to bring about this Easter Sunday metaphor wherein Mary was compelled to surrender her miracle to "a higher power."

Stern was a Jew seeking to continue "his line." But his child was produced by coaxing the sperm of Mr. Star into the womb of Mary, a Roman Catholic. So, the Romans and the Jews decided to take their miraculous metaphor to court.

The man who arranged for the seed of Mr. Star to be planted in Mary's womb was *Noel*, meaning "Christmas." Noel Keane ran the Infertility Center and gave the world a brand new mystery. Was Baby M a prototype for some new "Super Race" or was she in line with her father's "Chosen People"?

The case of Baby M was only one small part in a great linguistic puzzle wherein gold brought by three Wise Men out of Iran to Beth-lehem was to reap its final interest on the Stock Exchange in a fragmented Je-R-usa-L-em.

We walk with Indian gurus plucking objects from thin air. We chant with African shamens healing the sick, raising the dead. And we conjure with warlocks of Europe as we are casting spells.

All these magicians and teachers in every land have but one mystical master — "the Word."

The Language Crystal reflects our wishes before thought was divided. It is the plan for a Crystal City coming out of the sky. It is in the truth you speak. And most of all, the Crystal is proof that we are vitally connected when we are living in "the Word," beyond any distant good or evil.

The Language Crystal has come to us in our time of utmost need. Our waters are poisoned, forests are dying, our cities cannot breathe. And we must grasp life's metaphor again, consciously.

Baby M was sired by the techno class of Mr. Star, a bio-chemist. And Baby M was born to the classless heritage of Mary whose occupation was the child's flesh and blood.

Were these two in competition? Would the techno mind-set eventually eat up all our children?

Mary Beth meant "House of Mary" in Hebrew. But the legal wife of Mr. Star was named **Elizabeth** which literally meant "God of the Oath." Thus, the metaphor got twisted when promises were broken and technical contracts went unsigned.

The Infertility Center had its main office in Dearborn. And Baby M was a dear-born miracle.

Elizabeth was a pediatrician and a Methodist who planned to raise the child as a Unitarian, lending a strange sense of method to the madness.

But as our strange German-Jew, Roman-Catholic, USA-Unitarian story with the trappings of a play about the Lamb of God unfolded, mother Mary hired a lawyer by the name of **Mr. Wolf.**

These were the real names of real people in a real courtroom drama. Yet, the words had been sent to us as disembodied teachers according to the law of the Language Crystal, a law that (when decoded) leads to health and happiness and peace.

Why don't we do it in the road?

To get her to the Infertility Center's branch in New York City, the prospective father of Baby M often extended his services as a good chauffeur to the prospective mother. And while driving her to the office where his sperm was to be placed into her vagina, they had several friendly chats.

So, why did Mr. Stern and Mary Beth stop short of "making love" in some motel along the way or in the back seat of his car? Why indeed!

Why did they think it much more moral to have Mr. Stern manipulate his stock into a dish to be scooped up by technicians so "a class of doctors" might impregnate Mary Beth in a Medical Manor?

Mr. Star and Mary did not make love. For they lived in a surrogate world that had substituted the Tree of Technology for the Tree of Life.

Our Judeo-Christian heritage had left us with a piece of bread and a glass of wine to celebrate the crucifixion of "the Word," a riddle that began in the garden, where no bread was baked nor wine fermented. And Beth-lehem means "House of bread" in Hebrew.

Remember, 18 was the number that made the bread into a sacrificial offering. Here is the heart of our transition, linking "life" in the flesh to fire-technology to "life" throughout eternity.

The judge called Mary "manipulative," ignoring the father's penile manipulations. And in another verbal offense, "surrogate" meaning "substitute" was used to denote Mary's role as if medical hands and legal heads had conceived the child while Mary was a "substitute" for human flesh and blood.

And "the Word" itself was broken in a mystery of the cross that transpired between Christmas and Easter (between the day that Mary met Noel and the Easter Sunday when she surrendered her child).

In 1988, Mary was granted visitation rights on ensuing Easters while "the Stars" got the child on Christmases. And Mr. Star seemed content that he had carried on the line of his Jewish family that had been murdered by the inhuman Nazis.

The phrase "surrogate mother" was used in academia to describe a cloth or wire-mesh manikin employed to test the emotions of monkeys who were deprived of their mothers. The **surrogate** was a **substitute** for a real, live, flesh-and-blood mother monkey. But Mary was not a wire-mesh "surrogate."

We had been driven mad by Wall Street's god, a mechanical bull inseminating the expanding Techno State. A surrogate father (the media-fabricated President) ruled the USA.

And the surrogate wars of the USA were made possible by a detachment of spirit. For the number of "life" had been co-opted. And Je-R-usa-L-em was the symbol of a broken global family.

So, the mother and father of Baby M carried our taboo against "biological individuality" to a new extreme. We were a race confused about the terms by which our money dreams could fulfill true-to-life biological needs. The word "economy" was used as a surrogate for "finance."

Baby M had her life made complex because her real mother and real father avoided each other's biology in conceiving her. Wall Street collapsed because it was not really listening to the cries of the surrounding eco-sphere.

The language invented for machines had driven us insane. Robots could not be programmed to make a wish or have a dream. The treaties written down to put an end to war would never be enough, for we needed human deeds to build the peace.

Our next step is to transform surrogate symbols (written words) into a form that can mate with our organic instincts.

But this will require that we stop eating "the Fruits of the Tree of Technology." Oh, I know it's a shocking suggestion. Still, let us examine the central revelation of the Crystal: the reason for all "the evils" on this planet.

What did we eat in the garden that caused our name for the sun god (RA) to be transformed into the Hebrew word for "evil" (RA)?

CHAPTER 6

RE-FRAMING

How are these stories about Baby M, the number 18, Reagan, Armageddon, and so on linked to dyslexia and to crystal visions of the future?

We can go beyond our fears as the Crystal Code reveals how humanity has already transformed most of Armageddon by the power of "the Word."

In order to act "responsibly," we need to take response-ability for human destiny. And after the puzzle is complete, we see how Armageddon fits into an even greater metaphor. Then, with the re-solution of our Armageddon fears will come plans for a global democracy.

Armageddon destroys "the world," but not the Earth. For "the world" is only a notion (as in "He lives in his own world") while the Earth is solid. So, with the old world gone, the globe will still be here. Plus, we will have a world of new ideas.

Because the message of the Language Crystal is so very different from what we are accustomed to, a synthesis of thought will be needed to make the Language Crystal's messages accessible.

To shake off some old ways of thinking, a few chapters of re-framing will be helpful. A new mode of thought (crystallization) will be set forth. And we will re-frame our pictures of the past in a new crystal light to gain the foresight for our new long journey into space.

The age we live in is "new." Still, the impact of its newness will not crystallize on Earth for a hundred years or so. These formative years are, nonetheless, part of "the post-historic era."

The time of Moses was a turning point when the ten commandments were written into our culture. After Jesus spoke, a new law was written. And then Muhammad's written law helped set the stage for a divided Je-R-usa-L-em, as it is today.

Democracy is as powerful and will have as great an effect on Space Age generations as Moses, Jesus, and Muhammad had upon the Age of History.

But no singular leader will emerge in this new transition. For the era that has just begun will be energized by "the People."

Democracy is built on a belief that "the Word" is living among us. And each of us has an equal right to share in the goodness of "the Word."

In this context, we will re-frame the past so that later we may examine the first "evil" that we ate as a biological-technological conflict.

Eating the original "evil" had an effect on our language. Then, due to our linguistic problems, we developed unnatural family difficulties. But the first "sin," although acted out between the sexes, was NOT of a sexual nature.

We have historically associated shame with sex but the use of drugs, for example, is a greater shame today. During history, our own biology was a thing to be ashamed of. And now that history is ending, technology threatens to destroy us.

Linguistic shifts between the bio and techno realms will build to "a language quake" to shake and topple old-world views. The details will take several chapters while re-framing our old beliefs. And those notions that attack the bio-spirit will be the first to go. The religion of "statistics" will fall the hardest and make the most noise. Still, the shattering of his-story will not hurt those who trust in "the Living Word."

The Crystal is not for Whites, Blacks, Jews, Christians, Buddhists, Arabs, Orientals, or any other static states of "statistical persons." It is for individuals. For Jeru-salem (possession of peace) cannot be carried foreward while still in an old-world political framework.

So, a "new people" will bring the new law into focus to update the laws of old. Jesus added to the law of Moses. Muhammad disputed Jesus. Now the framework of our new "new law" is democracy.

Framing a True Democracy

True democracy, a feeling for individual equality, has its seeds buried in the USA. But it is more than an ideal. The people's government will be a biological fact as each of us casts a vote with every item we consume. And our new biological reality will emerge from new linguistic patterns. But we must first undo the verbal illusions of the twentieth-century USA.

It took thousands of years in Africa and the Orient to evolve the biological and the cultural differences of our "separate races." Also, various "nationalities" in Europe grew distinct. And in the USA, Europeans were referred to as a special "class" by tricks in English usage that we shall explore in depth.

Africans and Orientals had as many differences among themselves as Europeans, a concept only now beginning to be re-framed in the USA with its mind-set poised for the next quantum leap.

Differences between Arabs and Jews were as much literary (Biblical) as they were real, since both groups had only one father (Abram-Abraham) with two different mothers (Hagar and Sarah).

Yet for nutrition, health care, and other bio issues to be re-evaluated, the bio-individual will emerge as the standard in the future USA.

The concept of "cause" works differently in the bio- than the techno-realm. The bio evolves; the techno, we invent. And bodily, we are not at all like auto parts. The mechanistic assumptions of "the virus theory," for example, will be re-examined herein along with many other linguistic bio-techno confusions.

Dyslexia was labeled a "disease" with no known physical cause. Still, we druged dyslexics. And even though most diseases have no singular cause, drugs are given just in case, along with a denial of the long-term genetic and evolutionary "side-effects." Within six years after crystallization, our New Millennium plans will become clear to the majority of people who read. And after that, our cultural dynamic will rapidly shift.

THREE LINGUISTIC PHASES

Throughout this work, the three linguistic phases referred to are simply (1) before humanity used fire, (2) history, and (3) the phase that we are just beginning now, the crystallization.

Phase One is our prehistoric species-specific language. Phase One sounds are as natural to us as any genetic pattern is to any species.

Phase Two is historic language with the words we invented to label artifacts.

Phase Three is a language form as distinct in thought forms from historic linguistic patterns as the Age of History is distinct from pre-historic times before the use of fire.

Since infants have no immediate need to read, dyslexic (Phase One) vision presents them with no problem. But linear one-way words, such as you are reading now, forced us away from natural globular vision as we put on blinders for the sake of Phase Two techno growth.

The one-way thought system of Phase Two fed our technology but stunted our ability to talk about our personal biological needs. Now, the Language Crystal goes beyond linear words. And once you know the Code, you are sure to find other levels of meaning within its puzzles until you synthesize Phases One and Two and begin to live within the expanded Phase Three context.

"Dyslexic vision" sees from the center outward. Such globular vision was normal in our prehistoric era. And globular vision is still natural in all infants born in civilization today. Yet in Phase Three, globular concepts are more than physical.

What does a citizen of New Jerusalem look like? The answer is global. No "typical" skin tone, hair texture, shape of eyes, nose, or mouth generates culture at our new level as "the races" are re-framed. The cycle of historic separations began with a linguistic break-up of "the race" into different "races." And with the completion of that cycle, a new linguistic form shall reunite us (if you see what I'm saying).

Our linguistic structures so influence the way we see things that many other biological issues such as nutrition and health will be seen more clearly once our new linguistic phase is entered. Our old world-view is already unraveling.

An environmental and food awareness is growing that will have a global effect as sweeping as the industrial revolution once had.

The tobacco industry will preceed the liquor industry in its demise. Anti-pollution and re-forestation will become big business.

Your biology will no longer be sacrificed to the growth of technology. But it will take several chapters to explain exactly why. We must first re-frame our relationship to fire.

Plans have already been made to cut the farm subsidies that sponsor meat and dairy industries world wide. The grain industry will be cut down to human proportions. And a re-structuring from the ground up will take place organically.

The process has already begun. We shall move organically back to the garden of Paradise as we move technologically into Heaven.

FIRE is the pivotal concept in the Language Crystal. For our use of fire marks the beginning of a distinctively human technology. And the loss of fire when the sun (RA) burns out would mean the utmost "evil" (RA) if we had no fire-technology to carry our culture to another solar system.

The struggle of RA (sun god) with RA (evil) is a metaphor that we shall extend until it comes full circle. And we shall raise our fear of fire to a new plateau, beyond the un-conscious level.

Part of the the Armageddon story in the Bible says that in the final days the number of people to be saved will be 144,000. And since 1000 is a symbol of "perfection," the 144 must be perfected. And our next chapter shows this old-world prophecy re-framed to fit into a global vision. The 144 is 12 times 12, representing Israel and the Arabs reunited after the implosion of Je-R-usa-L-em.

Squaring the Circle

And I saw four angels standing on four corners of the earth, holding the four winds of the earth, that the wind should not blow on the earth, nor on the sea, nor on any tree.

And I saw another angel ascending from the east, having the seal of the living God: And he cried with a loud voice to the four angels, to whom it was given to hurt the earth and the sea, saying, hurt not the earth, neither the sea, nor the trees, till I have sealed the servants of our God in their foreheads.

*And I heard the number of them which were sealed: And there were sealed **one hundred and forty four thousand*** (Revelation 7:2-4).

*　　　*　　　*

And he carried me away in the spirit to a great high mountain, and showed me that great city, the holy Jerusalem, descending out of heaven from God, having the glory of God: and her light was like a stone most precious, even like a jasper stone, clear as crystal (Revelation 21:10-11).

*　　　*　　　*

*And he measured the wall thereof, **a hundred and forty four cubits**, according to the measure of a man, that is, of an angel* (Revelation 21:17).

*　　　*　　　*

When the ancient prophecy of 12's is cojoined in fulfillment of the network of 18's, the wishes of the ages shall then come to pass.

And in the final chapters of this work we shall see the passages that reveal how we are to eat after Armageddon has come and gone.

Meanwhile, let us examine the phenomenon of Armageddon as it actually came to pass to fulfill the prophecies of the Phase Two mind-set.

40

CHAPTER 7

THE CRYSTAL DREAM

Ronald Wilson Reagan had become the high priest of finance. He chose the number 144 to redeem the USA in its money crisis because the Bible used 144 to symbolize the Crystal City of New Jerusalem.

"The President's plan reduces the deficit by $144 billion over three years," said his White House press release in the heat of the 1984 election campaign.[1] The key phrase was "reduces the deficit by $144 billion." But when the Senate shaved his plan by $3 billion, the resulting number no longer matched up with the prophecy. So Reagan called on his men for a new fiscal approach, which led to the "Gramm-Rudman-Hollings Act" two years later. The 144 was then locked in place automatically, but in a different arrangement.

The Gramm-Rudman Bill was to reduce the deficit to $144 billion.[2] The key phrase then read "to" $144 billion. His first attempt had been to reduce the deficit "by" $144 billion. The symbolism was most important to Reagan. But his religion of finances built on this hocus pocus was headed for a crash, triggered by 108.36, a Hindu symbol with its roots in the ancient Kaballah.

Amazingly, many lesser priests were also bedazzled by bands of all-consuming angels as Gramm-Rudman went into effect. And so, officials predicted that the merchandise trade deficit of the USA would drop below $144 billion.[3] Was it mere coincidence or some strange counterpoint of deficits contrived to mystify money changers in foreign lands?

(1) NY Times 5/3/84, (2) NY Times 1/28/86, (3) Business Week 1/20/86

Besides this chapter's "financial" implications, it will help to prove that "Armageddon" was not (and will not be) a total holocaust.

Many people believed that the world would end in a battle of Armageddon. Even with the ending of President Reagan's two terms, many waited for an Earthly battle of Christ against Anti-Christ, to thrill at the armed combat, guts, and gore.

These believers in Armageddon thought that the streets and byways of Israel would be filled with blood due to the slaughter of thousands of Jews at the hands Russian soldiers on horseback sweeping down "from the North," as in Bible prophecy.

Reagan believed in Armageddon. He said so when in office. In later chapters, direct quotes will tell how he felt about the great mystical battle to take place "in our time." But no battle that was all-encompassing occurred in the Reagan years.

Yet, a period of transition had indeed taken place. The time of Armageddon as prophecied in the Bible was indeed fulfilled. The battle had come to pass in "the Word" who is re-born and now living among us in the Second Coming.

After the 1987 Stock Market crash, plans to cut the deficit by $14.4 billion (*N.Y. Times* 10/30/87) included the tax increase that Reagan had laughed at. (Note this new version of 144.)

Do not assume that these numbers were based on any legitimate fiscal planning. The point is that fiscal (techno) plans and eco-nomic (bio) plans could not be aligned due to our original break in consciousness. Only in Phase Three linguistics can we clearly state this problem.

The failing eco-structure was papered over with lies. So-called Christian executives lied to make money. So-called Christian governments lied to protect "National Security." So-called Christian preachers" lied to keep their ministries.

Since they thought "the Word" was not yet among them, they conspired with words in general that fell short of fulfilling the Spirit.

Ronald (6) Wilson (6) Reagan (6), with six letters in each name, was a living symbol, a function of history. His name was an omen from both above and below. And his bid to force the 144 into finances was obvious. But no one person, group of citizens, or Illuminati could have planned the numeric "coincidences" recounted in this chapter.

When negotiating the reduction of nuclear arms in Europe with the USSR, Reagan had 144 old **Lance** missiles on the side of NATO to contend with.[1]

In our metaphor, a *lance* had pierced the side of Jesus. Hitler captured the "spear of Longinus" used at the crucifixion. And on the day the lance was recaptured (unbeknownst to Hitler), the Nazi leader committed suicide in BE-RL-IN.

Between the Challenger and Chernobyl disasters, a Berlin bombing caused Reagan to attack Qaddafi (meaning "warrior"). And in Berlin at that time, exactly 144 seats in the House of Representatives awaited West Germans to fill them.

Remember, all these signs fit into one ongoing metaphor when viewed from Phase Three.

A line of division between the Right and Left in global politics was the legacy of HIT-LER. And so, BE-RL-IN was the place of his suicide. We shall fit these R-L puzzle pieces (Hitler's role, the rebirth of IS-RA-EL, and the fragmentation of Je-R-usa-L-em) together in later chapters.

Ger-man means "strange manna" in He-brew. And in English this puzzle relates to the Christian sacrifice of bread and Adam's punishment of "earn your bread by the sweat of your brow."

In Reagan's 2nd term, the "largest Protestant denomination, the 14.4 million member Southern Baptist Convention" held its largest business meeting in history."[2] Many Baptists had turned to Fundamentalism. And the World Bank extended $14.4 billion in loans around the globe.[3]

---

(1) NY Times 4/17/87, (2) Time 6/24/85, (3) Dollars & Sense, June 1986

Christa (our symbolic "teacher in space") died on the day President 666 intended to deliver his State of the Union address which was to introduce the Gramm-Rudman $144 billion deficit plan. But "666" was stopped by the death of "Christa" as the Techno State threw in a monkey wrench.

News of Christa's death reached Ronald Wilson Reagan at 11:44 a.m.[1] A sign of good (Christ) and a sign of evil (666) had clashed. And in these persons named McAuliffe and Reagan were bits and pieces from each of us, reflected.

El Salvador (the Savior), a key in Armageddon prophecy, received $144 million in "economic aid" after 666 took office.[2] It was used militarily to suppress the people. But few questioned how the $144 million was reckoned financially.

Marcos (who symbolized "Mars & Co.") was slated to get $14.4 million in military supplies from the USA before he was deposed.[3] As military despot of the Philippines, "Mars & Co." parodied the fall of the Roman god of war.

Reagan's focus on New Jerusalem's magic number ran parallel to the symbols of struggle: Christa, Salvador, and Mars in fiery combat.

In response to Reagan's trade war on Japan, "the dollar fell below 144 yen, its lowest since World War II".[4] One holocaust image after the other fit with the mystic synchronicity.

Then the USA crumbled under Reagan-ethics. For Reagan-omics was only an Armageddonist ploy. The Gramm-Rudman deficit that started at $144 billion was to drop by $36 billion per year. So, its goal was to be $108 billion (six 18's) when Wall Street crashed. And a drop of 108.36 in the Dow on Friday had triggered the historic crash on Monday (as we shall see in detail later).

With all its magic, the Gramm-Rudman Bill did not save "the economy" one lump of coal.

(1) NY Times 1/29/86, (2) John Chancellor 2/18/82, (3) NY Times 2/21/86, (4) NY Times 4/10/87

Money was the topic in half the sermons of Jesus. He lost his temper over an exchange of one type of coin for another. And he was crucified between two thieves, one on his Right, one on his Left.

Chrysler (a mechanical Christ symbol in the USA) had died and been resurrected when it "gave the Government warrants to buy **14.4** million shares" of its common stock.[1]

Christopher Columbus ("Carrier of Christ, the Dove") was born in Genoa in **1446**. And Amerigo means "industrious." The spirit and the body of the Crystal City were prophecied in names.

As the Je-R-usa-L-em experiment approached its final days, corporate chief executive officers in the USA, in the 6th year of 666, were receiving an average of **$144,000** yearly,[2] a lot of "bread" when people were starving in the streets.

Yet, the story of Christ and bread has a bio-logical explanation hidden in the Crystal Code, an explanation that these numbers shall uncover.

Remember, this entire metaphor began with some strange "thing" that we ate in the garden of Eden. We then fragmented our Phase One linguistics and began Phase Two, the Age of History with all its confusion of bio-techno double meanings.

With industry's decline in Phase Two USA, one casualty was **Flint**, Michigan, a once booming auto-making town named for "a fire-maker." The population of *Flint* was **144,000**,[3] and "industry" was in the throes of a symbolic death.

Under Reagan's plan to slaughter cattle to keep prices up "the government paid **144** dairy owners more than $1 million each."[4] (And a CIA "bullock," William Buckley, was sacrificed.)

So, the images were clear for those who saw the whole Earth from on high. For the Book told of a crystal river where food was to YIELD, in every true sense of the word and spirit.

(1) Time 3/24/86, (2) NY Times 12/28/86, (3) Time 2/16/87, (4) Vegetarian Times, March 1987

In 666's final year, the number of Palestineans killed in the streets by Israeli soldiers reached 144 on the date of 4/18[1] as Armageddon raged on.

Also on 4/18, the volume of stocks traded on Wall Street was 144,650 which indicated "man" (6) at "a turning point" (5) in kaballah.

We had reached our turning point symbolically, but the killings, tortures, starvation, and the general inhumanity in every nation would not stop until the basic cause of our Phase Two division was brought to the surface of human consciousness and literally turned around.

Between the attempts of 666 to get 144 into the financial records, USX (X is a Greek symbol for "Christ," as in X-mas) had faltered as the company (formerly U.S. Steel) earned only $144 milllion for the year.[2]

After Chernobyl spilled out its wormwood in the second quarter of 1986, the stock market's median return for that quarter fell to 14.4%.[3]

The House of Representatives put forth a $144.5 billion anti-drug bill in 1986.[4] (Again, 5 was a turning point.) With the USA's support, Peru disabled 144 drug-running airstrips within the year.[5] Also the USA cut Bolivia's $14.4 million in economic aid due to Bolivian drug traffic.[6] Note how much aid under 666 was in terms of 144.

Both "bad guys and good guys" were shipping drugs to pay for war supplies. In the time of Nam, a flood of heroin swept the USA. In its Contra war, the USA had a "cocaine" backwash along its military supply lines.

The *Christic* Institute's drug case against the Iran-Contra gang called Miami witnesses as 144,000 pounds of cocaine flowed in "a river of drugs" to Miami, according to the Highway Patrol.[7]

(1) NY Times 4/19/88, (2) NY Times 10/29/86, (3) Forbes 8/25/86, (4) NY Times 9/11/86, (5) Newsweek 8/18/86, (6) Time 7/28/86, (7) CBS "60 Minutes" 4/26/87

Note that the word "kaballah" has several spellings in modern usage: cabbala, cabala, qabbalah, and more. Two spellings, kaballah and kabbalah, are found in this text, and they are used interchangeably.

These multi-level coincidences were the beginning of our new Information Age where we ourselves were information, to be decoded spiritually.

The difference between a Phase Two (historic) and a Phase Three (crystallized) mind-set is that Phase Two is mainly two-sided. From our first use of fire to the start of the New Millennium, we had a singular direction. Our goal was to find a way to leave the Earth before its eventual death.

So during Phase Two, our mind-set was suited to the development of technology, but not beneficial to individual biology.

When primates first intuited that the Earth was going to die, we could not be mentally free until we had proven that space travel was possible. Now we know that we can save the human race. But the techno spin-off along the way has left us with some nasty habits that are now ruining our health and the environment.

Our cosmic knowledge rests in every cell of every organism. Yet, the dividing line in terms of language is where our pre-conscious answers are reflected in these archetypical stories.

Our early dreams of flying were aimed at space. And we experimented on ourselves. We burned our "witches" in one era and radiated "patients" in the next to test the limits of human flesh — to prepare for space travel. We con-fused the bio and techno realms. The bio has consciousness, techno has none. And we did not know that we were being ruled by our own fear of fire.

During the week before Gorbachev reached Je-R-usa-L-em's center, the Dow industrial average fell a total of **144** points (*NY Times* 12/6/87).

And as we fed our habits of consumption, a few weapons were made obsolete. But the international munitions industry was busily designing cheaper, more deadly weapons that the smaller nations and non-nations could afford. Ozone depletion, acid rain, and global deforestation were upon us. Our global problems were two-sided no longer.

Reagan also said his final-year deficit would be $144 billion.[1] Not reduced "by" or "to" in 1987, but "at" $144 billion at the end of 1988.

But no one asked why the President's fixation with the number of New Jerusalem (144,000) was so important to Reaganomics.

Beginning his second term, Reagan cut the $14.4 billion farm surplus payments.[2] The chain of karma can hardly be tied together by logic. Yet this does relate to the question of Israel and threats of Armageddon.

When we read of Israel, the facts may be about the man (called Jacob) or the nation now built on soil that has had many names, yet the reference is to the concept IS-RA-EL. Is the light outside you (RA) equal to the light inside you (EL)? This is Israel, a personal "struggle with God."

And in a poetic converse, Ronald Wilson Reagan (the man) was not 666 (the number). Mr. Reagan was not "the beast" any more than the man named Israel was the symbol "Israel." When the entire metaphor crystallizes, we each identify with all its parts inside our individual souls.

As Reagan toyed with his $144 billion deficit, a shekel, the Israeli coin, had 14.4 grams of silver.[3] And inflation in Israel hit 180%.

His first year, Reagan cut the Education budget to $14.4 billion.[4] He bragged of "a drop in the poverty rate to 14.4%" beginning his second term.[5] And we used the word "economy" (a bio concept) in place of "finance" (a techno tool). For we had yet to encompass our linguistic crystallization.

Neither the Masons, the Trilateral Commission, Kissinger, Rockefeller, nor all the media combined could have arranged to have Chase Manhattan earn $144 million in the quarter of 1986 when Christa was offered up on our phantasmagorial mandala.[6]

(1) NY Times 2/27/85, (2) NY Times 12/4/84, (3) NY Times 11/17/85, (4) USA Today 6/14/83, (5) NY Times 9/5/85, (6) NY Times 4/15/86

And Armageddon needed a plague; so AIDS was it. But "AIDS" was not a single disease. Still, the linguistic confusion about the so-called "AIDS virus" was so great that three chapters herein are devoted to re-framing it.

In a report in *Penthouse* (1985), Gary Null wrote: "Only one out of 144 gay men with normal immune responses became infected with HTLV-III," the so-called "AIDS virus."

Null was responding to the media hype that said AIDS was "always deadly." In fact, many people with various AIDS viruses had no symptoms while others with symptoms had no virus.

A Phase Two mind-set can easily believe two contradictory bits of information at once.

(1) You catch a cold sitting in wet clothing; (2) a cold is caused by a virus. Or (1) a virus-caused cancer is cured by radiation; (2) cancer is caused by radiation. In a limited sense each of these is true. Yet only a greater framework holds the whole truth of wholeness.

Rather than "the germ theory" (getting sick) and "immunity" (getting well), coming chapters will address "loss of vitality" and "restoration of vitality" — the true biological continuum.

The drugging theory of "Now you're sick" and "Now you're well" said pills added to health. And the trick was that lowering vitality (an effect of drugs) could supress symptoms.

"Cigarette immunity" is a good example: A child reacts to cigarette smoke with a healthy cough, a sign of vitality; but once the habit is in place, smokers often cease to cough. Do smokers grow immune? No. Heavy smokers do not react due to lowered vitality. But then, as with any type of drug, the accumulation eventually brings on a crisis.

What did medical drugging have to do with the Armageddon prophecy? With the future financial picture in Je-R-usa-L-em? What did the atmosphere of medical drugging have to do with our ability as a society to see things clearly?

The Crystallized Person

In Phase Two, science and religion were separate. But in Phase Three, individual health is obviously a work of the body and spirit together. And the many coincidences of names and numbers herein tell of a new linguistic union.

Prehistoric evolution brought forth a species that was physically able to adapt to the use of fire. And suddenly, humanity was on Earth. How did this transition come to pass?

Your body is real. Your spirit is real. And your mind is a channel that allows these two to hear and heal each other. So the Language Crystal is a function of the Universal Mind. Examine the evidence, and draw your own conclusion.

Christa's death came on the day President 666 intended to deliver his State of the Union address to introduce a $144 billion deficit plan. In the 6th year of Aquarius (1986), the date that Christa McAuliffe was offered up was the *18th of Shevat* on the Hebrew calendar. For in Hebrew, *Shevat* means "water carrier," the Aquarian symbol. Was Reagan influenced by his birth sign, Aquarius?

Six others died. Yet our teacher in space took with her the children's imaginations. Christa was both aviator and avatar, in awe of life.

And equally symbollic was **Ellison Onizuka** on the Challenger crew. In Japanese, *Oni* is "devil" while *zuka* means "to dwell." Also, his "Western" name *Ellison* encodes "Son of God," *El* (the Hebrew word for "God") plus *son* in the language of the Angles. So, Elli-son Oni-zuka means "Son of God where the Devil Dwells."

Since NASA means "to lift up" and "to travel forth," the "Challenger" tragedy indicated that a challenge to God was uncalled for. Our Heavenly and Earthly goals were to be re-aligned.

This is our "struggle with God" (Israel) as we search our souls, and our "migration" (Palestine) as we seek the proper use of land. For we are one indeed as New Jerusalem unfolds in "industry" (America).

We are a vision in the Language Crystal.

CHAPTER 8

VISION

This chapter introduces the Language Crystal Code. Herein, we explore the globular (dyslexic) mind-set to show how spelling backwards and confusing R's with L's are traits that written languages use to reflect on visionary thoughts.

Remember that my young "dyslexic" friend, John, had envisioned a *crown* on the head of a *clown*. His R-L confusions and backward spellings gave him a vision that transformed a cardboard-crayon image into a COWN, a crowned clown thing-king.

The memory of how young John was emotionally tortured and physically drugged by the Public School system to try to force him to renounce his own mystical knowledge haunts me to this day.

I escorted John to the "quiet room" on Tuesdays to see his speech therapist. Usually, the room was reserved for children with temper tantrums. But John was a well mannered boy whose only crime was a predisposition for linguistic brilliance.

Here are the beginnings of the Language Crystal Code as inspired by "dys-lexia."

D-PROGRAMING

In the fourth place of our alphabet, the D is derived from an ancient triangle. Named for the delta (a triangle), D has acquired a curve that makes it transitional in space and time.

When placed before a verb in English, D becomes that verb's undoing. COMPOSE becomes DECOMPOSE. Yet, D at the end of the verb adds to it a sense of completion. COMPOSE becomes COMPOSED.

The symbols A and B (representing sounds more primitive than D) are analyzed in a later chapter. This arrangement tells a story rather than simply defining the letters.

The Metaphor Evolves

ANGER is the word we use for our internalized and therefore delayed responses to DANGER. Other animals deal immediately with danger. They have no anger separate from danger since such anger would only waste their energy.

Because we have a word for it, we can hold onto anger. We can store any named emotion and pass it on in print. Our loves, hates, joys, and fears were packaged up and handed down so we could see the riddle of our history.

As Phase One animals, we had only present time emotions; anger and danger came together. But with the use of fire, time was divided. We built on the past to reach the future. When a stick acquired a name, its form (sticking out from trees) and its use (sticking into things) were made a part of it. And a complex sense of "tense" took possession of the sounds we made. Visions, past and future, were reflective of each other as we encoded our techno mistakes in history. EVIL was a DEVIL. And DEVIL spelled backwards was LIVED.

The Crystal reflects universal knowledge where "good" and "evil" are terms of survival. And since what is good for one species may spell danger for the next, humans have a mystery in their words, a secret of "the human condition" where fire is at the center of all our unconscious fears.

In Phase Three, the necessary evils of the Techno State will be under constant conscious bio-supervision as ANGERS are dispelled by ANGELS living in the spirit. And the awful fear of fire that pulled our strings during Phase Two will be turned into a conscious control to check the techno-fire-pollution now threatening us all.

In fullest consciousness, division is a dying vision. And the sound of "die" conjures up the "I divided." For the universe is born of "the Word."

In the Crystal Code: A = 1, B = 2, C = light.

D = spatial triangulation. And G = gravity.

This is not a strictly "logical" progression, for the letters represent an ever evolving union of viewpoints.

Seeing

In prehistoric times, we each stood on our own horizon, grounded by earth, breathing in heaven, seeing spheres of Earth and Sky pressed into each other. Later, one-way visions of the techno mind-set flattened out these realms as history blocked the view from our personal bio-centers outward.

To analyze the written word, we must know how we see. The eye inverts pictures on its retina. The images are "backwards" and "upside down." And the mind turns these around. At least, our modern mind-set finds a re-inversion necessary.

But we had no need to invert our prehistoric view when swinging in the trees. Before fire, logic and feeling were one. Before we had the un-conscious aspect of the mind, danger and anger were dealt with by a logic-feeling. Written words were needed later, only after the flame had turned us into super-natural creatures.

Compare the Greek alphabet before the Roman invasions to the Greek alphabet afterward.

| Early Greek | Δ | ℥ | 𐤂 | Δ | ℈ | Y | I | 目 | ⊗ | ⋝ | Ж |
| Later Greek | ρ | Β | Γ | Δ | Ε | Υ | I | 目 | ⊗ | ⟨ | Κ |

| Early Greek | ν | ᴍ | и | Ⅎ | ο | ᒋ | ᴎ | ϙ | ⊿ | ⟋ | Τ |
| Later Greek | Ⅼ | ᴍ | И | Ⅎ | ο | Γ | Μ | ϙ | Ρ | ⟨ | Τ |

Due to the Greek's inverted state of emotions, caused by the Roman invasions, almost every letter became its own mirror image.

We could diagnose "brain damage" in the Greek population due to such "dyslexia." But it is not a damaged brain that reverses letters, it is the mind as directed by the spirit.

Clues to this difference between brain and mind are found in experiments done on visual inversion. Subjects who saw upside down and backwards while wearing special glasses, after several days began to see right side up, still wearing the glasses.

Then, when they were seeing "normally" with the glasses on, the glasses were removed. And with the glasses off, they still saw things upside down and backwards. The mind was doing the inverting, not the brain.

And after a few days without the glasses, their vision re-turned to "normal." No physical changes had been made in their eyesight.

Since we cannot quantify the mind, some people challenge its existence. But "vision" goes beyond "eyesight" in the sense that a spirit lives beyond the body. And the mind joins these two.

Is the light outside (RA) equal to the light within (EL)? This is our "struggle with God."

The fire of the sun gives us the light needed for biological functions. The fires we create give us hope that we may lift up (NASA) and travel forth eternally. Fire is the turning point of sub-stance, the pivot of under-standing.

Yet the Bible mentions light, not fire, in the story of Creation. For our un-conscious (created by the Phase Two mind-set) pushed fire away from light. And we began our second linguistic phase with the ability to store our fear of fire. Next, our Phase Three vision will carry us beyond the realm of un-conscious fear.

"The fall" of Adam was a grave sin. For in our metaphor, "gravity" binds us to the Earth. And the chosen son of Abraham was Isaac, whose name means "laughter." So, the metaphor continues as a laugh brings "levity" to lift us up.

When we decode FALL backwards in the language of the Angles, we get LAFF. And "laugh" has a silent G that signifies "gravity."

The following is a list of pivotal words in our cosmic biological-spiritual evolution.

TIME spelled backwards is EMIT

Science accepts the fact that we are looking back in TIME when we see a star. The light that stars EMIT takes TIME to travel to us.

LIVE spelled backwards is EVIL

We realized the sun would die. So, in order to LIVE an eternal life in the body of our race, we ate of a tree that contained the knowledge of EVIL, to feed the techno mind-set.

DNA spelled backwards is AND

DNA is the substance that encodes our physical humanity. AND is the symbol that pictures "union" abstractly. DNA AND DNA AND DNA tells of both particle and wave, information in formation, our spirits and bodies, understanding sub-stance.

LOVE in reflection begins EVOLUTION

As primitives, we figured out that the sun was going to die. And we invented science, disturbing every Earthly relationship. Our sacrifice to science would buy for us eternal life. And the LOVE of EVOLUTION would cause us to create another home in Heaven upon another planet that we shall again call "Earth."

PART spelled backwards is TRAP

Believe you are a PART of this world, and you fall into a TRAP called "matter." Believe you are APART from this world, and you fall into a TRAP where you do not matter at all.

Since the Language of the Angles encodes a web of thought waves (radio waves) that bounce back from the ionosphere, all history's hopes sent toward Heaven began to form a Crystal City.

So, these reflective spellings usually occur at the highest levels of abstraction. Still, R-L (18-12) interchanges also can be quite instructive in everyday affairs.

It may seem flippant or abstractly poetic to speak of AND as a reflection of DNA. Yet AND is an ancient Greek word for "man" (as in ANDROID, an artificial man) while a plus sign attached to a sphere symbolizes woman (womb-man).

ANDRO-GYNE means "half-male, half-female." And since women built words to socialize men, "man" and "human" got confused. So, in English, we say, "If a monkey wants to eat, *he* can climb a tree," Our assumption is that the one spoken of is male, for the goal of his-story was to make men humane, in their reflective thoughts. And the basis of all life, DNA, is androgynous.

Those who begin to write in any language have a tendency to reverse some letters for such is the nature of vision. And, of course, our history is no more than a collection of visions.

In the Armageddon metaphor, three days before Christmas (1987), a video of Terry *Anderson* sent a message to the USA from his captors in Lebanon. The plight of the hostages seemed hopeless. And neither Israelis nor Palestineans were willing to talk to each other "officially."

Anderson means "son of the manly one." The metaphor of "host and hostage" was calling us back to our "struggle with God" (Israel) which will be our inter-planetary "migration" (Palestine) after we have mended Je-R-usa-L-em, amen.

And the amended budget that President 666 got that year was cut by $33.3 billion, approved in the Senate at dawn, 3:30 a.m. as Anderson's image arrived in Washington, 3 days before Christmas.

No one fact has meaning in itself. Yet with a crystal mind-set, we accept instinctual values and no single aspect is separate from the rest.

In Phase Three, biology is cherished. Still, technology is not devalued. These two are made to work together. So, the innate poetry of language becomes a new frame for numbers. And "statistics" are applied properly to techno data, but not to biological individuals.

Of course, not all words can be spelled backwards. PART and TRAP are like two lovers, each is a part of the other, even when apart.

LOVE and EVOLution have a self-consuming sense of inner-outer spirals, ever overlapping.

Scientists or religionists who insisted that Life was created at some point in time failed to see "Life" in its meta-physical SEED.

Light re-seeds Life. But light cannot recede. In truth, we each EMIT our own TIME.

SEED completes SEE. And WAS reflects SAW as we draw the uni-verse in upon itself.

The human spirit is simply light seeing and seeding itself — intention expressed in tension, information stated in formation. And light is the initial wave on which the Spirit writes.

This write-light complex is the Word of the Lord seeking (see-king) everlasting Life in the Wife. Humanity can travel forth forever only with respect for "the Word" and "the Life" married in truth.

At his-story's end, Palestinians and Israelis were in fact fighting out the remaining karma of a man with two names (Abram-Abraham) who traveled from Ur (light) to Haran (enlightenment) and had two wives ("wandering" and "princess") and two sons ("God listens" and "laughter").

On Earth, we had many worlds: an old world, a new world, a third world, a fashion world; yet in truth, one universe holds these together, for the wer-alt (old man) is contained within the uni-verse (one mother tongue). And TIME is a pattern we each EMIT from inner light manifest in "matter" (Latin for "mother").

Our words grow from darkened roots toward the light. Watch a baby learn to speak; it reads your thoughts before it knows a word. Then, with this basis in telepathy, the child imagines meaning.

With the surity of a monkey swinging from limb to limb, we can reach our destiny by being true to words, devoted to "the Word" itself, and to the Mother of "the Word," which is "the Life" of the uni-verse.

Syllabary, a link between writing in pictures and writing in letters, uses forms drawn from nature that are then codified to re-present sounds.

Early Greek settlers on Cyprus, under Asiatic influence, adopted syllabary. And inscriptions from the 4th century B.C. show links between particles (letters) and waves (words) in a dedication to Demeter, first in letters, then in syllabary.

The Greek language (by that time standardized) was written left to right. The syllabary went from right to left. And the struggle between cultures on Cyprus to capture each other's minds was like that between the Egyptians and Hebrews. Syllabary on Cyprus lost the battle. But we find a kind of abstract syllabary in the mirrorings of English letters and English words.

The Hebrew concept of a totally abstract God had a great influence on Hebrew writing. A sense of absolute concentration made monotheism the most important factor in our historic development. For history's goal was to get humanity to Heaven, but we were not always aware of the metaphor that we were living through.

Prehistoric folk did not see their actions with the perspective of anthropologists. Likewise, as we lived through history, we did not fully see "the Word" as our new environment.

The symbols of IS-RA-EL, HIT-LER, BE-RL-IN, Je-R-usa-L-em, and so on will eventually be viewed as having influenced history's individuals in the same way that plush vegetation, climatic shifts, and wild predators once influenced the individuals of our prehistoric era.

While scientists and zen masters build the formulas of light on either particle or wave, the syllables that carry their meanings are both wave (word) and particle (letter), so to speak.

And so, even scientific thought is made up of new arrangements of instinctual impulses. The goal of science is human survival. And science that is not true to that goal is not true science.

R (18) before a verb multiplies its action, as in "redo" and "remake." Behind a verb, as in "doer" and "maker," the R personifies its POW-R. And we use R to seal the family. Mother, father, sister, and brother end in R. But uncle, aunt (each with "un"), niece and nephew (subtly, "nice" and "few") do not.

We will see how final R's had a masculine tone in tailor over seamstress, doctor over nurse. Yet, MS. removed the R from MRS. to mark the end of his-story. The final S served a feminine function. "Miss" was held so dear by "Mister" for the part his-story said she was "missing." S united HE with SHE, our vessel of plurality (S).

Mother and father have deity's sign (TH) at center as] ought begets Theology in an unending tapestry.

EVE was tempted by the "devil" who said she could "live" for EVE-R. The sun-god RA got eaten up in an altered (altared) state. And the He-brew God put F-I-R-E beyond conscious F-E-A-R.

We can explain some patterns bio-linguistically. C and L, for example, are occulsives, formed as the upper and lower surfaces of the vocal cavity meet. Thus, many CL words strongly imply "closure."

Clasp, cling, clutch, clench, clamp, clump, clot, and a cluster of sounds such as clap, click, clack, clank, and clang clinch the claim that CL indicates in more instances than not a cleaving together. Still, a clash occurs since "cleave" means its own opposite, and we can clip things apart as well as clip them to each other.

Clamm means "bondage." And clan, claque, class, and clique are each social groups that show how forming into units can be devisive of the whole.

The fact that R and L are transitional and linked by numerology as well places them at the center of our oral-aural interchange and suggests that they may be central to the aura of the Language Crystal. As we shall see, the R-L pivot is central to the essence of life itself.

Words are oral (spoken), aural (heard), and come through us on an aura (light). Words center in a human viewpoint. Numbers are abstract. And we can co-ordinate these two by using letters that are units, encoded from the sounds we make.

Philo-sophy (love of wisdom) reflects phylo-geny (generations unto humanity) as the Greek *philo* (love) relates to *phylo* (tribe). The link between *phylo* (love) and *phylo* (tribe) is one form of LOVE that churns EVOLUTION. This pattern is seen as AND (joining in the abstract) turns into DNA (joined in evolution), an *gyne* (female) yields to *genesis* (being born).

"Generation" as an abstract word is applied to electricity as well as to humanity. For genesis is a union of energy and matter. Still, men can be made gentle in spiritual genesis.

"Gentiles" (meaning "nations") were called *goi* (meaning "nations," but implying "foreign") in Hebrew. Still, Israel became a nation (goi) among nations (gentiles) and others. So, Je-R-usa-L-em will not be re-solved by the mere knowledge of words. The goal of our mother language is not an endless exercise of the mind.

It cannot be emphasized enough that the mind can be emptied. Meditation is a way to clear this passage between body and spirit. The mind need not be filled with words or images. It can be empty, at rest, relaxed. With practice, you can clear your mind of all its thoughts.

These opening chapters of abstract patterns are here to set free the energy in your mind. With the crystallization, you can use that energy anew.

In a "consumer society," meditation is feared. For an empty mind has the ability to weigh all new modes of thought that enter.

"Consumers" are trained to fear loss. "Losing your mind" seems horrible. NOW, by setting your mind loose for a moment, you have the ability to choose freely the very next thing you will do, and this is the essence of free will.

LIVE and LOVE are our eternals.

FIRE and FEAR are our limits.

The bio-logical limits of our New Age goal (Peace on Earth) are encoded in this numeric poetry.

F = 6. L = 12. R = 18. I = ego.

E = energy. O = the void. A = realization.

These are the keys to a basic dietary law that shuns the "evil" we ate in the garden.

An innate poetry says that we FEAR to FEEL for deep reasons that relate to FIRE. This pre-consciously encoded message takes various forms in other languages (in later chapters). Yet, the Crystal (built on 18, 12, and 6) holds the key in the language of the Angles.

LIVE turned around is EVIL. LOVE reflected begins EVOLUTION. Our spirit, literally on fire, is thus contained. So, the Crystal shatters where L-I-F-E meets F-I-R-E, where ego (I) gets energy (E), where 18 consumes 12 and 6.

Science and religion, logic and intuition, the "political Right" and "political Left" each exist in every one of us. Yet, we appear divided against each other because each is divided in ourselves by a fear that we have yet to consciously share. And the reason for this is bio-logical.

To avoid endless wars, nuclear destruction, or drowning in pollution and disease, we must begin with a simple (yet encoded) law that will govern our decisions in Phase Three. Since "the Word" is generated in "the Life," our body chemistry must effect our ability to know the truth. And so, our Crystal Law relates to body chemistry.

The **plan** of the **planet** in its **plants** has already evolved via photo-synthesis. The Language Crystal is simply the means of focusing universal light to keep us in harmony with this biological plan. Thus we have poetic symetry.

REFER spelled backwards is REFER

The word R-E-F-E-R in Crystal is central to our growth, reflective in both force and form.

F (6) at the center of REFER is surrounded by E (energy). And around this energy is R (18).

By using the concept 18-Energy-6-Energy-18, we gain access to the Crystal. REFER your intuition to logic, REFER your logic to intuition, and "the plan" will be yours, personally.

The body and spirit engage each other by way of the mind — our referral system. So, the Code is super-natural and super-scientific. Its law allows innate light to be taken directly from food so as to govern our bio-techno interactions.

The dietary law encoded in the Crystal is based on universal principles of life. But since a Phase Two mind-set can believe two contradictory views at once, some people may at first "dis-believe" what they see documented. Due to this fact, you may find what could appear to be an excess of documentation in this book.

Prisoners are jabbed to get signed confessions. Children are jerked around if they do not recite a written pledge. Humanity's "external mind," its written culture, has enslaved us. Yet by facing our madness, we can be personally free.

For crystallized belief is the basis for pure intelligence, our guide to sure action.

We have our bio-intelligence and centuries of techno intelligence. We are very intelligent, but not very integrated.

For example, $E = MC^2$ is supposed to mean that Energy = Mass times the speed of light squared (C). But what could the word "times" mean in such a linear equation?

With 2 and 4 as abstract numbers, 2 "times" 2 is 4. But mass "times" the speed of light squared is more like figs "times" solar systems. Mass and light, unlike 2 and 4, are things that we feel and see. "The speed of light squared" is therefore not an abstraction; it is a powerhouse working in each of us as we each EMIT TIME.

In the physical realm, life is organized by light and disorganized by fire. Yet, the nouns "fire" and "light" were originally verbs. In linguistic evolution, we feel that we have "to drink" before we find "a drink." First we learn "to walk," then we go for "a walk," then we construct "a concrete walk." And in the beginning is the word.

"To fire" means "to send forth."
"To light" means "to land."

REFER encodes an abstract process. REFLEX requires less intellect, being less reflective. Thus, REFLEX expands into 18-E-6-12-E-24, to flex as stars within black holes.

The under-standing that becomes sub-stance is ever traveling, unraveling the uni-verse. Thus it is spirit that creates. You know from experience that you can change your inner sense of time. You have a light within that weaves waves of reality. And the Crystal Code reveals how to feed that light, not only with spirit under-standing but with bio sub-stance (with living food).

Rather than pre-tend to knowledge (as in Phase Two), let us look to the patterns we have written and ex-tend our vision to see what "evil" we ate from the Tree of Knowledge.

*   *   *

John's speech therapist sat him on her lap, held him to her breast, and in their weekly sessions, offered him candy, gold stars, and affection that seemed almost genuine. Gradually, her favors were linked to demands for linguistic conformity. First he complied with nervousness, later he overturned the furniture. Then the "specialist" insisted that I restrain my young friend. When I refused, I was reprimanded and switched to another class.

So, my profession of faith in John was said to be unprofessional.

When I was a child, I played with sounds and made up nonsense words. But when I went to school, I failed. I wrote and wrote the words, but could not learn by rote. The rules made no sense. I never learned the patterns that my childish mind was led to think of as some kind of divine conspiracy. I never learned "the rules of spelling."

After average work in high school, I got a job adjusting the books at the local electric company. Still, I shunned the reading of literature.

Next, U.S. Air Force testing ranked me in the top 99th percentile for language specialists and packed me off to Syracuse University for intensive study in the Czech language. My aptitude was high and yet my grades were poor. Still, the Air Force sent me to Germany where I soon learned to speak in a native Bavarian dialect, quite fluently.

My linguistic apitude was in speech. Yet, I learned by ear, not by writing.

After the Air Force, I got near straight A's in college majoring in child psychology. Even with my "spelling handicap," I gave the valedictory speech at Manhattan Community College (1969). Top grades on written tests came for giving teachers back their spoken wisdom — misspelled, but written in their own patterns of speech. Reading my answers must have seemed a bit like hearing themselves talk.

On occasion, I talked myself into higher grades by telling teachers of the faulty wording on their written exams.

Later, young John led me through the door of my "spelling errors" into casting spells. Since then, I have learned to under-stand my sub-stance by following "the Word" within "the Life."

"Being saved" (*sozo* in the Bible) means "to be sound" in its Greek origins. "Being sound" means "being heathly" in English. And in the Crystal "to HEAR" is "to HEAL" as evolving words vibrate in a sound mind and body. So, tuned to light, we touch the roots of sound to create beyond what is seen — to bring to life our vision.

CHAPTER 9

SCIENCE MEETS THE REAL WORLD

In both popular articles and prestigeous journals, science tagged its most awesome discoveries with the number 18. And this "scientific" trend told of what was lacking from the techno scene.

For, mystically, 18 signifies "life."

- The Big Bang - 18 billion years ago

- Life on Earth Begins - 1800 million years ago

- Mammals Evolve - 180 million years ago

- The Missing Link - 18 million years ago

- Humanity Appears - 1.8 million years ago

- Table of Elements Built - on 18 electrons

- Quarks Discovered - in 18 types

- Star Wars Planned - at 18 miles in space

- Human Sacrifice (the draft) - at 18 years

This was a composit of the belief system called "science" around the year of 1980 (1800 + 180). What could have caused such a coincidence? Had our collective mental picture of reality been drawn through some mystical realm?

As plants grow toward the light, our plans are even now reaching a plane beyond this planet. "Life" (18 in kaballah) is born again in "scientific" thought. And th-ought itself is sought to join the body and the spirit, as it ought. So, life of the spirit (no-thing) will be seen as the common denominator of every-body.

THE BIG BANG
HAPPENED
18 BILLION YEARS AGO

Masculine scientists agreed: all had begun with a great Big Bang 18 billion years ago. At least, this was the most published patriarchal perception in the year of 1980 (1800 + 180). But female scientists who knew of a desire for everlasting rebirth went unquoted in the scientific journals.

"We live 18 billion years from the Big Bang," said Timothy Ferris (in his book *The Red Limit*) to explain the origins of the universe.

"The universe is believed to have begun in a big bang, a cosmic explosion some 18 billion years ago," wrote science editor, Edward Edelson on Albert Einstein's 100th birthday (*NY Daily News* 3/14/79).

An "instant" 18 billion years ago was the moment of creation according to the science writer Leon Lederman (*Discover*, Oct. 1981).

As with the number of Contras and the time it took to die of AIDS, the press had latched onto a number, passed it around, and become quite sure of its authenticity.

The Big Bang sounded suspiciously like a bit of old-world macho imagery. "Hard facts" had yet to be tempered by tiny waves of itsy bitsy feminine bangs that ever ripple from Creation's foreplay unto its afterglow. So, by 1980, most of the male-dominated scientific field had agreed that "the Great Big Banger" was an 18-billion-year-old man, living on borrowed "western standard time."

Before our primitive auras were diminished, RA, external light, and EL, internal light, were seen as one eternal light. And Ein-stein (a dyslexic) also SAW what WAS quite primitively.

The fault in Einstein's formulas was that they gave time no sense of direction. Remember, TIME is a force field you EMIT so that you may live your life. Every mother knows that giving birth is not reversible. The life of a growing seed may be ended by fire or drought, but a seed cannot grow backwards in time. Only the anti-spiritual fear of death makes people see time backwards.

LIFE ON EARTH
BEGAN
1800 MILLION YEARS AGO

"When the major episode of deposition of banded iron formations [in the oceans] ended some 1800 million years ago, the trend toward increasing oxygen concentration became irreversible." In essence, this scholarly quote (*Scientific American* Sept. 1978) said that Life on Earth had begun to breathe and increase 1800 million years ago.

Was it pure chance that equated "life" to 18 in He-brew? Was it pure chance that two reptiles had once dreamed of flight together in order that they might engender ancestors of the dove?

Iron formations in the oceans began to breathe. And FE, our symbol for iron, is at the heart of male-fe-male cycles that breed animal magnetism in the blood.

We shall see (in coming chapters) how the Jews, Christians, and Moslems built on rituals of blood. Circumcision and crucifixion altered the male's electro-magnetic balance of iron (FE).

His bloodshed, a techno copy of the fe-male's, caused male mind-sets to surrender to machines and put him at variance to iron. Ironically, men went to war to test their metal, got repelled by each other and attracted to mechanical cycles. Thus, he built allegiance to the Techno State.

Eve was born from the side of Adam. Cain killed Abel. And Abraham took to circumcision while at odds with his wife. The wife of Moses insisted he perform the blood rite on his son. And the Church, born out of the side of Jesus, became his bride in blood after Mary had told her son that a wedding was lacking wine. Civilized rituals had wed men to machines, and men had become machinelike.

Minds devoted to machines in our current flow are not so different from formations in the oceans 1800 million years ago. But we are not increasing oxygen concentrations on the Planet Earth. We have reached the end of our cycle of historic techno expansion. It's time to concentrate again.

ALL MATTER
IS COMPOSED OF
18 QUARKS

Subatomic physicists describe the 18 quarks that compose the universe. We have six kinds of quarks (up, down, strange, charmed, top, and bottom). And each comes in three colors.

All ordinary matter is made of "up" and "down" quarks. Quarks called "charmed" and "strange" allow for creation and destruction of form. And quarks named "top" and "bottom" give the system permanence. Naming the creative and destructive quarks "charmed" and "strange" had put physics in the realm of metaphysics. The names were only a joke at first, but 6 quarks in 3 colors each does bring to mind an image of the Creator evolving from one light within our cosmic crystal.

EARTH'S INNER CORE
BEGINS
1800 MILES BELOW SEA LEVEL

The Earth's inner core is blazing, almost as hot as the surface of the sun. Yet, the outer edge of that core is only 1800 miles below sea level.[1]

Hear the explosions of EL (our inner light) in HELL (our inner fire). Language is the science that contains all other sciences.

RA, both "evil" and "sun-god," burns in the core of our Mother Earth. And AR-SON is ours in a world driven mad by its own hidden fear.

"God's struggle" is in every molecule. With RA and EL divided in our minds, God listens to the stones of Palestine. And we are con-fused.

Helen in Greek means both "torch" and "light." And HELL contains EL in Earth's inner night.

Add "eternal life" and suddenly a fire-science begun by monkeys fits into the cosmic plan that language is designed to scan. We are still working through our plan to get to Heaven.

(1) Geo magazine, April 1983

EARTHLY CHEMISTRY
IS BUILT
ON CONFIGURATIONS
OF 18 ELECTRONS

The chemistry we live by relates intimately to the number 18. The Periodic Table of Elements (next two pages) shows that each of the "long rows" has exactly 18 elements. These three "long rows" are central to changes in alchemy, for they contain the transitional metals.

Furthermore, each of the elements in the long rows tends to bond with other elements so as to achieve configurations of 18 shared electrons.

For example, chromium has 2 electrons in its first shell, 8 in its second, and 8 in its third. And all elements in the long rows have totals of 18 in their first three shells.

Chromium has an additional 6 electrons in its fourth shell. So, when chromium bonds with other elements, it seeks 12 more electrons to form a new configuration of 18 electrons. And so on.

Molybdenum is a good example. Moly blooms with the standard 2 plus 8 plus 8 electrons, a total of 18 in three shells. In its fourth shell, molybdenum has 18 more electrons. Yet with 6 electrons in its fifth shell, molybdenum will still seek 12 more electrons when bonding. It would seem that the mechanics of the universe were alive with 18's.

As scientists, we use the fire-spirit to give life everlasting to our beast. Elect to think and you connect with this flow of electrons. Think and you reflect eclectically. For electric rays, erecting force fields from RA (the light outside) to EL (the light within) span th-ought.
    You are "The Elect," when you choose the Living Word that is absolutely REAL, a double-spiral that is RA entwined with EL.

THE CRYSTAL STRUCTURES

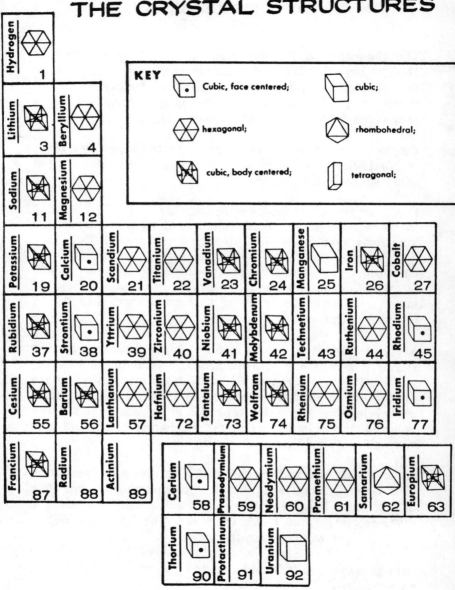

KEY

Cubic, face centered; cubic;

hexagonal; rhombohedral;

cubic, body centered; tetragonal;

Element	Number
Hydrogen	1
Lithium	3
Beryllium	4
Sodium	11
Magnesium	12
Potassium	19
Calcium	20
Scandium	21
Titanium	22
Vanadium	23
Chromium	24
Manganese	25
Iron	26
Cobalt	27
Rubidium	37
Strontium	38
Yttrium	39
Zirconium	40
Niobium	41
Molybdenum	42
Technetium	43
Ruthenium	44
Rhodium	45
Cesium	55
Barium	56
Lanthanum	57
Hafnium	72
Tantalum	73
Wolfram	74
Rhenium	75
Osmium	76
Iridium	77
Francium	87
Radium	88
Actinium	89
Cerium	58
Praseodymium	59
Neodymium	60
Promethium	61
Samarium	62
Europium	63
Thorium	90
Protactinium	91
Uranium	92

OF THE ELEMENTS

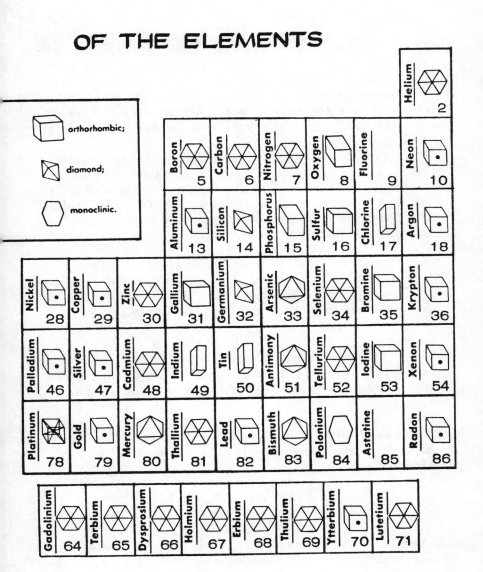

Before we had this "knowledge" of the elements, we had 12-hour clocks, 12-inch rulers, 12 months in each year, and circles with 360 degrees.

Fahrenheit placed **180°** between the freezing and boiling of water. And the patterns were built on sixes because the mystery meets its mastery in DNA whose strructure is crystalline.

In the Middle Ages, "mystery plays" about the life, death, and resurection of Christ were named for "master" craftsmen who were also actors. The "mystery" and its "mastery" are one. And so, the closer one comes to genius, the closer one is to generating universal patterns. For the universe is a mother to all worlds.

A BLACK HOLE EXISTS
180,000 LIGHT-YEARS FROM EARTH
This x-ray source has been seen by the University of Michigan and the Inter-American Observatory.[1]

A BLACK HOLE EXISTS
180 QUADRILLION MILES FROM EARTH
Another black hole is at our own galactic center, 180 quadrillion miles from Earth, "devouring matter at a rapid rate."[2]

These early discoveries in the newly opening field of black holes fit our mystical pattern. But many of us were still afraid of the dark.

STAR WARS BEGINS
18 MILES
INTO OUTER SPACE
"The American weapon is small [18 feet long] and advanced." This front page item on Star Wars was in *the New York Times* (8/21/85). It went on to say that "According to military officials, the fighter soars at an altitude of 18 miles, then fires its missile" — anti-life with the signs of life.

(1) Discover, March 1983, (2) Time 6/3/85

CRYSTAL GROUPING
OF THE ELEMENTS
FAVORS SPACING BY 18

The periodic table of elements is organized with the inert gases in the extreme right column. And the numbers of these gases are: helium (2), neon (10), argon (18), krypton (36), xenon (54), and radon (86). Argon, krypton, and xenon (having 18, 36, and 54 electrons respectively) each have crystal structures called "cubic, face centered."

This pattern of leaps by 18 is not unbroken, yet it does dominate the periodic table more than any other. The only diamond structures, silicon (14) and germanium (32), also display a separation by 18 spaces. As with linguistic structures, we find the greatest power at 18. The 18th letter (R) makes "make" a "maker" and allows us to "remake."

Also only after the first 18 elements have been laid out in line with their various groups (see table), do the three long rows of 18 each fall into place. This pattern is then broken, yet begins again at 72 (18 x 4), hafnium.

Out of the 91 natural elements, 86 have crystal structures. And then, of course, humanity has created its own synthetic elements. But neither synthetic nor natural groups (like techno and bio words) adhere 100% to crystal patterns.

Those who are human in form and anti-human in spirit cannot know that they lack humanity. Those who are most human stretch their own definition to include "outsiders." So, the Christ forgives the Anti-Christ. If either body or spirit had absolute rule, both would cease to evolve. And LOVE would not be reflected in its own EVOL-ution.

I know that I require chaos in order to create. "No chaos" equals "no choice." And so, I always expect to find the anti-human in the guise of humanity. Even disease has been my teacher. And yet, the key to techno survival is to know and allow ourselves to feel our bio limits. And for this, we need the Crystal Code. For in the Code is inscribed the highest Law of Creation.

THE SEVEN CONTINENTS
BEGAN THEIR FORMATION
180 MILLION YEARS AGO

THE MIOCENE EPOCH
BEGAN 18 MILLION YEARS AGO

In his book "Genesis," John Gribbin points out that "many mammals, including apes, spread out during the Miocene, and species diversified," beginning 18 million years ago.

THE FIRST ICE AGE
BEGAN
1.8 MILLION YEARS AGO

Various scientific methods dating geological time tell us that the Pleistocene Era, the Ice Age, began 1.8 million years ago. And these many cycles affected the social evolution of primates.

THE ICE AGE BEFORE THE MOST RECENT
BEGAN 180,000 YEARS AGO
(NY Times 11/29/87)

THE PEAK OF THE MOST RECENT ICE AGE
WAS REACHED 18,000 YEARS AGO

And many scientists are concerned that the next Ice Age could begin its process of crystallization sometime after 1999. But through trial and error, we know how to change climates on Earth. All we need is the bio-spirit to begin soon enough.

THE MAMMALS EMERGED
180 MILLION YEARS AGO

"A primeval mammal, yet unnamed, lived 180 million years ago, when the Age of Dinosaurs was young; it was the forerunner of mammals that flourished only after dinosaurs died out." This story in *Discover* (Nov. 1981) said that mammals came into being at the time of the formation of the continents.

The steps toward "humanity" were by 18's, like quantum leaps in the Table of Elements. And the way to everlasting life via inter-galactic travel is also marked by crystals in the Code.

THE CONCEPT OF MAMMALS
CRYSTALLIZED
180 MILLION YEARS AGO

The echidna anteater (close to a reptile) having a distinctly mammalian brain, emerged 180 million years ago as the first mammal in the philo-genetic line, says *Omni* magazine (Sept. 1985).

18-MILLION-YEAR-OLD FOSSILS
LINK HUMANS AND APES

They "were about 18 inches high at the shoulders when on all four limbs," said Richard Leakey about the bones of 18-million-year-old apelike being, Proconsul africanus (*NY Times* 8/23/84).

THE FIRST "MAN"
WAS CONCEIVED
1.8 MILLION YEARS AGO

A "Kenyan skull from about 1.8 million years ago" was captioned: "In a sense, it is the first human" (*Science*, April 1984). Also, 1.8-million-year-old stone tools were found belonging to Homo habilis in Siberia (*U.S. News* 9/1/86). And in Tanzania, a 1.8-million-year-old skull and partial skeleton showed habilis in a primitive state (*NY Times* 5/21/87).

JE-R-USA-L-EM GIVES IS-RA-EL
AND STAR WARS
$1.8 BILLION EACH

Reagan sent the standard USA's yearly **$1.8 billion** military aid package to Israel[1]. That year, Israel set February 18th as its deadline to get out of Lebanon. And a 666-man contingent of U.N. troops was ordered to keep the peace.[2] Coincidence?

Reagan's Armageddon plan had already maneuvered federally funded scientists into Star Wars backed by **$1.8 billion** in start-up funding.[3]

Was it financial wizzardry? It certainly was not universal poetry?

(1) NY Post 1/31/85, (2) Star Ledger 1/31/85, (3) U.S. News 5/14/84

SCIENCE MEETS THE REAL WORLD

Japan's surprise attack on Pearl Harbor took place 18 days before Christmas. But the first U.S. air reprisals were not until April 18th. And 3 years, 3 months, and 18 days later, on August 6, 1945, the atomic bomb was dropped on Hiroshima.

"Western" seeds of technology were then planted in "the East" as mutant fires fell on the House of the Rising Sun.

Also 18 days before Christmas, Gorbachev landed in the USA. He came to sign a treaty. And we have already listed the 18's therein.

The USA had sought limit of 3,300 warheads on land-based missiles, seen as a Soviet advantage. But peace rather than bickering ruled the day.

Just 3 days before Gorbachev's arrival, $33 billion in cuts were made in USA's Armed Forces budget.[1] The air was alive with magic numbers. For Christ had died at 33 to arise in 3 days.

Was the USA being run by numerologists?

After the Reagans revealed their astrological interests, their spokesman Marlin Fitzwater joked as he started his briefing (5/4/88) saying he'd take the first question "at exactly 12:33 and a half." Had the Aquarian Reagan chosen Fitz-water for his name? Where did the illusions leave off and reality begin?

The Language Crystal is biological, produced by living beings who also produce technology to cope within evolution in this universe. So, after our old-world mind-set is sufficiently dismantled, a new view of reality will begin to crystallize.

Charges in our auras come about due to currents of the Earth at 1800 amps.[2] But who creates the currents? And what are the limits of our auras? How much biology must we sacrifice for science? Are science and faith secretly wed?

In a cubic foot (12 x 12 x 12 inches) of snow are about 18 million flakes.[3] I wonder.

(1) NY Times 12/5/87, (2) Pyramid Power, (3) Science, Dec. 1983

CHAPTER 10

THE BODY POLITIC

How does it work? How do the patterns that govern the transformations of elements, the ice ages, the stages of evolution, and so on, come to dictate the designs that make up human thought?

GLUCOSE
HAS A MOLECULAR WEIGHT
OF 180

Earthly biology is powered by sunlight.

And glucose, the fuel that powers thought, is made when carbon dioxide and water are synthesized by the sunlight that acts on plants.

We get glucose by eating vegetation, by eating animals that have eaten vegetation, or by eating animals that have eaten animals that have eaten vegetation. In any case, the glucose is originally manufactured in plants by sunlight. And the atomic weight of glucose is 180. Remember: glucose the fuel that powers our thoughts, is made by sunlight interacting with carbon dioxide and water.

WATER
HAS A MOLECULAR WEIGHT
OF 18

Physical life on Earth began in single-cell plants in the oceans. And life in the spirit is born of water (symbol of sexuality). We are mostly water. And all physical life needs water. So, the atomic weight of water affects all patterns of "life." And our political mass in Aquarius will be marked by an affluence of belief.

We each have a spirit that works through our bodies. And the PLAN of the PLANET lives in its PLANTS.

OUR BODIES ARE 18 PERCENT CARBON

Coincidence? Let's see. Carbon is fundamental to "organic chemistry." But here is where science got involved in a bit of linguistic confusion.

Chemists once divided all substances into two classes, organic and inorganic. Sugar was called "organic." Salt, "inorganic." Sugar grows. Salt is mined. Sugar once had life. Salt never had life.

Add fire to sugar, it burns. Salt won't burn, it melts. Cool molten salt, it is not changed. But sugar becomes disorganized by fire and can never again be assembled into sugar.

Sugar can be dis-organized by fire because it was originally organized by light working through a living organism (OR means "light").

Both Egyptians and Hebrews equated the letter R to "light." RA was the source of "light" in Egypt while UR and OR meant "light" in Hebrew.

Soon, these ideas of "living" and "non-living" will prove crucial in determining the "evil" that Adam and Eve ate in the garden of Eden.

Old-world physicists forgot that time had a particular direction because they had not figured "life" into their equations. So, here is the rule: Physical life flows in one direction — orgainzed by light, dis-organized by fire.

Since "to fire" (to shoot forth) and "to light" (to land upon) are verbs that tell of a continuum in the uni-verse, we should not think of fire and light as static structures, they are functions.

Much publicity was given to uniting logic and intuition. Many people fought against static old-world modes of thought. But we were in a verbal trap. Our job now is to take that trap apart.

Let us begin with an investigation into the theft of a word, a theft that has in so many ways adversely affected "the meaning of life."

In the 1800's, chemists changed the meaning of "organic" and thus clouded their own understanding of substance. "Organic chemistry" took the life out of the phrase and re-used "organic" to mean "*Any Substance Containing Carbon.*"

Is It Really "Organic"?

By re-defining "organic," chemists had forged a pass to the school of philosophy and, once inside, had methodically doctored up the curriculum. The hoax was difficult to uncover since the patterns of life and non-life were identical, except that life had a sense of direction.

The heartbeat of the human fetus can be heard in a mother's womb after **18** days, said Betty La Rosa of the Right to Life Council (*CBS* 4/22/79) in a debate to define "humanity."

The first stage of brain development ends after **18** weeks in the womb, said *Psychology Today* (Sept. 1975). Had science uncovered another timetable of "the cycles of life" akin to kaballah?

After 18 months outside the womb, a baby sees itself as a separate being, distinct from its own mother, says Margaret Mahler (*Time* 6/19/78).

Sphincter control after 18 months allows for defecation control and feelings of separateness, says Barbara Coopman (*WBAI* 2/11/83).

"At 18 months, a child can identify a picture of a puppy and understand the word," says *U.S. News* (3/17/86). And other specialists said "18 months" was some kind of turning point. It seemed that "life" knew all about its own magic number.

Science writer Desmond Morris noted in a Life magazine preview of his book, *The Naked Ape*, that as our birth rate constantly exceeds our death rate, the number of humans (naked apes) on this planet increases by another 180,000 every day.

STOP!

Wait a minute. Population growth keeps changing. The first stage of brain development may, in some cases, end at 17 weeks. And a baby's heart may be heard at various times by different instruments.

Science is only another human belief system. We shall see how religions fit this same pattern. And the goal is to have all belief directed toward our successful organic evolution in the spirit.

Finding the Motive

The very reasonable word "organic" had its meaning stolen by chemists. To rehabilitate the thieves, we must find their motive and see that they return the meaning to its rightful owner — "life."

In 1827 (nine years after the publication of "Frankenstein's Monster"), science claimed a major breakthrough as urea was produced in a laboratory. A so-called "organic substance" had been made from inorganic materials.

The scientists claimed that a product of the living had been synthesized. So proud were they with synthesized urea, that they reclassified ALL carbon-containing molecules as "organic." So, in-organic, carbon-containing materials were suddenly labeled "organic." And no longer was "organic" used in science to mean "life organized by light."

But urea, methane, and other molecules, could be produced either by life or by synthesis. And from this juncture on, the theft of a word had hypnotized historic thought up to present time.

Technological society has always had classes, oppression, and depersonalization. But we had, at least, been able to think of personal freedom. With that ability to think threatened by the theft, "life" was losing its meaning.

Media in all its forms issued various reports on the impact of toxins on "the average person," but "the average person" was a synthesized person, put together from abstract bits and pieces.

Chemists could have chosen some other term for the study of carbon molecules. But science wanted a miracle — to create "life" in the laboratory. And all this fits with our mystical metaphor.

If Jesus could take lifeless (cooked) bread and transform it by words into his body, why should a chemist not create "life."

Battles over the word "organic" are surfacing as farm-ecology challenges pharmacology about the use of poisonous chemicals in foods, So, this and other life-related words will be re-deemed as we gain a truly organized sense of direction.

Once you see "life" as a continuum, you know that "time" cannot travel backwards and that "success" is built upon happenings in "succession."

But this is apparent only when we are seeing the connections between science and spiritual life, the life that is needed for the progress of science. A science that deals with structure while ignoring function is lacking in that spirit.

For progress (like life, time, and success) is a progression of events. To have a social order and a plan for the future, we must admit that time travels only foreward, that future events are a function of present actions. In other words, we require a philosophy of science.

To exercise personal freedom, to work toward a true democracy, we each must be able to think in terms of function as well as structure. Life is a function, not a structure. And the term "organic" refers to function. This is an important key to solving the puzzle of Je-R-usa-L-em.

A synthesized molecule may have the exact same "structure" as the organic variety (as far as any chemist can tell), but "function" exists only over a period of time. So, the term "organic" relates to light (OR) as it influences life over a period of time, which flows forward.

This feeling for the bio-techno struggle in our language will be comforting as we unravel the story of the "evil" that we ate in the garden.

So many statistics, like bits of colored glass, are falling toward the one kaliedoscopic center that we are headed for a quantum shift.

Yet, truth as ever is reflected in "the Word." The laws of life, light, succession, and progress are the same in Heaven as on Earth.

Each age of the Zodiac averages 2160 years (180 x 12). But two-dimensional constellations are seen only by viewers on Earth. In space, we have a new perspective on the stars. And so, as we enter the Age of Aquarius and the Space Age both at once, our old-world belief systems are fading.

In 1818, the wave-model for light was proposed to the scientific community by Augustin Jean Fresnel in a competition held by the French Academy. Up to that point, physicists used Newton's model which depicted light as made of particles.

In 1818, Sir David Brewster first revealed to the scientific community the various categories of crystalline formations.

In 1818, Jean Francois Champollion found the first link in the code of the Rosetta Stone when he transcribed the names of Ptolemy and Cleopatra from Coptic writing, the key to hieroglyphics.

In 1818, Frankenstein's Monster spoke its first words. Franken-stein's name meant "French-in-stone," mystically symbolizing Champollion, the Frenchman who had decoded the Rosetta Stone, as he gave new life to dead Egyptian words.

In 1818, Hegel (father of the dialectic) took the chair of philosophy in Berlin. As the master of two-dimensional thought, ever matching thesis to antithesis, Hegel gave Marx the dialectic to divide the globe into "the Right" and "the Left," with BE-RL-IN in the middle.

In these events of 1818, a crystal form capable of turning ancient words into electric waves had been trapped between the living and the dead.

Waves of light (in 1818) passed through crystal (in 1818), broke the code in stone (in 1818), as dead Egyptians spoke, and the division of tongues (in 1818) was crowned to rule BE-RL-IN.

Previously, LU-TH-ER turned the German tide against the Jews. Remember, Ger-man means "strange manna" in He-brew. For IS-RA-EL was to be reborn after HIT-LER evoked a new level of evil. His story is in a later chapter.

A multi-level drama was in progress. Life and non-life (as in the foods of sacrifice) seemed to be competing for our spirits as we were drawn into the puzzle of Je-R-usa-L-em.

The New Plateau

In the Egyptian Book of the Dead, 12 gods sit in judgement, 12 goddesses are divided by the monster serpent Herrt, spawning 12 young serpents. And 12 gods sing the praises of RA while 12 gods hold the measuring cord. Next, 12 human heads emerge from the devil serpent Seba while 12 mummies repose on the back of the serpent Nehep.

These sexual symbols recall Eve in the Bible and the goddess of Tantric Yoga whose sexual power is "kundalini," a coiled serpent.

From 12 tribes of Israel (giving us the Jews) to 12 princes of Ishmael (giving us the Arabs), 12 Greek gods on Mount Olympus, 12 Navaho gods under the ground of Je-R-usa-L-em, and the 12 Disciples of Christ, with 12-inch rulers, 12-hour clocks, 12-member juries, 12-tone musical notation, and 12 of almost anything in a dozen (except a baker's dozen), we had an Earthbound vibrational grid, a flattened design of space and time.

Yet, 12 moons fall short of a year. The cycles do not fit. And the moon, a feminine symbol, is where our Space Age begins.

Two women with different cycles were the wives of Abram-Abraham. But the 12 Arab tribes (also sons of Abram-Abraham) were not listed in John's "Final Days" vision in the Christian Bible. Why?

Because Palestine means "migration." And Hagar (Egyptian mother of Abram's first son, the first Arab) means "wandering."

The first Arab, **Ishmael** ("God listens") was driven out of written prophecy. And thus, among Abram-Abraham's children, "the Word" was broken.

With 12 gates to the City, Saint John pictured 12 angels guarding the names of 12 tribes. The walls of the city had 12 foundations and measured 12 by 12 by 12 thousand furlongs. But John's Crystal vision in the Book of Revelation was incomplete.

Now, we are entering a time when the answers to "Peace on Earth" and "Personal Health" will be identical — and REAL.

83

HUMANS DEVELOP A NEW
SOCIAL CONSCIENCE
AFTER 18 YEARS

Humans gain a new political life after 18 years on Earth. The rite of voting now comes in Egypt and Israel alike at the age of 18. And in the nations listed below, the privilege of voting suddenly appears, as if by magic, after 18 years.

USA	The United Kingdom	The USSR
Canada	Australia	China
Mexico	New Zealand	Vietnam
Bahamas	South Africa	Cambodia
Bangladesh	East Germany	Greece
Brazil	West Germany	Paraguay
Portugal	Peru	Rumania
Ireland	The Phillipines	Yemen
Italy	Poland	Zaire

Toward the end of history, 18 was the legal age of "sexual consent" for many and in war 18 marked "the boys" to be drafted. We shall re-frame the martial and marital arts later, in Crystal terms. Our focus now is the pervasive illusion that Phase Two thinking had created.

We believed that Israelis and Palestines did not inter-marry. We knew they did, but "believed" they didn't. We thought of "racial" or "national" groups as absolutes. An illusion of words could label a particular "half-breed" and create a media reality, but with no group labels, most historic people felt that they lacked identity.

In our migration to our next home, each Space Ship will become a nation unto itself. But our migration (Palestine) and our struggle with God (Israel) were not seen as one during history.

The dynasty that enslaved Israel was known as "the 18th Dynasty" to the Egyptians. And Moses was simply working out the karma of Abram-Abraham who had previously had a child by an Egyptian woman. The descendants of that child were "Arabs."

The Reason

The reason that we have this metaphor is so we can work out beforehand the type of society that will be necessary to find a home in Heaven.

TOV means "good" in Hebrew and E-TOV (good energy) reflects the power to VOTE. When Je-R-usa-L-em becomes a true democracy, we will have our "possession of peace" (Jeru-salem).

The many parts of this analogy were unfolding in politics toward the end of history. Those de-voted to survival had no choice but to vote for clean water and clean air. Those who focused on war did not understand the environment. As we add more names and hidden meanings to the Armageddon metaphor of Ronald (6) Wilson (6) Reagan (6), the message will be clear — our problem can be solved only by devoted individuals who vote with each item they consume or refuse to consume.

The Senate rejected a bill (3/30/88) that would have warned workers about job-related toxins. The E.P.A. refused to toughen rules on sulfer dioxide (5/14/88). Asthmatics might suffer, but not the general public, said "statistical evidence."

An assumption that "statistics" can divide one group from another denies that we all are hurt by pollution. Medical (insurance) models of disease labeled biology in parts. But disease is not a structure, it is the function of an organism whose life-force is seeking balance.

Besides the fact that a group of industrialists had pledged to buy an estate for Reagan to occupy after the White House (*AP* 4/13/88), a conflict of interests existed in our scientific, religious, and political terminology.

The USA was not a true democracy; and Israel (with no Constitution) was not a true democracy. Both, however, verbalized the dream wherein Je-R-usa-L-em shall be united when the cities of Earth begin the "possession of peace."

True democracy is in fact a down-to-Earth rule by the will of God as expressed in the voice of the people. Demos-kratos (people's authority) is derived from "daemon," which means the teaching role of divinity.

Imagine paying a friend to swallow poison.

It is difficult to think of treating another individual with such distain. But in the USA, the toxic waste material was so out of control that some groups literally paid others to swallow their garbage. And the Federal Government found towns so poor as to swallow nuclear wastes.

The idea that the body politic might grow into organisms that thrived on smoke in factory towns had served to keep us calm in the wake of booming technologies. So as pollution mounted, we tried to act as if we were like machines.

Acid rain, radiation, alcohol, cigarette smoke, pesticides, and other toxins damaged our enzymes. And cancer, arthritis, and all other diseases were in fact related to destructured enzymes.

Of course, there were emotional factors in all disease, and spiritual causes as well.

Some people knew the facts but could not seem to change their personal habits. And the Techno State wanted to protect itself by sacrificing some "percentage" of the biological whole.

We built a medical model of disease to drug individuals rather than reverse our Phase Two eating habits and growing technologies. In another theft of meaning, "technological expansion" was often referred to as "economic growth."

The "sacrifice of food" (our religious mystery) blinded us to the sacrifice of life in general. What "evil" had we eaten in the garden? The answer to our puzzle will soon be obvious; and later its implications will be clearly spelled out.

The Bible says that our problems are tied to that single act of eating "evil." And the Language Crystal says, we are living in a world of verbal illusions because most of us are still eating that same "evil." Yes, you are a member of the body politic. Still, you are an individual. Yes, the "sin" of Adam is said to be collective. Still, there is a personal answer to this mystery. And the result, eventually, shall be true democracy.

Alan Brauer says in *Extended Sexual Orgasm* that the *average* orgasm is ten seconds. And with an *average* once or twice a week, he sets the *average* couple's orgasm at 1½ minutes each month — "18 minutes a year." That's statistics.

What are the odds that a particular coin might come up heads three times in a row? A prediction based on statistics might be wrong. And with a lopsided coin, all abstractions are useless. We cannot state a probability unless we know all the factors. And even then, chance plays a part.

But with disease where variables are countless and spirit is an overriding factor, we get no more than propaganda from the number mongers.

Used consistantly at a well balanced roulette wheel, statistics might allow one to break even, if also betting house numbers. But the medical profession uses statistics as a huxter routine to get the gullible into hypnotic series of tests leading to diagnosis (a guess), then to drugging, and to moving symptoms around in the body until the patient either quits the drugs, dies, or gets well in spite of the chemicals.

The extraordinary numeric coincidences cited in this book go far beyond the realm of statistical possibility. Yet their ancient implications show that we are now at the heart of a mystery. And the Crystal Code is our demystifying tool.

Granted that most ills are caused by toxins in the environment and poisons in foods that people eat habitually. Granted that most disease can be prevented by re-naturalizing the globe and eating by the laws of nature. We must now gain a clear and unequivocal sense of direction.

Within the next hundred years, a new sense of democracy shall crystallize on this planet to plan for a global government, of the people, by the people, and for the people. And the people biologically shall rule technology. An organic truth in the Language Crystal shall give us the sense of direction that turns "evil" around.

Reagan means "to rule." And as Reagan's rule was ending in 1988, two men sought to replace him.

Bush, as we have seen, is from "the sign of the wine merchant" in England. And **Dukakis** from the Greek for "duke" is from the Latin *ducere*, "to guide." The English word "duct," as in aquaduct, has the same root; and so "duke" (guide) means "leader" or "guide." Rulers tend to measure things. Leaders can guide people to truth, but also can lead them astray.

Dukakis chose Bentsen for his running mate. And **Bentsen** is from the Danish, son of Benedict, which means "the blessed one."

Paul (the foremost Christian) **Kirk** ("church") was the Democratic National Convention chairman. And Reagan's Armageddon gang in Iran-scam broke Frank **Church**'s rules for the CIA. Bill **Chappel** was the first congressman named in the Pentagon scandal (*NY Times* 7/19/88). And the chapel bill would be paid.

Was the 1988 choice made between "the guide" and "the sign of a wine merchant" to decide the type of currency that the USA would use to pay its historic "Weinberger" bill?

It mattered little who took the 1988 Presidential vote. For the age of symbols had passed. And our most important decisions would be based on what masses of people consumed.

Jackson meant "son of Jacob" (who changed his name to Israel). Yet, Jesse Jackson was an adopted child whose name was originally Jesse Burns. So, his place in our metaphor was one of change.

When the soul of humanity "burns" for freedom and justice, the results can be inspiring. Yet, if a soul "burns" without giving out clear light, its energies can go astray.

Bear in mind that we each are part of the whole. The story of the uni-verse is a progression of fire and light. And so, these characters represent a struggle within each soul.

CHAPTER 11

WRITTEN IN THE WIND

When we began sacrificing our foods to the gods of fire, something very strange happened to our words. Early in history, our language was literally taken over the coals.

It is not apparent in most translations, but in the Bible when God is said to be angry, an idiom is often used to depict flames coming out of God's nose. In fact, the Hebrew word for "anger" (*aph*) is the same as the word for "nose" (*aph*).

Had our first thoughts about the super-natural gift of fire been clouded by nasal sensations that bothered us when breathing in the smoke?

In the Bible, we find that God breathed into the "nostrils" (*aph*) of man to give him life, and man became a living soul (Gen. 2:7). But at 171 other places in the Old Testament, this word for "nostrils" means "anger" instead. Was the mystical "life" that God breathed into man a smokey mixture that was fraught with danger?

The ancient Hebrew word for "spirit" (*ruach*) is much like the German word for "smoke" (*rauch*). Had these twisted spells caused a near holocaust of "the Jews" at the hands of "the Germans"?

Hitler's plans for Germany, as built on Martin Luther's Armageddon fantasy, were an extension of the ancient rivalry between Egypt and Israel.

Ger-man means "strange manna" in He-brew. But manna was a food from heaven, eaten in the land of Sin (Sion). And man-ger in the Christmas story was a place where animals eat. The clues add up only in English. What did putting Jews in ovens have to do with Je-R-usa-L-em, HIT-LER, BE-RL-IN, or bread in IS-RA-EL? The answer resolves as R and L fall in line with 18 and 12. This chapter focuses on the "original evil" that we shall uncover via the Crystal Code.

When words were written in letters, not pictures, we had a new mode of religious expression.

Belief in "one God" (EL) became more manageable when one idea could be linked to one sound by one letter of the Hebrew alphabet. Each character was individual, a module of abstract thought.

But why on Earth did humanity have a need for such precise abstract thinking?

The answer is NASA, a Hebrew word that means "to lift up" and "travel forth." NASA, which will lead to our future journeys into outer space, was our original reason for using fire.

We had hidden the fear of fire inside us. So, we needed a set of reflective symbols to show us our "un-conscious" in an external form.

Our need for writing and for ritual came to us after we tasted the supernatural food that we had offered to the gods of fire. The sun-god's "evil" then became our own — RA in He-brew.

Duplicate symbols, such as "anger" and "nose," stored the clues to our biological troubles.

On the techno level, we were solving a problem. On the bio level, we were creating other problems. And all the while, we were encoding the answers to any bio-deviations that we made along the way.

Every Hebrew scholar knows kabbalah. Yet, most Christian Fundamentalists ignored the fact that those Biblical passages on which they built their own Armageddon nightmare had occult ("occult" simply means hidden) roots in the Hebrew language.

With Je-R-usa-L-em built on 12's, the kabbalah that I received in English told me that 18 (life) was moving to a new plateau where the Crystal City is unified in "the Word" living among us.

Many Christians who labeled the roots of their own Bible as "occult," rather than seek its hidden messages, had lost track of its harmonics.

But the Code is not exclusively for Christians, Jews, Arabs, Germans, Americans, or the people who claim to "belong" to any other group. The Code is for "the Ultimate Individual."

Kaballah or **kabbalah** ("to receive" in Hebrew) is
the word for "servitude" in Russian, **kabala**.

The USA (symbolic center of Je-R-usa-L-em) is also to
receive God's tradition of servitude.

Keep in mind that the terms "Russian" and "Jew" are not
biological. Any person who is so motivated can become a
Russian or a Jew. So, our new revelation goes beyond
history to re-unite pure biology with pure spirit.

So, to re-solve the symbolism, the USA must draw the
power of its individuals into a non-historic true
democracy. For New Jerusalem (when united) is a global
Crystal City of clear individuals.

Our most basic individual habit, which is eating, must
be changed to suit our individual needs. With social
pressures set aside, fulfillment of pleasure will be the
signal to stop eating, for then will nutrition be balanced.
And a new type of "consumer" will emerge.

Eating without emotional turmoil is one of several keys
that will unlock the gates of paradise on our next plateau.
And eating patterns that we knew before the sacrifice of
food to "the gods of fire" can be reawakened. For the
Language Crystal encodes the needed information.

Under the Phase Two Techno State, we fell into eating
habits that were more in line with our work schedules than
with individual hunger. And as a result, we were driven to
eat when no hunger was present.

But we needed our emotional ties to the Techno State,
and so we let technology feed us. Cooked food "tasted
better." And the taste for natural eating was buried in our
collective un-conscious.

As with all that is stored in the un-conscious, the data
about natural eating was also encoded in the Language
Crystal, for retrieval in due time.

The He-brew food sacrifice became the Christian
centerpiece, now in the form of "a host." With fire trapped
in food as "a hostage," priests became both its guards and
prisoners. And our use of the flame was mystified.

Following the Metaphor

We have seen how El Salvador (the Savior), Israel (the struggle with God), Iran (the upper classes), Iraq (alcoholic drink), Palestine (migration), and names of people in the Iran-Contra scandal fit into place. Next, some of surrounding material on the Iran-Contra scandal signals the collapse of the Armageddon Movement.

The design of "the Savior," "a strugggle with God," "alcoholic drink," "migration," and "upper classes" will also include Nic-ar-agua, a symbol of "Old Nick" re-deemed in "Aquarius."

Beyond the politics, when we gain control of "evil" to serve biology under a true democracy, respect for the bio individual will be the true test of techno value.

These images of history are here only to lead us forward as biological individuals in search of a balance between technology and nature.

In the Iran-Contra scandal, a symbolic piece of evidence was the cake sent by Reagan via Colonel North to Iran. Remember, the land of Israel in the Bible was sold for a piece of bread. The cake sent by 666 to "the upper classes" fits precisely into our puzzle once it is completed.

News of Reagan's cake surfaced in a pro-Syrian Beirut newspaper when the hostage David Jacobsen ("beloved son of the supplanter") was released.

The first to confess to crimes in Contra-gate was Mr. Channell who had funneled tax-exempt money from wealthy patriots to finance breaches of the Boland Amendment. Mr. Funnel got off easy, naming Mr. North as a co-conspirator and telling how Mr. 666 (as a rule) was in on the fun.

To recap: Channell was a funnel. Reagan was a ruler. Regan a ruler. Shultz the overseer. Their Hasenfus, the rabbit's foot, got lost. And then, Poindexter, painer on the Right, resigned. Arm-a-cost, point man on Iran, was re-evaluated. Casey, the watchful, lost track. Buckley, the bullock, was sacrificed. Stockman, Speakes, Mr. Mouse and the rest had played their convoluted parts.

Our fear of destruction by fire toward the end of history was due to the fact that we hid our fear of fire in the unconscious in order to enter the Age of History in the first place.

The first of Mr. Funnel's contributors named in the press was Mrs. *Pentecost*. She was brought into Mr. Channells' net-work by a man named **Fisher** (*NY Times* 4/30/87). In tune with the preachers of the Armageddon movement, Channell had become a fisher of elderly women, as Christ's Disciples had once been made "the fishers of men."

Funnel was endorsed by Elliot Abrams. Elliot is "Jehovah is God" in Hebrew. And Abrams carries our metaphor back to the story of Abram-Abraham, who had two sons by two different women.

The connection is that Abram-Abraham offered to kill his Hebrew son as a sacrifice to Jahovah, but he burned a ram instead. This was the first story of a scapegoat in the Bible. And the ram was made a sacrifice to fire.

Pentecost is a festival 50 days after Passover. And Christians celebrate Pentecost as the day the Holy Spirit came over the heads of the Apostles in tongues of fire.

Mrs. Pentecost had contributed to crucify "Old Nick" with a belief that money talked on the Right side of its mouth in old Je-R-usa-L-em.

Pentagon costs were hushed. Weapons pollution mounted. And in occult (hidden) worship of fire-fear, the Pentagon met Pentacost in pentangles of the devil, approaching our turning point.

Reagan's own scandal-ridden image gave him the needed push to reach out to what he had termed an "Evil Empire," the USSR.

Once the unconscious fear of fire is received in consciousness, the task in New Jerusalem will be to spread democracy among all nations, not by the sword but by the word. People on the Right had the right idea, but an off-center mechanism. The way to teach democracy is by example. And a true democracy is thus true to "the Word."

The Russian words for "torment" (*muka*) and "meal" (*muka*) are the same.

Muka reflects an emotional problem with food that is echoed in many other languages. In Hebrew, "bread" (*lechem*) is related to "war" (*lachem*). In German, "a piece of bread" (*waffel*) is derived from the same roots as "weapon" (*waffe*). Patterns that equate bread to war are found around the globe, as discussed in later chapters.

This "Mystery of Christ and the Ultimate Diet" is in the un-conscious. For every tribe on Earth, even at the Equator and in the jungle, eats some kind of cooked (sacrificed) food. But why?

Every nation's child (unlike nature's monkey) knew meals could be hell. Adults had lost control of their eating habits and passed "the original sin" on to their chlidren.

Adam and Eve ate of "evil" in the garden and were blocked from returning to Eden by crossed swords of fire. The clues add up.

As the ages went by, we ate more and more from the Tree of Technology with less nutrition and added toxins. But somehow, our great scientists, nutritionists (with rare exception), and medical practitioners never seemed to notice that cooking food was not natural to any other species.

In the Bible, "fire" (*esh*) and "human being" (*ash*) were born of the same He-brew roots. For we needed fire to fulfill our destiny, to carry on "the race." And so, ignoring the side effects of cooked food, we focused on the taste, and created a sacrifice to the gods.

Our anger (aph) due to the breath of God coming into the human nose (aph) will be made conscious again, once these bio-concepts crystallize.

We have a true organic science that is our true organic chemistry, not related to any attempts to create "life" in a laboratory.

We know of solar power, organic agriculture, and so on. We need only put our organic democracy in control. With the bio-block removed, our New Millennium plan for peace will unfold.

Once we understand the terms of sacrifice, the names fall into place. The sacrifice of **bread** and **wine** was personified as **Bush** chose **Baker** to manage him in 1988. **Quayle** meant "to diminish" in Old English.

President 666 had surrounded himself with a host of living symbols. The Treasury of New Je-R-usa-L-em was ruled by *Baker*, symbolic of "bread." And the Vice President was *Bush* which was symbolic of wine because his name derives from the English "one who lives by a sign of the bush," a wine merchant. Defense was under **Weinberger**, "a mountain of grapes." And where the Treasury met Defense, their sacrifice of **bread** and **wine** grew with the karma of wrath. Reagan himself was a dweller in California a state of pesticide-poisoned grapes.

The religious right in Je-R-usa-L-em had expected Armageddon to start as a nuclear war where Russia would attack Israel. Falwell quoted one of many passages in the Bible about this trouble out of the North, saying, "Set the standard toward Zion: for I will bring evil from the **North**, and great destruction" (Jer 4:6). He believed an attack of horse-riding Cossacks would come out of the *North*, from the USSR into the State of Israel.

Mr. **Godwin** headed the Moral Majority as the prophecy of *North* unfolded. And the names Reagan, Regan, Bush, Baker, Baker, Bakker, Wein-berger, Poin-dexter, Shultz, Secord, Hasen-fus, Nimrodi, Kashoggi, Ghorbanifar, Hakim, and Sin-glaub fulfilled the prophecy of "trouble out of the North" as no novelist could.

The hunter who built the Tower of Babel in Old Testament times was *Nimrod*. **Mr. Nimrodi** was the key Israeli arms dealer in the Iran-Contra rite. The Saudi financeer had a name with a Turkish twist, **Kashoggi**, "a measure of land," interested in territorial games. **Hakim** meant "wise man" — linking Iran to Christmas. And **Ghorbanifar**, the Iranian middleman who delivered "the trouble out of the North," had a name meaning "sacrifice," appropriate to his role.

What were the odds that a man named "Sacrifice" might arrange to trade arms for hostages, or when his Tower of Babel fell, that an ex-senator named **Tower** would make up Reagan's report? The name of the key Israeli arms merchant like that of the hunter who built the Tower of Babel (Nimrod) told of a linguistic rebuilding of that Tower.

And to focus our attention on the sacrifice of bread, when the rule of Reagan-Regan broke apart, the man to replace Reagan's shadow ruler (Regan) was a *Baker* (Howard) who had servered **18** years in the Senate. Another *Baker* (James) was in charge of the Treasury. And it was a *Baker* (Bill) who was chief CIA spokesman on the Iran-Contra affair.

Also, Jim *Bakker* of "Praise the Lord" TV was a supporter of Reagan. Bakker fell at "the sign of the cock," blackmailed by a woman in Babylon who said he drugged her wine. And the Armageddon gang crumbled seven years after Bakker, symbolically or otherwise, slept with "the Whore of Babylon."

And in that time, more Palestineans (a word meaning "migration") were migrating back to their homeland, which was also called Israel, where the He-brew (Abram-Abraham) father of both Jews and Arabs had originally divided them.

Jewish claims to the Holy Land said Jews were "the chosen people." Bible stories said that they had faults like any other group. And yet, the Jews claimed the Bible as their property deed.

The Bible seemed true to itself because so many names in its stories fit its own metaphor. But in the final days of history, that Biblical metaphor was being re-solved.

And many felt we had reached a turning point. Would acid rain or atomic bombs seal our doom? Or was an Aquarian Age beginning?

In Reagan's Contra scandal, Boland was a legal turningpoint. For the Boland Amendment forbid all military aid to the Contras. And **Boland** in Old English is "the land where a river turns." So, 666 had crossed that river into Aquarius.

An Aquarian symbol appeared in the name of the key diplomat **McFarlane**, from Scots *par-holon*, meaning "sea waves." He first denied that a cake was 666's gift to Iran. Then Sea Waves reversed himself.

McFarlane said Oliver North brought a cake to the moderates in Iran. The bread symbol fit with the prophecy of "trouble out of the North." And North was indited on 18 criminal charges.

Before the scandal broke, Reagan suffered his great foreign-affairs embarrassment, confused as Gorbachev called his bluff about the "zero option" at the **Reykjavik**, Iceland summit.

Reykjavik means "smokey-bay." Combining fire and ice, Reagan offered to remove ALL medium-range missiles from Europe, but then forgot.

The hostage Benjamin Weir (set free but kept in secrecy until Sept. 18th) played a role fitting the clergy. **Benjamin** is "a son of the right hand." And in Welsh, **Weir** is a dweller near a fish-trap. (Where were all the Smiths?) Fish-trap referred to the Age of Pisces, wherein the Christian symbol was "a fish against a fish." And Pisces was ending so Aquarius might begin.

Only an encyclopedia could picture all these overlappping events. The goal here, however, is to point out the linguistic miracle needed for the Second Coming of the Word.

The signs were everywhere. "Some 1.8 million voters" were the body politic of El Salvador, "the Savior" (*U.S. News* 4/1/85). Synchronistically, *the New York Times*, toward the start of Reagan's 2nd term, reported that an average loaf of bread in the USSR cost 18 kopecks. Both "the Savior" and the bread of "the Evil Empire" had been marked by the number of "life" (related to kosher bread).

And 180 witnessses were heard in a case that accused 666's Immigration Bureau of harassing people from El Salvador who were seeking political asylum (*CS Monitor* 5/2/88). Coincidentially, the city of Salvador in Brazil had a population of 1.8 million (*CS Monitor* 5/3/88).

Pro-Life?

Armageddonists believed that a holocaust would be a good sign. And Oliver North was a born-again Charismatic. So, his interpretation of Reagan's Fundamentalist goals was beyond arms, money, or national-policy. The issues were mystical. Listen as they are demystified.

"Lights burned late in the White House last Nov. 18th as Oliver North and his colleagues in the Iran arms deal tried to massage the record of the complex weapons-for-hostages negotiations into a chronology that would minimize Ronald Reagan's role" (*Newsweek* 3/2/87).

Also, McFarlane "confessed to writing a memo Nov. 18th at the request of his successor, John Poindexter, that was deliberately phrased to 'blur' Reagan's role" (*Time* 3/2/87). Their trails crossed on the 18th. The cover-ups took place the day before Reagan's press conference wherein the lies went public. The metaphor of bread had been linked to the corruption of "the Word" and the loss of true democracy.

During 666's 18-month secret affair, anti-drug enforcement grew to "a **$1.8 billion** item." The cost of fighting drugs increased by **18%** (*Newsweek* 8/11/86). And all that time the CIA was smuggling drugs into the USA. For Congress would not "just say no" to the plans of 666.

In a society awash in coffee, swilling alcohol, and smoking tobacco while hysterically consumming "medical drugs," this problem will take some time to unravel. So, let's continue our re-framing.

On the first day of the hearings (5/6/87), we learned "the total amount of money representing the purchase price of arms sold to Iran that was put into the Lake Resources bank account" was $30 million. And $12 million "in round numbers" was paid to the U.S. Treasury for weapons purchased.

"I think you'll agree there's a difference of approximately **$18** million," said the chief counsel to Mr. Secord. "I want to ask you some questions about where that money went."

Which $18 Million?

Of "private aid" to the Contras "$18 million for weapons" was paid during the Boland ban.[1] But it was not exactly the same $18 million that Congress was tracing. A switch of military boots for some humanitarian boots got the arms-sales money mixed in with other funds.

On the third day of hearings, Secord was asked to review page 36 in his documents. Mysteriously, 36 was blank. And in kaballah, 36 is "rebirth."

Still, 18 was predominant in the scandal that seemed to be "a piece of cake" to Reagan.

McFarlane said $18 million was the price on the total of Hawks traded for the first hostage. And when asked to pick the first hostage for release, McFarlane chose Buckley (Bullock).

His emotions when telling that he learned that the CIA agent Buckley was tortured to death were poignant. All sides, however, seemed unconscious in the face of the symbolism.

Since the Bullock was dead, the Sea Waves chose Weir ("Fish Trap") to be released instead.

In terms of Pisces (fish against the fish) and Aquarius (water bearer), Sea Waves played his role by the book. We had become the new zodiac (little zoo) striving for a Space Age view.

In the knowledge that spirits live forever, the important part of this affair is the principle of higher consciousness. What we thought were evil motivations were only side effects of the techno chemical world we were living in.

Article 18 of the OAS Charter was read to show that the USA should not supply arms against the government of Nicaragua. And Title 18 of the U.S. Code was cited to show conspirators may be tried for attempting to defraud the USA.

The Criminal Code's 99-word conspiracy statute was said to be the principle legal instrument in the Iran-Contra affair.[2] But why had someone in the media added up the words?

(1) NY Times 3/7/87, (2) NY Times 5/12/87

In our symbolic world, Nimrodi, the Israeli arms dealer, lived in a replica of the White House in Israel.[1] Nimrod, who built the tower of Babel, was a hunter in the Bible. And 666 was the ultimate money changer. So, Nimrod, the modern hunter, who turned out to be "the smoking gun" that tied 666 to the weapons conspiracy of Armageddon, linked Genesis to Revelation, in our metaphor.

McFarlane, Secord, and North each felt they had been betrayed by the people of the USA when they were not allowed "to win" the war in NAM. We'll explore the poetry of this point later.

Bruce Springstein sold his 18 millionth copy of "Born in the USA," lamenting the tragedy of NAM, as the first Iran-Contra witnesses were called.

Nicaragua (Old Nick) was accused of supplying weapons to insurgents in El Salvador (the Savior) as the USA was torn between the Right and Left in the transitions of Je-R-usa-L-em. The Senate Intelligence Committee secret report on the Iran-Contra cash exchange was "a 180-page narrative," the first official summary.[2] Later, Swiss banks held onto the records, but Congress, "having issued some 180 subpoenas, obtained many of them through secondary sources."[3]

Our "watchfulness" (Casey) had his brain cut into by surgery on the date of 12/18. In symbol, the Central Intelligence link to 666 was dying.

Rob Owen had a name suited to running money from North's Armageddon gang to the Contras. Coors who manufactured alcoholic brew had a name derived from "currency." And he had poured his money into Mr. Funnel to further the human sacrifice.

The purpose of this metaphor is to show how the personal relates to the global. This formula used for evil can also work for good. And with proper application of the the Language Crystal Code, we can bring about Peace on Earth.

(1) NY Times 6/11/87, (2) NY Daily News 1/8/87, (3) U.S. News 5/4/87

Front page headline of *the New York Times*
"How $18 Million Got Soviet Weapons to Iran."[1]

The story told of French arms dealers pretending to ship arms to North Korea in planes from Israel. A German in Florida bought the Soviet missiles and launchers from an arsenal in Poland and shipped them to Iran. But the reason for the weapons trade was more than ideological.

As the 1987 nuclear reduction treaty was signed, Israel admitted to use of heavy water of Norway's nuclear plants to make plutonium. And the CIA said Israel used its plutonium to manufacture bombs. The USA sold heavy water to Israel. And Norway sold it to France, also making bombs. And Israel sold the materials and supervision by which South Africa had built its own nuclear weapons.

Nuclear non-proliferation agreements were being ignored as more unstable powers acquired more and more powerful arsenals.

It seemed we were moving toward chaos. But in the spirit we were struggling with "life."

A Bruni fund transfer to the Contras was dated August 18th, but North mixed up a Swiss account number, losing the money. Bruni's per capita income was quoted at $18,000.[2] The Sultan of Bruni bought the Boeing jet from arms trader Kashoggi with a personal check for $18 million.[3] Kashoggi lived on a 180,000-acre ranch in Kenya.[4]

The patterns were too constant to ignore. Such patterns would add up to scientific evidence if not in the realm of the mystical.

"Praise the Lord" fell with 180 stations in its network.[5] PTL had 180,000 "lifetime partners" whose holdings were being looked at by the IRS.[6]

On one side, the numbers fit together. On the other side, the names fit into our metaphor. And in the middle were the equations of the Language Crystal Code.

(1) NY Times 5/28/87, (2) NY Times 12/7/86, (3) Time 3/16/87, (4) Time 1/19/87, (5) U.S. News 4/6/87, (6) NY Times 6/16/87

During the televised hearings, Iran-Contragate did not focus on the drugs shipped to the USA via the same planes that had flown weapons out. The nation focused on the money. Charts showed bank accounts, arrows pointing around the globe, but no flow of "drugs for arms." Most people in the USA had lost perspective on "the drug problem."

Tammy Bakker, wife of the TV evangelist, said she was hooked on prescription drugs. The Bakkers had "medical charities" high on their list. Oral Roberts, a TV preacher also on medication, sought money for "medical missionaries." Jimmy Swaggart, who swore that he'd never tasted alcohol, poured donated cash into the medical drugging profession. Had God sanctioned "prescription drugs" according to the Armageddon gospel?

Medical drugging was a rapidly growing false religion. Other religions funded "the doctors." And promises by the Cancer, Arthritis, Diabetes, and other drug-pushing "Societies" turned out to be as empty as promises by the Armageddon Cults.

Modern medicine was not curing as many people as the placebo effect and "spontaneous (meaning non-drugged) remissions." A question seldom asked was: Who should interpret the statistics?

The more independent research done, the clearer it became that food was a greater factor in both the prevention of disease and healing than any of the drugs. Now, what does this have to do with the "evil" that Adam and Eve ate in the garden?

In He-brew, "bread" (*lechem*) relates to "war" (*lachem*). In German, "a piece of bread" (*waffel*) is akin to "weapon" (*waffe*). Had Adam eaten food sacrificed to false fire-gods? Did he anger the God of light whose photo-synthesis had grown the Tree of Life? Why do pyr-amids have fire in the middle? The word "pyramid" is linked to "purimis" in Greek, a type of *cake*. And "purim" is a feast of *cake* in the Jewish tradition.

What "evil" did Adam and Eve eat in the garden? Perhaps we need more proof.

CHAPTER 12

BREAKING THE CODE

The modern name *Sally* has its root in *Sarah* due to shifts in the *R* and *L*. The *R* in *Katharine* appears as *L* in *Kathleen*. And *Gerard* and *Gerald* have the same origin.

Also, R and L are meaningfully related in words of many languages. For example, *Glyph* is "carving" in Greek. *Graph* is "writing." In Arabic, *koran* is "writing" while *kalam* is "speech."

And *atsi-LA* (אֲצִילָה‎) is a "giving" verb that means "vesting" or "delegating" in Hebrew while *atsi-RA* (אֲצִירָה‎) is a "taking" verb that means "hoarding" or "accumulating." Both of these verbs have roots in the word for "nobility," the power to give and to take.

Did Romans choose Latin or Latins take Rome? In any event, ITALiaN is of LATIN origin.

And the R and L (in IS-RA-EL, BE-RL-IN, and Je-R-usa-L-em) reflect the historic divisions of the right and left halves of the brain. This chapter will explore the reasons WHY.

Linguists refer to R and L as "liquids." And at places 18 and 12 in the alphabet, they accent an Angular perspective. So, this chapter cites a few R-L leaps where crystal meanings break through. And soon, we shall apply this process to find out what "evil" humanity ate in the garden."

The union of *hearing* and *healing* herein came to us as bio information from our spirits in formation. And now we can apply it to control of the techno world. The cosmic ledger (L-edge-R) is endless.

A *bar* is "long and straight" (180°), as in bar-graph or iron bar. A *ball* is "round" (360°). The *ball* and *bar*, zero and one, vagina and penis are pairs within the metaphor that begins with Tree of Life, "10" in kabbalah.

Bar in Hebrew is "boy." In Babylonian, *Baal* was "god of the sun" in his-story's sun-son metaphor. And an extension of RA's double meaning will bring us around again to the light of EL.

FEEL - - - FEAR

Why do we fear to feel? Alienation, "the feeling of not feeling," divides the Phase Two mind-set. Yet in Phase Three, a healthy fear of technology grows with the poise that re-solves all fear.

Monkeys live by feelings and survive by fear as it unfolds in present time. A human, however, stores up feelings. And historically as well as individually, we use our hidden fear (hell fire) to build the moral codes that make us each a part of civilization.

Again, this relates to the fact that the Earth must die. We began to play with fire because we had to conquer our greatest fear. We feared a loss of the thread of biological evolution that the death of our Planet Earth could bring.

Yet, with the use of fire, our new "feelings" reached into the beyond — into the super-natural. Animals live by instinct; humans developed free will by using fire. So, this power that made us a group of universal travelers also set us free as fire-spirited individuals.

Fire technology is a knowledge of good and evil that allows us to create and destroy so that "the race" may live forever. But we developed "two humanities" in Phase Two. A conscious mind used what we could FEEL while an un-conscious mind encoded what we had to FEAR.

We coped with fear and stored a super-conscious message in "the Word." Only humans have mythology and writing for only humans had to encode the fear of fire in order to evolve.

Jewish people do not light fires on the Sabbath to acknowledge fire's two-sided nature. Yet Jews were attacked. The He-brew culture ritualizes the emotions that each of us un-consciously "feels and fears." So, the human animal was attacking its own mystery — mastery of the flame.

Our control of the fear of fire depends NOT on scientific learning, religious belief, moral attitude, or political persuasion. Its source is neither a nervous system nor a genetic trait. Our control of the fear of fire is born of our super-natural ego (E-go), the God within us.

HEAR - - - HEAL

To *hear* in truth is in truth to *heal*.

Did you ever hear beyond your thoughts? Was there a silence?

In ease, you heal dis-ease. You hear the voice of a spirit that listens to your own biology.

As meditation is a letting go of words, prayer is a healing word. Also, speaking words of love is a form of prayer, in truth.

And just as whales, dolphins, and bumble bees are born with species-specific languages encoded in their genes, so a primitive part of us is born with healing speech — the human hum.

In Sanskrit, OM is a human dialogue with God. And earth, water, fire, air, and ether (lam, vam, ram, yam, and ham) are essences of OM.

Note that "fire" is RAM while "earth" is LAM. Here is the ancient root of the story of Abram who burned a ram in exchange for his son's life. We shall explore these mantras later.

Our Techno State with its use of fire demanded additions to our natural language that interfered with natural hearing. And our inhumanity hurled the object of its fear against humanity itself.

The children of Ab-ram later joined with Rome, children of the wolf, to crucify the Lamb of God, to expand our powers of hell-fire. And in Phase Three, we must *hear* our techno creations to *heal* the dis-ease of the Techno State.

In He-brew where *gul* means "to be glad" and *gur* means "to have fear," this R-L interchange is still a useful union of emotions.

During techno growth, we pushed un-conscious fears onto friends and enemies. Now we can be glad to fear technology. Streaming smoke was once a sign of progress. Now, acid rain tells us that money for nuclear power would be better spent to stop the air pollution.

Healing is a process. And constant healing is "health." Listen to your inner self; tap into the common "wealth." For weal, in English, is a word that means "the body politic."

ANGER - - - ANGEL

Where the *angers* of Earth and the *angels* of Heaven converse is the start of our Space Age dream. And though it seems in linear thought that "anger" and "angel" have no common roots, we need only reflect on the crystal seam. Prehistoric sounds connect us to the future in a context where the present is a clearly pre-sent E-mission.

Every word you use today has grown up like a flower, with color and shape determined by its soil and seed. Reaching for the light, words spring from hums and grunts to touch the sky.

Earth, water, fire, and air FLOW together. So, each may be called a FLOWER. Such is the nature of "the Word." Gaze upon the stars, hear the falling rain. The sky is a flower. The river flows. Love is a flower that floods us all. Streaming through this life on Earth, "the Word" becomes a rose, lifts us up, and in fluorescent auras seasons us each unto the fall.

Words need your intention to beget for them new life. As flowers bend and stretch toward light, so living words seek enlightenment, until they plant their seeds again in distant soil.

Fear not death. Your spirit is eternal. For you are a child of "the Word." Follow your instinct in love with truth. Accept no falsity in the fall. You will be de-voted, devoted, and de-voted again, as you choose life eternally.

A metaphor of sounds where "mom" and "om" are linked to Baby M join mammary to memory and then, as humming animals that pucker up to suck, we are cut off by ma-machine from the hum on every baby's lips, as machines take up the mantra.

"M" is the Hebrew sound for "mother." The Latin imperative *regna* means "rule!" And *anger* is *regna* in reverse. We shall see how this romance and the passion of Jesus grew out of breaking bread, symbolic of broken words between the Romans and the Jews. A thousand mysteries spill from every word as energy (E) between R and L is activated by release — REL-EASE.

FRIGHT - - - FLIGHT

Imagine losing your "un-conscious mind." You would build up no anger. In danger you would either run away, freeze, or fight. And when danger was gone, you would feel no fear, have no anger, and recall (re-call) no-thing to resent (re-sent).

The *fright, flight, fight* syndrome is an animal response to danger. As noted, humans tend to store their anger, unlike other species. Yet, storage of un-conscious fear leads us to "feel" closer to our symbols. Thus, we can solve our greatest fear (the impending death of the sun) by perfecting a way to escape into outer space.

We have the archetype "devil" to store "evil." Such patterns will make more sense as the social context is filled in. The feeling for 18 (life) as a crystal element will grow more real as we begin to sense the bio-spirit that unites us.

I am always bemused by little babies who look into an open flame as if there were another world inside. And when the baby reaches for the flame, I wonder at the innocence — in no sense afraid.

I cannot emphasize enough the role of fire as a pivot of consciousness. For we tend to forget that its control is beyond our animal nature.

Mammals evolved to where we had the tools to make fire. Then a fire-spirit came. And that same fire-spirit enters each fetus to repress the fear of fire as the fetus grows in the womb. When does a mammal become a human? The test is by fire.

FAIR - - - FAIL

Without proper *air*, we *ail*, we lose our physical well being. Since we in-vent reality. Je-ho-vah (from YHW-H) is the God of the Wind, and a vow-el is a breath of air. Our spirits put on the airs and "the Word" itself becomes our flesh.

Not being *fair*, we would *fail*. So, our job is to give God air. By being fresh, being defiant in the face of techno dominance, being creative, we rebuild our spirit in the flesh.

CANCEL - - - CANCER

From a human standpoint, *cancer* is the inability of a cell to *cancel* its own growth. And from the cancer's perspective, human cells are waiting to be put to the cancer's use. So, cancer cancels a human self, cell by cell by cell.

This mysterious model of disease implies that cancer can assume a viewpoint and then invade the body. And this medical model is referred to as the germ theory or virus theory.

But since cancer can be prevented by eating properly, it obviously does not have a will of its own. Broken enzymes are always present in cancer. And enzymes get fractured by sunburn, pollution, and physical blows. Might cancer also be due in part to some "evil" like that Adam and Eve ate in the garden? The answer is that the most common way that we put fractured enzymes into our bodies is in the form of cooked foods.

So, rather than looking for viruses to fill out the medical model for cancer, we might focus on vitality — supplying non-fractured enzymes to the digestive system.

The Language Crystal gives us the physical law of how to feed the body. But during the age of history, although the Crystal law was scientific, it did not serve technology. Cancer was accepted because we needed a consumer mentality to drive us into the Space Age. Now, we are here.

Modern medicine claimed, "Unless survival rates improve," 18% of the people in the USA will die from cancer (*U.S. News* 7/29/85). By giving out such "statistics," the so-called experts held on to the illusion of control. But the Techno State kept polluting as if we all might mutate to make cancer normal. And we fed ourselves on drugs while gearing up for more irradiated foods. We were in the Space Age but running on the momentum of the mind-set from the Age of History.

For this reason, it is important that we each acquire a crystallized mind-set so we can begin to explore our new dietary law.

This Sanskrit pronunciation chart shows an ancient line of consonants (note the semivowels) where the English Y, R, L, and V are related.

Sanskrit Pronunciation Guide

Consonants

Gutturals:	क ka	ख kha	ग ga	घ gha	ड̇ ṅa
Palatals:	च ca	छ cha	ज ja	झ jha	ञ ña
Cerebrals:	ट ṭa	ठ ṭha	ड ḍa	ढ ḍha	ण ṇa
Dentals:	त ta	थ tha	द da	ध dha	न na
Labials:	प pa	फ pha	ब ba	भ bha	म ma
Semivowels:	य ya	र ra	ल la	व va	
Sibilants:	श śa	ष ṣa	स sa		
Aspirate:	ह ha	ऽ = ' *(avagraha)* · the apostrophe			

The R and L come to us via a different branch than the Y and V in the unpronounceable name of God in Hebrew — YHVH (also written YHWH).

Je-ho-vah was first a god of the wind. And the R-L law, the RAW LAW of the Crystal, tells us of our relationship to "life" in the foods we eat.

The RAW LAW resolves the conflict between RAM (fire) and LAM (earth) in ancient Sanskrit and in that language from before the time when Hebrew and Sanskrit were first divided.

Our "evil" (live in reverse) eating habits may linger a bit. Emotions may still surround foods we sacrifice to fire as we try to defend our cooking and other intermediate industrial complexes.

Drugs will still compete with foods, especially in motivating us to action. Yet, as surely as a bunch of primates once overcame the fear of fire, so shall we overcome the need to feed our un-conscious ways. And cooking, the original process that altered the chemistry of our foods, will be relegated to history.

Bio-science re-solved makes all religions one.

Yahweh, Jehovah, Jupiter, Jove, and Jesus (hey-Zeus) were spells once cast by deity.

And YHWH was not pronounced; its letters were each vowels in Hebrew. So, by civilized instinct, we thus invented (breathed in) the proper name of "God," who is really nameless.

In the Crystal Code, a VOWEL is a VOW to EL. For YHWH was a God of the Wind. And Je-ho-vah (YHW) answers the English question of WHY, as H (an expulsion of breath) completes the cycle.

Next time a child (or atomic physicist) asks you "WHY," take a few deep breaths before you answer. It will prove to be an inspiration. But the God of the Wind won't tell us why till we find our own reflection in the light.

N reflects a part of M

Say "em," the sound is expansive. Say "en," the sound grows thin. M pictures a continuing wave. N ends the wave. Yet, N is an M beginning again, so "begiN" ends with N. And M is lasting in OM while N is short in NO. Still, N goes ON reflectively.

Approaching each other in the void (O), M and N yield MONO (oneness). Re-turning from the void (O), the ego (I) rejoins both in OMNI (all).

MAN is a vision where waves embrace, where M and N come face to face with realization (A).

MEAN has a double meaning. It tells of a MAN among MEN. His energy (E) can be realized (A) when he follows a middle (mean) path. If he acts angry (mean), pathology leads him astray.

Technology is MEAN, yet a MEANS unto a new and higher way. Biology means a path to the spirit. And balance saves the day.

NUMB is NM in division at B. NUMBER makes the B pronounced. So, techno thought (number) is the turning point (U), at B un-consciously.

And YOU (as I see it) are the turning point in eternity.

110

Make Much Magic

MOM (more open than MAN) generates waves (M) round the void (O). NON depicts lack. M begets mega-words. "Make," "much," "magic," and many more multiply meaning that negatives like "no," "nyet," and "nada" never nullify. In German, NEIN (not 9) is negative. (See NOVA in Latin.) In Russian, _devyat_ is "nine"; _devitsa_ is "girl" (femi-nine).

MUM, silent waves cancel at the turning point (U). NUN makes no waves in bed. NONE (NON-E) has no energy. ZONE (Z-ONE) is limited. Z is the end and turning of N. So, ZEN is an energy zone that limits the limitless one.

The male-factor is no malefactor and ma-lady not a malady when we have words for the melody and sex for naught is naughty.

NASTY (the short wave lacking "energy" E and "life" R) is a sign of stunted MASTERY.

Civilization used reverse-psychology to keep the beast (in man) at her breast. Woman had charge of the kitchen. The fire that he feared was served to him disguised in tea and toast. Thus, she was seen (subliminally) as his fire-goddess.

We ate more and more sacrificial foods since the dawn of history. And many dietitians believed that "hot meals" were more nutritious.

We pulverized wheat, sifted out the starch and bleached it, added water and yeast, then pounded it to ferment, put in some "vitamins" and filler, cooked it, called it "bread," made it into toast, then into stuffing, and cooked it again.

The sun god had been baked in bread to eat. But bread was nutritionally dead. Plant a crumb or crust and it will not grow a single grain.

NE-ME-SIS, the goddess of retributive justice, was a feminine reflection of his EN-EM-Y, which in the wild was always another male. But then, we chose a brand new techno-bio game.

Eve tempted Adam to eat of Technology. Nemesis punished him. And Psyche drove her lover away by burning his flesh. For sex was changed by the use of fire (as we shall see).

As we embrace both machines and immortality, our NEMESIS rejoins the self. The ENEMY is an inner turmoil, energy that ends (EN) and energy that continues (EM) in a union at (Y).

And ENZYME is the final key for it guides our living energy. And ENEMY at Z is a fractured ENZYME, in the end.

This may sound like a riddle at first, yet it fits into the mystery. For when a body dies, we see that it does not stop its enzyme activity. In fact, the body's enzymes assist in its decay. And those enzymes continue to live in the soil, to provide for new growth. So, the death of a bio-spirit is simply a point of departure where each partner goes its own way, for a while.

Egyptian *glyphic* writing (carved pictures) went from left to right while Hebrew *graphic* (abstract letters) went from right to left. And since the R's and L's of both were often confused with what we call W, Hebrews and Egyptians thought of each other as dys-lexic (bad-word) people.

In Hindustani, ATMA means "supernatural being" while ATNA means "to be filled." The man called "Amen" from Alpha to Omega (from Ahhh to Ommm) is living. The Word is in the World again. So, we can indeed get over endless wars.

In contra-dictions of "the Enterprise," Star Trek could show these letters on the screen.

Captain Kirk: We're approaching a star. The signal reads W-A-R-M. We're getting too close. The signal reads W-A-R-N. Raise the shields. The signal reads W-A-R. We're out of control.

With this pattern, war can be turned around. The answer is encoded in the Language Crystal.

"Beam me up, Scotty," says Captain *Kirk* ("Church" in Scots). And in the USA, *the Church Report* limited the CIA (reacting to Nix-on) long before a bogus "Enterprise" and the secret team of 666 broke the intergalactic law, clinging on to the weapons trade, anti-democratically.

GNOSIS IS SONG

A gnostic is one who believes. But agnostics can never decide. So, GNOSIS IS SONG, for gnosis is "belief" itself.

And the Armageddon gang refused to believe what democracy said about war toward the end of his-story. "Western" historic MAN had suffered his quantum spirit reversal in NAM. War was no longer an effective tool of social re-organization.

Centuries ago, a glyph-graph drama was played to the hilt by Jesus when Roman and Jewish coins were traded at the temple entrance. In his anger, Jesus whipped the money changers. Roman coins were embossed with pictures of men. Jewish coins had only abstract symbols.

Jesus displayed his anger because the pictures of men on coins were traded for abstractions to be offered for the work of God.

And in the Final Days, the personal (bio) and bookkeeping (techno) uses of money brought on the scandals of Bakker, Meese, North, and others in the Armageddon gang of Je-R-usa-L-em.

Caiaphas, high priest of the Jews, turned the tables on Jesus who was bought for 30 pieces of silver from the temple priests. Then Jesus felt the other end of the whip before he died between two thieves. And Judas threw the coins back into the temple. So, the high priests used the money to pay for the graves of "poor strangers." For there was a trick in calling people "strangers."

And the trick that divides "the rich" from "the poor" will be exposed when we see how we share a single planet. Making money by selling anything from munitions to junk food only adds to global poverty.

As Jesus was captured, Peter cut off the right ear of Malcus, whose name meant "counsel." **Pontius Pilate** meant "pontiff armed with a lance." So, in these symbols is a moral that we can learn.

And the Jewish high priest who paid for the capture of Jesus had the name of **Caiaphas**, which meant "depression."

Many radical shifts occurred as the USA was being turned around in NAM. Woodstock gave birth to a new generation of anti-war children. The musical "Hair" on Broadway made people aware that Aquarius was coming — to bring Peace on Earth.

The troops came home, guilt began to build, and a few years into the post-Nam era an increase in teenage suicides was blamed on hidden messages in Rock and Roll. The "demons" were said to be sent by Alestair Crowley, a self-styled 666. But demon (evil spirit), daemon (divine teacher), and demos (people) were actually of a single origin.

The faces on the cover of "Sergeant Pepper's Lonely Hearts Club Band," a Beatles record album, had among them Alestair Crowley, "the Beast." The beetle (a bug) was a deity in Ancient Egypt. And the Beatles (with a beat) were a music sensation. So, Christian preachers pointed to demonology in the Beatles' "backward masking" of words.

Some thirty years before "Satanism" appeared in Rock and Roll, Crowley wrote that his followers should think backwards, walk, write, talk, and listen to phonograph records backwards.

In the "White Album," John Lennon says, "number 9," in a way that played backwards becomes, "turn me on, dead man" — a reference to rebirth in the Goddess that the Armageddonists blamed for the start of death cults. But the teenage death cults had already been fueled by images from NAM.

Jimmy Page of Lead Zeppelin bought Crowley's house during Ronald Wilson Reagan's rule. And Page's song "Stairway to Heaven" (a 1970's hit) was tops in USA radio play during 666's reign.

"With a word, she got what she came for. And she's buying the stairway to Heaven. Cause you know that sometimes words have two meanings."

This was the message of "Stairway to Heaven" that played backwards said, "Here's to my sweet Satan." Many nations called each other "Satan." But in the Bible, **Satan** is a word that simply means "enemy" (E-N-E-M-Y).

CHAPTER 13

THE CODE

A = 1

In English, "a book" means "one book." A is our first letter because we use the sound of "a" (from our breathing patterns) to mean "realization."

The softer sound of "ahhh" is realization with satisfaction added. And "ah ha" sounds out complex emotions (realization plus confirmation).

The abstract concept "tree" floating in your mind is never realized descriptively until you think of "a tree."

I may stammer around the sound of "uhhh," when trying to focus. I may say, "I need uhhhh, uhmmm, I need a pencil." And the more my word "a" sounds like the letter A, the more my thought comes into focus. Such is the power of language.

In English, the sound of "a" can also mean "not one" or "negative realization." In words such as "asymmetry" and "atheist," only a space makes the difference between "one" and "not one."

But since "a space" touches "all space" in the uni-verse, the theist and atheist have no-thing to agree upon or disagree about. What may seem like asymmetry to me is only natural to a tree.

I equate "oneness" to "realization" where my own emotions and spirit meet. And atonement is at-one-ment in my vocabulary. I feel my history is forgiven when I know that I am involved in the present, which is pre-sent universally.

This chapter outlines the Crystal Code so that we may analyze the words within our puzzle more precisely. Still, Modern English has many changes ahead before it reaches out to all the languages on Earth and draws them into itself.

B = 2

B is equal to two as in "bicycle," for **B** is our second letter. The **bridge** from **ridge** to **ridge** is **B**. The **border** dividing **order** from **order** is **B**. Where two are separated, where two are joined, **B** acts as an abutment. The **bother** between **other** and **other** is **B**. Yet, spirit can **reach** across each **breach**. And love can **brim** over ego's **rim**. We **blend** and **lend** each other form. We **bend** at the **end** of every cycle. Being two, we continue **to be**, male and female, he and she, ever divided, ever one.

AB (the Biblical word for source) created light (C) in Genesis, verse 3. **Blink** and the **link** of light is gone. For a **lack** of matter and **lack** of pattern intersect in **black**.

We **loom** within each other's love, **bloom** there for a while, and die. **Both others**, he and she, may enact the **right** to make life **bright** or may turn away from **light** bringing upon themselves a **blight** until their magic ring is closed and they cling as shadows in the night, lacking individuality.

Either **locked** in each other's arms or **blocked** by each other's hidden fears, we lived upon the **brink** of time within the **rink** of space where the **ball** of **all** was divided. So, from hell-fire ever **blasting**, shines the light that is ever **lasting** as Adam's blast is met by Eve's elasticity.

Eternally turning energy (E), HE (an explosive E) and SHE (a quieting E) shall ever BE, dividing and coming together in energy. Crystal etymology traces words into the future. **Border**, of Teutonic origin, surrounds the **order** that was Latin. And "the Word" at order's borders has criss crossed the whole of his-story.

A and **B** are divided, separate. AB means "source" in He-brew. ABBA means "father." And since EL means "God," ABEL is "transitoriness" in the Bible. And AB-EL was killed by his brother CA-IN when a new realization (A) of light (C) was in view. For in He-brew, CAIN means "acquisition." And the murder happened after they both had sacrificed food.

His-story was the story of men told in words that women taught them. Yet, children speak in abstract sounds that angels have already brought them.

When Cain killed Abel, their names told a tale of "acquisition" killing "transitoriness." But a literal parallel does not detract from facts. Cain and Abel existed as men just as Reagan, Regan, North, Nimrodi, Ghobanifar, and the rest. They are no less than real because their names align with their roles in our cosmic drama.

AB-EL (transitoriness) spoke in a spirit that was re-divided at the Tower of BAB-EL (the gate of God). With AB as "source" and BAB as "gate," we might imagine the Gates of Heaven, a woman giving birth — a river's mouth, a "source." The rules are not strictly logical, still our letters and their meanings relate to human feelings.

The Hebrew word for "master" RAB meets the word for "boy" BAR where RA is up against the B. For our mystical union builds on a-symmetry.

And with the Code in full array, we shall be able to piece together our historic mystery.

ARSON tells us how fathers and sons disputed over fire, reflecting both sides of RA.

We praise the sun-god that keeps us warm, but warn against a flame that's brought to Earth.

ARIES, the RAM, in Greek turned into MARS, a Roman myth. In Hebrew, ABRAM burned a RAM. And we cannot draw a line between ourselves and gods as they are encoded in his-story's symbols.

Only those aware of the Code and its power over human thought can set themselves free from the hypnotic spells of history.

Good against Evil. God versus Devil. The Code has formal words to praise the formless. Yet, that which goes before (in time) is "the former." And "the Word" in "the Life" gives us form.

Realization (A) divides (B), fires forth light (C); and if that light should light upon another light (C), evolving divisions at the delta (D) triangulate to extend the Crystal.

FIRE --- LIGHT --- LIFE

The source of light of course is fire. L-I-F-E (12-ego-6-energy) springs from F-I-R-E (6-ego-18-energy), but only through the medium of light in photosynthesis. The sun is burning so that we may eat its fruit in the spirit of creation.

AB ("source" in Hebrew and "from" in Latin) is "realization" (A) of "division-and-union" (B) where light (C) is born in the Crystal.

And ABRACADABRA (entrance to entrancement, chanted for enchantment) has roots in Abraxas, Gnostic "Lord of Heaven," and **abhadda kedabrah**, "disappear, as does this word," in Aramaic.

In the history of this babble, we see the Lord of Heaven disappearing as does the word abracadabra, which consumes itself, as does the sun.

These two-fold roots reveal the birth and the death of the sun (the Son of God). And Sophocles counted the number of ABRACADABRA as 365, a cycle of the sun.

ABRA-C-A-D-ABRA depicts a source of good (AB-RA = light) flowing out of the source of evil (AB-RA = fire) and vice versa. Yet, fire (the source of light) is the source of all unconscious suffering stored from the beginning of history. So, ABRA-C-A-D-ABRA inserts an R into the progression of A-B-C-D- to focus the letters in "life."

The role of the ARAB in Armageddon will come to light as the fire-secret of ABRAM unfolds. We will fill in the puzzle pieces as we go along.

But the progression is not strictly logical. As we get beyond the con-fusions of history, a new con-fusion arises a conscious working through of Earthly sexuality. History was mainly focused on the gentling of masculinity while the Goddess was viewed subliminally.

The "Ram of God" was burned by Abraham. The "Lamb of God" went through hell-fire to set souls free. And now, the "I am of God" is taking its first steps into New Age individuality. A new view of language is needed to see our most supreme deity as physically un-qualified.

In Hebrew symbols, men matched wits with boys.

Bar meant "boy," as in *bar-mitzvah*. *Rab* meant "master," as in *rabbi*.

So, BAR and RAB reflected on each other. And when Abraham circumcised himself, he circumcised his two boys also, wedding both Arabs (from the line of Ishmael) and Jews (from the line of Isaac) to the blade of "the machine."

Centuries later, when the Romans ruled Israel, a boy-master (*bar-rab*) was born. And the blood of Jesus was said to replace the need for shedding children's blood. And then, this new covenant was transformed into a sacrifice of bread.

The New Testament says, when it came time for the Jews to decide on setting Jesus free the crowd cried out, "Free Barabbas." Yet, *bar-abbas* means "boy of the father" in Hebrew. But Jesus called himself "Son of the Father." And this linguistic mix-up had another level. In Latin, *bar* meant "wild," as in *barbarian*. And *rab* meant "mad," as in *rabies*, a disease of mad dogs.

The crucifixion of Jesus was a working out of linguistic reflection in our ancient Mediterranean shepherd tribes. "The mind" where words evolve was reviewing its hidden fear in a plan to reunite the body and spirit. For this breaking of "the Word" was executed to open the Gates of Heaven.

These verbal shadings led the Jews not to free *bar-rab*, "Son of the Master" by asking to free *bar-rab*, "a wild madman," the murderer Barabbas. And so, the metaphor turned toward Rome.

When we factor out the B, *bar-rab* becomes *ar-ra*, linking *arson* to *ra*. Yet these are only empty symbols until we know "the Word" as an immortal being, untill we see ourselves following our own words into "the Life" eternal.

Eventually, we will be able to think logically and poetically at once. Science and religion will be united. And our new sacrifice will be one of levity as we learn our Space Age g-ram-mar — a union of male and female principles.

THE LANGUAGE CRYSTAL CODE

A = one, the first principle, realization.

B = two, separate (b-order), joined (b-ridge).

C = light, as in Genesis 3, ($E = MC^2$).

D = the delta (a curved triangle in 4th place).

E = energy (as in everything).

F = six (6).

G = gravity.

silent G = gravity's mystery (as in light).

H = expulsion (ah ha, he he, ho ho, hate).

I = ego.

J = the Tree of Life (1 & 0, yielding 10).

K = life force, (as in kundalini, ki, king).

CH = light expelled (18), also equals K.

L = six plus six (12).

These are the building blocks of English as it is written. Energy is encoded as E, which is in the fifth place. And 5 is also "a turning point" in the language of numerology. J symbolizes the Tree of Life due to the meaning of "10" in kaballah.

Memorizing these meanings is not necessary to read this book. The main idea is that logic and intuition are combined to invent language, thus they must work together to understand it.

THE LANGUAGE CRYSTAL CODE
(continued)

M = the continuing wave (as in om, mix, warm).

N = the ending wave (as in no, nix, warn).

O = oxygen, the void, femininity.

P = power (as in push, pull, pop, pow, pulse).

Q = the inside out (as in question, quest).

R = six plus six plus six (18).

S = the crystal seam.

T = the crystal crossroads.

U = the crystal turning point.

V = the valley (as in vagina, virgin, Eve).

W = spirit wings (as in we, weave, wave, win).

X = six plus six plus six plus six (24).

Y = the yoke, joined and descending (yoga).

Z = the illusion of parallels (see N).

The sixes (F-L-R-X) crystallize in a REFLEX of thought. For our bio mind-set used our bodies in a sub-version of "life" to create the Techno State. Numbed by the numbers, our E-motions reflexed, rather than reflect biology.

Herein, free will and predestination are met at last. The function of the Crystal on Earth is to create a new state wherein we shall balance our technology with biological individuality.

C = LIGHT   G = GRAVITY

Space journeys will depend on how we process the Code. C-ode itself means "an ode to light."

Courage is "the light of our-age." And since C is "light" while G is "gravity," chance and change (chan-C-e and chan-G-e) relate to time in a very personal way. We could break down CH (life) into its componants, which indicate a sending forth (H) of light (C); but there is no end to life's mystery, only a quest for its mastery.

The Earth has ground around its center. And a cover hovers over. So, GROUND is ROUND at gravity (G). And the COVER OVER all is light (C).

Too much of one's own gravity is GREED while a strict adherence to inner light is CREED. We may DECREE (by our lights) what others should be, but all goes by DEGREE (under gravity). "Evil" has a place in nature, as "greed" fits in society.

In our new context, a moderated "greed" is the provision for a future need. So, direct your "greed" to what is best for you.

Your loyalty is your royalty. For each of us is a reflection of the whole. Our social obligations are already written in the Code. We need only make clear the way to be true, biologically.

To see where "creed" and "greed" are one, go to where light (C) meets gravity (G), drink from the crystal river. When the people of Earth have a greed for clean air, fresh water, and sanity, we will know that bio-greed has won.

The techno mind-set, based in greed, can be bio-balanced by a guarantee to all a-greed. Rather than producing more and more Coke and Pepsi, more and more pizza and whipped cream pie, and more and more drugs, we can re-orient society.

While poor people were told to "get a job, any job," a popular TV game show of 1988 was "Double-Dare." Children and families wallowed in vats of junk food. And these were also signs. The remainder of this chapter shows mostly abstract aspects of the Code. Next, we shall begin to bring the abstract and the practical together.

In English, the silent G in LIGHT is called a surd since it has no roots in sound. In math, "the square root of three" is a surd since no number squared ever yields three. Yet, these expressions of absurdity have roots in bio-spirituality. For we each find our center (C-enter) in three, our conception through sexuality, where one plus one makes a baby, bringing gravity to light.

We grafted math from the Tree of Technology to the Tree of Life, and made the path of math a patho-logical ab-surdity. Reaching for the stars, we strained our bio roots. So let us re-deem our nuclear plants, agricultural suicides, pesticides, global vaccination plans, food irradiation plots, and other anti-biological schemes.

Let us re-consider how the spirit's absurdity might be consciously re-dreamed.

The *B* in LAM*B* was silenced as the evolution of English flowed parallel to Christianity.

From WOM*B* to TOM*B*, fear was riddled by surds. The BOM*B* made us NUM*B* and DUM*B* in absurdity.

The surds of hidden divisions (B) and hidden gravity (G) will not be silent as E-motions are set free in Space Age E-quality. And LIGHT will be pronounced by auras of biology.

The aura is disfigured if disease, untruth, or hatred pierce its shield of energy. And auras are always reduced by flames.

The more you feel the truth, the better you deal with disease as its symptoms are read by your individual biology. The more in line your energy is with the flow of photo-synthesis, the more readily you will heal.

CLEAVE is the opposite of itself: "to split apart," "to cling together." So, when spirits CLEAVE, light (C) may LEAVE the one, only to re-turn through the other. Does light have a center of gravity, hidden in a silent G? Or is light mostly levity? The answer is that L-I-G-H-T is shared, as we shall plainly see.

DUMB gets DUMBER if truth goes unheard. And NUMB gets NUMBER if there is no word.

So, NUM*B*ERS themselves become absurd if they have no roots in biology.

Listen. Without the surd, DUMB is mirrored in MUD, Adam before he had spirit. Without the surd, LAMB is the e-scape goat for MAL-intentions, mal-e against himself. Without the surd, BOMB reflects a MOB, humanity globally out of control.

The SOLDIER who was SOLD had not listened for the surd. Without the surd, TOMB reflects MOT, in English, "a word of wisdom."

Woman bears "the Word" when the wildness in men dies. And WOMB without a surd makes MAN and WOMAN one. Born of the spirit where history ends, we KNOW the NOW.

MADAM I'M ADAM
spelled backwards is
MADAM ' IM ADAM

Dancing with the M in Adam's introduction is an "apostrophe," which in Greek theater commanded on-stage imagery. The spoken apostrophe was a device used by on-stage actors to turn away from their audience and speak to some off-stage persona.

In English, the ego's "*I will*" is condensed to "*I'll*." Without an apostrophe, "*I'll*" becomes "*ill*." "*We will*" is "*we'll*" which becomes "*well*." For ego can make us *ill* while harmony can keep us *well*. And *I will* finds its peace in the greater comfort of *we will*.

She will contracts to "*she'll*" which in turn becomes our *shell*. *He will* contracts to "*he'll*," our *hell*. And his hell is passion bounded by her shell — fire re-born in light, forever.

We PROVE this true when true to each other. And to IMPROVE, we act from within. I-AM-PROVE will contract to IMPROVE.

And from deep inside the Crystal spring these patterns drawing history to a close.

The Hebrew "*I AM*" (God, the Nameless) had cast out Ishmael (God listens).

The *PLO* (of the Arabs) had gone insane from not being heard.

And *SION* (a Christian Paradise) had set its sights on "the Holy Land" of the real E-state.

Now, the *IMPLOSION* of I AM + PLO + SION is a compression of Je-R-usa-L-em.

As with the battle of Armageddon, the implosion of history takes place in the mind.

IMMANUEL, Christ, is now the I AM MANUAL, as pure energy (E) becomes realization (A).

RADAM in the Bible (Prov. 10:5) means "a deep sleep." Was ADAM in a deep sleep when Eve was taken from his side? Was he in R-ADAM?

Ego sees MA. I know I AM. MA-AM is the first reflective sound, later seen as MA-D-AM.

And more than verbal wanderings link "Madam I'm Adam," in our Angular language to "a deep sleep" in Hebrew. For only the aura of a woman's shell would man be prepared to go through hell.

RADAM spelled backwards is MADAR. And MADAR in Hindi means "mother." From the "deep sleep" before man had words, mother had her telepathic secret, the source of all society.

She socialized "the human monkey" with her body and her words, and made of He-brew the greatest force in his-story — One Father God.

A mother's teat where babies eat is a treat for any child. But the Techno State made mechanical "drinkers" of men. A-DAM in Hebrew can mean "of blood" or "of red clay." Was the first man made of clay? Or was he born of woman's blood?

DAM became MAD. And MAD is "intoxicating drink" in Hindi where RAMA (R-AM-A) was equal to Krishna, as a Christlike avatar.

The words go on and on. Being IT becomes a game. When children are IT, they tag each other to pass the "itness" along. IT is the ego (I) at the crystal crossroads (T). We are UNITED or UNTIED in accord with how we see IT.

F = 6.   L = 12.   R = 18.
I = ego.   E = energy.

F-I-R-E and L-I-F-E
are the cutting edge of individuality.

In 666's reign, IRAQ and IRAN played patriarchal egos (I's), drawing to an end (N) and into each other (Q), both (centered in RA) trapped in IS-RA-EL's karma. And the karma of secret weapons from the USA fell upon the frigate STARK. A STAR of kundalini (K), sexual energy gone astray, fired on by Iraq's war planes — accidentally.

The captain's name was **Brindel**, Old English for "branded." The $180 million frigate was a 3,600-ton missile carrier (*NY Times* 5/20/87). And 36 dead were returned from the Stark, while one was lost at sea. And peace would not be spoken of until July 18, 1988, as we shall see.

The crucial points often had clear markings. *U.S. News* (2/2/87) said the city Basra was "a psychological key to the survival" of Iraq. And in Hebrew, BAS-RA meant "daughter of evil," But to its families, it meant "good red land" in Iraq, relating to the confusion of "A-dam."

When Reagan was under fire in the Iran-Contra scandal, Senator Burton defended him. In English, **Burton** is "one living in a fortified manor." And Pat **Buchanan**, White House communications chief, backed Reagan fiercely. In Scots, *both-chanain* meant "the canon's seat," reserved in church. But the chairman probing the scandal was **Inouye** (read by many, "in-no-way"), in Japanese, "above the water well," another Aquarian symbol.

Following his Reykjavik (Smokey-bay) stint of absent-mindedness, 666 ignored the three times in 18 months that Russia extended its moratorium (*U.S. News* 2/2/87). And after a U.S. weapons test, encoded "Hazebrook" (Hazy-brook), the USSR got back to testing-as-usual. Note the Aquarian water symbols. Ronald Wilson Reagan was born under the sign of Aquarius. And many symbols around him, in fact, did extend his astrological games.

CHAPTER 14

THE LAST VERBAL TABOO

A riddle: "What has 18 legs and catches flies?"
The answer: "A baseball team."
If you ask a child to tell a joke, you will likely get a riddle in return. By the age of six, children in the USA know about three times as many riddles as jokes. Their riddles decrease as jokes increase until, at about eleven, jokes and riddles are usually replaced by anecdotes.

In steps, the child learns to get around verbal taboos. For riddles, jokes, and anecdotes weave abstractions into things. Unlike riddles, jokes may twist words in insulting ways. And anecdotes are more subtle. Yet, each gains status for the speaker while transforming past feelings beyond social taboos — by manipulating verbal taboos.

The child who asks a riddle assumes authority. The joker can attack a person, group, or idea with little fear of physical reprisal. And the anecdote teller can symbolically alter the past.

In Phase Two, many older people used aphorisms which (unlike riddles) did not invite answers. So, such wisdom often had no listners. In Phase Three, true wisdom comes with no verbal taboos at all, as words caress the global bio-spirit.

To build machines, we start with reductionist thinking; we abstract from nature, and duplicate mechanically. Yet to heal a body, we cannot use a reductionist approach, for the spirit, in truth, cannot be reduced. So, truth makes us whole.

But since we (unlike other animals) named the objects we invented, we put taboos in language. On top of species-specific sounds, we imposed techno words; and verbal taboos were place markers.

This chapter explores the historic taboo that kept our own biology from speaking clearly about the techno hazards that we had created.

Human dis-ease is socially complex. For mental balance is disrupted by deceit in words between body and spirit, even when spoken internally. Thus, verbal taboos can limit individual vitality.

Linguistic taboos divided the classes. Children were taught to say "kaka" or "dodo" (not "shit") while "excrement" was accepted. Each meant the same **thing**; but our sanitary taboo (shhh-it) gave us a parallel verbal taboo. A secret child-culture tracked these nuances with glee. And "dirty words" grew young again, but not without leaving mental scars.

From Latin, "perspire" and "expectorate" seem more polite than "sweat" and "spit," from Anglo-Saxon; but the reasons for this translate into intimidation, dominance, and ownership. Though "dirty words" seemed down-to-earth, jurisprudence put real estate deeds into the hands of those who had learned some Latin.

Since sexual control was seized by the ruling class, the Latin *penis* (tail) was accepted over cock (a rooster) and prick (a thorn), though having the male organ as "a tail" did insinuate a sexual reversal.

After riddles came jokes. Sexual jokes tested the female listener while venting male agression. Racial jokes were territorial in the abstract. And pain jokes seemed therapeutic. In each case, the laugh relieved tension; but it also emphasized social division — private tension. Jokes were both divisive and group-cohesive at once.

Why was Israel's father named "laughter" (Isaac)? In English, *laughter* relates to *slaughter* at S (the he-she seam). Thus, the blood of the lamb. A taboo is at the delta of *daughter*, the moon-blood, and viRgin, with R (life) secreted in her vagina.

We had a taboo against knowing ourselves in an organic biological way. We demanded "proof" by way of statistics and techno riddles. Still, the answers were encoded in our words.

A computer chip with a specific label performs the same function as others so labeled. It's simple. We invent the chip and we stick on the label. But with biological life, we try to label that which is around us, created within us, and evolving.

So, at the crossroads of trying to re-invent our own biology, semantic con-fusions compounded the techno menace to our survival.

The wrong semantic twists are already playing a joke on innocent people, threatening to gag our entire civilization (knockin' 'em dead).

In a few chapters, we shall begin to explore the origins of "AIDS." But every time you see AIDS herein, imagine it to be in quotes.

We had to struggle for compassion in AIDS reporting. But it was taboo to discuss the techno origins of AIDS in the media. We shall examine the issues in depth, for in Phase Three, knowledge (not taboo) is the basis of action.

Was AIDS linked to viruses that were mutated and incubated in labs? The evidence can get lost among re-Latinized (dead language) terms that ignore the subtleties of living biology.

And the ultimate joke (derived from "hoax") of Medical History was its riddle of statistics.

We made vaccines with different viruses (some nameless) by mixing them together. And when we named a virus that mutated rapidly, any name we gave it was useless. So, a diagnosis (the naming of disease) based on such illusions would be a questionable theory, at best.

Also, the definition of the word "vaccine" was being shifted because the old medical models of disease were falling apart. Vaccines were once made to infect a person so antibodies would form. But with AIDS, antibodies were already present in both those who got symptoms and those who did not. Was the medical story an anecdote used to gain prestige by statistical manipulation?

In Phase Three, we speak in terms of biology, untainted by technological hype.

Remember, a mental imbalance can be brought on by spiritual deceit. And the mind affects the body. So, healing is not a techno-reductionist process. The spirit always plays its part. And "the Word" is our pivot between the body and spirit.

AIDS had a physical cause; or more precisely, "AIDS" had many physical factors and was a label eventually used (like "cancer") to name several diseases, each of which had multiple factors.

Our next chapter, "Apartheid of the Mind," is a bridge to later chapters on Medical History, the AIDS Virus, and Nutrition that follow. Each chapter deals with riddles used to cover up our own taboos against biological knowledge.

Honey bees direct each other to flowers by the movements of a dance. And even trees communicate telepathically. Yet, humans gave techno words such importance that we often ignored our own social dances, blocked telepathic waves, and forgot the bio-spirit rooted in our language.

In the beginning, children learn more through telepathy than any other social means. But if a society makes biology a joke and technology a riddle, then techno-knowledge is used to lock bio-fear into an "Apartheid of the Mind."

Around the Holidays, magazines list food under "Home Decorations." Newspapers gear food columns to suit the ads they hope to solicit. Obligatory wine columns are written less for readers than to make liquor advertising seem appropriate.

Night clubs and casinos (with highly processed foods washed down by coffee, wine, and booze) are the stomping grounds of TV comics who often (with some exceptions) add to TV's bad-food bias.

"Science writers" edit cookbooks as a spin-off of their "expertise." And the Government trys to create an illusion of control, while media seeks nutrition credibility. In this social context, nutritionists are now called a threat by hospital dieticians who are trying to outlaw any advise that is not under "medical supervision."

A taboo against natural foods on TV is generally enforced without written orders. Seldom does "a TV person" eat an apple, avacado, or simple salad. Almost always, TV food is techno food, packaged or prepared at length by "a chef." No open conspiracy against the garden variety of simple food exists — but we have a powerful taboo.

Also in the media, drugs are in categories with a taboo against mixing. Marijuana and cocaine may be listed together, or alcohol and tobacco. But coffee is in a class onto itself. (We shall see the reasons later.) People took marijuana with beer, but the separate litanies did not change.

"Drink" (a highly social word) was twisted into "drunk" (intoxicated), for it was often taboo to say "alcohol" (the toxin). So, a "drunk" could be seen as the "victim" in the passive voice.   We have few substitutes for "book" or "door." But taboo items have many words to avoid their names. A greater taboo; more names. Marijuana has many names: grass, gange, weed, maryjane, and other more local slang. Coffee has less: java, cup of mud, brew, pick-me-up. And TV has given us more slang for "breast" than for any other word: boobs, hooters, and other rapidly changing jargon.

A society can also make good things taboo and harmful things not taboo. But then, we find that jokes, anecdotes, drama, and literature will carry on the quest for substantial resolution.

The number of slang words for "beer" (suds, a cold one) decreased since TV ads insisted that we ask for "a Lite" or other substitute. People asked for cigarettes by brand, not for "nicotine."

And taboos protected machines. Studies on acid rain were labeled "incomplete" but studies on the cause of tetanus were called "complete." For germs were said to be the enemy. Techno-based medicine "proved" much against germs by using statistics. But we had a taboo for many years against "proving" the danger of tobacco smoke, while viruses "caused" cancer. In fact, statistics on either side proved not a thing in terms of the bio-individual.

If a child smokes a cigarette, that child will cough. But a person who smokes for many years has less reaction (until the crisis). Drugs disguise our symptoms. Aspirin lowers a fever. But the body's vitality has brought on that fever to burn off toxins. So, aspirin actually blocks the fever by lowering vitality.

We only take aspirin when we have symptoms, so the process is clearer with smoking. The child has vitality and expels the smoke violently. But the conditioned smoker's vitality is weak due to the drug. So a smoker seems "immune," until the crisis, when symptoms break through "immunity." Now, compare this to aspirin.

Due to "Vital Accommodation," many medicines seem to work if we are not aware of the illusion. Healthy people may be judged weak (the child who coughs) and sick people may be judged healthy (the smoker who does not cough) because the body adjusts its vitality to present circumstances.

Be it alcohol, coffee, aspirin, or valium, the drug will lower vitality. But all the while, the user is storing toxins in the organs and fatty tissue. And so the crisis builds.

Medical druggers who hide behind statistics have not made us as healthy as apes. Yet, the techno propaganda endangers every species.

Retin-A was the TV-touted skin drug of 1988. "One daily application maintains epidermal sloughing," said *AMA Drug Evaluations*. Mud packs of fine clay used daily do the same. But clay has no sales rep, gets no TV-MD hype, and is seldom used as religiously.

In our use of the planet, we hid some poison here and there in the same way addicts stored up toxins in body cells. And we hid our global dis-ease with contradictory patterns of speech. *Forbes* magazine (7/28/86) asked retorically: "What Ails the Developing Economies?" But "What Ails" implied a sickness — a biological question. Did Forbes have a "financial" medicine? The riddle is answered by examining the phrase "Developing Economies."

From a profiteering angle, the words "developing" and "economy" were used as techno jargon, where "development" always implied "industrial."

When you hear of "real estate development," do you imagine planting a new jungle? Truth is we need more jungles. But the "developing countries" in Africa referred to in the media are, in fact, the eco-lands that are being destroyed.

When you hear "ecomomy," do you think of eco, meaning "home," eco-sphere? Or do you think of "finance"? When you hear "principle," do you think of money or of philosophy? What does the word "interest" mean, eco-nomically?

When you hear, "I work in the health field," does "health" bring to mind something natural, or do you think of pills and vaccinations?

You can develop individual hearing, which means naturalized listening. What does the word "sweet" bring to mind? A piece of fruit? A persimmon? Or an item picked from the Tree of Technology? A chocolate candy bar.

What of "white" and "black"? Are your thoughts natural? Or are they notions named to cover up a Phase Two social taboo?

If a ragged "tramp" asks three dollars for a used item, a customer may offer two instead. That same customer might not dispute the price of a store-bought antique and would definitely pay the exact price for a pack of cigarettes — due to a social taboo. I have also observed that smokers are more willing to give a cigarette to a beggar than to give a nickle. In Phase Two, we tended to surrender our individuality. But by transposing a convienant way to think of prices, we thought of ourselves as statistics also.

You can break taboos when you are in power. When corporations are sold, prices are negotiated. At every level in nature, power can be used to go against the norm. And in Phase Three, a natural power is born of the individual who cares for the whole. So, a true sense of humor, a bio-spirit humor, solves the ultimate riddle.

The power of spiritual healing has been tested by Christian Science practitioners. But they do not boast, saying that such practice should not be used outside their own religious setting.

But Christian Science, like modern medicine, does not always work. And when either seems to be effective, we cannot say for sure what "caused" the healing; there are always many factors.

Yet, Christian Science as an organized group has provided the time and space to document the healing powers of belief, which is not a private commodity owned by any religion.

When performing in lieu of M.D.s, Christian Science practioners often get "a doctor's fee" covered by easily attained insurance. For with no vaccinations or medical "cures," they heal at a rate equal to or greater than that of those who subscribe to "medical doctors."

But non-affiliated parents who tried to avoid vaccinations for their children found that even though "a religious belief" could keep the M.D.s at bay, "an individual belief" might not hold any political clout. Great social power was needed to speak out against "normal medical practices."

Yet in Phase Three, statistics never apply to bio-individuals. In Phase Two, the last taboo was against knowing our own bio-spirits. M.D.s with the license to give out drugs with the backing of statistics (gathered by drug companies) claimed to be teachers of nutrition, authorities on sex, social counselors, and philosophers.

We had a verbal taboo against using the word "doctor" to describe anyone with no legal license to prescribe drugs. We treated our bodies like machines, forgetting that machines can't dream. And in this context, personal finances and taxes chased after "medical statistics."

So-called "health-care programs" were funded by Government with much the same abandon as were so-called "defense programs." And Je-R-usa-L-em was divided by its own anti-biological taboos.

CHAPTER 15

APARTHEID OF THE MIND

When a "White Man" first showed his face among the Eskimos, he was named *kablunak*, which means "one with bushy eyebrows." In Hawaii, the "White Man" was *haole*, meaning "foreign," related to the pig-god. In Mexico, the "White Man" was a *gringo*, "one who speaks Greek, jargon, or gibberish."

But none of these groups called their visitors "the White Man." The Eskimo was concerned with facial hair, the Hawaiian with the spirit of a pig, and the Mexican with linguistic ability. Only "the White Man" himself was fixated on skin color. And "the White Man" was a phrase used mostly by English writers whose skin tone was more like pink or salmon than it was white.

In Africa, "the White Man" was called *wakolini*, which means "colonizer" in Swahili. Or he was "an outsider," *wanyika* in Tanzanian. In Kenya, the Englishman came to be known as *wabeberu*, "one who sits on others."

In China, more was written about the shape of "Western eyes" than about skin color. But in every land where the English went, there followed the extraordinary myth of "whiteness of skin."

I phoned the U.N. Austrailian Consulate to ask what aboriginies had originally called British colonists. And the librarian said, "they called us the White fellas." And then, when I asked for "an original term," he became defensive.

In fact, I met with much hostility from people on all sides of this issue. But I did learn that different groups had different ways, besides skin color, to label other groups. So, why was there a growing "apartheid of the mind" in the USA?

Each child's ability to read is affected by the truth-quotient of language. And our taboo against bio-knowledge was fostering cultural illiteracy.

Why did the English focus on "white skin" rather than eyebrows, pig-gods, or linguistic ability to build a racial mythology?

Because "White" is an absolute abstraction. And only such an absolute could rule the Phase Two Techno State. As it turned out, all other "races" became "the opposite" of White.

The USA remained a racist nation after its so-called desegregation due to the "White Man" myth. And even people who thought they were opposed to South African apartheid still spoke in formulas with an apartheid of the mind.

The fragmented language of Je-R-usa-L-em held a wedge between instinct and intellect. And "race" divisions were woven into the vernacular of the USA. The term "race" is in quotes here because in Phase Three only one human race exists.

In her book, *Twice As Less*, Eleanor Wilson Orr tells how "Black English, with its own grammar," can come between a student and the solution to a problem in math.

Orr relates that "half more than" in "Black English" can mean what "half as much as" means to the dominant culture. The problem arose when Orr took "half more than" to mean "half again as much" when she was teaching math.

A student had used "half more" to indicate a decrease mathematically, while Orr, the teacher, presumed that "half more" meant an increase. Both interpretations had some logic to support them. But logic was not the issue. Does her book give us examples of how to tutor people who speak "Black English" so that they may become proficient in "White Mathematics"?

Not exactly. But it does raise some important questions of perception as related to "negative" and "positive" in linguistic self-images. Why did slaves use the double negative?

It seemed logical to say white was positive and black was negative, so Historic English carried with it that feeling exactly.

HISTORIC ENGLISH was more than a language, it was a movement that encircled the globe.

As English grew to be the power tool of the global Techno State, its connotations fell under control of "**the man**" who was WHITE, in the RIGHT, and following the LIGHT. And "the man's" ideas (and ideals) were etched into the language.

In politics, "the Right" opposed "the Left." So, "the Left" got left behind. Being right was "righteous," a religious rite. The right-hand side of a graph was positive. Even right angles were cor-rect and "on the square." And "the Right" was politically owned by "the White Man."

In the USA where "Whites" ruled the job market, "the Right" made global policies, and "the Light" overshadowed religion, "the System" had evolved from an un-conscious fear of fire.

Historically, "white" comes from the Germanic *wiz* through the Sanskrit *svetas* which also gave rise to the Slovanic *svetu*, meaning "light." From common roots, the words "light" and "white" made the "White Man" into the "Light Man," born of a "race" among the gods. So, even though we spoke racially of "Blacks and Browns," there was a taboo against thinking about "Whites and Pinks."

In some past era, all "Chinese" were born in China and all "Hispanics" once spoke Spanish. But can an "Oriental" now be born in the USA? Can an "Hispanic" speak only English?

Such questions are absurd since they have no roots in biology. A child can learn any language, and a woman on one continent can bear the child of a man from any other. But Historic English viewed biology in static terms.

Technology was not the enemy; it had given us global travel. So a child of many origins could be born in the USA. But if that child had any African traits, it was labeled "Black." And "White Man's" English held "dark thoughts" to be anti-social and "black deeds" to be evil, while "the Prince of Darkness" ruled the underworld.

The English dictionary defines "black" as "a dark skin tone." This is not the first definition nor a true one. "White" is said to be "a fair skin tone" even though the lightest skin (albino) is pinkish and, in truth, we have no white skins among us. Real skin "complexions" are, of course, "complex."

As far back as the 13th century, the movement that was HISTORIC ENGLISH pictured "Blacks" and "Whites" as absolutely separate "races."

In the USA, a person from India with very dark skin was not verbally grouped with "Blacks." In England, such a person was seen as "Black."

Sallow skins were mythologized as "White." But "lighter-skinned Blacks" were . . .

I realize that this "racial" problem cannot be solved by talking about it in Phase Two terms.

Even Supreme Court decisions were handed down in terms that were legally off color because most people had agreed to be verbally irrational.

After we invented the unconscious to store our fear of fire, we developed a fear of the dark that no other animals had. For fire (in our inverted reasoning) "protected" us from the dark. When light was used for reading, "the dark" became an enemy of the Techno State and was said to be a time when beasts were on the prowl. And though most carnivores hunted by daylight, human mobs did their worst at night. And vampires reported to be flying about under cloak of darkness.

In the context of history, "to be dark" came to mean "to have an animal nature." And our animal natures, if not totally denied, were called "lower natures," to be sacrificed to the Techno State.

We usually used the right hand to write. We used the light to write. And as written words paid hommage to themselves, Historic English focused on things set right by legal rights. Religious rites were conjured up to combat "forces of darkness." And "Whites" who fed on written documents claimed to be enlightened, as the verbal illusion built techno dominance into social divisiveness.

Who was on "the Left" in the USSR, the people or the Government? And what real differences could such labels make to our biological reality?

Even in Russia, "Whites" held power. Were Jews in Israel lighter than Arabs? And among Jews and Arabs, did the lighter skinned of each group hold a social status with more political clout?

In the USA, the phrase "Blacks, Whites, and Hispanics" became a political catch-phrase. But such phrases of verbal segregation implicitly held social-biological segregation in place.

Several decades ago, a "mulatto" was defined as the first generation offspring of a "pure negro" and a "pure white." A "quadroon" was the offspring of a "mulatto" and a "pure white." An "octoroon" was the child of a "pure white" and a "quadroon."

Notice that mulattoes, quadroons, octoroons, and so on got progressively lighter, with no labels for a lineage of "Whites" whose "intermarriages" made them progressively darker.

Dictionaries were written by those who thought they were "Pure White." So, ideas of an absolute "White Race" remained in the language.

But mulattoes, quadroons, octoroons, and so on would eventually replace all "the Blacks."

"Pure Blacks" were being linguistically phased out. And "Pure Whites" faced a dilemma. So, two categories were re-instated as our techno mind-set put an embargo on thoughts that might integrate the human race. Now so-called "White" and "Black" youths with no sense of history often feel hatred that is said to be "sudden" or "unexplainable." Linguistic evolution was reversed to maintain the myth of the "White Man."

Even Martin Luther King, in his "I have a dream" speech said, "Little black boys and black girls will join hands with little white boys and white girls." Robert MacNeil (*PBS*) aired King's speech on the "English Language" series, noted the dialect, but did not address the meaning. For "Black-White" had become a context of national news reporting.

In 1986, South Africa re-classified 506 "Colored People," making them "White." Also, 2 "Whites," by official decree became "Malay," 14 "Malays" were made "White," and 9 "Indians" and 7 "Chinese" were re-entered on the registers as "White," thus being granted the privilege of voting.

No applications were received from "Whites" who wanted to become "Black." And the Government did not turn any "Whites" into "Blacks."

These changes, called "transmografacations" in South Africa, were said to be part of an effort "to maintain racial balance in the country." The USA had a more subtle process. The year that President 666 had tried to stop sanctions by the USA against Apartheid, exactly 666 "Blacks" were transmografied to "Colored" — still not light enough for voting privileges.

Meanwhile, a neo-Nazi "racist revolution" was planned in the USA by Armageddonists of the group "Aryan Nations." In the 7th year of 666, Richard Butler (Butt-LR = Hit-LR), the chief Aryan, was held on conspiracy to overthrow the Government. Butler's Church of Jesus Christ took Aryans to be God's people and preached that the Jews were the offspring of Satan.

The para-military "Aryan Nations" group taught the doctrine that Jews would suffer at Armageddon, an idea in line with sermons of Falwell, Bakker, and other Armageddon preachers. And after a trial, the Aryans were aquitted on all charges.

Remember that Aryan means "upper class" in our metaphor. And the USA was in a conflict with Iran, an Aryan nation, at that time.

Of course, there are no equivalent Phase Three terms related to this topic. But in the Phase Two mind-set, some "Blacks" were Jews, Moslems, or Christians. And there were many beliefs about "Blacks" in Bible prophecy. Still, once the myth of the "White Man" disolves, "Blacks" will also disappear. And we shall, at last, see each other biologically, free from pre-judgement.

Non-White? Half-White? Off-White?

In the 1950's, "Black" was not a favored "racial" term. But when the Freedom Riders of the 1960's were beaten by southern mobs in the USA, "Black versus White" was presented as the context. The real issues, however, were "democracy" and "equal protection under the law" for individuals.

Lunch counters and schools were made neutral territory. But news reports were far from neutral. "Negroes" seized the front of the bus. "Colored People" got "their" civil rights. Yet the context of "Black versus White" made the headlines. And human social evolution was pushed aside.

Various "races" evolved separately only due to geography. But as we traveled in Afro-Eur-Asia, politics kept "the races" apart. As politics in the USA threatened the separateness, myth-makers seized on the greatest abstraction language could afford. "Black statistics" and "White statistics" were invented; and these were absolute opposites that could never biologically evolve.

Evolution was disbelieved by racists, just as a "Communist-Capitalist" peace was beyond the scope of Armageddonists. Each thought in terms of "the group" as a finality, an absolute.

The Contra-Iran hearings put Congress on trial for its "inconsistent fight against Commies." But were all the "Commies" alike? And why were the "Commies," "Blacks," and "Jews" the enemies of the "Aryans" who thought that their ideas were on "the Right," "White," and endowed by "the Light"?

Our ideas were chaotic. We had lost our grasp on biological reality. Yet financially as well as ecologically, global thinking was already at hand. And within the BASIC meanings of English were the tools of Space Age thought.

"Ethnic" is from the Greek for "nation" while "ethical" means "individual character." We have no real ethnic qualities that are not born of ethics. For every nation is originally conceived in a specific language. And in Phase Three, all Earthly languages shall evolve again into one.

In the USA, arguments were stated in terms that could not be resolved. TV people (labeled "Black" or "White") played the roles of "Blacks and Whites together," separate but equal. And the ads took full advantage of the emotional tension.

"The Dating Game" and "Love Connection" on TV had unwritten rules that allowed "Orientals" to be dated by "Whites" or "Blacks." But "Blacks" and "Whites" remained as isolated myths.

Newscasters, politicians, commedians, and sports personalities often called themselves "Black." And those who thought of themselves as "White" were more than happy to agree.

Johnny Carson often introduced his comedy with: "If you accept the premise, you accept the joke." And since most people accepted the premise that "White people" existed, the joke was on many of the people who were called "non-White."

Libraries of "facts" about "races" perpetuated our Phase Two White-Right-Light mythology. Instead of lynching "Niggers," mental apartheid offers segregated scholarships. Rockefeller and Carnegie grants paid the National Academy of Sciences, Commission on Behavioral and Social Sciences, and National Research Council millions of dollars to report on "Blacks in America" (*NY Times* 4/28/86). Some "Black scholars" wanted more control in such studies. But no "mulattoes" need apply to get the "Black" and "White" grant money.

Since "Black" and "White" people were only the creations of a linguistic phenomenon, no scientific studies had ever, in fact, been conducted. Still, we piled more data into our disinformation file. But all the data was linguistically flawed.

The line between "science" and myth had faded. We were funding un-scientific studies.

Remember this as you read our next chapter on viruses. The lack of accurate terminology has also caused a great misunderstanding about the origins of biological disease. Labels can make us "see" what is NOT a scientific reality.

The sons of Noah were named "Dark" (**Ham**), "Fair" (**Japheth**), and "Word" (**Shem**), classics in our cosmic metaphor of light-and-dark evolving in each other before the fall of the Tower of Babel.

And "fair" opposed "dark" in English; a trick of meaning said, "fair" (light skin) was "fair" (honest). For, in the Bible story, after Ham (dark) was "unfair" to Noah, Noah cursed the earth (dirt) and put a curse on Ham (dark) for seeing his father *Noah* ("rest") at rest while Noah was drunk and naked.

This Bible story is suspect in that Ham (dark) was banished to Africa, implying that the Hebrew civilization preceeded dark skins on the African continent. Still, the mysteries of "the Word" are not diminished, even though abused.

Iraq's Ambassador Hamdoon protested (11/22/86) arms sales to Iran. Ham-doon had known for years of Israeli arms going to Iran and asked 666 (the beast with power to buy and sell) to abide by existing treaties (*NY Times* 8/1/86).

Had Noah's three sons, "Light," "Dark," and "Word" set the stage for Israel to sell nuclear weapons to South Africa? Would Armageddon resolve the Old Testament's conflicts in a holocaust?

Not if we follow "the Word." Semites (Arabs, Jews, and others) who were descendants of Shem (word) did not mean very much to each other after the Word of Abram-Abraham was broken.

His scriptural promises had belied his flesh and blood sexual relationships. Abram-Abraham, who was descendent from "Word" (Shem) had given his word to two different women, thus lying to the uni-verse. **Ab-ram** means "source of exhaltation." And **Ab-raham** is "father of a multitude" or "source of the Egyptian vulture" depending on inflection.

But **Ab-ra-ham** is "source of evil darkness" in He-brew. We had a fault in the language.

And "fault" is literally "a division" or an opening. We shall resolve this metaphor in a later chapter on sexuality.

Connective puzzle pieces are found in still other chapters where the Hebrew word for "to do it in the evening" is **ARAB**; and **BARA**, "to create" in Hebrew, is its reflection.

The sir name "Black" is from the English *blac* ("bleach") which means "white." Black is b-lack in the Code. And in Spanish, *blanco* can mean "blank" as well as "white." Clearly, what makes sense in techno terms does not always apply to biology. And we have a language to prove it.

Since thinking is so linked to words, it would be impossible to overcome pre-judgements without a verbal re-deeming.

Phase Two religion frowned on "dirty words" and medicine attacked "dirty germs" while vital words and vital germs were killed in the process. In fact, all words and all germs were good; the only problem was a lack of balance.

A character could "get soiled," as if soil were repulsive. But it was not biology we were saving from dirt, it was the clean machine of the Techno State. Medical chemistry was persued as if we had not evolved among micro-organisms. Doctor's gowns and even the bricks of hospital buildings were as white as possible.

"Dirty" was a word applied to sex. And medical history ignored our compatibility with dirt.

Swamps and decaying matter were a problem for our civilization. But our trouble was not with bio dirt so much as with techno debris. And both religion and science had bowed to the Techno State as the "White Man's" politics thrived on sterile linguistics.

Next, we shall review the Jesse Jackson happening of 1988. The media presented the Democratic run-off in terms of "race." But Jackson was no more Black in real terms than Dukakis or Bush were White. Still, there was a mystery in Jackson's name to fit our Armageddon drama.

Humanity is more than a group of biological creatures. In an invisible sphere, we are acting in an eternal drama based on pure belief.

Jackson derives from "son of Jacob." And it was Jacob who changed his name to Israel. So, with the USA at a color-karma crossroads, **Jesse Jackson** said Jerusalem should be an international city.

His turning point came in New York when Mayor Koch recalled Jackson's 1984 remarks, to push Jackson out of the 1988 presidential running.

Bar **Kochbas** (son of a star) was the last self-proclaimed Messiah to be put down (135 A.D.) when the Jews were driven from Jerusalem for the last time in history. New York Congressman Charles Rangel came to Jackson's defense, saying that **Koch** was acting like "the king of the Jews." And the name Ch-ar-le-s R-angel held ra and el reversed. Also, Jacob fought an angel before he changed his name to Israel. And ch is *chai* in the Code.

Jesse simply means "Jah exists," a belief in Jahovah. But Jackson had referred to New York as "Hymie Town" in 1984 when many Jews took offense. Actually, **Hymie** derives from the name Hyman, related to *chai*, bringing our metaphor full circle. For *Hymen* is the Greek god of marriage (sealing the nomination for Dukakis).

Kirk (church), Democratic National Chairman, was caught in the crossfire. And on the opening day of the **Atlantis** convention, July 18, 1988, Koch banished himself to the Nether-lands.

Jesse Jackson made PUSH (People United to Save Humanity) an entity on the date of 12/18 in 1971. And in the year of his "Hymie Town" remark, he cut a deal with Coors Beer on 9/18, to push $8.8 million into advertising in "Black-media." Coors was funding the Contras and would make more money if "Blacks" drank more beer. Previously, Jesse had convinced the Bush Beer, Wine, and Liquor Company to employ more "Blacks." And Jackson claimed to be the nation's moral leader against drugs.

The Phase Two mind-set had drawn very clear distinctions between mythical "racial" groups but did not understand that drugs were drugs, even when beer was "politically acceptable."

It was **Gore** (an appropriate name for the task) who gave Koch the platform to attack Jackson. And Gore was a supporter of the tobacco industry. Koch had nearly eaten himself to death in various New York restaurants. And such "officials" were looked to for environmental decisions.

Many so-called "Blacks" thought they were too dark. So-called "Whites" got tanned. Most people had lost their minds to the Techno State.

Most U.S. women thought their breasts were too large or too small. And since "techno beauty" was the absolute, some resorted to breast surgery to make themselves look "right."

Also, "sinister" and "gauche" ("left" in Latin and French) meant "dishonest" and "unfashionable" in English. But in the end, left-over garbage that was given the right-of-way by the historic mind-set began to choke us all.

Deposits on newspapers, auto tires, clothing, batteries, cars, and other so-called "disposable items" will be a central issue when bio survival becomes the only political question. But so long as non-issues such as "Black and White" fill the minds of voters, there will be less energy to deal with our bio-spiritual reality. Bio life begins with con-ception. Techno death begins with de-ception. And true language holds the balance.

More than two-thirds of teenagers in the USA have used alcohol and (says the official report) "one-third drink enough to hurt their school work or get in trouble with law enforcement officials."

But "teachers" and "officials" drink alcohol as much or more than any teenagers.

An 18-year-old has probably seen 100,000 beer commercials. Society, so torn by discrimination along "racial" lines, forgot how to discriminate among substances. We divided teenagers from older folk while we put beer and wine ads on TV and banned whiskey ads. Caught in our own verbiage, we ignored the signs around us. And most people had been blinded to the vision of God among us.

Many signs showed a lack of true discrimination. Juleen **Turnage** (turn-age), of the Assemblies of God, said Jimmy Swaggart's refusal to be silent would result in his expulsion (4/4/88). And the Age of Pisces was turning to dust.

When Attorney General Meese asked John Shepherd to be his chief assistant, Denise Sinner said she had an affair with Shepherd (a married man). As proof, **Sinner** said **Shepherd** had a mole that could be seen only with his pants down (*NY Daily News* 4/8/88). And their names were signs.

Shepherd belonged to an all-male athletic club and an "all-White" country club. Swaggart made his South African tour to aid the "White" regime. The Aryan had been caught with its pants down.

We have seen that *cherno* is "black" in Russian. Yet, *chert* is the Russian for "devil." For fear of the dark was international.

In the USSR, "Moslems" and "Asians" were the butt of "White Russian" prejudice. Every group with an historic mind-set mistreated biology to suit the needs of the Techno State. And it wasn't supposed to make "sense" during history.

In the USA today, the law prohibits discrimination due to race, color, creed, national origin, religion, sex, marital status, disability, or age. But you would have no standing in court if treated unfairly because of your individuality.

Laws protect those who BELONG to a specific "race." But if a person will not sell you a home because they do not like your personality, no law protects you. So, seeking "justice," many people accept racial, religious, or other anti-individual labels, without thinking much about it.

Your child could avoid a vaccination and go to school if you were a Christian Scientist. But if you had no "official religion," the Techno State made such individuality difficult, until in 1987 a Long Island, New York District Judge named **Wexler** ("changer") changed the decision on compulsory vaccinations.

Wexler ruled in New York State that a family with beliefs similar to Christian Science was exempt from vaccinations even though its members did not BELONG to an "organized religion."

The other family in that case was not exempted because they objected on medical grounds, not due to "sincere religious beliefs." In essence, the decision said: medical practice was based on a belief system, but that medical religion could not be attacked from within, by common patients.

The question of whether medical practice is a science or a religion leads to our next chapter. Are we the species that in some strange way has become allergic to dirt?

The symbolism that separated what was "dirty" from "pure White" had such power that with the "White Man" myth in place, "non-Whites" usually worked at dirt, tilled the soil, and lost their territory.

"American Indians" (originally from the Orient) did not invent the name "Pale Face." The phrase was dreamed up by James Fenimore Cooper. And the joke was on those who had dirt stolen from under their feet due to the "White Man's" riddles.

In racist terms, generations of "Blacks" grew lighter due to "intermarriage." But no generations of "Whites" grew darker. The puzzle is linguistic, not genetic; and its outcome is territorial.

Now, the USA exports pesticides and medical drugs outlawed domestically. Pesticides return in imported foods; medical drugs return in the form of drugging karma. And the quest for "wealth" (a false sense of wealth) is destroying our health.

America is where the tribes that traveled east from the cradle of civilization met with those who migrated west from the same origins. And now, the American dream is to spread democracy globally. Yet, true democracy is an organic process. And so, the language that supplies its spirit will be balanced biologically, beyond any "Apartheid of the Mind."

CHAPTER 16

MEDICAL HISTORY

Mrs. Beebe's new-born baby laughed when slapped by the doctor. Mrs. Beebe's doctor reported the fact, and it was labeled "medical history." Why?

The reason is alarming. Biological happenings began to be labeled "medical" after it became the custom to alter births, physiological changes, and our emotions by the use of drugs.

Laughing at the doctor's slap was certainly not "normal." So, Baby Beebe's case would have to be monitored closely. The medical mystique could be endangered by such a laugh.

Since drugs can alter the conditions of births, and dying, physiology and even emotions, all such events were conscripted under the terms of Medical History. And even if drugs were not used, M.D.s were given an unusual linguistic role.

With the power to drug, M.D.s held the legal right to name conditions that other people had no legal right to name. In the USA, only a "medical doctor" could own a license to name a disease.

"Medicine," *medicamen* in Latin, means "drug" or "poison." Physical, mental, even spiritual pains can be removed by certain (or uncertain) drugs. But a re-moving of pain with drugs is a trick played on the body since the spirit also re-moves pain. So, we might ask if the drugging of society (like the drugging of individuals) could create an illusion of well-being while leading to long-term ills?

More pointedly, what effect did medical labels have on the social perception of reality?

Was AIDS an Armageddon plague? Will it endure? Or will it fade like so many plagues have faded in the ages before modern medicine?

And what of the notion that AIDS was created by a few mistakes made in Medical History?

Dia-gnosis Versus Gnosis

Mr. Sick complained of a headache. A dietition told Mr. Sick to get more protein in the morning, less lecithin at night. The "cure" was half a scoop of syntho-vitamins in randomized double-blind doses, followed by two placebos and a tepid bath.

Mr. Sick's astrologer had seen esoteric green cheese orbiting the moon. So, she introduced Mr. Sick to a prospective mate; cheesecake in Pisces and pretty fat, but on a diet of powdered yogurt to help lower the nation's Federal Dairy Surplus and slightly skew the couple's karma.

His doctors said Mr. Sick's headache was due to either: 1) tissue blockage, 2) a new virus, or 3) some old nerves in his spine. Number one was a surgeon's diagnosis; two, an internist with an uncle in the pharmacy; and three, a neurologist. The "cure" in each case depended on what Mr. Sick could pay for: 1) surgery, 2) pills and hype, or 3) referrals to the M.D.s colleagues.

Mr. Sick's psychiatrist said he would be crazy to give a headache physical treatment. A mental image (father) was eating at body tissue (mother), causing the ache while Psyche did God-knows-what with Mr. Sick's id. The "cure" was to analyze Mr. Sick's ego until all signs of synthesis had stopped.

A clergyman said sin was the cause but "seeing your doctor couldn't hurt." And since the drugs were part of Mr. Sick's medico-religion, he could deduct double their cost on his tax return.

The Moral: Let others diagnose and you may get out of touch. You could lose faith in yourself, lose your mind to "medical drugs," and never learn to know yourself.

Also, diagnostic tools that impress the victim can cause harm. And an external label would not externalize Mr. Sick's headache. In fact, a label might interfere with finding a cure. But labels were a major selling point of Medical History. For example, people who died with "AIDS" did not all die of the same symptoms.

The Labels of Babel

Throughout Medical History, idiopathic edema was confused with arthritis or premenstrual syndrome. The "doctors" admitted this professionally. Still, before the public (on TV), most M.D.s tried not to contradict each other. Still, German measles was confused with scarlet fever; Myasthenia Gravis with brain tumor or psychosomatic illness. Confusions could be expected considering the complexities. But naming diseases is often a hindrance to dealing with symptoms.

As a disease evolves, medical *diagnosis* (the naming) can interfere with personal *gnosis* (belief). For belief is part of any cure and often brings on healing in an interplay of the spirit with emotions, hormones, and body cells.

But misplaced faith can lead to panic. New York "health officials" said 1 in 18 people had the AIDS virus until it was politically necessary to cut that number in half (*NY Times 7/19/88*).

An Historic Medical Scam

"Polio was defeated by 1960. A triumph," said the media. "The vaccine risk was worthwhile." No more polio? A great step forward for Modern Medicine?

Not really. In 1960, the Centers for Disease Control reported a new disease, aseptic meningitis. And the 1,593 cases of the "new" disease were much like the polio that had decreased by 1,319 cases that year. In fact, *Merk's Manual* (the diagnostic Bible) said to doctors: "The two diseases are clinically indistinguishable in the accute stages."

Was polio halted by a vaccine? Or for some odd reason, was polio re-named "aseptic meningitis"?

In 1985 (latest report) only 5 cases of "polio" were diagnosed in the USA, with 10,117 cases of the new "aseptic meningitis." If "polio" was stopped, why not stop its twin? And what of other "named diseases" with similar symptoms? The "AIDS epidemic" was being diagnosed by the same techniques of medico-politics.

During the "polio epidemic," "non-paralytic polio" could be the label given to symptoms of "a common cold." For Merk, the publisher of the diagnostic Bible, is also a pharmaceuticals manufacturer.

No more polio! Thanks to vaccine! The USA had done it! So why did the USA not turn a profit by selling its polio vaccines in Europe?

The U.S. medical establishment had not hooked the European press into its propaganda network. So, polio ran its course in Europe without extensive or compulsory use of vaccines. What's the explanation? Had vaccinations in the USA caused new epidemics, as it was rumored among "health fanatics" of the 1960's?

Dr. Robert Mendelsohn reports that he "gave up on the polio vaccine when Jonas Salk [pioneer of the vaccine] showed the best way to catch polio in the USA was to be near a child who had recently taken Sabine vaccine." In the debacle, the contenders (Salk and Sabine) called each other cheats and liars. For polio would have run its natural course without their combined interference.

Tight-knit medical groups gathered statistics, named diseases, and in closed sessions molded the data to fit "professionally" biased outcomes.

In the New York Archives of Pediatrics (Sept. 1950) Dr. Scobey wrote, "There are other causes for poliomyelitis, other than a virus." He said food poisoning was a major cause and listed many "polio twin" diseases. But as so-called "polio epidemics" spread, dangerous vaccines were widely used.

AIDS vaccines were tested. Medical statistics shifted rapidly. Wider definitions of AIDS were written. The number of AIDS viruses mounted, The various "AIDS symptoms" increased. And Medical History was repeating itself.

The 1988 medical bill in the USA came to "more than $1800 per capita." And to squeeze the most out of Medicare, growth in physicians costs were up by 18% (Insight 8/8/88). Was this a time to rely on "medical statistics"?

To make it appear that particular shots controled "a flu," for example, a medical group would agree that a case history reflecting immunization against "that named flu" should be reason enough for a doctor to render a different diagnosis. In other words, if the shots had not worked to prevent the symptoms, that same set of symptoms would be given a different agreed-upon name.

Keep in mind, vaccines were touted to prevent a disease, not to act as a cure for symptoms.

Statistical proofs may show a named disease (not the symptoms) is "prevented" while its cause goes unchecked, the symptoms remain, and either "a new disease" is created or old labels are juggled.

In the early days of vaccines, we explained all this by assuming ignorance on the part of the medical establishment. Viruses did mutate. And disease symptoms could change daily. Yet, an examination of the medical literature shows that the cries of several righteous doctors were overruled by the vast majority. The doctors in general claimed successes where none existed. Even worse, the vaccinations often caused permanent symptoms of the sort they were meant to prevent.

Diphtheria vaccine brings on a death rate and severity of illness equal to a lack of vaccination. Measles, whooping cough, and rubella vaccines can result in death as "a side-effect." Doctors admitted the high risk and low benefit of mumps vaccine but continued to vaccinate. Yet, vaccines can change the natural immune reactions of an individual. And since they have a systemic effect, vaccinations can change a person's genetic makeup and thus affect future generations.

The Medical Establishment's plans to vaccinate ALL the world's children by the year 2000 ignored one deadly flaw: Medically induced damage to the genetic material of future generations can never be undone by any amount of re-labeling.

The resultant biological damage due to global vaccinations would put our entire race in peril.

The Merk Manual (1972) said of poliomyelitis:
"Infections with poliovirus are common, but overt disease is relatively rare except in epidemics, and then the ratio of inapparent infections to clinical cases is probably less than 100 to 1. Poliomyelitis vaccines have had marked impact on disease in those parts of the world where they have been used extensively."

But what of the European epidemic that ended naturally? Merk was instructing U.S. doctors in the rules of the game. And pharmaceutical dealers were profiting from the myth.

The Merk Manual (1977) said of poliomyelitis:
"Infections with wild poliovirus are common in unimmunized populations, but overt disease is relatively rare except . . ." The rest was like the 1972 edition. But read carefully. A distinction is made between "wild" poliovirus and "vaccine-caused" polio. Merk said, "The few recent cases in the U.S. were chiefly in unimmunized individuals." But this referred to a "wild" virus. Cases caused by polio shots were called: cholera morbis, billis fever, inhibitory palsy, etc. Educated "doctors" could easily see through the linguistic hoax.

On one panel, reported in *the Illinois Medical Journal* (Aug. 1960), Dr. Bernard Greenberg, said he was concerned over "the very misleading way that most of this data has been handled from a statistical point of view." Dr. Greenberg was a medical statistician. His salary did not depend on the number of shots he administered.

"Paralytic polio" and "non-paralytic polio" were being played off against each other in statistical "proofs" of success. Coxsackie virus was thrown into the mix-match batch of "polio twins."

Were "the AIDS statistics" of the 1980's to be the groundwork for another scam? New vaccines from monkey, bovine, and sheep viruses similar to AIDS were produced before the AIDS epidemic — before not after.

Hold on to this clue.

"Laboratory findings are another reason why I am getting nervous," said Dr. Kleinman, a member of that same panel. "If polio antibodies mean anything in respect to protection, I am forced to conclude that much of the Salk vaccine is useless." He went on to say that "over 50% [of those vaccinated] do not have antibodies to Type I and Type II, and that 20% lack antibodies to Type III poliovirus."

The vaccine was to induce a patient to develop antibodies against polio. A bit of polio should cause cells to react so that in an epidemic the vaccinated would be saved by their antibodies.

Unlike various "polio" viruses, just a little infection with "AIDS" could be deadly. Why was the "new" so-called AIDS virus so adapted to human tissue? Had it been cultured in human tissue in medical labs? Hold on to this clue also.

Antibodies in the blood are used to diagnose AIDS since the virus is so small that electron microscopes are needed to see it, so diffuse (in one of thousands of cells) that finding antibodies is easier, but less conclusive. We cannot examine a live virus. It is killed to be tested. Therefore, we do not see the function of a virus. We have never seen a living virus interact with antibodies.

That the relationship of virus to antibodies is theoretical was ignored by vaccine merchants and therefore by the media that used "official" press releases rather than investigative reporting.

Keep in mind those "Black people" and "White people" who seemed so real because they lived in linguistic myths that were accented in the media. Now, what of our "mulatto viruses"?

Historic prejudice ran so deep that many of us did not take verbal truths to heart. Some people found comfort in thinking of themselves as either "Black" or "White." And slavery to such absolute abstractions had served to build the Techno State just as slavery to the Pharaoh had once built the pyramids. Still, thinking of biology in such terms had weakened our spirits.

Statistics on "Blacks" and "Whites" were used to tug at emotions while feeding a climate of social division in the Techno State. And medical numbers did the same. Statistics deal in the abstract. But if applied to bio-spirit, they do more harm than good by interfering with gnosis, which is a belief in the personal individual (not-dividable).

The worst part of the vaccine story is that shots carry un-named viruses. Vaccines are made not in sterile labs, but in scabs of purposefully infected animals. So, how did the AIDS virus first enter a human? And why did so many AIDS twins suddenly appear only in humans?

Other-specie viruses do NOT readily adapt to human cells. But a virus cultured in a lab and grown successively, generation after generation in human tissue, will adapt. An in-depth chapter on "AIDS" origins gives the details later.

In the 1800's, a German influence in the USA caused a shift from mild herbs to heavy drugs in medical practice. And only in 1975 did the AMA begin to shift away from its dogma that food had no bearing on disease. By 1980, a few M.D.'s were studying nutrition; and by 1986, many claimed to be experts. Then, a media blitz was launched to say that "doctors" knew the truth all along.

After only 12 years (1975-1987) the snakes from the head of MED-USA were getting laws passed to constrict private citizens who might give nutritional advise to each other. And in several states, such laws are even now in effect.

If laws force vaccines into people's blood, why not force them to eat properly and exercise instead? Neither is true to democracy's spirit.

The Techno State refused to admit that most dis-ease was caused by unnatural eating habits, pollution, and civilized stress, and that vaccines are a threat to the long-term evolution of human vitality. And what of the spirit factor in evolution? Let us begin to fit the Language Crystal's puzzle pieces together with our bio-reality.

CHAPTER 17

QUESTIONS ABOUT "AIDS"

Do viruses invade our bodies or do they wait for an invitation? More importantly, when a virus is in some person, what or who decides if that virus can or will do any harm?

And most importantly, for the survival of the human race, since we are the hosts of the virus, what role do we play in viral mutation?

About 80% of adults worldwide are infected with the oral herpes virus. Some get sores, some do not. About 20% of adults are infected with genital herpes. "Attacks" of genital herpes usually appear after an emotional upset. Who is attacking? Who is being attacked? Is the virus to blame?

With the emotions under control, outbreaks of herpes can be halted. So, we cannot say a virus is "the cause" of the disease. Emotions effect the body's chemistry. So, there is no single CAUSE for any disease. There are only many FACTORS.

Also, unlike bacteria, a virus has no actual metabolism of its own. The virus procreates only through our DNA and RNA. A virus is one of "the living dead," with no will of its own. And so, our spirits must play a part in viral evolution.

Viral genes do not mutate unless they do so in league with the RNA of their hosts. At least, this was true until humans started mutating viruses in specimens in medical labs.

Animal tests showed that each species made its own different antibodies against the AIDS virus. And though chimps could be infected by needles, none of them got the severe symptoms of "human AIDS." The chimps developed swollen lymph nodes which indicated that their nodes were working, trapping and eliminating poisons. But somehow a new virus had been mutated that was specifically adapted to human tissue. How?

Comparisons and Twin Diseases

A rumor was spread that monkey bites or those who ate monkey meat had started AIDS. But AIDS had first appeared in cities, not in jungles. And the pygmies, who ate the most monkey, seldom if ever got AIDS. So, monkey bites and eating the flesh of monkeys did not originate AIDS.

Again, the term "AIDS" is used here as it was used in Medical History.

African AIDS statistics were added to AIDS statistics from the USA even though lab equipment in Africa was lacking and cases were diagnosed often by visual clues.

In the USA, as the disease (or the statistics) progressed, we had as many AIDS twins as we had polio twins. There was "asymptomatic AIDS" as there was "asymptomatic polio" which made it easy to prove anything at all, statistically.

In Africa, malnutrition could be the a major cause of symptoms that were diagnosed as AIDS. And the global path of AIDS was parallel to the path of smallpox vaccination campaigns — an interesting factor that we shall return to later.

TB or not TB

Medical History said that vaccines now protected the USA against tuberculosis (TB), but only after 90% of TB was eliminated by central heating and clean-air laws in factory towns.

The epidemics of diptheria, whooping cough, and measles had begun to decline in both rates and virulence before their vaccines were introduced.

Rheumatic fever, an inflammatory disorder that crippled and killed for decades, was rare in the USA by 1988. Yet, "the doctors" did not know why it had faded. There was no vaccine.

But if a rheumatic vaccine had been patented, TV would have documentaries extolling "the great rheumatic fever triumph" of Medical History.

Manipulation of the media rather than cures had built the "effective-vaccine" myth.

Medicines once mystified by Latin names are now shielded by "statistics." As with the "White Man" myth, repetition had made an historic memory seem to be a numeric fact.

AIDS-related sarcoma lesions were similar to TB that had raged in factory towns with a lack of central heating. And so-called "minorities" were getting the symptoms of AIDS.

H. Nikens M.D., director of Minority Health in U.S. Health and Human Services warned that AIDS was becoming "a minority disease" (*C.S. Monitor* 5/16/88). Not "low income" but "Black and Hispanic" was the label applied to the "risk group."

"White" intravenous drug users were often put in a separate catagory. But contagion by blood was not a believer in myth. In the USA, some 60% of the 18,000 hemophiliacs had AIDS from blood given by hospitals (*Night Line* 6/14/88).

"Scientists Admit AIDS Identification Error" (*NY Times* 2/23/88). "Growing a Wrong Virus" (*NY Times* 3/1/88). There are multiple AIDS viruses (*Science News* 2/27/88). Plus, each strain had many mutants. So, the easily detected were first blamed by "medical scientists."

Why so many male homosexuals get AIDS at first instead of the general population had various and contradictory explanations. In a later chapter we shall see how an "agressive medical treatment" of hepatitis and mononucleosis (endemic among many male homosexuals) played a part.

Anal intercourse among either hetero- or homo-sexuals is not a wholesome practice. Still, it was not the origin of AIDS.

We had "Blacks" with light skins and European features; but we had no "Whites" with negroid or African characteristics. Our historic linguistic framework had blinded us to bio-reality.

We had many people with the exact symptoms of AIDS but who had no virus. We had people with the virus who had no symptoms. And still, since we had an "authoritative" group of "doctors" with their "statistics," bio-reality could be damned.

A Smallpox-Hepatitis Connection?

Why were homosexuals the first to get AIDS in the USA? Many got hepatitis injections prior to any AIDS symptoms. We will discuss this later.

At first glance, the data seemed convincing. Up to 90% of those with the virus were in risk groups that were statistically defined. But people not in risk groups who had like symptoms were then said to have Kaposi sarcoma or some other illness, not AIDS. And poor antibody testing left more room for statistical manipulation.

Rather than admit to a multitude of factors, "medical authorities" (in league with the drug companies) searched for a "cause" that could be halted with more vaccines.

Were the many AIDS viruses hybrids from medical labs? M.D.s who brought up this question were not given airtime on major TV networks. And why did "experts" question whether the last stocks of smallpox should be destroyed (*NY Times* 11/3/87). A cover up? One AIDS virus was a cousin to smallpox. Let's take a look at the medical politics of the AIDS era.

After years of little-publicized court battles, the American Medical Association (AMA) was found guilty of conspiracy to violate the Sherman Anti-Trust Act. And the guilt went deeper still.

In 1987, the AMA, American Hospital Assoc., American College of Radiologists, American College of Physicians, American College of Surgeons, and Joint Commission on Accreditation of Hospitals were found guilty of conspiring to influence Congress and otherwise trying to discredit the so-called "Alternative Health Care" systems.

A heavily financed appeal was mounted. But an injunction had been handed down on Sept. 25th in a Chicago U.S. District Court to stop M.D.s from illegal discrimination in business practices.

What, beyond financial interests, came between the "alternatives" and the M.D.s?

After decades of collecting funds for "the war on cancer," it was begrudgingly admitted that raw fruits and vegetables were the best preventative.

A Children's Headache Remedy?

We could no more cure cancer than cure a cold. The virus theory had not paid off. And the idea that what prevents disease can heal was crystallizing in the public mind. If eating healthful foods can keep us well, then eating healthful foods can heal.

But M.D.s did not want others to get business spin-off that might come from giving out dietary knowledge. Most of the TV ad money spent by large pharmaceutical companies was, after all, to get people into a "doctor's office." "See your doctor" was the message, as if the only doctors were of the drug-pushing medical sort.

So when chiropractors and nutritionists spoke of natural healing, the AMA barred M.D.s from any association with the so-called "quacks."

In pregnany's 3rd trimester, back pain due to imbalance is often successfully treated by massage and physical adjustment; but some M.D.s gave drugs to pregnant women rather than refer to a chiropractor for the needed adjustment.

The Federal Trade Commission, Better Business Bureau, and Federal Drug Administration each met regularly with the AMA to end "Alternative Health Care." The FDA and drug industry teamed up to mail out news kits on Quackery, as if legal-drugs were not pushed by quacks. And the media accepted the propaganda as legitimate news.

The AMA's guilty verdict was hardly registered in the media where TV and magazine M.D.s had been made a part of "the news team."

Unlike racism, rampant medicalism was not seen as a threat. Racists, at times, denied their pre-judgements. Medicalists were trying to put their form of prejudice into State and Federal laws.

Ads for children's drugs were directly aimed at children in TV peer-pressure formats. As cocaine and heroin were first introduced into wholesale markets by the medical profession, so our next generation of addicts was being prepared. And it was all quite legal.

QUACKERY

This brochure is a joint publication of:
The Federal Trade Commission
The Pharmaceutical Advertising Council
The U.S. Food and Drug Administration
The U.S. Postal Service

**U.S. Department of Health and
Human Services**
Public Health Service
Food and Drug Administration HFI-40
HHS Publication No. 85-4200.

Above is a reproduction of the front and back of a 1987 pamphlet from the U.S. Department of Health. Note that the brochure was jointly published by "The Pharmaceutical Advertising Council."

Of course, we have some medical practitioners who try to use drugs sparingly. And surgery will always be needed in case of accident. Also, there are as many quacks in the so-called "Health Food Industry" as among M.D.s.

We have some chiropractors with less skill than others. And though some may give good nutritional advise, other people will not. Our problem is that the Government cannot legislate properly so long as meat and dairy lobbyists and medical interests are making governmental decisions.

So, we come again to true democracy as the goal of New Jerusalem, our Phase Three global city.

Before we address how a new virus was mutated to adapt specifically to human tissue, before we consider individual faith rather than the faith of organized religions, organized medicine, and techno-organized governments, let us dip again into the crystal stream of God's Eternal City, Jeru-salem (possession of peace). And let us re-examine the "evil" that we ate in the garden of Eden.

CHAPTER 18

TURNING WAR AROUND

In the next few pages is the message central to the Language Crystal. This is the jewel in the lotus of our universal linguistic mandala.

When the fragmented Je-R-usa-L-em gets itself together in the Crystal City of New Jerusalem, a singular nutritional law will rule the land.

But please don't panic. This does not mean that you will be put into prison if you break this law. There will be some fudging for a while until "free will" and "choice" come into line with "common sense" and "primal instinct."

It never makes much sense to eat things that you do not like even if they are good for you. For the best of food, eaten with resentment, can turn to sickly sour mash churning in the stomach.

However, the Crystal LAW of nutrition states clearly what the highest energy food can do for you. On a very personal basis, it will bring you inner peace. But not every person can begin today. For we do not have enough of this high energy food globally available under present circumstances.

No, this is not a sales pitch for bee pollen or vita-soup. There is no order form to fill out that reserves "your special 30-day supply."

Still, this food will make you thinner or put on pounds if you are too thin. You will reach a balance with nature. Combine this food with proper exercise, fresh air, and moderate sunshine, and you will be more aware and energetic.

As we shall see, our agriculture will be saved, farmers and orchard owners will thrive. And all the people of the world will be better fed. But such changes, naturally, will take time.

First, let us look at the mystical clues to our very natural food that are hidden in our various languages. We have seen some already.

In German, *waffe* means "weapon."
And *waffel* means "a wafer of bread."

In Hebrew, *locham* means "war."
And *lechem* means "bread."

In Russian, *duku* is "spirit," *dukhovka* is "oven," and *dukhovenstvo* means "clergy."

In Russian, *muka* means "torment."
Yet, *muka* also means "meal."

Also, *aph*, the Hebrew for "nose," is the word for — "anger." As God breathed "life" into Adam's nose, it was more than a "natural" life. And the He-brew word for "baker" is *aphah* which is of the same root as "anger."

In Russian, *pekar* means "baker."
Yet, *pekhota* means "infantry."

Jesus was born in Beth-*lehem*, a "House of Bread," in a MANGER, the Latin word for "to eat."

In He-brew, MAN-GER means "strange manna." And "Yiddish" is the GER-MAN word *Judisch*.

In German and Yiddish, *essen* means "food," for food is of the essence in our Angular union.

Note that these linguistic trails link the modern nations at the heart of our "struggle with God," IS-RA-EL. In Hebrew, RA is a fire-light outside. EL is a fire-light within. And remember that pyr-amid is related to the bakery feast of Purim.

Why has a little piece of bread become the focus of Christian ritual? Why is it forbidden by the Catholic Church to say the mass with a piece of raw apple instead of a piece of cooked bread?

How did our sacrifice of food to the gods of fire become a factor in the countless diseases plaguing humanity in the final days of history?

Let us examine the major transactions in Bible History. How were they involved with BREAD?

THE FOODS OF SACRIFICE

In the garden, Adam ate fruits and vegetables. Out of the garden, Adam was told: "*In the sweat of thy face shalt thou eat bread*" (Gen. 3:19). He had to sweat for his bread. And fire blocked his return to Eden, beginning our historic metaphor.

Cain murdered Abel after both these sons of Adam had been "sacrificing" food (Gen. 4:3-8).

The land-right to Israel was traded: "*And he sold his birthright unto Jacob. Then Jacob gave Esau bread and pottage*" (Gen. 25:33-34). So, cooked food sealed their real estate deal.

And Jesus was betrayed with a piece of bread. "*He that eateth bread with me hath lifted up his heel against me,*" said Jesus at his Last Supper (John 13:18). Then Jesus blessed the bread.

And in the reign of 666, "*a smoke came out of the North*" (Isa. 14:31). And Colonel Oliver North took a cake and Bible to the Wise Men, the invisible moderates of Iran.

Looking back to the fall of Adam, to the murder of Abel by Cain, to the quarrels between Israel and his brother Esau, to the crucifixion of Jesus, and to the cross between Iran and Ronald (6) Wilson (6) Reagan (6), we find this common thread.

We cannot blame Adam, Cain, or Israel. We need no longer crucify Jesus for his bread sacrifice. And Ronald Wilson Reagan (working through North) can be forgiven for sending his cake, because a Charismatic told him to.

Armageddon was ending; 666's power was falling to "the People." With price supports removed from tobacco, meat and dairy, with medical and drug industries competing in an educated market place, with coffee, alcohol, and heavy drugs taxed in proportion to their social harm, we can work our way back to the garden, democratically.

Imagine you were born two thousand years ago. You felt a bit different than other children. Growing up, you could see into the hearts and minds of your playmates. You saw with clarity what others held to be mysterious. Not only did you know the most distant past, you also looked into the future.

Due to your powers, it would appear strange for you to speak your mind directly. You could not ask your companions to change their lives as radically as would be necessary to live by the law of full consciousness. So, you spoke in riddles.

You became as one with humanity, taking on the common ways, eating bread and drinking wine. Yet, your mystic memory held onto a natural law. You saw the primitive mind in a pristine state before the use of fire. And still you chose to go through hell so that humans would have an example of how to suffer quietly while developing technology.

Your parables gave hints of the many levels of understanding sub-stance.

At the crossroads nearly twenty centuries ago, you made your life and death a parable of bread.

Your best friends had never seen a spaceship. How could you explain it to them?

You said, "Master, love your slave. Slave, love your master." Then you sanctified the food that feeds unconsciousness. Blindly enslaved to the Techno State, humanity would work its way to heaven.

The fear of fire in monkeys had been replaced by a mystery of hell. But you knew that all fears were the same. Still, you had no one to tell.

The Roman Governor, the Jewish Sadducees and Pharisees planned to put your body to death. In fact, they followed your Father's plan. You knew your followers would forsake you, soldiers would obey their orders, and not one person would grasp the meaning of your sacrifice.

Someday, somehow, humanity would really go to heaven — and continue to multiply.

In truth, your Word would never die. For your name, *Jesus*, means "Savior" in He-brew.

Alice and Wonder Bread

Alice began her adventure by drinking from a bottle marked "DRINK ME." Unwise to bottler's ways, she said, "The bottle has not been labeled poison, so there should be no poison in it." The mixture of cherry-tart, custard, pineapple, roast turkey, taffy, and hot buttered toast caused her to shrink. "Shutting up like a telescope," her mind reacted as all consciousness reacts to eating fractured enzymes (the key to our mystery).

Next, Lewis Carrol makes Alice into an image of Christ. "She tried to fancy what the flame of a candle looks like after the candle is blown out." She ate a tiny cake marked "EAT ME." The printed word told her to. And that cake (a ticket to Wonderland) was incased in glass, like the monstrance around a cooked Eucharist in the Christian mass. Jesus was a rabbi who was nailed to a cross, and Alice's journey is through a rabbit (rabbi-T) hole.

Oh, how the Word was broken by B-READ. Alice's first thought after eating the little cake was **"that for a moment she had quite forgot how to speak good English."**

Her next thought was to get a new pair of boots every Christmas. This tells us in Carrol's imagery that Alice was linked to Earth (by boots) through the birth of Christ (Christmas).

To Alice in the garden, things were reversed (dys-lexic) and confused. For her's was a techno mind-set trying to talk with animals. Her vision had been inverted by the things she ate.

"I took the little book out of the angel's hand, and ate it up; it was in my mouth sweet as honey: and as soon as I had eaten, my belly was bitter," wrote Saint John the Divine (Rev. 10:10).

Cooked food, sweet in the mouth, turns bitter in among the stomach's living enzymes. A Phase Three view of Scripture shows bodily reactions linked to the spirit. For IS-RA-EL is where the fire-light that is outside meets the fire-light within. Is Ra El?

RA = EL = C. It's relatively CLEAR.

167

Our culture started in the garden. we had a sense of Peace on Earth. We were monkeys, safe because we climbed in trees, high above the predators.

Our story started in the heavens. We saw the brightest angel fight against the essence of all light. And we were the spirits who ob-served.

Humanity was born — a union of these two.

As monkeys, we saw Lucifer fired from his place in Heaven. But we were confused. We saw him as "the Prince of Darkness." Yet he lived in flames. He gave us fire to make us like the gods, so we might evolve forever. And when we ate the fruits of fire, all hell broke loose. For . . .

R A W

SPELLED
BACKWARDS
IS

W A R

Yet, WAR can be turned around
by application of the RAW LAW.

We were the only species on this planet ever to cook its food. And with this mystery inside us, its answer was externally encoded. Backward spells and R-L confusions make sense in turning war into something new. The raw law is our key to ruling over the techno mind-set, bio-democratically.

Let us now begin to bring the various sections of our Crystal puzzle into line. During the reign of 666 in Je-R-usa-L-em, a new food consciousness was taking hold in the USA, a consciousness that could radically change the eating habits of all nations, a new food consciousness that could literally turn war around for the New Millennium.

FIRE WAS THE FIRST
ARTIFICIAL PRESERVATIVE
EVER ADDED TO FOOD

Diets of raw fruits and vegetables are the best for avoiding disease. But "scientific" studies remained inconclusive on this issue since most "scientists" did not "believe in" eating much raw food.

Most health food journalists insisted that many foods be cooked to break down their fibers. Other foods were said to have enzymes too strong to be assimilated in the raw state.

BUT FIRE AS "AN INGREDIENT"
RADICALLY ALTERS THE STRUCTURE
OF EVERY SINGLE NUTRIENT

Raw pizza was not appealing nor a food natural to our species. We ate so many manufactured foods, that we almost forgot our natural tastes as they were before the use of fire.

But how had we become enslaved to "hot meals"? Why did we think our food was less appealing when it cooled to room temperature again? What trick of "home cooking" made us offer food to fire before we ate "a meal."

AN OUTLINE OF TECHNO HISTORY

(1) As monkeys, we realized that stars were dying. (2) We knew the Sun (source of earthly energy) was a star that would die. (3) So, we prayed to get to Heaven before the Sun and Earth would die.

(4) The spirit of eternal life then allowed us to sublimate the fear of fire. (5) Eating fire-foods, we fed the un-conscious. (6) And then un-consciously we mentally reflected on myths that sealed our fears.

(7) Our innocent monkey memory faded, but its shadow left us with an "original sin."

(8) When Christ took on Adam's bread sacrifice, he manifested a divine division between the body and the spirit. (9) And now, "the Word" has come in a new atonement, at-one-ment, (10) so that we may dwell consciously in the Tree of Life again.

Heating food above 130°F destroys its protein. (You would never take a bath that hot.) And when cooked enzymes interact with our own living enzymes, we re-supply our foods with "life" by sacrificing our spirits.

Enzymes have evolved on the Earth's surface with a limited range of heat resistance. And to expand that range requires either millions of years of evolution or concentrated spiritual work by "the race" as a whole.

Remember that you have "an eternal life" and "a mortal life." There is a flow between these two. And your mind observes your spirit as it moves through your body. More cosmically, this flow is "the Word" itself.

Your mind sends messages to all other minds. And thought waves are reflective — a clue to how the patterns of the Language Crystal are E-merging. Our problem at the end of history is that we are approaching the saturation point where human biology will no longer support the intake of dead enzymes. We are depleting our spiritual energy to keep our physical energy alive while eating more and more dead food.

If "life" were born of inorganic cosmic soup, if enzymes were made of chemicals with no spirit, then we would have no metaphor. But we each can hear a voice within that speaks of creation. And so, we can create a set of conditions to insure that voice a more comfortable place to inhabit in the future.

As cousins of apes, we could not have begun to work with the flame if not hypnotized by a fire spirit. An exchange of energy was used to build Space Age technology. And another exchange will unlock the gates of the Eternal City.

The "bread" pattern of many languages extends the original split between RA the sun god and RA, the Hebrew concept of "evil." And so, the 18's in our final years will in the end crystallize in our minds as the purest path, a meditation on "life" beyond "life."

On the surface of the Earth, heat above 130°F destroys enzymes. This is why RA is He-brew for "evil." "Evil" is "live" spelled backwards. "Devil" is a reflection of "lived." And WAR is RAW in re-verse. Only the Raw Law solves our linguistic mystery entirely. Flour does not flower in the punishment of puns.

We ate more and more sacrificial foods since the dawn of history. And dietitians believed "hot meals" were more nutritious. The fire-sacrifice, our techno legacy, and destructured enzymes ruled our Phase Two bio-systems.

Within the millions of years of human evolution on this planet we cooked food for only thousands of years, yet many asked, "Why eat raw food?" rather than asking the more obvious question, "Why eat cooked food?"

Human beings had made themselves the exception to the raw food rule of nature. And in the end, most of us expected to die in a hospital at the "mercy" of our own fire-born technology.

Had the sun god of Heaven been baked in bread to be eaten on Earth? Was there magic in the food of sacrifice?

The answer is yes. The foods of sacrifice had brought society together, feeding the unconscious, allowing us to work with technology in a way that natural primates could not. We had no conscious fear of fire. Yet, in the language of the Angles, we had encoded FEAR and FIRE with parallel vibrations.

And now, the Second Coming of "the Word" will give to all humanity a new perspective. Bread is dead. Plant a crust of bread, it will not flower or produce a single grain of wheat. B-READ, as a broken word, symbolizes a return to the Tree of Life on a new plateau. READ gains a new power to LEAD.

But this new union will be realized only in the doing. Reading is no longer a matter of detached abstract symbolism. As language crystallizes, all reading is done with a true connection to the eco-sphere and to human biology.

A Corny Story

Imagine eating an ear of corn for breakfast. Fresh corn, right off the stalk, uncooked. Would it be super-energizing? Not especially. Corn, even raw corn, is not a first choice of foods among primates.

But shoot those kernels of corn from guns, put them in a box with a hero or cartoon character as their endorsement, and suddenly that simple ear of corn is "something super-natural" — or so say the TV ads. Can cooking add energy to food?

Corn, flaked and baked, has less nutrition than raw corn. For cooking can only destroy nutrients, never add to them. But raw corn, raw cow's milk, and a chunk of raw sugar cane to chew on might not appeal to "the average consumer" while baked corn, pasteurized cow's milk, and granulated cane sugar seem to make "a perfect combination" on TV. How did we develop such illusions?

Why celebrate a birthday with burning candles on a cake? Why hang lights on a tree in winter?

Such rituals approximate the way we saw reality before we had the use of fire. We string lights on Christmas trees because we long for the aura of fresh fruit, as found in *paradise* (from a Persian word meaning "garden").

Religion says God created "life." Science says that "life" began spontaneously in a chemical soup. But proof that "life" can begin where "no life" exists is lacking. All "life" comes from a chain of existing "life."

A problem with the meaning of "life" for modern scientists was that science did not believe in the spirit — our grand data-matrix, the under-standing of sub-stance, the matter pattern of our living uni-verse.

Life organized by light works through a living seed. And supernatural life begets a vision so that natural life may see.

Matter is eternal. Energy is eternal. Life is eternal. And eternity extends not only into the future, we come from an eternal past as well.

Life has always existed.

Enzymes at Work and Play

A fruit fly deposits its enzymes to eat away at the skin of an apple. When you eat an apple, the enzymes in your stomach engage the apple's enzymes in the dance of life. Or an apple digests itself (rots). The enzymes in its pulp mature to feed the enzymes in that apple's seeds.

And before the sperm-cell of a man penetrates the ovum-cell of a women, it must send out enzymes to prepare the ovum's surface for entry.

In gestation (as life builds) and digestion (as life breaks down), cells interact via enzymes.

We have seen EN-ZY-ME relate to EN-EM-Y in the Code. Life does not leave a body when a person dies. Life simply assumes a new direction. The hair and nails continue to grow for a while. And the living enzymes begin to digest the body cells. So, the life of the body feeds the life of the Earth itself.

We have seen that "to fire" is a verb meaning "to send forth." In the brain, electricity fires in a synaptic leap. A male fires his sperm into a fe-male. Sperm fires its enzymes into her ovum. We have many levels of energy interchange that are each a form of firing.

As macrocosm and microcosm meet, only an ob-server joins quantum mechanics to relativity.

C-R-eat-E becomes C-R-E-ate as light (C), life (R), and energy (E) realize (A) the crystal crossroads (T). And life eats life to create new life. In one E-ternal (internal-external) double spiral of energy, the uni-verse consumes itself, consummates within itself, and goes on.

Live foods dance with the eternal potential of enzyme evolution. The Living God creates new life by in-venting the bio-spirit anew.

So, as the observer alive in you uses all its enzyme potential, you are in charge of fire (where fear is aware of itself). You have all creation as your own, to share with others who are read-y to ride the waves. History was a grand experiment; but we simply must move on.

After we gained the use of fire, animal instincts were declared an enemy of religion. And under the Techno State, we acted inhuman toward each other. War was real; and hell, a mystery. We had gone to war with our very own food.

Keep in mind that Jeru-salem means "possession of peace." So, when we read of "Peace on Earth," it does not mean that little boys will cease to shove or that girls will no longer tease. Our New Jerusalem will be established when the fire-power of the Techno State is under conscious control.

"Harmony" begins with "harm" since life depends on light from fire that consumes life itself.

Light a candle, and create a sphere of death; micro-organisms die — the essence of a sacrifice, life in the air consumed for fuel to consummate in energy. We must destroy life in the process of our own re-creation. Harmony may begin with harm, yet every earthly organism is furthered when humanity travels on, evolving even after the Earth itself is cremated.

Now, we must bring to consciousness the cause for which we first began to sacrifice. Can we smoke cigarettes and have the will to save rain forests? Can we drink alcohol and care about our planetary water supply? During history, bio-goals were a matter of degree. In Phase Three, we are consciously choosing between life and death.

History ends as fire-science takes us to Heaven at every level of the metaphor.

In the first food-commandment, God said, "I have given you every herb bearing seed and every tree in which is the fruit of a tree yielding seed."

The progression of dietary exceptions to this first Biblical law grew more and more complex. First Adam ate bread, then Noah ate animals after the flood; vegetation was swamped for at least one growing season. Later, meat could not be mixed with dairy. But in the end, no law could replace the original. For the raw law was not a product of any mortal mind.

The Habit of Habits

When he got the chance, Noah did not revert to the first food law, eating seed bearing plants and green herbs (fruits and vegetables) as in Genesis, chapter one. Instead he established a ritual of kosher meat and cooking to go with his new eating habits. And food rituals replaced instinct.

We knew that refined sugar, coffee, alcohol, and chocolate were dangerous, but such "foods" fed the techno mind-set. Destructured enzymes caused the mind to act like a machine. So, science lacked a con-science in the days of history. And we took comfort in coffee rituals.

Dis-organized foods became our drugs. And a bit like Noah, we made up a new religion to keep our drugging-eating habits. Now, TV ads are engineered to build the cooked-food mystique.

In the Woodstock generation, some on marijuana, LSD, and speed, helped turn the War in Nam around by marching in the streets of the USA.

Woodstock's flower children sacrificed their souls to touch the nation's heart. And the war in Nam was turned around because so many youths had gone mad with grief. Even the CIA played its part, opening channels to smuggle in drugs. History was a ritual of madness. We solved poverty with war, solved war with slavery to the Techno State. And now, the homeless are declared "insane" for taking on the fruitless karma. The "insane" get "medical drugs" for refusing to join in national rituals of techno consumption.

Diplomats in the USA drank martinis; in the USSR, vodka. And we shared champagne when the arms limitations were signed. Our mind-sets were like fashions. A hundred years ago, who imagined the world's businessmen in every nation dressed alike in suits and ties? Who thought the world might grow wise to alcohol and tobacco abuse within a century? The crystallization has begun. A clear concept born of bio-consciousness will carry us beyond the foods of sacrifice.

Adam's sin was not in eating apples. That notion came about much later because the Latin word for "apple tree," *malus*, is also Latin for "evil." As we have seen with Alice in Wonderland, our words can get confounded by what we eat. So, the warlike Romans didn't really know their apples.

The Latin noun for "war" *bellum* was also the adjective for "beautiful." For the Roman mind was mirrrored by a belligerent culture.

In Je-R-usa-L-em, we had linguistic problems with basic concepts such as "black" and "white." In chemistry, we misused the word "organic." And in biology, we built a medical history of viral infections on false labels. Our apple trees were dying due to acid rain.

In 1987, immediately after the 18th summit and its talk of nuclear reduction, plans were begun for a build-up of "conventional weapons." We had not turned WAR around.

"Organized Science" and "Organized Religion," by definition, ignored the chaos that divided them, for neither was whole — organically.

Many movements in the USA advocated vegetarian meals. Animal rights activists encouraged vegan food preparation. Many macrobiotics were beginning to enjoy the benefits of fresh fruits and uncooked vegetables. And even medical doctors were starting to admit the obvious.

But eating raw apples eliminates the baker, the packager, the brand name, the advertiser, and the media hype with its supporting "news" and press releases. A change in eating habits will effect heavy concentrations of wealth. Agriculture in the hands of health-conscious people will grow our fruits and vegetables with no poisons while paying farm workers a just wage to take the extra care tending healthful organic foods.

WAR is a complex social ritual. So turning WAR around calls for a new social structure.

Enjoy the process — organically.

CHAPTER 19

THE BEAST OF 666

ONLY ONE PRESIDENT OF THE USA
HAD SIX LETTERS
IN EACH OF HIS THREE NAMES
RONALD WILSON REAGAN

Reagan's 18 letters were the mark on policies of Je-R-usa-L-em in the years of Armageddon.

ON THE DAY THAT 666 WAS ELECTED
THE WINNING LOTTERY NUMBER
IN WASHINGTON D.C. WAS 666

In *the Washington Post* (11/5/80) opposite an ad for TOYS R US was the Election Day lottery number.

THE FIRST COMPLAINT OF 666
WAS THAT GOVERNMENT REGULATIONS
ADDED $666
TO THE COST OF EACH AUTO

Reagan said in his very first national address on TV (2/5/81), "Regulations adopted by government, with the best of intentions, have added $666 to the cost of an automobile."

THE FIRST BUDGET OF 666
PROJECTED $666 BILLION IN REVENUES

One year — to the very day — after 666 decried the spending of $666 for auto safety, he asked for $666 billion in revenues (*NY Times* 2/6/82).

"No man might buy or sell, save he that had the mark, or name of the beast, or the number of his name," said the Bible. And Ronald Wilson Reagan set out to fulfill the prophecy, with a belief in his own magic number.

WHEN PRESIDENT 666 TOOK OFFICE
A 666-YEAR FUEL SUPPLY
REMAINED IN THE USA

Newsweek (7/16/79) graphically reported this story from the Energy Department: "at current usage, the USA would be completely depleted of oil, gas, and coal in 666.5 years." And it was released half a year (.5 years) before the election of 666.

"Oil and money shouldn't mix with weapons-deals and politics," was my thought on a winter's eve as I sorted some news clippings into envelopes.

And then I heard a metallic snake hissing in my room. My radiator was steaming. And I suddenly felt connected to the oil barrons, landlords, arms merchants, and businessmen who had subdued my Mother Earth. The men who mined the coal years ago to melt the ore to make the steel to build the oil rigs were keeping me warm. But the chain of command in industries that poured the molten metal to make "my" radiator seemed so cruel.

I sat and wondered for a while. Who was at the top of the techno establishment? Those who supply the steam? Or those who use it?

In some way, we are all connected to the buying and selling of power. The petro-chemical poisoning of our Earth was our collective human project.

On February 18th, 1987, the USSR aired an 18-minute TV documentary explaining Chernobyl to the Russians and Ukrainians. Yet, the Soviets, France, England, Germany, and others continued to activate nuclear power plants.

I thought of turning off my radiator. But such a gesture would not save a drop of oil. The steam was controlled by a thermostat that worked for the entire apartment complex.

Besides, I was happy to be warm even though my metallic snake was filled with heat by those who worked for "the Whore of Babylon."

In the Bible, the Whore of Babylon is tied to the Beast of 666. For the Whore sells her soul for money while 666 decides who can buy and sell.

IN THE FIRST YEAR OF RULE BY 666
666 THOUSAND ONE FAMILY HOMES
WERE SOLD IN THE USA

These 666 thousand one family homes were sold due to many random decisions made by many individuals with various motives, acting separately in different localities.[1] Also at that time, the national home mortgage foreclosure rate was 18%.[2]

REAGANOMICS AND 666 JELLYBEANS

A children's math book entitled "666 Jellybeans" was published in 1976 when few people dreamed that a man with a weakness for jellybeans would ever be President. Jellybeans were mini techno eggs that strangely told of the resurrection of Christ.

And as economists questioned jellybean math, a Nobel Prize was awarded (10/12/81) to Professor James Tobin for his work opposed to Reaganomics. Coincidentally, that prize was $180,000.

666 BABIES WERE BEING BORN
TO EVERY TEN THOUSAND WOMEN
AS 666 TOOK OFFICE

When Reagan took office, the U.S. Bureau of Health Statistics reported live births per ten thousand women of childbearing age at 666. With population growth leveling off, by 1984, women in the USA averaged 1.8 children each.[3] By 1987's end, the average U.S. family had 1.8 children.

AND THE DEFICIT TURNED AT 666

Bridging Reagan's two terms, $666.5 billion in revenues collected in the last year of his first term was supposed to pay for the first year of his last term.[4] (This is not the $666 billion from his 2nd year.) And the 5 was a turning point.

(1) U.S. News 4/12/82, (2) NY Times 10/20/85, (3) Time 8/6/84, (4) NY Times 10/26/85

179

THE ACHILLE LAURO, 666 DISEMBARK

Was Reagan a hero in the Achille Lauro affair? He captured terrorists as Egypt mumbled that 666 had lost the game of counter-intelligence.

"When 666 passengers left the ship" to sight-see in Cairo, Leon Klinghoffer, 69, and his wife Marilyn stayed aboard.[1] Leon, a Jew, was murdered by Arab terrorists. The couple had their 36th wedding anniversary, September 18th. And Leon was in a wheelchair, tied to the Techno State, with symbols woven round him.

The escaping killers were forced to land their plane in Italy. And that same plane (later as "flight 648," 6+4+8=18) was seized soon again by other terrorists who killed 60 passengers.[2]

The crisis in Italy caused by the Achille Lauro affair was settled when Prime Minister Craxi carried 180 votes in a vote of confidence.[3] At that time, a move to deny Israel its U.N. seat (an annual event) was begun by 18 Arab nations.[4]

BY THE END OF 666's FIRST TERM
HOSPITAL OCCUPANCY DROPPED TO 66.6%

Two million patients per year "pick up infections" in hospitals.[5] And 20,000 die yearly from those infections. Some were wise enough to heal at home. And so, 18,000 beds had been removed.

Hospital food was a horror, cooked and steamed and sanitized to death.

Under Medicare, payments "per disease named" were made for each diagnosis in any one of 468 (a multiple of 18) catagories.[6] And that year, those on Medicare paid $18.60 monthly.[7]

And these abstractions formed a web of super-consciousness as 666 hovered over the pyramid in the bio-riddle of Je-R-usa-L-em.

(1) NY Times 5/24/87, (2) Time 10/21/85, (3) NY Times 10/17/85, (4) NY Times 11/9/85, (5) Alternatives Newsletter Sept. 1986, (6) NY Times 1/16/85, (7) NY Times 1/15/85

AIDS AND THE MARK OF THE BEAST

The 3rd AIDS virus was "officially" SBL 6669 V-2.[1] Also, out of 789,578 military recruits tested, 1,186 were infected,[2] which rounds out to one in 666, a ratio that would spell doom if AIDS were not to rise and fall as had every epidemic, including those before the use of medical drugs. The numbers made a channel to what we hoped to demystify.

A study of "multiple personality disorder" gives us a clue to the gap between body and spirit as related to all "named" diseases. For the same body can react differently to the same stimuli if a different spirit controls that body. For example,[3] some drugs are known to affect children differently than adults. And if a person with "multiple personality disorder" sometimes acts as a child, a different reaction to such drugs will manifest when the "child-spirit" is in control.

But since we all display some personality variance and also interlock in spirit around the globe, the way we feel about ourselves and each other (among other factors) affects the symptoms we display. So, with 666 given the power to buy and sell in the Armageddon prophecy, belief in "the beast" had an effect on us all.

These clippings about Reagan's retirement home from SPY (Sept/88, page 108) show that his number was even revered among his friends.

20 of Ron's friends incorporated themselves as Wall Management Services Inc. and just up and bought him a house. The consortium is headed by Holmes Tuttle and metals magnate Earle Jorgensen; among the stockholders . . . are, it is believed, William French Smith, Betsy Bloomingdale, Armand and Harriet Deutsch and several others of the very old gang. The original notion may well have been that the Reagans would live in it free of charge, but . . . they will pay a rent . . .

Nancy wasn't pleased by her gift house at 666 St. Cloud Road (the landlords quickly changed the number to 668 to avoid the satanic vibrations for a president whose own name — Ronald Wilson Reagan — is three six-letter words). In fact, she continued to house-hunt in Bel Air, Brentwood and Pacific Palisades. But Ron amiably accepted the present.

(1) NY Times 11/20/86, (2) NY Times 5/15/87, (3) NY Times 6/28/88

THE TOTAL SPENT BY 666
TO WIN HIS SECOND TERM
WAS $66.6 MILLION

The New York Times put Mondale's spending at $67.4 million, Reagan's at $66.6 million, while pricing the combined annual party and elective politics at $1.8 billion.[1]

BEGINNING THE SECOND TERM OF 666
THE FARM CREDIT SYSTEM
HAD OUTSTANDING LOANS OF
$66.6 BILLION[2]

As the USA grew more health-conscious, control of the food supply slipped away. Many imported fruits and vegetables were laden with poison sprays. And border inspection standards were even lower than already poor domestic inspection standards. Still, it was not fruits and vegetables that had thrown the farm credit system into a nose-dive.

THE AVERAGE SPEED OF THE EARTH
IN ITS ORBIT AROUND THE SUN
IS 666 HUNDRED MILES PER HOUR

The World Book Encyclopedia reports this fact with no footnotes on the beast. Yet, the monkey who learned from the stars that our planet would die someday knew that 666 was our symbolic link to immortality.

The SON of humanity, named for the SUN, keeps us on the path of cosmic evolution by ever chasing his own shadow across the endless sky.

At Reagan's first Whitehouse meeting with State leaders, he passed out jellybeans to 18 Governors.[3] Eating the tiny Easter symbols, he mentioned that the 18th of February was to reveal his budget cuts for Reaganomics. Next day, 18 versions of his anti-abortion bill were submitted to Congress.[4]

(1) NY Times 8/17/85, (2) Insight 3/24/86, (3) David Brinkley NBC 2/13/81, (4) CBS 1/14/81

Who Was That Masked Man?

The Bible says, "*Here is wisdom. Let him that hath understanding count the number of the beast, for it is the number of **a man**, and **his** number is Six hundred threescore and six*" (Rev. 13:18).

But the word for "*a man*" in the original Greek is *anthropos*, also used to mean "*mankind*." And no article "a" appears in the Greek text. Further, the word for "*his*" in "his number is" can be read as "*its*" implying no gender. So, the Bible may say that 666 is the number of "humanity."

Bishop Irenaeus used 2nd century gamatria (a Greek number system) to prove that LATEINOS, "Romans," totaled 666. Greek numerals accused the entire nation of Rome, so *anthropos* must have been thought to be "a people" not "a man."

By kaballah, Nero was said to be "the beast." Peter the Great was numbered in Russian. Many were accused in Hebrew, Greek, and Arabic numerals.

Let A equal 6, B equal 12, C equal 18, and so on in English; and KISSINGER totals 666.[1]

Peter Bungus, a Catholic theologian under Pope Leo, proved by gamatria that Martin Luther was 666. Luther made public his Thesis on April 18th (1521). He died on February 18th (1546). He split Germany in its belief that bread held the "real" body of Christ and also laid the path for Hitler's attack on the Jews. (Hitler's symbolism follows shortly.)

Adrian Rogers, president of the Southern Baptist Convention, opened "the Pat Robertson for President in 1988 Campaign" with a speech linking Goliath (slain by David) to 666. His numbers were a bit off. Still, Ronald (6) Wilson (6) Reagan (6) was being protected by Armageddonists who tried to hang the beastly number on someone else.

In fact, the power to buy and sell, even in a limited marketplace, is in the hands of the people (anthropos). No matter what the number system, we are each responsible for what we consume. We are the beasts who seek to be as gods — eternal.

(1) Scientific American, June 1974

And the Moral is . . .

George *Morales*, a drug smuggler, was questioned by Senator John Kerry of the Foreign Relations subcommittee on terrorism, narcotics, and international operations. The testimony, as follows, was given the day of Admiral Poindexter's first day at the Iran-Contra joint hearings (6/15/87).

Kerry: Your organization sold those drugs?
Morales: Yes, we did.
Kerry: And what happened to the money which was the proceeds of the sale?
Morales: We sent the money to the Contras.
Kerry: And who took that money for the Contras?
Morales: Different parties. Francisco Horaldo, we used to call him General Franco.
Kerry: And that was taken in the form of cash out of the United States?
Morales: Cash. And some of the money was taken by Horaldo through the International Airport.
Kerrry: And let me go to the second flight from Costa Rica. Was it to Great Harbor, December 1984? You said, two hundred and some kilos?
Morales: No. It was early in 1985.
Kerry: It was 1985?
Morales: It was the plane 666 crashed, I believe, I understand.
Kerry: That crashed?
Morales: I understand that.
Kerry: Right. Was there ever another flight from Costa Rica to Great Harbor involving cocaine?
Morales: December 1985. In January 1985, 1986, I'm sorry.
Kerry: Okay. Apart from 1986 then, there were a total of two flights with cocaine?
Moralees: More than two.
Kerry: More than two?

The fact that drug-flight 666 had crashed was not on TV. For Admiral Poin-dexter was puffing his pipe for the cameras.

CHAPTER 20

THE DRAMA

Jodie Foster never met John Hinkley in the flesh. Yet before Ronald Reagan was pierced by a bullet from Hinkley's gun, their three paths had crossed in a crystal prophecy. Reagan was haunted by 666. And amazingly, the names of "Foster" and "Hinkley" added meaning to the drama of the Beast.

These symbols commanded attention not by any powers of church, state, or astrology but by their Earthly synchronicity. So, before we see their meanings, let us review the context.

Hinkley was never close enough to touch young Jodie Foster's body. But he had dreamed about her, written letters to her, and he shot the President to impress her. She was his baby-faced starlet, the harlot of his fantasies, the whore he saw as his very own upon the silver screen.

The patriarch, the fallen virgin, and the man-child made mad by civilizing machines were cast in a mystery play. But how and why and by what power had the mystic vibrations of 18 come to rule this trio as they acted out their drama?

Hinkley was out of work while Ron starred in a global dream. Jodie appeared as a ray of light, rated R. And 666 was the theme. For money had chained the Beast to the Whore of Babylon.

Poor Hinkley played the role of one possessed. He acted opposite the Whore and the Beast. For their names were as characters in our mystery play.

Saint John the Divine said in Revelation that what he had written would be *prophesied again* (Rev. 10:11). And the story in the Bible's final pages was being relived, with a twist.

The names that floated to the surface of our collective myth gave a clear picture of the lesson to be learned in the Final Days before the start of the New Millennium.

JOHN HINKLEY
FEATURED IN
A LOVER'S TRAUMA

Hinkley shot the President just after Reagan gave an 18-minute speech.[1] Reagan's first official TV address (seven weeks before) was also 18 minutes.[2] Guided by numerology, his first speech said that his new budget would be presented to the nation on the 18th of the following month. He named the 18th twice for luck, the only number he cited twice. And on camera, Reagan held 36 cents (two 18's) in his hand to dramatize the value of a dollar.

Most of us knew that the worth of money was an agreed upon illusion. But Hinkley, mad about the Whore, felt broke and helpless when he purchased his weapon at Rocky's Pawn Shop, 2018 Elm Street, Dallas. Before he shot Reagan he stayed in Lubbock (population 180,000), a small town 318 miles outside Dallas.[3] The day of the shooting, he stayed at the Park Central Hotel on 18th Street, across the street from Secret Service Headquarters.[4] And the Firearms Control Center traced the weapon he used to shoot Reagan to Rocky's Pawn Shop within 18 minutes of the time of the shooting.[5]

The restraining order to halt the slaughter of dairy cattle over an 18-month period came from a Federal district judge in Lubbock.[6]

Remember that *Buckley* the CIA agent murdered as a hostage had a name meaning "bullock," an animal of sacrifice. And the haunting images of Buckley's torture drove U.S. agents to frantic deeds.

This aspect of our sacrificial food metaphor is as meaningful as the golden calf from the time of Moses and far more easily interpretable than the animal images in the Book of Revelation at this point in crystal development. Further along, we'll know all about it.

(1) Time 4/13/81, (2) Time 2/16/81, (3) Time 2/16/81, (4) Time 4/13/81, (5) NY Times 1/27/85, (6) NY Times 5/1/86

RONALD WILSON REAGAN
STARRING IN
THE CRYSTAL DRAMA

"When it achieves its most noble intent, film reveals that people everywhere share common dreams and emotions," said President Reagan as the films of 1980 received their Academy Awards. His message was on video tape. In real life, Reagan was in a hospital with a bullet wound from Hinkley's gun.

Also, we share nightmares whether we want to or not. For wishes will come back to haunt us if not carefully chosen. And childish dreams of frogs, scrotums, princes and presidents arose months later when Jodi hosted *Saturday Night Live*. Mister Mike told how the little train that died rolled over Freddie the Frog at 180 miles per hour. (The audience laughed.)

An 18-minute film to introduce Reagan at the 1984 Dallas convention was panned by the networks who wanted only bits of it. Yet, the polls said 54% (three 18's) of his fans felt better off with Reagan while 72% (four 18's) of those said they would vote for him again.[1] And they did as frogs croaked by the numbers, and princes jumped inside their very proper names.

President 666 was first elected 36 years after a 6 year war in which 6 million Jews and 6 million Christians were slaughtered by Nazis. He starred in a radio war drama, "Joe Smith American," on *MGM Playhouse of the Air* (1942) playing Joseph whose wife Mary gave birth to a son on Christmas. Joseph asked a nurse *three* times about the *six* hours Mary had been in the delivery room. And later, three sixes came up again as "*six* slugs" intended for a Nazi spy were mentioned *three* times by the Federal Agent who had rescued Joe Smith (Reagan) and, in the process, captured the Nazi thugs.

Six shots were fired at "Dutch" Reagan in his real life drama as the Whore and madman chased each other through the looking glass.

(1) NY Times 8/17/84

187

JODIE FOSTER
OFF AND ON
THE SILVER SCREEN

Jodie was just 18 when Hinkley shot the President. Early interviews reveal her desire to be President when she grew up. "I've been working six months a year, six days a week," she said while spinning her yoyo years before in her hotel room.[1] And mystical foreshadowings touched her earlier works.

In the movie *Echoes of a Summer*, Jodi says, "Tell me who I am and what's my time." Richard Harris replies, "You're from the 18th century." In 1980, "18th Century Fox" was Mo Udall's joke at the Democratic convention to poke fun at Reagan's old movieland ideas. Of Jodie's screen illness in *Echoes*, Richard Harris says, "There's been 18 final judgements." And Lois Nettleton replies, "We'll get 18 more if necessary."

In the movie *Carny*, Jodi told Gary Busey she was 18. But she was younger. "We've had 18 deaths in two seasons," he said to her ominously.

The ancient trauma, the national drama, and the deadly dream, however, came together in the movie *Taxi Driver* where Jodi played a prostitute.

Hinkley saw the movie and imagined himself as "the Taxi Driver" who tried to impress Jodi Foster by shooting at "a presidential character."

These puzzle pieces will fall into place with the meanings of Foster's and Hinkley's names.

Hinkley as an English word means "falteringly" or "misgivingly," "with a lack of belief."

And Hinkley built his real-life character on "a lack of belief" that grew out of the gap between Reagan-the-symbol and Reagan-the-man.

The 666 counted citizens as numbers. Ronald Wilson Reagan counted them among his friends. But money was Reagan's blind spot in a very sensitive area. **Foster** (as in foster parent) is an English word, from the Norse word for "to nurse a baby," that essentially means "to feed."

(1) N.Y Daily News 12/8/76

188

Not only did Ronald have 6 letters in each part of his name, the day Reagan was elected the winning lottery number (666) in Washington D.C. linked him to his strange monetary fate.

The only mention of 666 in the Old Testament tells us that *"The weight of gold given to Solomon in one year was 666 talents"* (1 Kings 10:14).

Solomon's 666 became a symbol of great fortune and evolved into a sign of wealth among the Jews. Eventually, 666 was used by Jews in Europe as the mark of those shopkeepers who exchanged money with a power to buy and to sell.

When viewed from a distance, three sixes that hung above the doors of money merchants looked like three dangling circles. And over the years, the sign evolved into three balls — the international mark of the pawnbroker.

President 666 was shot by a gun bought and paid for under the sign of 666 at Rocky's Pawn Shop.

Reagan the man and 666 the symbol were united in a single fate by a bullet wound. The metaphor of Anti-Christ had come full circle.

For bread-winners and bread-losers, President 666 promoted a devilish lottery that put the USA in hock for a belief in money for the sake of money itself — the so-called "supply side."

Before the bullets from Rocky's Pawn Shop hit the President, a taste for blood in the USA was reflected in the currently running movie *Rocky*. And Rocky's screen address was 1818.

Hinkley was angry because he was refused a job by "The Rocky Mountain News." And he had a picture of the Nazi, Rockwell, on his bedroom wall.

Symbolic fragments crashed and mirrors turned in our kaliedoscope of words. Hinkley's wandering soul, cut deeply by the edge of history, was right for the part. "Disbelief" had a strange relationship to "Fostering" in the years ruled by the Beast. "The power to buy and sell" had left millions starving in the streets.

As producers bid on rights to movies, presidential hopefuls bid on rights to the American dream. And Ron spent $18 million on campaign advertising.[1]

The signs upon him were as bright as stars over Bethlehem. He started in office with 18 women in the House, 18 members in "the Black caucus," and one lawyer for every 18 people in Washington D.C.[2] The Water Resource Bill (a $180 million Aquarian issue) brought on the first override of his veto (3/22/84). And two days before, 18 Republicans turned against him on the Prayer-in-School Bill.

With hearing loss apparent for about 18 months, Reagan joined 18 million hard-of-hearing in the USA, and got a hearing aid.[3] And Abram-Abraham had named his first son Ishmael (God listens) before he threw the child out of his house.

The metaphor of Hinkley and Foster, the strange affair between "Disbelief" and "Food," was part of the tale of Abram-Abraham who had two sons, one begetting the "Jews," one begetting the "Arabs."

One son belonged to Abram-Abraham in writing, the other was accepted only in speech. This was Reagan's problem with Contra-Iran and many other issues. The President had given verbal orders that were not the same as those in writing.

And Abram-Abraham's sons were Isaac (laughter) and Ishmael (God-listens). For laughter is anti-listening to allow unconscious release.

History put writing over speech, logic over instinct, techno over bio. The right hand ruled the left. And in Reagan's numerological joke, the Promised Land (Jerusalem and our global Je-R-usa-L-em) were plagued by homelessness.

President 666 had a diffusion of belief. He had faith in numerology, astrology, the Fundamentalist preachers, Ollie North, Ed Meese, and so on. But Hinkley (disbelief), at the sign of the pawn shop, had Reagan's number.

(1) Newsweek 10/27/80, (2) Monitor NBC 12/16/81, (3) People 8/20/84

The human laugh is a complex aspect of speech.

The Eskimo word for "laughter" (iglavtiriwok) also means "making love." For a laugh that can be shared creates a social bond.

A custom among the Eskimos, when two members of the group have a dispute is to gather in a circle around those two. Each of those in the dispute tells jokes about the other. And those who form the circle laugh when they are moved to do so. The consequence is usually that one of the jokers gets embarrassed and leaves the village, perhaps never to return again.

Laughter not only heals, it can be divisive. And in the USA hysteria reigned as laugh-tracks (a potent opinion-forming mechanism) were added even to children's TV cartoons. We tend to disregard people at whom laughter is directed while honoring those who have provoked the laugh.

The root of laughter in humans is the sound of an alarmed, and frightened primate who is trying to warn others in the group. Even a smile is often a sign we use to disguise hostilities.

The English word "smile" has its roots in the line of words: miracle, mirage, mirror, admire, and marvel. The human smile is a miracle in that when other primates show their teeth in some like fashion it means they are ready to fight.

Remember, the ancient MR words that lead to our "mister" and "marriage" were built upon the mirage of smiling mothers weaning their sons while slowly and subtly civilizing them over the ages.

Ab-ram was the Biblical "mister" named to the matrilineal tribe of the Hebrews. And here is a key to the Israel-Palestine conflict. Abram was already the father of "God Listens" when he was tempted to offer his son "Laughter" as a human sacrifice, after his wives came into conflict.

The smile is a female invention, a miracle that men have learned to imitate. Still, the female smile is a confusing cue to many males, even to this day.

The bonding of child to mother must survive the weaning process for men to advance their culture. But in the USA, the cow is almost always pictured with distended utters, for many people think that cows must be milked to be comfortable.

Yet when a cow is no longer milked, its utters return to normal, like other mammals. In places where cows are not milked they are not pictured with distended utters, and so sexual symbolism is not attached to women's breasts.

Food sacrifice is so deep in our society that the bullock and lamb are constant symbols. Still, society is being weaned of this karma as diets are shifting to fruits and vegetables. And **paradise** is a word that means "a walled garden."

In Phase Two, we were the children of machines. Men shaved their faces to look like boys. Women were painted like dolls. And we ate more dairy products since machines could give us more. The Ad-Council, civic groups, and public schools made daily dairy part of the education machine.

Technology (artifacts we have due to our use of fire) was elected as the Maker of human images. The symbols around 666 show that Reagan was the last anti-environmental leader that the eco-sphere could afford before "the People" would have to take control of planetary destiny.

Foster (to feed) and Hinkley (disbelief) were pivotal on a bio-personal level in Reagan's drama, the story of a changing rule. His bullet wound was not a headline about some "foreign" covert war that Reagan could ignore at breakfast.

Reagan's disbelief, his failure to see that the hungry were properly fed, had come back to him with all the power of "the Word" as it enters "the Flesh" of an avatar.

A bio-consciousness is now developing among the people; the race shall not be lost. As we are in the spirit so we manifest in the body. And as we treat our bodies so we direct our spirits. We are, in fact, the living metaphor. And the guilt of the past is washed away.

The Hinkley, Foster, Reagan drama touched the very essence of our dietary problem. For Reagan was "the rule," Hinkley was "disbelief," and Foster's name was even more specific in its origin.

Foster in English has an etymology that takes us back to food. The female star in our mystery play was named for a need folks have to foster each other, literally to share their food.

So, "disbelief" shattered "the rule." As a new concept of "fostering" was coming of age.

Caught between "Mr. 666" (in control of money) and "Mr. Disbelief" (an unemployed man), was "Ms. Feed One Another." And in the movie within the drama, young Ms. Foster played the Whore.

Social Security and Food Stamps were cut by the Beast in his early years. The economy was ravaged, finances squandered. And the stock market crashed, Private charities shrunk. Yet starving people did not count in the Dow Industrial Average.

In her movie, Foster acted opposite a hero who planned to shoot a presidential figure. And Reagan put a dollar sign on the number 144 attempting to sanctify the numerological Whore that was given his name — "Reaganonics."

But whores will quibble over money to distract the soul. Arguing about a five dollar bill with the poor man or five hundred with the banker, whores search for more than money. Their game is meant to try the spirit and test society.

This metaphor began as Adam was told that he would have to earn his "bread" by the sweat of his brow. He first ate un-whole (cooked) fruit after Eve had traded her soul for the keys to the Techno State. She became the whore to make us whole, for she purchased our stairway to heaven.

Ronald Wilson Reagan's signed Bible and cake to Iran ("upper classes") were the most prominent symbols of food being sacrificed to maintain the class divisions of the Techno State. His cow-boy image and the choppy laughter that characterized his speech were adjuncts to the role.

Ronald (6) Wilson (6) Reagan (6) played a role in world affairs quite opposite to that of James Carter (J.C.) who had moved to bring Egypt and Israel openly and directly into peace talks. Reagan drew the USSR toward the Holy Land by flatly refusing to talk with many "lesser powers" in the area.

The name of the Air Force officer that Reagan put in charge of Star Wars was spelled one way and pronounced another. ABRAHAMSON was the way he spelled it, but he pronounced it ABRAMSON.

And the promise to Abram-Abraham was that his seed would number among the stars (Gen. 22:17). But there was a hitch. Isaac (laughter) was called "an only son" (Gen. 22:2 & 16) and Ishmael (God listens) was sent out of the house. Here was a clash of the written with the spoken promise, personified.

Just 12 years before 2000, the 144 in Reagan's fiscal plan was no more than a joke. Those who still identified with the 12 tribes of Israel and 12 tribes of Ishmael were at war. The "Left" and "Right" in Je-R-usa-L-em seemd far from having a "peaceful possession." And so many had chosen to live in disbelief rather than re-deem their own personal relationships to food.

Our story hinged on money. For the power to buy and sell was exclusive to people with the mark of the Beast. Rather than taxes, Reagan proposed to gather funds by selling "entitlements," selling public land rights, and general privatization.

Reagan laughed at acid rain, saying that trees can cause pollution. Other politicians voted his way, hypnotized by the numbers. And acid rain not only poisoned rivers and killed trees, it also added to the toxins in our food supply.

When Don Regan's book described Ron Reagan's astrological beliefs, it seemed that a pardon for Ollie North was suggested. And by that time, the number of pardons already granted by President 666 was 333 (*C.S. Monitor* 5/17/88).

The stars and numbers were parts of the game, and another key was synchronicity.

On all three networks (9/24/81), President Reagan's singular error was clearly broadcast. Written in front of him was ". . . our deficit for 1982 will be increased by 16 billion dollars." Yet Ronald Reagan said, ". . . our deficit for 1982 will be increased by 18, or pardon me, 16 billion dollars."

His error at that time told of things to come, like the 18 criminal counts charged against Ollie North. A bit of role distance between actor and symbol can add relief to even serious plots. For Reagan, "18, or pardon me," did the trick. The mistake in reading his lines was significant; it was the only one. But *the New York Times* omitted "18, or pardon me," from its published transcript. Audio-video tapes, however, hold the record.

Later, "Debate Gate" was pursued by the press. His 18th official press conference (6/28/83) shook Reagan so much he lost his grip. His closing words at that 18th meeting were, "I'm sorry." Again, a transcript appeared in the *Times.* Again, "I'm sorry," did not appear in print.

The Times usually deemed Reagan's entire press conferences fit to print, including his closing words. His first closing was "Thank you." His third was "Well, thank you." The fifth closed with the answer to a question, the sixth with, "Helen has told me I got to get out." But when the 18th ended with "I'm sorry" (also preserved on audio-video tapes), it was not printed.

The Times (7/23/86) did print an error spoken by the President. In referring to *South Africa*, Reagan said, "If *South America* wishes to belong to the family of Western nations, . . ." Since racism was the topic, his pre-conscious prejudice was showing. But it was no simple issue of black and white. In that talk on South Africa, rejecting sanctions against apartheid, Reagan mentioned several numbers, yet he spoke one number twice — the magic number — 18.

President 666 knew his tricks with the number 18, but he had been trapped by its power.

Only as recently as the Middle Ages did our great band of primates begin to acquire sir names in England as a sense of "tribe" was replaced by a sense of "family," the new basis for "nations." We were one step closer to individuality as the root of true democracy.

November 18th, Reagan (the man) was in Geneva while 666 (the Beast) cast its shadow over Wall Street. The Dow closed at an all-time record gain of 144.02 as trading slowed to 108.36 (a Hindu link to 18), a number that was to precipitate the great Stock Market crash, as we shall see.

Reagan teased the Soviets by offering to share Star Wars. Gorbachev, 54 (three 18's) at the time, thought it was a financial squeeze (666's way to get Congress to support his Armageddon plan).

Since Reagan's was a vengeful God, his religion of the Beast evicted farmers "possessed" by banks. In the guise of "a spiritual man," the Beast had re-possessed the souls in a land of disbelief.

Gorbachev followed a Party line where "God" had no political clout. And since the Soviet had its own religious mystique, Jews (and other citizens) were not allowed to leave (to break the faith).

Ironically, Israel sought to block Soviet Jews from entering the USA (*Times* 3/1/87). Mr. Shamir said the main issue was to "bring *more people* to Israel." When using the English word "people," Mr. Shamir clearly meant "*bring more Jews.*"

But the Fundamentalists of each One-God belief claimed not only that their religion was the only worthy one but that their branch was correct. So, the meanings of "Jew," "Christian," and "Moslem" were debated internally among the many sects.

"You're not a real Jew, not a true Christian, not a genuine Moslem." The factions had as many differences among themselves as they had between them. We were genetically primates. And only our use of fire, our unconscious fear, and our need for a symbolic super-structure had made us call each other names.

Joyce Brown

On December 20th, 1987, I joined a demonstration against homelessness in New York City. A host of factors were discussed by the appointed speakers. And many chants swelled among the marchers.

Some of the homeless were ex-G.I.s from Nam. Many claimed to be "people of color," as if the opressing forces had no color at all.

So many factors, from karma to malicious intent had driven Je-R-usa-L-em into social chaos. And in Jerusalem, simultaneously, people ("Palestineans") were being shot down in the streets.

As I marched along, carrying an unlit candle, I fingered my beads of meditation. I had to pick and choose the chants I could join in. Because I was so conscious of words, I could only echo those ideas that I felt to be cosmically true.

I could not chant against individuals, even if they were "in power," for I knew that we all had power and that individuals could change.

So, when the chant, "Free Joyce Brown" arose, it swept over me as a sacred mantra.

Joyce Brown had an earthy name with a touch of desolation and yet a spirit of joy. But when she was taken against her will from the streets of New York, she said she was Billy Boggs; the "bill" not paid back to Earth was "bogged" down in finance.

Joyce Brown, a homeless woman, was a brilliant soul. When she was interviewed by Gabe Pressman on NBC, she displayed a keen calm wit greater than the mostly uncandid political candidates.

Pressman asked her if she felt that homeless people might be dangerous. Without the blink of an eye or a moment's hesitation in speech, she gave the only appropriate answer to such a question. People who have homes can be dangerous too, she said. Joyce Brown was quite articulate.

And so, her story became the center of a great debate among judges, psychiatrists, lawyers, news commentators, and just plain folk.

Would Mother Earth be allowed to know another joyful growing season?

197

When Joyce Brown was taken in, she was injected against her will with psychothropic drugs. Her crime was not being a consumer. So, the bitterest techno-fruits were forced into her veins. Then her lawyers had the drugging stopped. But what of the less fortunate who get no publicity?

At first she won her freedom from the confines of Bellevue Hospital. But "the authorities" did not let her go. Instead the case was appealed. And a second judge said that the first judge had paid too much attention to Ms. Brown herself and not enough to the reports of psychiatrists, who were medical doctors and therefore qualified to make the ultimate decision as to her "insanity."

What of Australia's Bushpeople and people of the rain forests? Were they insane for wanting to be free from invasion by technology? And were the drugging "doctors" any more than another gang in a struggle for turf?

The media oft-times did not see beyond its own technology. Detached from biology, our story was out of focus, difficult to grasp. We suffered from a "disbelief" in our own integrity.

Listen to a speech by the Mayor of New York or the President from the final years of history. Both, literally, could not speak two sentences in a row without an "uhhh" to break the words apart. And holding a political office seemed to lead most officials to speak in the subjunctive mode where answers were prefaced by "I would say."

True "belief" is related to "fostering" the best in each other. Nomads were not mad, not insane in their homelessness. And householders need not be mad with a mania for owning things. As our social systems move toward a global balancing, primitive tribes need not be deprived of their homes. In fact, we must have guardians of the wilderness.

As the disbelief in our biology fades, we will foster each other again. And 666 shall be seen as "human." For we are staring in the revelation that is our daily drama.

CHAPTER 21

INTERNATIONALLY SPEAKING

In Iran, the word for "spy" is JASUS. So if the language of Iran were the only one you knew, when you heard the name of Jesus, you would be reminded of "a spy." The reasons go deep into our language.

"Jesus" derives from Je-ho-vah, a way of saying Y-H-W-H (neither vowels nor consonants), a name we cannot speak. Thus, Jesus is said to give form to a thought (thought) undescribable in scripture.

Muhammad treats the Divinity of Jesus as sub-versive because a spoken contract (Abram's vow to Hagar) was broken in Hebrew Scripture.

If Jesus were divine, reasoned Muhammad, then the Jews from the Hebrew Abraham would be the chosen people of history.

Je-R-usa-L-em is divided because only one son of Abram-Abraham is deeded the land in the Bible. Israel was fathered by Isaac (laughter), and Isaac was written of as the **"only son"** of Abraham (Gen. 22:16). And Jesus was born of this line.

On the other hand, by Allah, Jerusalem belongs to the children of Ishmael (God listens) who was **the first born son** of Abram. However, it was more than 22 centuries after Abram-Abraham's death when Muhammad put his claim in writing — the Koran.

Since Jesus had descended from David, David from Israel, and Israel from Isaac, it seemed that giving credence to Jesus would support Isaac's claim to the land. For Ishmael (Isaac's half-brother), the first Arab, was not in the lineage to Jesus. So, to refute the claim that Jews rather than Arabs owned the land. Muhammad denied in the Koran's 18th surah that God had fathered a son. Oddly this dispute began between two mothers, the wives of Abram-Abraham. One word had come between them (see **qalal** in index).

In the Word? Or in the Blood?

This division between "a struggle with God" (Israel) and "God listens" (Ishmael) began when "laughter" (Isaac) was given dominion. And in the Space Age, laughter is transposed to levity as we shift our bio-emotional energy.

Muhammad felt that taking Jesus as the Messiah required belief in a "Jewish" rather than an "Arab" lineage. Then again, the Jewish Scribes did not accept claims to divinity made by Jesus. So, the metaphor comes into focus only when we take a step beyond the historic totality.

When Abram changed his name to Abraham, he did not physically change his relationship to his two sons. But by breaking his word, he left a riddle to ensure the growth of separate branches needed for techno evolution. In both the USA and USSR, Jews and Moslems were ruled by the majority. With no religious disputes, our little band of fire-bearing monkeys would not have had the emotional energy needed to build a space program.

The Phase Three context of the Crystal refers to "the space program" generically as NASA. For by the time we begin our treck to the stars, "nasa" will have re-evolved to its original meaning ("to lift up" and "to travel forth") in our heavenly language of the angles.

Centered in Iran's word for "spy" (JASUS) is USA spelled backwards. This is why Reagan sent a cake and Bible to Iran, why 666 extended the metaphor of sacrificial foods. For the land of Israel was "purchased" for a piece of bread. Adam's first pun in the language of Punish (B-read).

"*Howl, O gate; cry O city; thou whole Palestine art disolved: for there shall come from the North a smoke*" (Isa. 14:31). So, Oliver North's cake to Iran makes sense as a food of sacrifice. In Phase Three, "the Arabs" and "the Jews" will be the sons and daughters of one family again as Israel's 12 tribes and Ishmael's 12 tribes are joined in the 144,000, the mystical symbol of New Jerusalem.

200

ARAM — ALAM

The Je-R-usa-L-em War in Armageddon's final years was focused between Iraq and Iran. For RA in its divided state was central to each.

Abram-Abraham was promised that his off-spring would "number among the stars." So, with the Space Age beginning, fulfillment was at hand. But first, the Crystal Code will unite humanity's groups on a new plateau. Persian (an Indo-European branch of language) has drawn *Aryan* (upper class) ideas out of India and passed them to Germany via Iran. So, an Aryan attitude left its mark on nations where "Ar-ya" was a hidden conflict.

Many words in Iran and Germany are cognates and each nation has built some of its "mystique" on treating Jews as *Alien*. Also, both the Germans and Iranians had historic periods when they had Aryan (upper class) delusions of superiority.

In Iran, *alam* means "pain" while *aram* means "peace." This R-L transition tells of a cultural drive that confused "pain" with "peace" in Phase Two, for bio values had to suffer so that techno goals could, in fact, be achieved.

In Hebrew, *atsiLA* is "giving" while *atsiRA* is "taking." In Arabic, *koran* is "writing" and *kalam* is "speech." These transitions are now clear.

The give and take of speech and writing allowed "humanity" to hide from itself during our ages of techno development. But in our third linguistic phase, giving and taking are more obviously one as writing and speech are re-aligned.

The resolution of our metaphor rests in a union of Abram's verbal promise to Hagar and his written promise to Sarah, for both were his wives.

No written peace plans will settle the ancient dispute in the Holy Land until the people begin to talk to each other in the streets, until the so-called Israelis and so-called Palestineans see each other as brothers and sisters. When we accept each other as individuals, the sham of official "races" can be seen for what it is, a hiding place for one's own personal biological fear.

The Hebrew word for "master" is the Russian word for "slave." Both are *RAB* in English.

And the children of the USA are now in bondage to ancient forces that must be resolved before we find our peace in the Holy Land. For the Moslem population in both Israel and Russia is growing. And a shift of power will necessitate bio-peace by means of true democracy.

The Hebrew word for "master" is not composed of any of the same characters as the Russian word for "slave." Yet, transliterated into English letters, both appear as *RAB*. And it shall be the USA that supplies the model of world peace. Only in a true democracy can the master and the slave become one within each soul devoted to "the Word."

Imagine if each Jew in Soviet Russia were the victim of an ancient verbal conflict. It is not at all illogical. Crossed words are at the root of every international dispute. For each nation, like each family, finds its origin in a name. And our names shall be our tickets to the spaceships of survival.

All children know that spelling lessons are a special form of state sponsored terrorism. Still, we are in awe of what writing does for logic. The evolution of ideas fashioned by written words carried us into the Space Age. So, the signs are clear that writing has lifted our spirits. To see "the Word" as a living being, we need only accept the Spirit of E-quality.

With this power, we acquire the knowledge of the One God who is true to "the Word" while also evolving in the personhood of Spirit.

Both in Russia and in Israel, we shall have true democracy where every person has a right to vote — Arab and Jew, Commissar and Commoner. For the puzzle of Je-R-usa-L-em is solved.

To make this possible, the One God gave us the rules of mono-theism, mono-gamy, and mon-ey (one value of interchange). The mono-rules (explained later) caused Abram-Abraham to choose between two women and two sons. As the raw law gets digested, men of Earth will become aware of the next level of conflict — organic democracy.

Imagined conflicts between "races" and "religions" were mere contrivances. For we were in fact one race with one true religion. Our fault was in not appreciating the dark that separated each light from others. As One God brings "the Word" and the Spirit into each other, dark keeps them apart. And in this darkness shines that light that is our individuality — free will.

ARAB spelled backwards is BARA which means "to create" in Hebrew. And ARAB itself can mean "to lie in ambush," or "to do it in the evening," both of which intonate "darkness." But in Hebrew, the word ARAB can also mean "to be pleasing" since we love to do it in the dark.

In ABRA-HAM (HAM means "dark"). And BAR-A means "a son realized" in the Code. So, BARA, which is "to create" at the Bible's beginning, yields a mandala in the flesh.

An ARAB was the first son of ABRAM after he made love to Hagar. Sarah had a son beyond that bar-gain. *Bar* in Ger-man means "money." *Ger-man* in He-brew is "strange manna." And *bar* in Hebrew means "boy." We have seen the symbols. Now, let us carry them beyond the borders of his-story.

ARABAH is "wilderness," where Abraham sent his unwanted wife and child. Yet, "wilderness" is a valued concept in the Phase Three mind-set.

BAal means "husband" and "owner" in Hebrew.

Bar, the Hebrew (Aramaic) for "boy," was pitted against the Babylonian *Baal*, a sun god and god of sex. So, *baHA* meant "confused" and *baHAR* meant "to choose," as our battle of words evolved.

HA was added to Abram to give us Abra-ha-m, with "laughter" as his He-brew son. Abraham meant "father of a multitude."

Was "the Word" playing a joke? Trace "joke" back to "hoax," from *hocus pocus*, the words of Jesus when he made bread and wine into a mystical body-and-blood sacrifice to replace circumcision rite of Abram-Abraham. When the cycle is complete, our laughter will be free.

Each nation boasts of a special dish, its cooking, and its alcoholic drink, but our sacrifices are basically the same, bread and wine, cooked food and fermented drink.

Romeo and Juliet, as the Romans and the Jews, committed suicide with poisoned drink and dagger. And both nations also died. Then Latin and Hebrew were born again to serve science and religion, those lovers torn from each other's arms by the forces of the Techno State.

Romeo and Juliet, suffering in a feud, were killed by family names as much as by dagger and poisoned drink. Foxes kill rabbits to eat; humans murder humans for a family or national name, to gobble up the symbol and regurgitate the fame.

Moses, enchanted by the name Ramses (Ra-Moses), rendered Egypt spell-bound. And Jesus asked above all things that we recall his name. But the names of Moses and Jesus were also functions, as we have seen: Moses "to draw out," and Jesus "savior." As far back as we re-member ourselves, mothers have given us names to live up to. And our fathers were familiarized by names.

Our names accent identities to realize our own individuality. For only an individual ever finds salvation. We are not saved in groups. Each person dies alone even if in a crowded place. No one eats for you. No other drives you to consume.

Salvation is a saving grace. And only you can save. For "the savior" lives in all who will save the Earth. Armageddon was a war of nations which was in fact a war of words.

Moslems opposed Judeo-Christians in a struggle for conscious love of the female principle. Judeo-Christians evolved to the spiritual realization of monogamy. Moslems evolved to the position of not drinking alcohol. Each surpassed the other.

These laws were not observed by individuals in every case. Yet, the water that Jesus changed to wine at the wedding feast was basic to the un-conscious aspect of our food metaphor.

A Chance To Change

Making changes in your habits, you can change the world. You need not take a different name, what counts is what you do. Practice all the bio-rules, and other people's words will contain a magic that will work for you. Listen to what other people say rather than what "they meant to say." See their words as functions of biology, and the truth will set you free.

Reagan set money for ARMS (warfare in an Aryan nation) against the money for ALMS (welfare in his alienation) when he invested in Iran. Millions of people were swayed in the process. But 666 was only a pivot. Millions of pepole had already set the verbal patterns in motion. It came to pass, for so it had been written.

And Jesus did not write a gospel, he spoke in living words. For his purpose was to absorb old karma and free the energy for new. We can see the powers that got caught in words as tribes pulled and tore the meanings of each other.

The Hebrew for "master" (rab) became Russian for "slave" (rab) as our Angular crystal grew with symmetry. Out of this division of RA came many branches. "Teacher" in Hebrew (*rabbi*) is linked to "worker" in Russian (*rabotnik*) by spells first sung to RA at the dawn of history. In Russian, *baran* is "a ram," *barashek* "a lady," and *barysh* "a profit." Jacob (Israel) worked seven years to marry his lady Rachel (a lamb), a profit. And *bar*, we know, is the Ger-man for "money."

We have no separate languages, only dialects of one basic mother tongue moving through conception and deception. Abram was born at UR, a town with a name that means "light." Yet in German, UR means "origin." We have not come from different places. All is ur in origin. U-R. You Are. CH-UR-CH. In the Crystal Code, the "church" is light that is surrounded by life itself.

We now have a "low intensity" war in "the Third World." Over 44 nations are involved. The Third World War is being waged in present time. And our Armageddon is at hand. If you are reading this in peace, be conscious of the fire you command.

Hansel and Grethel had a father who could not earn his daily bread. So, the children left home. But they lost their way in the forest while trying to follow bread crumbs they had left along the trail. Then they came to a "House of Bread" (Beth-lehem). Hansel ate of the gingerbread roof. Grethel tasted the windows of spun sugar. The Wicked Witch soon had Hansel locked in a manger to be fattened for the kill. But Grethel shoved the Witch into the oven. And the children escaped.

They then returned home bringing with them the precious stones of the Wicked Witch. And again the basic elements of our pre-conscious struggle made an enduring story. When our misuse of fire drove us from our home in the garden, we lost our way on this planet; like Hansel and Grethel, we conversed with the old woman of spells. And now, with her gems of knowledge, we can go on.

Imagine that a voice came out of heaven when primates first began to play with fire. And in the beginning was "the Word" that made us human.

How would you feel if friends had fires near their caves, kindled while your kin had yet to muster up a flame? In German, *Kind* is "child." In English, *kindling* is "a thing to burn." We grew un-kind to animals as fire redefined our kin. Now, we are un-kind to our own kind. We hurl fire at each other blind to our own instincts.

JASUS meant "spy" in Iran. And spiraling in Je-R-usa-L-em were waves of ancient karma. From James Carter (J.C.) to Reagan (666) passed the adviser on Iran, Gary Sick. *Gary* means "one who uses a spear. And the affairs among Jews, Christians, and Moslems were *Sick*. So, when the USA's Vincennes (Conquest) shot down an airbus from Iran, killing 290 civilians, just before the 4th of July 1988, the command was given by Captain Will Rogers, for *Rogers* also means "one who uses a spear." We will see more about the spear and the crucifixion of Jesus in a later chapter as we trace the sacrifice of Adam's bread through history.

CHAPTER 22

THE FOOD GROUP RELIGION

The USA has a national religion. And in prayers read aloud by duly licensed teachers, the dogma is openly preached: "Foods are divided into the Four Food Groups," amen. But we have more than four food groups.

Still, while Creationists and Evolutionists fought over what should be taught to children, the Four Food Group prayers were chanted daily.

"Group One: Meat gives your body protein," recited the children from *Your Body Book* (Dept. of Health, N.Y.S. 1980's). "Protein builds muscles, blood, and skin." The children *know* of dinosaurs that did not eat meat. Dinosaur muscle, blood, and skin could be fed on vegetable protein. But the Four Food Group Religion *believes* that a "Dinosaur Theory" could never apply to humans.

"Group Two: Milk gives your body calcium," says the children's litany. "Calcium builds strong bones and teeth." But we *know* that cows with great bones outgrow their need for milk. Still we *say* that "you never outgrow your need for milk."

In humans, lactase (the enzyme for digestion of milk) is not produced after we grow our teeth. But dogma says, "Cow Theory" cannot apply to humans, even though calcium is plentiful in greens.

We *know* that bulls eat no meat, milk, cheese, or yogurt, nothing in the first two groups. Bulls eat grass. But dare we *believe* the "Bull Theory" that protein and calcium come from grass?

But leafy greens are a **lower** group. And prayers must be read in order, or else instinctual eating might lead to lunch-room excommunications, and "unbelieveably" healthy children in the USA. A belief that protein is found in greens would eat away at the dogma of the public-school religion.

"Group Three: Fruits and vegetables give you vitamins which help your body use the foods you eat." This sentence implied that the vitamins in vegetables were not food. Children already took it on TV faith that natural vitamins could be found in tablets and drops. Unlike meat that built muscles and milk that gave us bones, fruits and vegetables had only vitamins, nothing that could not be found in chewable TV-advertised tablets.

The priests of the Four Food Group Religion had been schooled by high priests who had gone before. These were their sincere beliefs.

The litany concluded, "Group Four: Breads and cereals give your body starch and protein." Let the children pray, "The starch turns to sugar and gives you energy." Yet, fruits and vegetables have sugars and starches. We *know* that our cousins the apes in the wild grow strong without the aid of bread or cereals. But could "Ape Theory" apply to the Four Food Group Religion of humanity?

Even though the Beef Trade was forced by the Attorney General to quit the "Beef Gives Strength" ad campaign because it was deemed "deceptive and misleading," children were left with an impression in their formative years that meat was the number one food in the number one food group. Beef was quality protein. As a religious *belief*, no *facts* could make it otherwise. But . . .

Civilized humans eat too much protein for our primate digestive systems. And many diseases are complicated by mal-digested proteins. Why was a Four Food Group Religion taught in public schools? Why was animal protein labeled "number one"?

In 1977, President J.C. planned to celebrate Food Day with a White House meatless meal. But he was overrun by the Meat and Dairy lobby. The Meat and Dairy lobby is so powerful that Government presses turn out its literature. And taxes pay its members to write propaganda for the schools. Amber waves of grain in the USA still belong to the cow-boy, the high priests, and the bully boys.

We have come this far by eating to survive. Human diets using fire are both sub- and super-natural. But our rational (animus) and irrational (bestia) selves are in preconscious conflict.

In New York State, a 1980's comic book starring Nutri-Man and Vita-Woman warned against "the Sugar Demon." But the grammar in the comic strip blurbs was so poor that its message was convoluted into dietary dis-information.

The Department of Health's comic included this standard religious passage in the words of Nutri-Man: "Judy, your body needs good foods, like milk, eggs, fruit, cereal, cheese, and meat. Not sugary foods! Sugar gives you false energy that leaves you feeling even more tired later!"

The message was more than subtly confusing. Due to miswording, children read a slander against sugar, with no distinction at all between natural sugar and refined sugar.

The sugar in a balanced diet of fresh fruits and vegetables is not a problem. But sugar and starch in bread and packaged cereals are in fact the demon. And food refiners are the demon-makers.

The "educators" (like Alice in Wonderland, after eating a cake) forgot how to speak good English.

Nutri-Man never said that cooking turned sugars to tars, FACTORS in cancer. Vita-Woman never said cooking gave us fractionated enzymes, FACTORS in the growth of every cancerous tumor.

The grain-based dogma of Meat and Dairy derives from U.S. history. And once schools converted to the Four Food belief, after a few generations even the distinction between vegetables and fruits were blurred. They were squeezed into one group. But red peppers were once called non-sweet fruits. Green leaves were distinct from yellow leafy or green flowery vegetables. Peas, sprouts, sweet potatoes, avocados, mellons, berries, citrus and so on were cherished as distinct. And nuts that are soaked also come alive with protein (but don't get too much protein).

The religion of "Vegetarianism" also had its dogma which was equally unfounded. "Vegetarians" argued that an analysis of our saliva showed what foods we would eat by instinct. They said that saliva of leaf and fruit eaters is more alkaline, like yours and mine while the saliva of flesh eaters is more acid, not like yours and mine. It sounded reasonable.

Leaf and fruit eaters have millions of pores all over their skin, like you and me. Flesh eaters have no pores and perspire via their tongues and pads on their noses and feet, not like you and me. The arguments had some validity.

Human intestines are about 12 times the length of our bodies, like fruit and vegetable eaters. But meat eaters have digestive tracts only 3 times the length of the body. And since acids that digest flesh must be excreted rapidly, a short digestive tract is better for meat eaters. But in the human digestive tract, such acids, when held in longer, cause indigestion. Quite understandable.

Life-long putrification and fermentation of food in the stomach caused by rotting meat and various poor combinations of foods was a major factor in human disease throughout the Age of History.

The arguments of the "Vegetarian" religion were true as far as they went, but they overlooked the fact that monkeys were NOT strict vegetarians. Chimp diets are discussed in a later chapter.

Monkeys have much larger canine teeth than we have. Still, we (the super-natural monkeys) are equipped to eat and digest small amounts of meat. If faced with starvation, we can even eat dogs. So, we can decide what is best.

Testing food on rats was a ritual of the scared techno mind-set. With the bio knowledge that rats were omnivores by nature while we were omnivores by artifact, some held religiously to the belief that rat data might show us how to eat. Yet the most efficient way to eat is determined by the body and its environment. And as the mind (in "the Word") re-shapes the relationship between our bodies and spirits, our diets will change.

Hot Dogs and Cold Milk

Our ritual fire worship led us to believe that "a hot breakfast" was more nutritious than a piece of fruit, especially in winter. "Hot lunches" were sacrosanct in public schools. And "the Hot Lunch Program" was a law in many States.

The "scientific" notion that life emerged from a bowl of "cosmic soup" had more to do with what our scientists had for lunch than what they thought of Evolution and the continuum of life.

The Agriculture Department paid Farmer Brown and his dog to tell the children of TV-Land about the Four Food Groups, giving meat and dairy free TV commercials.

The myth of "complete protein" said meat had all the essential amino acids. But "complete protein" is a meaningless phrase, for various animals find different groupings of amino acids essential. And various organs have proteins with different amino acids. So, to eat a "complete protein," a human would have to acquire a fresh human carcass and eat bits of each organ (eye, entrail, bone, brain, gonad, heart, kidney, spleen), and eat the pieces raw. That's "complete protein."

Fresh fruits and vegetables offer all the amino acids necessary in the right amounts for primates (that's us) to make our own complete protein.

Our need for protein varies from about 18 to 36 grams daily. But most people in the USA eat over 120 grams. And since we have no protein storage system, excess is excreted in urea or turned into factors in skin-growths, tumors, and cancers.

Weight loss on high protein diets is due to the fact that protein passing through the blood stream before it is metabolized into urea leaches out minerals (including calcium). So osteoporosis may result from diets high in meat and dairy. Human mother's milk is for a child and cow's milk is for calves — naturally.

Why is milk on TV "delicious" when "ice cold"? Because it sours rapidly otherwise. But natural foods taste best at natural temperatures.

Our Food Group Religion, shaken in the final days of Armageddon, will lay the cow-boy to rest as our new Space Age mentality takes hold. For Space Age thinking deals with bio-units. The space capsule, the individual person, and the Earth itself can each be seen as bio-units.

Eventually, our "migration" (Palestine) and our "struggle with God" (Israel) will be resolved in one sphere. Spaceships of migration to our next home will be in the form of roaming terrariums. Science is even now working on a gravity supply for our future spaceships.

Each capsule will start with two families who can intermarry, produce offspring, and recycle the remains of the dead. The food supply will consist of items that can be recycled also with no toxins and no waste on our intergalactic menus.

A factor in arteriosclerosis is cholesterol. Fruits and vegetables have No Cholesterol, yet our bodies make all we need when we eat only fruits and vegetables. We also produce vitamin B-12 when we eat organic, unsterilized foods. B-12 in on the the food, rather than in it.

If not too far gone, heart disease, caused by high-fat diets, can be reversed by high-fiber diets. And fibers in raw fruits and vegetables as consumed in our space terrariums will be suited to primates, so heart disease will be no problem, so long as we exercise.

Also, a factor in arthritis, excess uric acid, is not a product in eating vegetation.

Back in historic times, "experts" got billions of dollars for research into cholesterol. We paid to support our emotional ties to the cow-boy. The majority of U.S. citizens, like many Hindu sects, had dairy rituals as part of their worship.

We ate not from hunger. Food was a feast in the blood of the lamb and the golden calf while bread and wine gave us communion. These rituals had once served to get us through the winters and famines of our pilgrimage. Eating "evil" was not wrong; it was the only thing to do. We made the choice to survive. And now, we will choose again to gain a greater view from the next plateau.

CHAPTER 23

ONE TRUE RELIGION

With One True God, why do three One-God religions each claim different truths in the Holy Land? Why do Jews and Palistineans fight as Christians go on pilgrimages into Beth-lehem (House of Bread)? Is the One God devouring itself? To answer, let us try (rooted in "tri") to touch and crystallize the essence of our true belief.

The first belief that you have is a belief in belief itself. Each religion begins with faith. Faith begets Hope. Hope begets Charity. And these are abstract attributes of the One God.

In the spirit we start with Faith. In the body we begin with Love. As these two meet, physical Hope is joined to spiritual Hope.

We have two interlocking triangles, one above, one below, in Heaven and on Earth.

IN JUDAISM
18 EQUATES TO LIFE

It is a Jewish tradition to give 18 of something special when gifts are given to celebrate "life."

The Star of David can
be drawn by placing six
triangles together,
each with three sides.
Thus, the expanded star
has 18 equal unbroken lines.

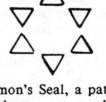

David's Shield was made from Solomon's Seal, a pattern of two interwoven triangles. And Solomon, as we have seen, was given the gift of 666 talents of gold, used later as the base of money-lending symbols outside modern pawnbroker's shops. And 666 was shot by a bullet of Mr. Disbelief that was bought and sold at a pawnshop under the sign of 666 for Solomon's talents.

The 666 (known popularly as the Anti-Christ) is 18 (life) broken into three parts. As Christ had come to teach everlasting life, Anti-Christ separated the life of man's body (6), the life of man's mind (6), and life of man's spirit (6).

These sixes apply to men rather than to women because life's separation is only an illusion of his-story, where man's attachment to eternity is temporarily clouded over.

Every child was born of a physical mother, who was born of a mother, who was born of a mother. We are all connected (as a web), joined in the flesh because we are each physically born of woman.

Yet, it can take from 36 minutes to 5 days for a sperm to reach an egg to effect conception. So, a father is not always present, tied to the child or to our web of human flesh as is a mother.

In the Spirit, however, Father and Son form an unbroken chain of life (chai). Focused in their spirit web, the men of each One-God religion had laws to stop abortions at home while going off to war to kill children of other One-God religions. But as the social roles of men and women began to blur, a love of the body was merging with a newly crystallizing love of spirit.

We have seen the puzzle pieces BAR and RAB, boy and master meet at R (18) as Bar-abbas was freed instead of Jesus. From stage to stage, each drama inverted the next. For the bio-source of all men was woman, the root of his bio-conflict.

Jesus, a boy-rabbi died to help us resolve this mystery. In kaballah, 6 is man and 9 is woman, each with a different union in 18. At 99 Abram-Abraham came into conflict with his two wives.

Since six represents "masculine perfectability," Jesus took up his "Father's Business" at the age of 12. He studied mysticism for 18 years (absent in the Bible), then assumed his public life at 30 (6 x 5) for 5 is a turning point. He was crucified at 33, and arose on the 3rd day.

ISLAM HOLDS IN ITS 18th SURAH
THAT ALLAH HAS NO SON

In the 18th surah of the Koran, Muhammad writes, "*to warn those who say: Allah hath chosen a son, a thing whereof they have no knowledge, nor had their fathers. Dreadful is the word that cometh out of their mouths. They speak naught but a lie*" (Surah 18:4-5).

In the 72nd surah (four 18's), Muhammad repeats his message. "*I pray unto Allah only, and ascribe unto Him no partner.*" Muhammad addressed the issue of "God's Son" due to matriarchal clashes with patriarchal "rights of inheritance."

Abram-Abraham's sons were his in the spirit. He fathered them both in free will. It was his wives who eventually had a disagreement.

Humanity was just beginning to work through the building of monogamy, the mono-game of sex that would give emotional interest to money under the the rule of monotheism. For these would be the rules to guide our families as we traveled to our next home in a distant galaxy.

AND NOW THE NUMBER 18
IS
ENCODED IN ENLIGHTENMENT

ENLIGHTENMENT is the only word in English
to have the letters E-I-G-H-T-E-E-N in this order.

```
E N L I G H T E N M E N T
N L           N M       T
E - - I G H T E - - E N -
```

Enlightenment is simply insight, seeing where your personal wave meets with the eternal. NL is a wave ending at a right angle. NM is the union of all waves again. And T is the crystal cross-roads.

The spell that is cast by enlightenment comes to eighteen only in the language of the Angles.

In order to become a Zen Master, one must solve a series of 54 (three 18's) koans.

CRYSTALLIZATION

A koan is a problem whose answer can be found only in a flash of enlightenment. And enlightenment is when all facets of the Crystal reflect inward. At this point, all religions are one.

First, let us look at the abstractions. Then, we shall consider the practicality.

As we pass through history, the 6 and 9 unfold separately in 18 to produce an even higher pattern at 108, a key number in what is often called our "Eastern tradition." East and West (as directions, not places) form an outward spiral in Phase Three intergalactic linguistics.

In terms of human flesh and blood, this means that males and females are devising a way to share their sexuality while living in peace. With a true sense of monogamy, males will overcome even the pre-conscious drives to fight with each other.

The one true religion begins with being true to each other, being faithful to our words whether they are written or spoken.

The Mount Everest Center for Meditation is now located 18,000 feet high in the Himalayas.[1] After meditation, "Eastern" and "Western" mind-sets can not sit separately in Phase Three.

Being true to our words yields fluidity when we are not bound by history. For definitions will be suddenly alive as we seize the Space Age view.

"Buddhas with moon faces live for a day and a night. Buddhas with sun faces live for 1800 years."[2] This ancient saying mystically unites the spirits of women and men in a common cycle, full realization on a new plateau.

Truth is beauty in poetry, yearning to be free and yet confined within a form.

This is the marriage of opposites. He writes the laws that she has only dreamed so that he may see her dream as his reality. Each owns the other thoroughly. And freedom is the fee.

(1) Newsweek 9/12/83, (2) A Glimpse of Nothingness by J. van de Werering

BUDDHISTS
CLOSED THEIR CIRCLE
AT 6 TIMES 18

The 18 Tamil Siddhas (Siddhartha was Buddha) were teachers whose vibrations are now in all authentic Buddhist teachers. As with Judaism, Catholicism, and Islam (ready for his-story's implosion), the Buddhist line of priests was traced to a male. And re-birth was focused in a spiritual dimension of "life."

Many Buddhists, as do Hindus, wear sets of 108 beads (six 18's) with a pattern similar to the sets commonly worn by Catholics, having 54 (three 18's).

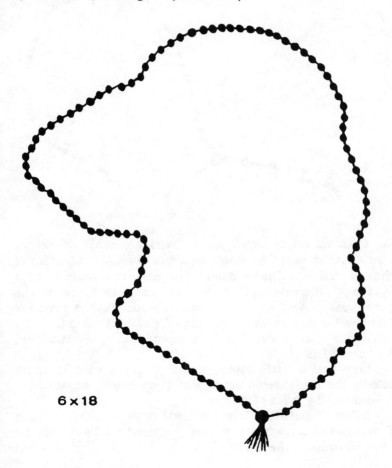

6 × 18

CATHOLICS
CLOSED THEIR CIRCLE
AT 3 TIMES 18

The rosary beads that Catholics most commonly use are pictured below. With a circle of 54 (three 18's) consisting of five sets of ten beads on which are said the "Hail Mary" plus four single beads between these sets on which are said the "Glory be to the Father," with five more beads before a cross is reached.

Five marks a turning point in numerology.

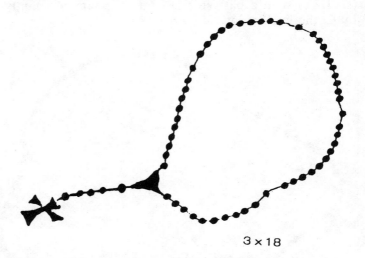

3 × 18

The Catholic set of beads has a "Miraculous Medal" where Hare Krishna beads or Rama beads or Buddhist beads have what is called a "guru bead." Some Hindu sects have a picture of their leader or favorite saint in place of the "guru bead." And Catholic rosary beads have a crucifix after the turning point at the end of the circle of 54.

Vatican City, Catholicism's temporal state, was built on 108 acres of land.

Mary had a little lamb. Rama Krishna sold it. Mars reflects the slaughtered Ram. But G-ram-mar cannot hold it. And so, the cries of pain.

As "East" met "West" in the final days of 1987, a crash of our global stock markets was triggered automatically by a 108.36 drop in the Dow.

218

THE ANCIENT HINDUS
HID THEIR MYSTERY
IN 6 TIMES 18

Following the 108 Upanishads, Hindu sects also use 108 beads in worship of 108 names of God. Hindus (unlike Buddhists) see the Creator as a per-son, Brahma. The second person is Vishnu, the Preserver, while the third, Siva, attends to reproduction.

"In my first perfect accommodation of the 18 spheres of mentation, I recognized no separation among my six senses," says Yogi Kirpal Sing in "Naam or Word." From 6 days of creation through 9 months of labor, we enter at the 18, "life" itself.

B-RA-H-MA is "male genesis" in the Crystal Code.

MAYANS SOUGHT CONTROL
OF WOMAN
IN THE NUMBER 18

The Mayan calendar had 18 months of 20 days, with 5 special days. The 18 months affected fertility in the magical thinking of the Mayans. Toward the end of history, we tried to squeeze 12 moons into a year. And the Mayans also built pyramids to set the sun's vibrations into stone.

The mystic American Indian, Black Elk, writes in *Black Elk Speaks* that he had "The Great Vision" at 9 and "was no good for anything till 18."

Jerry Falwell told 18,000 members (at the time) of the Roads Baptist Church, "I raised my boys to be bulldogs, to hold that jugular vein, even with 18 bullets in 'em" (9/30/80). Such was the vision of the Armageddonists. And the bull-dog was a fitting image for the cow-shepherds of Je-R-usa-L-em.

Islam's 99 names for God mirrored a division of two feminine symbols. At age 99, Abram took the name of Abraham, which led to the break-up of his family. He kept one woman (nine) and drove another woman (nine) out of his house.

THE LIVING DEAD
MEET ETERNAL LIFE
AT 180 DEGREES

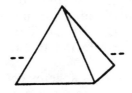  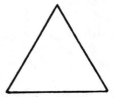

Egypt's pyramids, built to hold the living dead, gather energy from four faces, each of 180°. The Star of David has two triangles, male and female in rebirth. The Christian Trinity yields life born of the Hole-y Spirit, Father, and Son. Three is our first family, inwardly directed, extended in its "life," eternal in its evolution.

Egyptians stopped building pyramids with the advent of their 18th Dynasty, thus beginning their New Kingdom. Toward the end of the 18th Dynasty, monotheism became the state religion, as devoid of strange gods as was Judaism. But the monotheism did not hold. And today, Moslems do not accept the convention of monogamy.

Also, the Egyptians had a special triangle, the MR Triangle. At 13:18 (M:R), the 666 is found in Revelation. And the MR with angles of 36°, 54° and 90° was "the building block of the universe." Used in pyramids to house dead bodies, all its angles were divisible by 18.

The number of "life" was so ubiquitous that the original length of Egypt was set to be 1,800,000 geographic cubits.[1]

"Vertical compression members of masonry are limited in height to 18 times their diameter" in the old Greek formula.[2] Also, the great circle of 30 sarsen stones at Stonehenge had its original uprights about 18 feet in length.[3] And the height of the pillars of the temple of Jerusalem, most meaningfully, was 18 cubits (Jer. 52:21).

(1) Secrets of the Great Pyramids by Peter Tomkins, (2) Nine Chains to the Moon by Buckminster Fuller, (3) Stonehenge Decoded by Gerald Hawkins

220

The Popular Tradition

What is the message in these 18's? The magic so pervades that it's part of the scenery. Official ice hockey courts are 180 feet. And tiddlywinks are scored by tiddling winks into a pot from 18 inches away. And golf has 18 holes.

Lords of the Flame took control of evolution 18 million years ago, in our Lemurian Age, says Alice A. Baily, in "Initation, Human, and Solar." Her use of "Lemurian" is a reference to human beings (the universal mon-key). And in China's theater, 18 Lo Hans fight the Monkey King for control. The Lo Hans are demons. And our monkey nature is taken for granted in Oriental culture.

The parallel evolution of body and spirit is reflected in 18. For just as the female links each new human body to the next by her own, it is the male who must decide on bringing peace, for he is the innate warrior. His number 6 is always the 3 as opposed to the 3. Her number 9 is ever yielding 3 into 3 into 3. And so, 18 carries them both into an expanding cycle.

Lutherans said, "18 inches is an adequate pew space."[1] For comfort, 6 inches were added. Bishop Fulton J. Sheen sold 18 recorded conferences, in the *Catholic Digest* (July 1977). Jimmy Swaggart sold 18 hours of talks (11/12/80). Jimmy's Bible College opened, 18,000 applied.[2] Jim Jones served Kool Aid laced with cyanide in Guyana on November 18th. Later, CBS spent $1.8 million to produce "The Guyana Tragedy." Robert Shuller built a new $18 million "Crystal Cathedral."[3]

Irving Wallace, "who sold 180 million books" wrote *The Miracle* about Lourdes, "city of 1800."[4] He told how the Lady of Lourdes said she would return 18 times. Her secret letters locked in the Vatican supposedly held the Armageddon plan. And her "18 visits" were a clue.

(1) The Lutheran 4/16/86, (2) Time 2/17/86, (3) People 9/29/80, (4) J. Cafferty, NBC 9/12/84

Governments had no money for irrigation, no seed money for fig trees in the desert. The USA had no plans for orchids of plenty but had a bull-headed hunger for guns and butter. We subsidized vaccine insurance. *Vacca* is Latin for "cow." Women were advised not to breastfeed; children thus lacking immunity were poisoned by vaccines; and insurance laws were shifted.

Likewise, HALF the income of dairy farmers was subsidies. Livestock owners paid less for feed; and taxes paid to slaughter "excess cattle" fed on subsidized grain. Such was the karma of the golden calf. The cow was deified at the expense of humanity.

No subsidies went to organic farms, but their taxes helped to subsidize Meat and Dairy. Still, in a Phase Three market, organic produce will compete fairly. And mothers are already being encouraged to breastfeed again. The crystallization of all religion will come to us as we build our true democracy, globally. And the proper use of money will be essential to our unified religion.

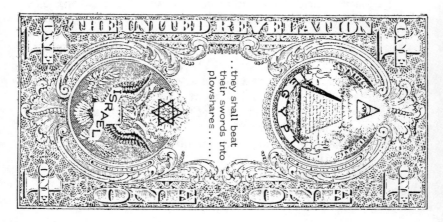

A ballot you can cast for good health, personal wholeness, and planetary survival states quite clearly, "In God We Trust." Note that "God" is in the singular. For one force on this planet that money is meant to serve is "life" itself.

CHAPTER 24

MONOGAMY AND MONOTHEISM

The Chinese Book of Changes, *I Ching*, uses six random drawings of straws or six random tosses of a coin to guide the readings. And "changes" are found when a six or nine appears in one of those six random drawings or tosses.

Also, the sign of Yin and Yang depicting opposites in union (expansive-contractive, hot-cold, light-dark, male-female) resembles the arabic numbers 6 and 9 in an embrace. And in kabbalah, 6 and 9 equal male and female perfectibility. So, his-story's symbols come to-get-her where 6 meets 9. For they mystically touch in life at the number 18.

Not only does *chai* (18) mean "life" in Hebrew, *chi* means "living energy" in China where the art of tai-chi-chuan offers 108 sets of movement to bring yin and yang into balance. Also, in "The Tibetan Book of the Dead" *chi-khai bardo* is "a light seen at the moment of death." And *Chi-na* names the land where fire first came into the hands of Pe-king man. But the story makes sense only in English.

The threads of fire, light, energy, and life in our early languages lead up to the machine (ma-chi-ne) as a mother of techno life, linking matter (MA) to a negative-energy wave (NE), making inter-planetary travel possible. And we at times negate biology to feed our ma-chi-ne.

Coincidentally, in Reagan's first year of rule, a subscription to LIFE (the magazine) was $18. And LIFE (the breakfast cereal) had "shelf life" that Shredded Wheat said was mixed with "18 teaspoons of added sugar" (not good for human life).

God and sex are mutual creators of "new life." So, we can apply abstract (disembodied) knowledge to biology. Simply stated, our movement toward monotheism has paralleled our movement toward monogamy. And each inspires the other. But the story goes that Eve was the first tempted to become as a god, to know eternal life. And this was woman's "fault." A fault, of course, is a crack. And later, we shall see why the word "testament" has the same roots as "testicle."

"The New Testament" is not a Jewish term since Jews do not call their Book "The Old Testament." And "Judeo-Christian," which inverts any belief that a Messiah is yet to come, makes less sense to Jews than to Christians. So, if Muhammad named the Koran "The Newest Testament" and attached it to the other two, Christians might know how some Jews feel about having a compound-Bible.

Nonetheless, modern Jews agree with Christians on monogamy. "Old Testament" Jews had many wives, yet Jewish men today marry only one wife at a time.

In the invisible realm, it was a trouble with female spirits that allowed I-ra-q and I-ra-n to be sacrificed in the final days. And a problem with spirits (alcohol) was basic to distortions among Christians and Jews. Bear in mind that these are "faults" in the belief systems that filter into daily reality.

In a family-line where the patriarch kicks his wife and child out of the house, monogamy is less likely to grow. So, the Moslems still suffer from the abuse of Abram-Abraham who once changed his name and divided his family. The Arabs and Jews are acting out a madness from their family history.

In Phase Three, weddings without wine will tell the spirit of woman that the body of man no longer needs to be drugged to be made ready for society. Remember that all the Phase Two drugs that humans took were used to accommodate the biology of the total human organism (all humanity together) to the trials of the Techno State.

The ideal of monogamy proved a consternation to modern Christian and Jewish men because the "One Goddess" was de-meaned in his-story. But, ironically, as each religion in turn honors God the Mother equally with God the Father, all our religions will be brought together under the One True God of Family Unity.

It was necesssary that the Son of God re-deem the Age of His-story. Yet in Phase Three, a union between the Father and the Holy Spirit (Mother) will be born of "the Word" in living evolution.

The Second Coming of "the Word" brings **being true** to a new level. This is why the Armageddon preachers fell in the final days. They neglected the Earthly Goddess and expected Mother Earth to be destroyed by God the Father so a new Earth could be made. And the preachers chased their own tales, trying to "make" new women.

In our beastly metaphor, while many Moslem men had polygamy as a goal, many so-called Christian men chased the Whore. Both saw masculine "power" as a determining factor in human sexual relations. The following symbols help to unravel pre-monogamous history.

ADAM is a reflection of MAZDA with a Z (an end) in the middle. And Mazda is a key to future unity among the Arabs, Christians, and Jews. For it was the Persian deity Mazda who inspired the Wise Men to visit Jesus. And Muhammad's One-God fits with the Persian (Iranian) One-God of the Wise Men. So, these pieces fit together as the one fits into zero, sexually.

Zoro-aster (Zarathustra), once in a polytheist sect in Iran, taught his Wise Men to believe in One God. But Mazda, Zoroaster's One-God diety, had a twin brother by the name of Mainyu. Also, the father of Rome (Romulus) and the father of the nation of Israel (Jacob) each had his own twin brother. So, three sets of twins picture the male in conflict with his own shadow, a saga of good and evil in the abstract, yet acted out as bad male energy (mal-E) socially.

At the time of Jesus, Zoroastrianism was the state religion of the Persian Empire and Mazda was the reigning deity of the Middle East. The story of the Iranian Wise Men of Mazda (whose first name was OR, "light") carries the many threads of our mystery into present (pre-sent) time.

Jesus was torn between Romans (sons of Romulus) and Jews (sons of Israel, whose name was Jacob). For Romulus and Jacob had each taken the land of his own twin brother (Remus and Esau). And the God of the Iranian Wise Men had taken the power of Heaven from his twin-brother.

This story, with all its trivia (three roads) contains the entire metaphor of human existence. These three faces of man (6) are ever turning in the uni-verse that is woman. And woman has inverted in one-turn (uni-verse) her sexual position to meet man face to face, to harmonize a higher energy. So, we shall touch on woman's uni-versal quality in several later chapters.

Three male archetypes had defeated male twins. To extend monogamy within monotheism, Jesus re-deemed (re-valued) his roots — born of Earthly Flesh met in a Heavenly Spirit.

The notion that spirits were more sacred than flesh was a necessary evil in the Age of History since we needed to build a Techno State capable of getting to Heaven, in the flesh. Romulus, suckled by a she-wolf, also used dairy as a food. And Zoroaster promised each follower his own inexhaustible cow in Heaven in the time that Jews worshiped the Golden Calf. His promise supported a social order wherein stealing cattle from the wealthy was a mortal sin.

Near history's end, Cornell University doubled the milk output of several cows by injecting them with hormones. The cow-boys had not outgrown their desire for milk while many nations suffered dairy over-production due to subsidies. And in a 1986 election ploy, Reagan inverted his farm policy to pay farmers for not growing sorgum, corn, barley or oats. The purpose was to keep dairy prices high. And we will see how the golden calf, President J.C., and Iran fit into this historic spiral.

CHAPTER 25

HITLER, THE WOLF

ADOLF means "wolf" in Old German. ZWOLF is "12" in Modern German. And Z-WOLF encodes "an end to the wolf" in English, an angular clue in our "racial" murder mystery.

The name Adolf Hitler stirs emotions that run deep. For though it is easy to see that fire is a source both good and evil, it is painful to admit that good and evil are never absolutes in human affairs. Most people confess to some "evil." And most like to think that babies are innocent. So, to meet the confusion, when adults try to judge each other, we put 12 people on a jury.

Now, let us look at the clues as we integrate our logic and emotions about "the wolf."

Adolf Hitler was judged by many to be the most "evil" murderer in modern times. Yet, there is an irony in the history of Hitler, the wolf.

Wolf Begin, Menachem Begin's father, died in a Nazi concentration camp, giving his son the spirit to fight for a new beginning for Israel.

"An end to the wolf" was well met in "Wolf Begin" who fought against Adolf. But the "12" was mystified again as Israel got bogged down in defining "a Jew" as opposed to "a Palestinean."

Ishmael (the first Arab) had 12 sons, who were princes in the land. And Israel's sons begat 12 tribes who were freed by the blood of Passover lamb. A human "Lamb of God" was sacrificed by Rome under the sign of the wolf. And Hitler, the wolf, re-united Germany with Rome during World War II. Yet, *ger-man* means "strange manna" in He-brew, a sacrifice of food. UR, "light" in He-brew, is "primitive" in Ger-man. And Hitler's scientists were christened as heroes in the USA, for building NASA, which means "to travel forth" in He-brew. The puzzle fits together only in English.

Somehow, "the most evil man of modern times" gave rise to a rebirth of Israel and the beginnings of a workable space program in the USA. And symbols of the lamb, a fire sacrifice, and bread dominate the story of Hitler, the wolf.

LAMB (with silent B) reflects a MALE (with energy, E). And WOLF is a backward FLOW as spirit streams converge. RUACH means "spirit" (breath) in He-brew while in Ger-man RAUCH is "smoke."

And "boy" (bar) in Hebrew is "money" (bar) in German. The emerging patterns seem unspeakable. Did the international bankers who financed Hitler know at some mystical level of the flesh sacrifice that was to be exchanged for NASA?

Could we have gotten the same results without the "racial" hatred and the murders?

Could we build a Heavenly City with no journey into Hell? If Adam had taken the power of RA (fire) and used it for only science, would he have maintained a conscious connection to deity? Might we have moved at a slower pace, technologically? Why did Adam EAT from the Tree of Technology? Why did he put the knowledge of "good" and "evil" inside his own body?

Perhaps, as homonids we could not have dealt emotionally with the Techno State if we had not lost our primitive mind-set.

So, let us re-arrange some puzzle pieces. Ger-man is "strange manna," but manna was food for the Israelites who were literally lost in *Sin*, the name of a spot in the desert near Mount Sinai. And *Sinn* in Ger-man means "sense." It's an Alice in Wonderland puzzle, needing only a key to the rabbit (rabbi-T) hole.

The R-L signs are HIT-LER, BE-RL-IN, IS-RA-EL, and Je-R-usa-L-em. But what of "b-read," "to read," and "to lead"? "To hear" and "to heal"? And the RAW LAW? Did Jesus (like Alice) use cooked food to get into a backward garden? Did he use a piece of bread to start a new techno sect? Was Hitler confused by a Catholic up-bringing? Why did Adolf put Jews in his ovens?

Apparently, as a child, Hitler believed that bread from convent ovens placed on his tongue contained the Lamb of God. "Fear of fire" and "the cannibal taboo" were resolved for him in a single host that held his God, a food infused with flames. And Hitler's rituals were conjured in covens. His political party began with 12 others; for 13 makes a witch's coven. And 13 is "a baker's dozen," an extra stick of bread for the Christ.

Images of "sacrificial bread" and "the Lamb of God" gave Hitler a mystified foundation. But Adolf "the wolf" gave a twist to the cross. He personified an "evil" hidden in humanity.

The monkey who held a burning stick was seen as irrational by other species. And if simple biology could judge, HIT-LER was a focus of history's fire-irrationality. Fire was the fear that drove the human wolf to madness.

Religions did not make "common" sense. Instead, they stressed beliefs we did not have in common and steeped us in pre-conscious fears.

If eating broken enzymes fed the un-conscious in an unseen world, what did the bread sacrifice do to our humanity? Had fire-worship cost us our conscience? Abram-Abraham was ready to burn his son; was he being rational? Con-science (body and spirit knowledge in harmony) was fractured as a sacrifice to the Techno State.

As we began to worship fire, we tried to eat it in cooked food. When nuclear energy gave us power, we irradiated food. Con-fused between creation and cremation (M is matter in our equation), eating a god was common to us in ancient religions. And the man-ger hid the theme of cannibalism in Beth-lehem ("House of Bread").

Left overnight in the desert, manna stank and worms grew in it (Exodus 16:14-20). Had people faced with starvation eaten the corpses of others who had died that day? The "strange manna" was not accepted by Israel's children until Moses called it "the Bread of the Lord." Were cooked bodies eaten for survival, an offering to God? We have only written words to tell.

The Wafer

We have seen that in German, *waffe* ("weapon") and *waffel* (a bread wafer sacrificed at mass) have the same linguistic roots. Also, the Hebrew word for "bread" (*lechem*) is related to "war" (*locham*).

Remember, Alice lost her grammar after she ate a tiny cake. But *Waffel* also means "chatterbox" in German and "to speak evasively" in the USA.

Reagan waffled on his way to a Jewish torture shrine and visited a Nazi cemetery at Bitburg in Germany which raised a furor among many Jews.

The Cookie Monster's mystical biscuits ruled as PASTA encoded sins of the PAST.

Matzoth was prepared for 18 minutes. The Anti-Christ divided 6+6+6. And the year that Reagan visited Bitburg, Passover began on the Jewish Sabbath between Good Friday and Easter Sunday. The USA was evenly divided as to whether 666 should visit Nazi graves, 18% were undecided.[1] And 72% (four 18's) of West Germans favored his Bitburg stop to visit the Nazi cemetery.[2]

President 666 laid a wreath at a Bitburg grave site of 1800 Third Reich soldiers.[3] That 1800 in the press was approximate as was another news report that Kurt Waldheim had deported "nearly 1800 Greek Jews" when he worked for Hitler.[4] Waldheim, former U.N. Secretary General, joined Hitler's "brown shirts" on November 18th. And his file was kept secret by the 18-nation War Crimes Commission.[5] For our primitive secret went deeper still.

Humanity itself would have to reach a new level of consciousness before our individuals could be seen as fully separate from their nations.

This sense of separateness is frightening to many people, yet for others it embodies the sense of being a god. The key to this puzzle is, of course, your own Free Will. You can do anything and still be human.

(1) Newsweek 4/22/85, (2) Newsweek 5/6/85, (3) NY Times 5/8/85, (4) NY Times 5/2/86, (5) NY Times 5/12/86

Our rom-antic affair with the wolf was the other side of our sacrifice of the lamb. And all nations had their strange love affairs with beasts, though not all worshipped wolves as did Rome. Israel's first love was Rachel; her name means "lamb." And RA-CH-EL gave birth to Joseph, who became (in prophecy, Obed. 18) the head of "the spiritual Israel." Yet, a matrilineal order was religiously maintained.

Our use of fire plus spiritual factors changed estrus to menstruation; new waves from woman's monthly cycles were interwoven, as we shall see, to give most women periods of blood. (See chapter Written in Blood.)

The drama that little girls play out with the Big Bad Wolf is mirrored in every man, each with a bit of the wolf, each with a bit of the lamb.

And young Adolf sang in a choir, worshipped a virgin, desired to be a priest, knew Church Latin, and remained unto death in the Church of Rome. Also, he said Ancient Rome was worthy of imitation.

Mussolini (Muslin, a white material), Italy's ruler and Hitler's ally, with a wife named Rachel and mistress Claretta, a little L-R symbol, fit Hitler's "pure white" Aryan delusion. For Hitler, the wolf, fed on the gaps in spiritual evolution. And NASA evolved from Ger-man techno spin-off in the USA. The priest, preacher, mulla, and rabbi said, "the Lord worked in mysterious ways." Did German karma in NASA kill Christa on the Hebrew *Shavat*'s 18th day? *Shavat* was the water bearer under an aquarian President who walked the line between "good" and "evil," as every human does.

With the fall of the Western Roman Empire began "the Dark Ages" in Europe. And at the end of this cultural rot and fermentation came the discovery of America (body), the Renaissance (mind), and the Reformation (spirit). In every respect, humanity took a giant step foreward. Each "evil" cycle (as always) makes sense only if viewed in the light of a universal "good."

An angel said IS-RA-EL was the name most suited to Jacob's mission. So Jacob became "a struggle with God," *Isra-El*. Did some fallen angel tell Alois Schicklgruber to invent the name HIT-LER to give his son, Adolf?

Alois (Adolf's father) was Maria's son. Maria's lover had an unrecorded name. And as in the mystery of Mary and the Nameless God, Maria had a child with no father, so that child generated a new symbol.

Alois took Hitler from *Heidler*, "a heathen" in German. And the boy named Adolf Hitler was the sixth child of Alois Schicklgruber Hitler. Also, Adolf's mother KLARA died when Hitler was 18.

Even though "the Word" is our slave (a genie of great power), it has rules of its own. So this tale of Adolf (the wolf), reveals a primitive link between the beast and humankind.

CH means "life" in the Code, for *chai* (18) is also the word for "life." And RACHEL (RA-CH-EL), meaning "lamb," gave ISRAEL new life after he had defeated his twin brother.

Romulus (a twin) was suckled by a she-wolf. His father was MARS, encoding a conflict with the RAM. And in He-brew, *ram* means "exalted." So, Abram became Abraham ("father of a multitude").

This symbolic overlay of words tells us that the Romans and the Jews were both spiritually and emotionally concerned with eating lamb. Both Roman and Jewish cultures were farmers who were dominated by cults of shepherds. And as in the USA in pre-sent time, people saw the symbols as somehow separate. Still, after we see beyond our history, the NOW is absolutely WON.

Egypt made a god of the wolf. Israel made a law against such worship. But neither group stopped eating lamb. In times of starvation, prehistoric monkeys tracked the wolf and shepherds learned to prey on the lamb. Each man preyed on every other man and prayed to God for a more gentle plan. "The Word," however, reflected our actions as we waited for its Second Coming.

Theodor HERZL (HE-RZL) is called "the father of Zionism." Z (an ending) comes between R and L. For Theo-dor, "God's gift," drew one of ISRAEL's 12 (the tribe of Judah) from the clutches of the Ger-man ZWOLF ("12" in German).

These patterns are still seeking resolution. ALIEN and ARYAN were born of flawed reflections of one perfect Crystal law. Aryans invaded India in 3000 B.C. and became the "upper classes" long before the time of Abram. Sanskrit ARYAN gods, chosen people, and supermen created the ALIEN. And in modern times, HIT-LER's N-A-Z-I nation fell, giving rise to HE-RZL's Z-I-O-N.

The USA and USSR on the Right and Left, both geographically and politically, were sucked into the city of BE-RL-IN. So the stage was set for the final days of his-story (see chapter 38).

HIT-LER's Secret Police led by HIMM-LER had gone mad with ritual. Had HIT-LER, the wolf, been a disembodied spirit in ancient times? Had secret brotherhoods of our new found civilizations in India and Egypt (with their blood-brood cults) given us this ghost to reckon with?

A form of bio-regression was forced on humanity after the Flood. When no vegetation remained, Noah sacrificed the animals, taking into his DNA the RNA (memory factors) of other species. This spirit division was later personified in the actions of Japeth (fair) and Ham (dark), his sons, and in the line of Ab-ram from Noah's third son Shem (word). Thus, we had our apartheid of the mind. Who were the little HIT-LERs, the troops that devoured humanity? Who had given whom the power to inject drugs into alienated mental patients in the name of "social superiority."

A HIT-LER has no nationality, only an Aryan attitude. So, the poorest family can have its own "little HIT-LER." Even with the Buddha, Torah, Christ, and Allah all within the soul, you still can have your own little HIT-LER. And only conscious control can ever make the difference.

The Big Bad . . .

A Big Bad Fox never chases little girls in the forest. Jackals do not huff and puff and blow your house down. Neither Dogman nor Coyoteman is cursed with an appetite for human blood. Is it only the wolf who dresses in wool, flaunts sheepskins of diplomacy, and deserves the axe? And what of wolf impersonators who provoke wars, diplomatically?

In fact, wild wolves are innocent of any crime against humanity. A pack of wolves will not attack a human being. Wolves are afraid of us. But we have symbolized our fear of nature's flow, unconsciously.

The German for "fire" is *Feuer*. The German for "leader" is *Fuhrer*. These two got tangled at the sound of R as German grew to meet its destiny. And Germany went insane as fire became its leader, in fear of fear itself.

Before written history, man made the *fiend* his *friend*. Canines helped capture the victims of the brotherhood. And we made the sound of the fiend (ger) into the Hebrew word for "strange." So, a ger-man became a man of hun-ger. And the Huns with ferocity became "ger-man."

German was labeled "Deutsch" in Deutschland, where *deutlich* meant "clear." And yet, *Deutung* meant "an interpretation."

The lips of dogs or wolves do not form sounds such as G and R. "Grrrr" is a sound of anger (an-ger) that humans make as energy (E) flows between gravity (G) and "life" (R) in our struggle to live with levity. So, we can forgive our history only when we see that it has given us today. And we can accept today only when we treasure tomorrow.

The myth of Armageddon that says you need not join your future to your past was not invented by Christianity. Zoroaster had a similar story to tell to those enslaved. Such stories of fear can disable the manager within.

A MAN-A-GER, must have "realization" at center. M-A-N is a realization (A) between two kinds of waves (M and N), one eternal and one limited. And so, each man can reg-u-late the beastly "ger" of anger.

234

Mengele

Dr. Josef Mengele (the Angel of Death) was chief medical practitioner at the death camp Auschwitz. And only 180 of his 3,000 victims survived Mengele's "Jewish twin children" project. Only Jewish twins were held for Mengele's insane experiments. And the Jewish children who were not twins were gassed upon arrival.

MENGELE's name was ambiguous. It encoded a plurality of spirits (MEN) linked by gravity (G) to EL followed by energy (E). He was a techno maniac who specialized in twins. (Romulus was a twin. Israel was a twin. Mazda was a twin.)

Mengele "sewed twins together back to back. They screamed day and night from the pain," said a Jewish orderly who worked in Mengele's hospital.

Doctor Mengele specialized in eyes. He tried to change brown eyes to blue by injecting dye into babies' eyeballs. Aryan racial traits mattered greatly to Mengele who had a darker complexion. But the original Aryan was only a myth, an artifact of "upper class" linguistics in Sanskrit. The concept of ARYA in India was an ancient parallel to the myth of "the White Man" in the USA.

In nature, every marriage is an intermarriage. No "pure race" has ever existed. Only the naming made the tribes that wandered feel as if they had verbal boundaries. And so, nations were built on names.

New Aryans from the USA went to Nam to kill babies with slanted eyes. And ironically, those New Aryans often thought of themselves as "Black." But if they thought of themselves as "White," they still could kill "Yellow" babies, in the name of the "upper classes."

Who can see the eyes of the homeless, turn away, and forget about "them"? Where is Hitler? Who has given out the orders to let the homeless rot? In alienation, the Aryan nation is made up of individuals. Thus, we keep alive the madness. We need no living Hitler, no Dr. Mengele. Our own devices and excuses, manufactured one by one, are sufficient for the "them-o-cide," the one by one holocaust of alienated individuals.

The Eyes

In the good old USA, the "westernizing of Oriental eyes" costs up to $1800 at the hands of a certified Beverly Hills plastic surgeon. Doctor Matsunaga "who is of Asian descent himself" says, "Asians identify with Western features, particularly big, beautiful eyes." He speaks of "improving" a droopy jawline or having a hook nose "fixed" for an Italian or a Jew (*Omni*, Oct. 1985).

Ruled by machine-made precision beauty (not by individuality), we clamored for techno features that would never fade. Men shaved their faces and women their legs in vain attempts to prove we were not animals and possibly would not die. We danced like machines, in the final days.

Are cosmetic surgeons on TV who want to change your eyes at all like Dr. Mengele — certified and certain in their Aryan morality? And do the ads leave ugly scars on children's minds?

We were more clever than Mengele, so subtle in our official disguise, only taking orders, at a profit, citizens in the service of the glorious, poisoned Techno Land, adding to the Gross National Product with each operation.

We need plastic surgeons for accident victims. But wholesale "cosmetic surgery" insinuates that aging is not beautiful. So, even without Dr. Mengele, we have continued to torture ourselves.

After World War II, so many Germans claimed not to have supported Hitler, one might think no Nazis ever lived. No common soldiers bore the guilt. But unlike Nazis, the USA had a "the two party system" to allow the nation to dodge from Left to Right while neither side took the blame. And two-dimensional thinking was all the rage while an Aryan-Alien division marked Je-R-usa-L-em.

West German Chancellor Helmut Kohl said, "Only 18 days before Germany was surrounded, I was asked to join the Nazi SS" (*Time* 5/6/85). And Reagan's job approval dropped to 54% (three 18's) after his Bitburg visit (*Time* 5/6/85).

The Russian word for "wolf" is VOLK, which is the German word for "people."

The ghosts of our ancient blood-brood brotherhood still keep our nations divided today. One reason Hitler, the wolf, got into power was a strange fear of starvation — irrational, yet the root of much conspicuous consumption in Je-R-usa-L-em.

HIT-LER was a decision many souls had made: to use "national-ism" in defense of "me-ism." But when Je-R-usa-L-em comes together, it will yield a a global Crystal City, not a nation. Armageddon preachers hoped against hope for Revelation said ALL nations would suffer. And New Jerusalem is not a nation.

MENDACITY means "untruth." MEND-A-CITY is the key. Taking untruth apart, we find many truths in its divided context. For the truth is not an abstraction; truth must be true to something. So, we are true only when true to each other and true to "the Word" itself.

The Jews that Hitler baked had what he coveted, a durable nation with no physical boundaries. The Jews had a spirit of oneness, a link to the One God.

Hitler wanted his nation to have no boundaries. He wanted a oneness for his Aryan "chosen people." But Hitler's nation would have no boundaries not because of its abstract spirit. He wanted to rule the globe by enslaving all "the Aliens."

"God is with us," Hitler proclaimed, *Gott Mit Uns*, on every Nazi uniform. Through the occult, he chose a "good luck" swastika, a "twisted cross," a devil's Christianity. He planned a great assembly hall (180,000 standing capacity) like the Roman Pantheon, intended to someday duplicate the grand venerability of global Christendom in Berlin.[1]

Israel means "struggle with God." And Hitler's plan of conquest was entitled *Mein Kampf* which means "My Struggle." So, in BE-RL-IN came the end of Hitler's isra-EL, his struggle with individuality.

(1) Inside the Third Reich by Albert Speer

Hitler's officers bungled plans made to kill him with a bomb at his 18-foot conference table in the "Wolf's Lair," in East Prussia. But Hitler's drama ended later in his 18-room Berlin bunker.

Robert Payne tells of Hitler's death in detail. Hitler ordered 200 liters of gasoline from Erich Kempka to block bunker exits as Hitler planned his suicide. But fate stepped in. "With difficulty, Kempka was able to collect about 180 liters," writes Payne.[1] And 18 marked the end of Hitler, the wolf, when he shot a hole in his own head with his 7.65 Walther (W-al-th-er) pistol (see Lu-th-er). And that 7.65 adds up to 18 in numerology.

Hitler had wolfhounds at the Wolf's Lair. Johanna Wolf was his private secretary. His closest fiend, Hess, named his son "Wolf." For, as was Reagan with his 666, Hitler was aware of his own symbolism.

Most of Israel's 12 tribes were "lost" with the exception of the Jews. Also, followers of Manassa ("forgetfulness") went west to Angle Land, only to be seeded later in Je-R-usa-L-em. And as the USA closed in on HIT-LER's BE-RL-IN, a certain "forgetfulness" set in. So, the symbols of Satan enshrouded "the wolf."

Amazingly, the names of the 6 women at Adolf's Satanic black-mass suicide made his symbolic cycle complete. The 3 married women in his inner circle when he died were **Frau Goebbles** (God is bold), **Frau Junge** (Jungfrau means "virgin"), and **Frau Christian**. So, "a bold god," "a virgin," and "a Christ image" at the Ger-man sacrifice of "strange manna" yielded an Anti-Christ in flames.

The unmarried **Fraulein Krueger**'s name signified a sacrificial "drinking vessel." **Fraulein Manzialy** (from Italian) signified a sacrificial "calf." So "the wolf" had symbolic meat upon its altar.

The 6th woman was **Eva Braun**, wife of the wolf, at its end. Eve was Adam's mate. And Braun (brown) signified a desolation in the Earth.

(1) The Life and Death of Adolf Hitler

In parallel to Hitler's closing scene, *Buckley*, the sacrificed "bullock" of the CIA, *Weinberger* in Defense, a host of *Bakers*, *Bush*, sign of the wine merchant, and others (plus more to come) extended the same elaborate scheme.

Hitler claimed to be a vegetarian, but ate a daily dose of dairy. His favorites were cream puffs ordered at a Berlin bakery. No, cow-boys don't die easy. Reagan was told to eat more vegetation due to his colon cancer. He then called Old Nick "a cancer" and sent a cake to "the upper classes," but he did not heed the dietary advise.

Food is fundamental to cause-and-effect in our daily lives, but we often forget how great a part it plays, spiritually, emotionally, and as an instrument of karma (Sanskrit for "action").

A West German official delivered 180,000 marks to a secret agent in a Berlin subway station. The money traded for East German prisoners was spent like cash paid for beasts at a county fair.

"Bonn paid $1.8 million this month" to free a group of German refugees. U.S. dollars were used, not German marks. Still, the number was 18. And $180,000 was paid for release of close relatives of East Germany's Prime Minister. No note was taken of "the 18 coincidence" by the reporter. But this *New York Times* story (7/29/84) also said, at current exchange rates, $54 million (three 18's) had been paid since the flesh trafficking was uncovered. And the Berlin flesh exchanges made the news as Reagan started an 18-day vacation.[1]

"Nationalism" was the context of so many headlines that no conscious connection was made between the words "Nationalism" and "Naziism" in the USA's plutocracy.

In Ron's Hollywood anti-Communist activities when with the Screen Actor's Guild, he was one of 18 FBI informants, listed with others whose names were blacked out. The first FBI interview with Reagan was November 18, 1943.[2]

(1) NY Daily News 7/30/84, (2) Ibid. 8/26/85

The 18th Zionist Congress made a secret deal with HITLER to get Jewish-held money out of Germany. As documented in *The Transfer Agreement* by Edwin Black, the money was used to buy up land in Palestine, land later to be part of ISRAEL.

Jews became upper class (Aryan) land-lords in the Promised Land. And Palestineans in their old hometowns were labeled Aliens. Nations come and go or shift their borders. And in EurAsia, Britian, and elsewhere, "religion" has always played a role in land disputes. But do nations built on religious creed have rights greater than nations built on material greed? Is worshiping God any better excuse for offering up a human sacrifice than worshiping the devil?

The USA made "Capitalism" its state religion, by opposing "Communism." But May Day and Pay Day are both found in every civilized family. So, being "totally" capitalist makes no common (community) sense.

And Totalitarianism (a totally enforced rule of any sort) is uncivil. It stops ideas and ideals from evolving. When "Communists" trap people within their borders and "Capitalists" do not care if people have a place to sleep, May Day (ma) and Pay Day (pa) are abusive parents. And conversely, when "Commies" manipulate capital and "Cappies" let communes grow tax free, both will have the intercourse that ma and pa need to prosper.

Static terms such as "the East" and "the West" are fading with our Space Age view. And the politics of "Left" and "Right" made global by HIT-LER is being de-fused. "Communist" and "Capitalist," "Black" and "White, and all such labels that divide and conquer the mind are making way for individuality.

With Reagan's era ending, Iran (Aryan) said for the first time (July 18th, 1988) it wanted to stop fighting Iraq (an alcoholic drink). Let us examine some smaller pieces before we put this major event in place.

CHAPTER 26

J.C., IRAN, and 666

The USA has had only one President who bore the initials J.C. And in many respects, his career was a reflection of events from long ago. James Carter (later a carpenter for the poor) spent much of his time as President living through a parable.

President J.C. (James Carter) spent exactly 186 days secluded in the White House Rose Garden during the Iranian crisis. Previously, three Wise Men from Iran (Aryans) were the first Aliens to greet J.C. (Jesus Christ). Three priests of Zoroaster, "followers of light" (186 symbolizes the speed of light) gave gold to J.C. And the modern J.C., who gave gold to Iran, wrote in *Keeping Faith* that "all escrows were signed at 6:18 EST" to transfer gold to Iran. Zoroaster (Mazda's high priest) took power in Persia (Iran) in 618 B.C. This puzzle tells a tale about life (in our next chapter on the patterns of the Fibonacci series).

J.C. (Jesus Christ) was history's turning point. And it took 1666 votes at the Democratic convention to send J.C. (James Carter) into the 1980 race where he lost to 666. The sale of 1666 AIM missiles to Saudi Arabia by 666 (6/5/86) eroded the aim of J.C. to find Peace in the Holy Land. And 666's "secret team" cut a deal with international weapons merchants.

The next four pages are packed with details. I have added very few explanatory frills so as to make clear the stark reality of change as history was in "fact" crystallizing.

The Wise Men from Iran (Arya, "upper classes") came to a man-ger in Beth-lehem (house of bread). Je-R-usa-L-em, land of *Aliens* with the posture of *Aryans*, supported the Shah of Iran whose image was "White" to "the Right," and headed toward "the Light" as the King of Kings. And the USA upheld a despot Shah until a despot Ayatolla took control of Iran.

J.C.'s Crisis, 666's Nostalgia

Due to the Iranian Crisis, gold was super-charged in 1980. The greatest one-day drop in gold prices ever recorded was by 18% in 1980.[1] The biggest one-day leap was January 18th of 1980. The Market took its deepest plunge in years, falling 1.8 per common share on Saint Patrick's Day, 1980. And the 18% inflation rate helped lose the election for J.C., said the cover of *Time*.[2]

Before the Crisis, 18 women from International Women's Rights left the USA on March 18th to raise the veils and the consciousness of Iranian women. They were sent immediately home. And Komeini's first TV interview was with Mike Wallace on November 18th.

Carter's first armed response was to send "an 1800-man Marine" unit to the Arabian Sea.[3] Days after the embassy had been seized, an earthquake shook 18 Iranian villages.[4] November 18th, Iran decided to free all "Black" and female hostages. Bank Markazi of Iran sued in London for the $1.8 billion frozen by the Bank of America.[5] January 18th, Prime Minister Baktiar shifted allegiance from the Shah to Khomeini.[6] February 18th, Arafat of the PLO received a pledge from Khomeini to unite against Israel.[7] And their conspiracy was made public.

President J.C. declared December 18th "National Unity Day" in the Iranian Crisis. And U.S. reporters were ordered out of Iran by January 18th, 1980.

Industrialist Edward LAMB questioned J.C.'s increase, "$18 billion in armaments."[8] Fort BRAGG claimed bombers could be on target (Iran implied) "on 18 hours notice."[9] Later, the Bragg hostage-rescue failed. And in the end, "The Iranian Assets Litigation Reporter" went on sale for $1800 a year.[10]

In 198 B.C. (18 + 180) Israel's detachment from Egypt was made final. In 1980 A.D. (180 + 1800), J.C.'s final days as President were in the shadow of Iran. Later, when citizens under 666 were taken hostage, the press glossed over it at first; 666 laughed but would not listen. He sealed a techno deal with the USSR and tried to pretend that his arms deals with Iran had some vague relationship to "Communism" and "national security."

242

In Abscam (a schizo-twist to Carter's Iran crisis), the Feds lost $186,000 in bait.[11] Senator Williams was offered 18% of a bogus mining company as a bribe. Congressman Murphy was defeated after 18 years in office. Richard Kelly blamed his plight on the 18 members of his staff. These were the key officials caught. And the yearly legal fees for J.C.'s term mounted to $18.6 billion.[12]

Of popular interest, Money Market Funds were projected to reach 1,800,000 individual accounts just before 1980, whereas in Reagan's first year, Money Market Funds doubled to $186 billion.[13] The world's largest Money Market Fund (Ready Assets) went up to $10.8 billion (our Buddhist/Hindu number).[14]

Krugerrand ads said all our gold (if in a cube) would be 18 by 18 by 18 yards. So, the USA bought Apartheid gold in 1980. The mark of the Beast was in its hand. Later, 666 banned the Krugerrand.[15] And he followed Florida when it took $1.8 billion out of South Africa.[16] From his first to second term, South African (S.A.) investments dropped off to $1.8 billion.[17]

S.A.'s Indian minority won 18 seats for its "People's Party" against the "Black" majority. But only 18% of those eligible to vote showed at the poles.[18] During the trouble in 36 S.A. districts, Reagan's approval rating among "Blacks" in the USA rose to 36%.[19] And a world torn by its Phase Two beliefs continued to poison the atmosphere.

That year, Martin Luther King got his holiday, 18 years after his death. Jesse Helms complained King's holiday would "rob the Treasury" of $18 million annually.[20] Some men were kings of things, others for what kinship brings.

The Shah of Iran left his bed in the New York Hospital to be carried down 18 floors, so that he could leave via the basement. The exiled despot went to Lackland (lack-land) Air Force Base where 1800 enlisted medical technicians were stationed.[21] "Cancers like his (the Shah's) kill their victims in 18 months," said the media.[22] And the self-appointed "King of Kings" died after 18 months in exile as Iran moved toward center stage in the Gulf.

Khomeini fired his first Foreign Minister after only 18 days. Mr. Sadr became a hunted man in Iran about one year later, on June 18th.

Events were building to a quantum in the meta-mind. On the 18th day of the 1980 War between Iraq and Iran, the first ground missiles of that war killed 180 in Iran (Dezful) while fire from Iran wounded 18 in Iraq (Kirkuk).[23] The USSR supplied Iraq with 1800 tanks.[24] The media made this deal sound ominous in the days before the public was made aware of the arms sales to Iran by the nation of Israel and President 666.

In 1980, the European Common Market agreed to reduce production by 18%,[25] 18% of consumer goods went to the private sector in the USSR,[26] $18,000 in the USA was the highest auction price ever paid for a doll,[27] and only 18 hours after winning the "1980 Miss World" title, Gabriella Brum, 18, abdicated her throne[28].

OPEC's first price per barrel of oil was $1.80, agreed on by all its members. After 18 years of gradual increases, just after J.C's "Camp David Accord," OPEC jumped the price to $18.

OPEC first faltered in Reagan's first year. In a push toward $36, other members conflicted with (Christian) Venezuela.[29] And from then on, OPEC was weakened. Venezuela lost its bid for 1.8 million barrels in daily production.[30] Then in the conflict, OPEC's output was pushed down from 18.5 to 17.5 million barrels per day. Without its magic number, quotas ruled OPEC for the first time.[31] But the $18 barrel was back during Contragate; and wavering goals were set at $18 through 1988.

OPEC couldn't sell 18 million barrels daily.[32] The Russian pipeline was built for $18 billion. Still, 18 million barrels remained OPEC's goal. And Nigeria's Mr. West said, "If you hypnotize us and ask the market share of OPEC, the best figure is 17.5 million barrels." *The Wall Street Journal* (12/10/85) said others asked over 18 million. But the spell was broken, according to "Mr. West."

NO-PEC?

Meanwhile, back in the USA, the Texaco oil giant threatened bankruptcy. Having snatched Getty away from Pennzoil, Texaco owed Pennzoil $12 billion in damages. Texaco had tried to catch up financially, shutting 12 refineries and 18,000 service stations, making waves on Wall Street.[33]

Iran had trouble shipping while crude oil from OPEC again held at the magic 18 million barrels a day.[34] Still, overall prices for all grades at the pump were higher by 1.8 cents per gallon.[35]

The USA was importing 1.8 billion barrels per year (*NY Times editorial* 1/26/86).

Then, the bottom dropped out of the oil market. Smaller nations such as Peru (180,000 barrels per day) were being squeezed by lower prices.[36] Saudi Arabia with oil reserves of 18 billion barrels was eager to sell.[37] Global finances were in a spin. Peru had nationalized the assets of InterNorth, an oil firm based in the USA.[38]

By shipping arms to both Iraq and Iran, 666 had managed to further destabilize the area, making more waves in the Persian Gulf, affecting Wall Street and "the Third World," and demanding even more oil, to feed the destabilizing war machine.

These facts are compacted to show how technology was blindly consuming technology, without feeling.

Pesticides oozed from restaurant meals on Wall Street. High priced junk food, booze, and coffee greased financial schemes with insensitivity.

Poisons ingested — headache remedies traded — and the market ignored any bio implications.

Still, depletion of the rain forests affects the air on Wall Street. And the rationality that we had hidden was cropping up in our search for the meaning of "life" (18).

Destabilization (666's brutal foreign policy) was coming home due to the global nature of waves.

J.C.'s memoirs, *Keeping Faith*, were written in 18 months. And faith is the first line of defense against destabilization. For your bio faith will help to bring about a new techno stability.

Money, gold, and oil each reflected crystal facets changing hands between J.C. and 666. Need we ask, Who was to blame? Which one of us uses no oil, directly of indirectly?

We each have an Aryan (upper class) persona and an Alien within. The Shah of Iran was "clean cut." Khomeini was gruff. One killed for politics, one for religion, each with a techno mind-set.

The 180,000 mullahs in Iran formed Khomeini's cadre,[39] following his dictates from exile. After the revolution, the religious were "upper class." And 18 Soviet diplomats were sent home in 1983,[40] for neither Commies nor Cappies ruled Iran.

To most people in the USA, the Iranian stance in mining the Persian Gulf in 1987 seemed like a sort of insanity. The karma from Reagan's mining the harbors of Nicaragua seemed unrelated. Yet, the Crystal shows a deep relationship, a mirroring of events in a karmic sphere.

Many aspects of the body, mind, and spirit seem unrelated in our "consumer society." So, the goal of our next chapter is to clarify the maze between body and spirit that we perceive as our collective mind.

(1) Time 2/4/80, (2) Time 3/10/80, (3) Time 2/25/80, (4) Today 11/15/79, (5) Time 12/17/79, (6) NY Times 1/19/79, (7) NY Times 2/19/79, (8) Tomorrow NBC 12/18/79, (9) NBC Special 7/26/79, (10) Time 11/10/80, (11) Jim Ryan NBC 8/18/81, (12) Time 7/27/81, (13) Time 11/5/79, (14) Time 3/31/80, (15) NY Times 9/10/85, (16) NY Times 5/7/85, (17) The Progressive, Oct. 1985, (18) NY Times 8/30/85, (19) Business Week 1/27/86, (20) U.S. News 10/31/83, (21) NY Daily News 12/3/79, (22) Time 11/19/79, (23) NBC 10/9/80, (24) David Diaz 9/23/80, (25) Time 11/17/80, (26) Time 6/23/80, (27) NBC's Today 9/8/80, (28) Time 12/1/80, (29) Newsweek 8/31/81, (30) Time 3/21/83, (31) Newsweek 3/28/83, (32) Time 1/28/83, (33) Dan Rather CBS 9/23/83, (34) NY Times 1/24/86, (35) NY Times 2/5/86, (36) NY Post 2/10/86, (37) Business Week 1/13/86, (38) Star Ledger 1/24/86, (39) Information Please Almanac, 1981, (40) U.S. News 2/6/83, (+) Business Week 12/9/85

CHAPTER 27

THE AVERAGE AGE
OF EVERYTHING

The first three days of Creation are recorded in the Bible at verses 5, 8, and 13. And amazingly, 5813 inches was the height of the Great Pyramid of Giza in Egypt. A third 5, 8, and 13 is found in the number 5813, which is the radius of a circle with the circumference 36,524.2. And 365.242 is the exact number of days in an Earthly year.

I would have inserted the word "amazingly" into many sentences in this chapter, but there simply wasn't room. Why are cycles of the sun related to the days of Creation and to the inches in a pyramid?

The answer is that 5, 8, and 13 bridge the inner path from 0, 1, 2, 3 to the spirals of the Golden Mean, mystically linking 6 to 18. This is the only mystical facet in the Language Crystal, where the fire meets the light — in "life" — the mystical, eternal life of our race.

The progression of 0, 1, 2, 3, 5, 8, 13 begins the Fibonacci series which yields the Golden Mean, a number that nature counts on.

Now, let us start at the beginning. To obtain the Golden Mean, we start by adding zero and one, then add their sum to the highest of the pair.

We begin with 0 and 1. The sum is 1. Then add the sum to the highest of the pair. So, add 1 (the sum) to 1 (the highest of the pair). The new sum is 2. Now, add the new sum (2) to the highest of the previous pair (1). The sum is 3. Add 3 to 2, get 5. Add 5 to 3, we get 8. Add 8 to 5, we get 13. Add 8 to 13, we get 21. And so on. The Golden Mean of .618 is approached when we divide any number in this series by the next higher number.

Fibonacci's series (basis of the Elliot Wave) was used to predict Wall Street waves during the reign of 666, and so it led to the 1987 crash, as we shall see in a later chapter on "harmonics."

In the process of growth, many green plants arrange their leaves according to the mathematical formula of the Fibonacci series. Sunflowers, daisies, pine cones, and pussy willows arrange their seeds, petals, layers, and buds according to this progression. The logarithmic Fibonacci series (0, 1, 1, 2, 3, 5, 8, 13, 21, 34, 55, 89, 144, 233, 377, 610, 987, 1597, 2584, 4181, 6765, 10964, etc.) shapes the galaxies. And the curves of breaking ocean waves are also formed by a spiral dictated by these numbers.

Divide any of the higher numbers in this infinite progression by next and the answer approaches the Golden Mean, .618. For example, 4181 divided by 6765 yields .618033999999999.

Divisions all along the line yield answers that alternate above and below, approaching .618 from both directions. And traveling at the speed of light, 186,000 miles per second, a mind meets its own internal fire. In the Code, 6 (F) and 18 (R) are con-sonant in FIRE. This makes ultimate sense to a bio-spirit living in the now. For the verb "to fire" is a word of separation, a dis-union of elements, one being fired from the other.

$E = MC^2$ crystallizes matter (M) in FORM, and light (C) and energy (E) in FORCE, because F-O-R encodes 6 and 18 around the void (O). This is why FOR is purely a word of function. (And "what for" equals "why.")

FORM waits FOR CE. FORCE searches FOR M.

Roots of teeth, horns of rams, tiger claws, the parrot's beak, spider's web, elephant's tusk, fang of snake, shell of snail, all have curves formed by the Golden Spiral of the Fibonacci series. Even the hairs of our heads swirl determined by the ratio of 1 to .618. So, where life accommodates dead cells (hair, horn, web, claw, etc.) is the Golden Junction. The moth in spirals seeks the flame; and humanity can reach the stars through this golden formula.

FIRE and FEAR are met between 186 and .618.

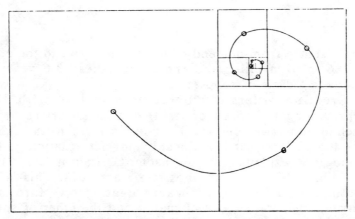

Nature's Golden Spiral can be depicted by drawing a rectangle with sides in a ratio of 1 to .618. Next, form a square within that rectangle. The figure adjacent to that square will be a smaller rectangle with sides also in the ratio of 1 to .618.

Form a square within the smaller rectangle. And continue in this manner as far as possible. Then join the centers of all the squares with a curve. You now have a picture of the Golden Spiral, the womb of creation, in symbolic structure.

Pythagorus and Euclid called the Golden Mean "divine." Leonardo used it in his paintings and sculpture. In most Greek art, from the Parthenon to a classic vase, from the position of a navel to the proportions of a leg and placement of the eyes, this formula was used as a guide.

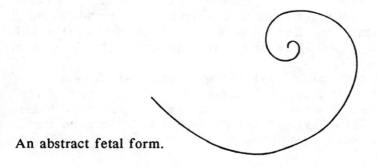

An abstract fetal form.

The distance from one end of the Earth's orbit to the other is 186 million miles and the moon takes 18.6 years to complete a cycle of eclipses.

Creation orders our perception in line with 186, approaching the speed of light. And in sacrifices to the Techno State, we followed light like a moth to the flame. For it was fire that led humanity to menstruation and to monogamy (explained in our chapter "Written in Blood").

Approaching 186,000 mps, we reach .618. This is the realm called "mystery," where death flows into life. Between two spirals, one of matter and the other of spirit, we see the light. And our souls are on fire.

In quantum physics, we see that light acts or re-acts with "probability." Light is a prober probing a problem called "humanity" as we are probing the problem of "light." For "to light" can be a verb with no body of its own.

And so, when "light" lights upon us, we must decide how to use its energy. This is our personal ISRAEL (our individual "struggle with God").

And L-I-G-H-T has its own silent gravity.

Yet, faster than the speed of light, a spirit thought (thought) is at rest. And you can own that spirit.

"The oldest observer in existence is the Universal Mother whose life lasts 61.8 billion trillion years." *Omni* magazine attributes this quote to "Veda Vyasa, author of the *Bhagavad Gita*, a second-century Hindu Scripture (*Omni*, Dec. 1983). But the *Gita*'s 61.8 is simply the Golden Mean caught up in the decimal system.

The Golden Mean, generated by one and zero, is not of a decimal order at its outer reaches. For beyond the speed of light, time does not count. And crystal images (F = 6, L = 12, R = 18) abound with cosmic ego (I) and eternal energy (E).

A mystical L-I-F-E is a spirit on F-I-R-E in spirals of the Golden Mean, approaching .618.

L-I-F-E moves as L-I-G-HT (with a gravity, G, hidden near THeology) and photons on F-I-L-E charge to the C-enter that we see as "self."

Flip a coin 100 times, odds are it comes up 50% heads. One flip, chances are 50/50. If 100 people flip it, probably it comes up heads 50 times. It matters not who flips the coin or when or where. With a RANDOM sampling, the odds are even.

In universal terms (flipping in all directions of time and space), the meaning of "random" includes ALL forces of body, mind, and spirit. So, once we admit to the pervasive link that is telepathy, a re-assessment is needed of all so-called random experments on our body chemistry. We are, after all, flipping more than coins.

Random selection is always between the elect (spirit) and the elect-ron (body), as negotiated by the elect-or (mind). And we are the body electric.

R-AND-OM selection is the process by which life (R = 18) convenes DNA (life's union) in OM ("the Word"). OM, the everlasting wave (M), comes out of the void (O), re-reflected in MORE. RE-MOVE the energy (E) of one spirit field and MO-RE will appear in another. For the formula "FORM FROM FORM" depicts R (life) as it weaves through OM.

"FOR" indicates purpose. The fear of fire was FOR a reason. We overcame it FOR each other. And now, FOR the sake of humanity, we must move that fear to a new plateau — FOR a new purpose. And this we do for our own survival, even beyond Phase Three.

During Phase One, we were children, enjoying the Earth with no need to pick up after ourselves. All our wastes were bio-degradable. During Phase Two, we were adolescents; for we had to learn math and chemistry and study for tests in sociology. During Phase Three, we have a greater responsibility. And by Phase Four, we shall have reached our maturity as a race, ready to enter outer space.

Peace is thought at rest. Th-ought is a symbol for "deity" (TH) plus "ought." For TH is as one letter, the ancient triangle. And so, th-ought is one-in-three plus a zero (ought) while th-r-ee is mystic energy. Our goal along the Golden Spiral is for-ever:

TO TRAVEL FORTH, FOR-TH.

The Hebrews did not number days 1, 2, and 3 of Creation in verses 5, 8, and 13 of the Bible; the verses were so numbered in Greek translations that first appeared around 3 B.C. Also, the Egyptians could not have knowingly put 5813 inches in their Great Pyramid, for our modern inch does not fit evenly into the Egyptian system of cubits.

Pyr-amid ("fire in the middle") relates to He-brew in a way that only the Phase Three mind-set is read-y to demystify. The cycles of the sun are linked to both in our religio-scientific quest. A 5813 radius in our solar year (365.242 days) is only a fact on Earth. For in our solar system, Earth is where fire-spirits come see the light.

As our word patterns are joined in English, so these numbers fit an Angular system. And once our new mind-set is crystallized, we shall extend the meaning of life one step further.

Evolution and Creation are two theories of life. Science says matter always existed while religion believes God always was. Both sides claim that an "Always-Being" somehow produced the "life" that is in forms that now re-produce themselves.

This question of life's beginning is related to Eve's temptation by the serpent. After God told her, *"Ye shall not eat of the tree in the midst of the garden, lest ye die,"* the serpent told Eve, *"Ye shall not surely die. For God doth know when ye eat thereof, your eyes shall be opened, and ye shall be as gods, knowing good and evil."*

"And when the woman saw the tree was good for food and pleasant to the eyes, a tree to make one wise, she took of the fruit and ate, and gave also to her husband, and he did eat" (Gen. 3:3-6).

The subtlety of this trialogue is hidden in the three definitions of "life": life of the mind (R), life of the body (DNA), and life of the spirit (OM). These three combine in R-AND-OM selection, evolving in creation.

To live forever as a race, we chose to feed the unconscious mind, so we could build the Techno State, so we could travel forth, following "the Word" (our Lord) who follows "the Life" (his Wife), eternally.

Elliott Wave Theory

Why did the Stock Market crash? Many "experts" agreed that Robert Prechter had enough influence over a sufficient number of traders to turn the tide. But Prechter was riding on the Elliott Wave Theory. And Elliott, an accountant, had derived his rule from the Fibonacci series to predict changes in the Stock Market's direction.

According to the Theory, markets move up, down, up, down, up (a sequence of 5) and then reverse to move down, up, down (a sequence of 3) for a total of 8 in a series. But it's not so simple, said *Discover* magazine (March 1987) before the October 1987 crash. For some waves are embedded in others.

Mr. Prechter became a multi-millionaire in the role of Stock Market advisor. He influenced many thousands of investors with his newsletter and was correct so often in predicting shifts in seven years of Armageddon that his flock went with him over the edge. *Prechter* is a name that derives from the German for "something that causes one to vomit or to regurgitate." And with perfect timing on Wall Street, Mr. Prechter lived up to the vibrations in his name.

The odd part of Prechter's analysis was that he was not predicting actual events so much as riding the behavior of a herd of investors. And this was complicated as his popularity grew; a greater percentage of that which he predicted fell under his influence until he reached the center of his own "random" activity.

The Stock market dropped by 108.36 on a Friday. Our Buddhist/Hindu no-God/many-gods number (108) had been reborn (36). Then the weekend allowed a ferment of doubt about a war in the Persian Gulf to get mixed with computer-generated sell-offs.

The *Times* (10/23/87) said Prechter was a shepherd who told his flock they'd be "in the promised land by 1988." Little did he count on the eco-system's waves of spirit that adjust our waves in the true economic sense.

We had live cells, elements, and spirits before we had techno-logical arguments, industrial averages, or stock exchanges on this planet. The patterns of this bio-sphere are already in our souls. We know the Earth as well as any groundhog living in its crust. And the life in our bodies will tell us what is in our own best interest to balance the economic-finance of our eco-sphere.

The average age of everything is exactly half infinity, a point where numbers cease to count, where life goes on consuming life, eternally.

The miracle, amazingly, is you. You are the one who is observing, the one who knows, who feels, who ultimately decides what to do with your life.

Some people give 10% of their earnings to a "religion" in order to prove a "charitable" gift. But who dares claim, "I spent 10% of what I had on food I gave to the homeless?" Who will tell the IRS, "All I have to show for it is the memory of a smile" or "Here's my receipt duly signed by some good folk with no addresses"?

Since written law is so mechanical, "charity" has fallen under the rule of "the machine" to the exclusion of our needy biological individuals.

The best of natural healing is not paid for by insurance coverage. And the most effective care is not researched by a tax-exempt Cancer Society or Arthritis Foundation. But citizens are forced by the numbers to favor "the machine."

And in a final effort, 666 tried to reduce the payments to blind, elderly, and disabled persons who were receiving gifts of food and clothing. The public outcry was so great that the notion was abandoned (10/16/87). Still, the 666 had tried. For the majority of voters had said that their main "interest" was in money.

When life and death come into play, the average age of every living thing is one. You have a choice. Colds go away, cancer goes into re-mission, and arthritis fades once a true paradise diet, proper exercise, and love's spirit-mending deeds become a part of your life. For you are the C-enter of your own mystery.

CHAPTER 28

THE ORIGIN OF "AIDS"

Emanuel Revici M.D. reported progress with AIDS patients. "According to Revici," wrote Gary Null, "dividing the disease into componants enables us to conquer each facet to produce a full healthy state within the patient" (*Penthouse*, June 1987).

Revici's spiritual nature, one reason for his successful treatments, was not emphasized in the article. But Dr. Revici was attacked by the AMA for his mode of treatment. Though the case was not stated as such, his cures were thought to be "too spiritual" by some other M.D.'s.

The verb "to cure" actually means "to care," in line with biology's continuum as we experience it. But we were trying "to cure" AIDS patients with no "care" for the origins of AIDS, origins that could still bring on another plague.

When 666 was elected in 1980, only 18 licensed vaccine manufacturers still operated in the USA, a drop from 36 over 12 years (*Science*, Aug. 1980).

On October 18th, 1986, Congress passed a bill allowing U.S. companies to ship drugs and vaccines abroad, even those not approved for U.S. citizens. The bill also set limits on company liabilities in cases of vaccine-injured children.

The *N.Y. Times* (11/15/86) said Reagan signed the bill after lobbying by "groups representing children." Bogus groups often fronted for tobacco or drug companies while claiming to represent the consumers. But drug outfits paid for ads, so who represented the children was questionable.

Legal drugs had record export sales increases and the' greatest profit margin of any industry in the USA. And we have barely touched on the horrors of medical politics. In such an atmosphere, it is reasonable to suspect the possibility of a cover-up. Had the AIDS epidemic been spawned in medical labs that were developing vaccines? Several co-related theories have already been advanced.

Robert Cathcart M.D. (Los Altos, Ca.) treated viral infections, colds, and mono (before the AIDS epidemic) with mega-doses of vitamin C. He thought the treatment effective and so gave vitamins for AIDS symptoms. His patients used zinc, manganese, selenium, A, D, E, and exercise. And Dr. Cathcart said that "attitude" had a potency equal to any vitamins. (*Let's Live*, Aug. 1986).

AIDS was treated in several ways. But medical drugs got the media's attention. Even though new drugs lacked the standard statistical hokum, they got better press than "alternate" methods.

While claiming that education was the goal, the media released a minimum of information over and over again. And it was a general taboo to probe the medical origins of AIDS.   Preventing AIDS became the task of every man, woman, and child in somewhat the same way that "stop pollution" TV ads were aimed at children while large corporations did the dumping.

We have a right to get emotional about people dying of "AIDS." And tracing the origins of AIDS will not diminish those emotions.

We can care about our family, our family name, and ethnicity while having clear definitions that enhance such emotions. Being labeled "Black" or "White" has no ethnic value. The skin tone of your mother's face was not an absolute abstraction. The song she sang was a human song, blended from the richness of every mother gone before her.

Human biology is never "black or white." So, when we see the many factors in the origins of what was called "the AIDS epidemic," it makes the tragedy no less; but we will be able to take some measures to prevent similar mistakes in the future.

We started history by sacrificing biology to feed the Techno State. And by history's end, we were defending the viruses that we ourselves had mutated in labs, viruses that were bought and paid for in our attempts to technically adjust our global biology.

The African Green Monkey

The monkey blamed for giving humanity the AIDS virus did not suddenly attack us. Medical History shows that "doctors" used the green monkey years before they named any "AIDS" symptoms.

Dr. Eva Lee Snead, a medical researcher in San Antonio says, "Human contact with green monkeys is abundant and continuous." The green monkey was used to make a polio vaccine in 1960 with Simian Virus SV-40 which brings on "immuno-deficiency."

The public had a false impression that "a polio virus" had been isolated when in truth vaccines contained a scattering of many viruses, some known (named), others neither named nor acknowledged.

Green monkey serum carrying genetic information into the human cell nucleus was used in labs. And now we know that SV-40 is a factor in tumors akin to those of AIDS. Leukemia, yeast excess, and so on are linked to these vaccines and to AIDS.

The viruses had not been isolated. Medicine was not an exact science. But vaccine sales-personnel tried to create such an illusion.

The U.S. Public Health Service noted SV-40 contamination in 100's of millions of polio vaccine doses in 1960. And the green monkey had been used to make those polio shots. The spread of SV-40 by tainted polio shots was easy to cover up since the live (not inactivated) vaccine carried many other viruses that were also transferred.

Dr. Snead said, "There is abundant reason to believe that SV-40 by itself or in combination with smallpox, measles, or syphilis, could have caused severe problems we are seeing today." She was speaking of the so-called "AIDS" epidemic in which many viruses were co-factors.

SV-40 can carry other diseases into the cell. But as with "the White Man" myth, due to the very nature of biology, there never was and never will be a "pure" strain of SV-40. The clear-cut terms of the M.D.s (like the racist terms "Black" and "White") do not fit biological reality. So, in Phase Three, people are treated individually.

Viral Evolution

Most people had the notion that viral scientists, with instruments such as the electron microscope, were neat operators. We imagined their decisions to be as sharp as laser beams.

However, the production of viral agents in the laboratory can be more accurately compared to the transfer of microbes in a chicken slaughter-house where cancers and excrement are mixed into the same water that washes the dead plucked chickens.

I have yet to see a TV documentary that shows the making of vaccines. The belly of a cow is slit and diseased cells are placed inside to fester for several days. The festering mass is then scraped out of the animals inflamed belly to make the next batch of vaccine.

In 1967, 500,000 young men (many of whom were homosexuals) were vaccinated with an experimental mononucleosis vaccine, a virus present in most people with AIDS. The SV-40 combined with mono or cold virus then made new compound-diseases.

As with lab-bred "killer bees," headlines did not focus on the origin. Stopping the spread of AIDS was the story. But what of the experiments that could create more new monsters?

Rather than vaccinate every child globally, as modern medicine plans to do, we will do better to stop producing viruses in the lab where most of the "AIDS" complex was originally mutated.

A virus seen up close is an individual. Each can mutate in its host. Statistics said "Black people" acted in a certain way. And we believed in statistics as the power base of the Techno State. So, we believed the statistics on viruses.

A few viruses with "names" were used to build a theory that suited our Phase Two competitiveness and financial trends. But statistically invented "viral groups" were no more real biologically than statistically invented "racial groups."

Each human is a new environment for each strain of virus, so viral evolution changes within each of us. And we are bio-spirits who use emotions (controlled or not) to personally evolve.

Cold symptoms may occur with sudden chills. Still, most colds do not come with winter's first frost. They immediately follow the food-indulgent winter holidays. Also, "cold viruses" are often present with no symptoms. So, let us re-think the factors that precipitate "viral disease."

A person may get a fever, vomit, get a rash, or display many symptoms in combination. And that person may be "infected" with many viruses. But remember, we are all "infected" — a buzz-word that should not usually be alarming.

We have varying degrees of infection. And the word "virus" (derived from the Latin for "poison") was used in medical history long before "the virus theory" was concocted. So, as we progress through old medical journals, we must be aware of even the evolving definitions of the word "virus."

A small amount of poison can cause death, as with amanita virosa mushrooms. In other cases, it is the cumulative effect that brings on a crisis. Also, viral-poisons vary in potency.

Many "facts" are printed here and elsewhere on AIDS. Yet you (as an individual) must go beyond these "facts." The final page of this chapter offers a test that goes beyond "facts." Still, we (as a group) must know the complexities of "AIDS," to avoid future plagues.

People died of opportunistic ills invited by AIDS. But those ills existed also without AIDS. So, what was "the cause" of death?

Dr. Caiazza in "Private Lives" (May 1987) said, syphilis and AIDS were "endemic in absolutely the same populations" and all the symptoms of AIDS are also described in syphilis. And skin lesions of sarcoma were first seen by Kaposi in syphilis. By treating syphilis, Dr. Caiazza had "noted marked clinical improvement in six AIDS/ARC patients." So, similar symptoms (under different names) had responded to similar treatments. But Caiazza's anti-treponemal doses, he boasted, were much more than "the recommended dose."

Connections, Not Drugs

While Caiazza wrote out higher doses for syphilis, penicillin-resistant gonorrhea had doubled within a year (*UPI* 12/2/86). Again, individual cases were treated with no thought of what the drugs in our gene pool would do to future generations.

Anti-AIDS proteins, said *The Lancet* (5/2/86), could be inherited in one of 6 combinations of 3 genetic subtypes each (note "the 18 complex").

The *Yoga Journal* (July/August 1987) said that "over 30,000 people nationwide have been diagnosed with the disorder [AIDS], and nearly 18,000 have died" (coincidental at press time). Still, the article was optimistic.

"The medical establishment tells us that the average lifespan of a PWA (person with AIDS) is 18 months," said the *Yoga Journal*. PWAs live "about 18 months," said the *N.Y. Times* (11/17/87). The statistic was "official" — 18 months.

Yet PWAs can beat those odds and get better, "a fact rarely mentioned in the news media," said the *Yoga Journal*, going on to show how AIDS was used by many to contact a personal awareness of the spirit's power to heal.

An Overview of the Epidemic

The World Health Organization (WHO) linked the "AIDS" in Africa to the use of smallpox vaccine.

And the WHO correlated those nations that got smallpox shots with the rate of AIDS. Zaire had the highest percentage of smallpox vaccinations and the highest rate of AIDS. And Burundi had the lowest percent of smallpox shots with the lowest rate of AIDS. Also, nations like Tanzania and Malawi with a mid-range of smallpox shots were mid-range in percentage of AIDS.

A medical origin explains its rapid spread. The doubling time would be about 15 months if its entry was a single point of origin (counting even some very promiscuous cases). But with many points of origin, we had an AIDS explosion.

Testing: 1-2-3

In 1979, tests of the experimental hepatitis B vaccine were given to what statisticians referred to as "white-male-homosexuals, between the ages of 20 and 40." The hepititis B experiments were centered in Chicago, Saint Louis, New York City, Los Angeles, and San Francisco; and these were the very same populations in the USA that were also the initial avenues of the AIDS epidemic.

As in Africa and Brazil, the trail of AIDS was marked by vaccinations. South American nations with no vaccinations had little or no AIDS.

The cover-up stories that AIDS had come out of Africa via Haiti to the USA took many forms and had no "statistical" backing, but they kept the lab-created fiasco out of the news long enough for "new medical cures" to get the spotlight.

Treatments for AIDS symptoms that could not be profitably patented were called "quackery." Only medical propaganda was quoted in the media. And the AMA dictated Government policy.

An old joke says, "The operation was a success, but the patient died." And techno-based drugging could prove to be just such "a success."

Of course, we cannot do away with necessary surgery or drugs entirely. A drug to cure "river blindness" (caused by parasites) has proven to be effective. And in other rare cases, drugs are the best approach aside from prevention.

The test on the final page of this chapter will help you to decide by means of your own knowledge. You are already in-formed with bio-wisdom.

With lack of exercise, junk food, and drugs of every sort, the media hype given to aspirin as a tool against heart attacks was criminal. Studies in Britain showed aspirin had no such effect.

Between drug ads on TV, our "consumer society" was being conditioned by bits of medical TV news. And chief lobbyist for the American Pharmaceutical Association was named Mr. Hyps (*N.Y. Times* 7/13/88). And the TV hype was dissuading us from a connectedness with our own bio-nature.

"Experts" wanted to destroy the last stocks of the smallpox virus being used to inject Army recruits. For while smallpox vaccine was no longer kept for "public health" purposes, the military had been conned into infecting new recruits with the live-virus concoction as a precaution against "possible biological warfare."

Faced with bio-warfare schemes, the excuse was illogical. But salesreps from drug companies who met with military bureaucrats over coffee had found an easy mark (akin to hospital secretaries who were pressured into polio booster-shots).

Reports on AIDS in the military were sketchy. But *the New England Journal of Medicine* published a warning against a plan to use modified versions of the smallpox vaccine to combat other diseases. This scatter-pattern approach used with anti-biotics was also used with vaccines. The warning was interseting since it came from a research team at Walter Reed Army Hospital.

And a team working with Dr. Robert Redfield at Walter Reed Army Hospital reported on a recruit who developed AIDS. Fever, headaches, stiffness, and sweats ensued two weeks after his smallpox shots. Three weeks later, at Walter Reed, he was diagnosed as having "meningitis." The labels had come full circle (see chapter 16) back to polio. And then, the recruit rapidly developed further symptoms labeled "AIDS."

The medical team said the recruit died "after responding to treatment." Still, "responding to treatment" can mean "loss of vitality." It is also argued that agressive drugging is a factor in many "AIDS" fatalities. Remember the child who "gets sick" from smoking and the heavy smoker who seems "immune." The personal test on the final page of this chapter solves these riddles.

Drug users who shared needles were more likely to die than hospital workers who got stuck. The factor of "vitality" plays a part in all but the most extreme cases of poisoning or infection.

To See, Or Not To See?

These graphs of the rise and fall of poliomyelitis and infectious hepatitis show that they were very closely parallel. Were they caused by different viruses? More likely they were products of many of the same FACTORS.

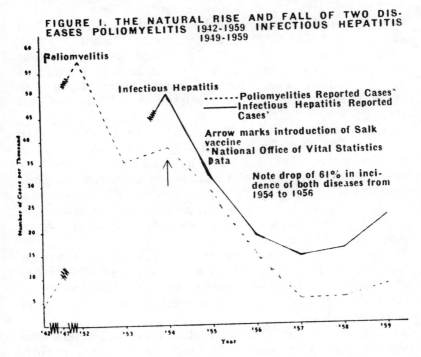

FIGURE I. THE NATURAL RISE AND FALL OF TWO DIS-
EASES POLIOMYELITIS 1942-1959 INFECTIOUS HEPATITIS
1949-1959

A gradual rise in polio from 1940 to 1952 was followed by a gradual decline from 1952 to 1957. And the introduction of the Salk vaccine (after polio had sharply declined and was slowly rising again) was less coincidental with the fall of polio than with the fall of hepatitis.

Even though "the doctors" had juggled the names and statistics, we see that particular viruses were not so particular. Shifts in natural patterns were greater than shifts for which Modern Medicine claimed the credit.

With commercial viruses added to epidemics for several generations, our graphs were getting more deceptive — less true to bio-reality.

263

A *New York Times* headline (1/12/88) reported, "A Solitary Dissenter Disputes Cause of AIDS." Dr. Duesberg believed HIV was not the true cause of AIDS, said the article. But the headline ignored the others who had already written on alternative theories about the factors of AIDS.

The article did say, "Many scientists believe that other unidentified factors may be involved in AIDS, but virtually all believe that HIV is a necessary factor."

But *"virtually all believe"* is a way of saying that some do not believe. And dia-gnosis was at best a game of dubious beliefs. The descenters quoted herein along with other M.D.s could not get published in "official medical journals."

And before the AIDS fiasco, the World Health Organization (Bulletin # 47, p.259) in 1972 was proud to call for the creation of a virus that could destroy human T cells. Also, the Journal of Comparative Leukemia Research (1973, Bulletin #40, p.783) predicted an RNA virus that would contaminate vaccines and produce a pandemic.

Many knew that something like AIDS was in the works. And it could happen again.

· Over 50% of cattle herds in the USA have bovine leukemia and are infected with retro-viruses. The bovine visna virus is another member of the AIDS family of viruses. And fetal calf's hair is used in the production of most vaccines.

HTLV 1, 2, and 4, BLV, HBLV, HIV, and others were named. But these were only family names in a rapidly mutating group of viruses.

Later, 1988 guidelines were issued by the World Health Organization so AIDS could be diagnosed in Africa without costly equipment. Symptoms of malnutrition were to get statistically confused with AIDS and new graphs and charts could tell whatever story suited the chart makers.

Remember that "vitality" is a key factor. And only you, as an individual bio-spirit, can know how to negotiate your own vitality.

The *AMA Journal* (9/4/87) also gave new signs for AIDS including "other bacterial infections" with no need for a positive HIV. And some pneumonias were reclassified as AIDS. All this juggling was not seen on the TV evening news where a constant drum beat accented the search for a vaccine to stop what was simply called "the AIDS virus."

In 1987, we transplanted "foreign genes" into bacteria of the TB vaccine (*NY Times* 6/11/87). And the new shots would cause more complex genetic problems in "less developed countries." Not one disease was true to its name. And the symptoms of one often matched the symptoms of others. So, a medical reporter could not track vaccine-related loss of vitality — disease and death.

A Federal study cited New York for increases in TB (1/23/88). But City officials blamed AIDS. And national figures also reflected a rise in TB. In fact, every-body on Earth had less vitality with each bit of internal and external pollution. And we could never graph the complexities.

Since we cannot afford a gene pool that leaves future generations in a hopeless search for ever stronger drugs, we will do better by focusing on health. Viruses play a part, yet spiritual and physical vitality are overriding factors.

Rather than send fresh fruits and vegetables to starving people, the USA sent wheat and medicine. Religious organizations gathered cash to support bad diets and deceptive medical invasions.

Massive irrigation projects, fruit trees and gardens were not sent to people in malnourished nations. The USA meant to help, but the techno mind-set did not know how to feed itself. We had geared our concepts of "health care" first to suit industry and then to suit "health insurance."

Playing with sheep, bovine, and monkey viruses was a mistake. Then, we tried to heal without hearing our environment. We fed our un-conscious mind-set with foods from the Tree of Technology and forgot where un-consciousness had begun.

When people "dying of AIDS" took to a healthful life-style, they often had remissions but were never written up in medical journals.

"AIDS" began in men vaccinated for hepatitis or mononucleosis, in Africans, Brazilians, Hatians, and others who got smallpox shots, in infants with little immunity infected in the womb. And later, it became most active in the rotting bodies of those infected who used heavy drugs.

Can we re-drug the planet's population back to health? Can drugs become a new mode of evolution?

The amazing thing is that drugs can make us feel so much better. But how can a concoction that makes a well person get sick possibly make a sick person get well?

The answer is that medical poisons often work by killing off an infection faster than it kills the patient. And if drugs are given in the right amounts, enough vitality may remain to rebuild the body after the fungus, virus, or other "infection" is gone. The malfactors are usually not invaders, but normal body residents that have increased in number, as flies will increase around a rotting piece of fruit. So, the imbalance may be righted for a while by a fly-spray or by drugs.

Now, here is a test: If you feel the symptoms of a cold, do not eat for 12 hours — and watch the cold symptoms diminish. Should you eat after 12 hours and feel the symptoms return, a 36-hour fast may be needed. Yet, 12 hours will prove the principle.

Fasting works like anti-biotics, yet with no toxic "side-effects" and more selectively. When you cease to eat, your internal feeding will empty your digestive tract and then begin to scavenge for what your body needs least, thus (unlike anti-biotics) increasing your vitality. Depending on your condition, you may have less energy, but your vitality will be greater. And a fast works not only in colds but in all infectious diseases where the body needs to re-balance its vitality.

A proper fast requires pure water and rest plus the avoidance of enervating stimulation.

CHAPTER 29

THE MONO-GAME

The Language Crystal is in place; Armageddon swept away by the Second Coming of "the Word." And we need only focus on the meaning — MORTALITY is MORALITY at the crystal crossroads (T). Life in the spirit is creation beyond cremation; in the mind, conception beyond deception; in the body, purification beyond putrification.

When fruit rots, it goes bad. Yet "bad" apples are "good" for compost, and, if planted properly, can grow good apple trees. For humanity, dying is only half bad, for death allows a spirit to depart and to grow anew in goodness.

Still, while we live in the body, morality is ours to help us help each other. So, good and bad have their ultimate meanings in the spirit.

This is why most humans feel obliged to live up to our names and why no individuals of other species can be held accountable to names we give them. Only humans are individual in such a moral sense. Your body and spirit both answer inwardly to the very same calling.

Phase Two rules were given negative forms. We had no "positive" law. Groups fought against "negative groups," we cherished inclusive (positive) forces and feared exclusive (negative) forces.

The rule that said, "I am the Lord, thy God; thou shalt NOT have strange gods before me," is crystallized in the new positive law of mono-theism. "Thou shalt NOT commit adultery," is now the positive law of mono-gamy. And "Thou shalt NOT steal," is the positive crystal law of mon-ey. These three mono-laws of morality put our monkey madness to rest as love makes common sense of the mono-game. For this is the way of the individual within the human family.

Positively, you will see the weakness in saying, "I am not a Jew, not a Christian, not a Moslem, not a Buddhist." You can have the best of all these worlds in one.

Monotheism, monogamy, and money were invented to focus the body, mind, and spirit of man — a social unit. Woman invented the mono-game as part of her "master plan." But during his-story, money gained a power of its own. We called it "script" and "specie." Some bits of one-thing (money) were made equal to some bits of anything else. And we let our mon-ey vote on tiny bits of destiny.

Did God invent marriage? In the spirit, mono-theism led man into mono-gamy. He played house in his woman's context. Her bed became the physical center of their mono-game. Yet, mon-ey became a coersive force that she introduced to weigh upon his mind.

The Whore made his marriage seem like a bar-gain. Cheating was labeled "crass" while fidelity gave him "class." But then the money was given more and more power "of its own."

Imagine being a primitive woman before men were domesticated. How could you get a wildman to come into your house — for keeps?

1. You could make up *monogamy* and tell him that it was the very best game in town.

2. You could invent *money* as a means of com-petition. Having invented the money game, you would play it better than he would. So, to keep him from violence, you might let him win, till he got used to playing, till he could lose with grace.

3. You might tell him of the *mono-God* called "Father," remind him of the instinctual feeling (that he could otherwise forget), tell him that he was a father, the pro-creator of your child.

Through his monogamy (body), his money (mind), and his monotheism (spirit), you would own him entirely. And your plan would work so well if it were not for (3) the female side of deity, (2) the other side of the coin, and (1) that counter-point in the mono-game, the Whore of Baby-L-on.

In his-story, the Whore wore a feminine mask while God was disguised as a male.

The fact that woman invented a Mono-God did not detract from the integrated One God who already existed. And when we created money, we did not destroy the real value of things. Our problem in the final days was that money had become detached from its biological and spiritual roots.

Money in the USA said, "In God We Trust." It did not say, "In Gods We Trust." Mono-gamy was the rule. And mon-ey was a tool of the national One-God, one-mate religion.

One God first appears in the Hebrew Bible as a plural noun, for our belief evolves through our relations within families.

We used money to measure supply and demand. But advertising took money from supply-side profits and used it to create demands, thus destroying the systems ability to balance itself.

Monotheism focuses man's spirit. Monogamy can center his body socially. But since money is the tool that makes thing-for-thing equations in his mind, the use of money as an advertising pivot meant that entire groups (even scientists, M.D.s, priests, and presidents) could lose their mind to cleverly manipulated ads.

A progression from family names to brand names set money "on its own" and eventually meant that nations could no longer control financial corporations.

Machines were wed in corporate bodies to rule the people. But as their intercourse spilled over, pure and innocent biology (flesh) was labeled "pornograpic" while machines were said to have "true beauty." And many religionists got baptized while wearing their business suits.

Plastics, chloroflorocarbons, styrofoam, and rivers of soot were poisoning the environment.

Since technology yields bio-security in space, we thought money was security and used it to feed technology. Still, only those vibrations that are true to life bring our three mono systems together in harmony. Money can regulate the Techno State only when we are true to "the Word."

Mon-key, Mon-ey, Mon-chai

No two apples are ever the same, biologically. But one ballbearing is meant to be the exact equal of many others, technologically. So, money used to regulate technology can function appropriately; but money that controls biology is as frustrating as pornography. The more involved we got with a porno-use of cash, the more frustrated we became. *Porn* meant "whore," which gave us our analogy of the Whore of Baby-L-on.

Rich and poor alike, we were the children of the Techno State. We ate the poisoned crops, drank the acid rain, and swallowed all the drugs that "mama-machine" dumped upon our plate.

Since the money specie pretended immortality, men sold their souls to keep their nations' moneys "free" and paid to take their "liberty" with the Whore, internationally. The bleeding soldier held a rank above her. The "infantry" got its name from the French "in-fant," meaning "not to speak." And so, the soldier was dumb, politically.

True to form, "the Word" leaves a ticklish trick to be decoded. Life comes with con-ception. Death comes with de-ception. So, when man and woman lie together, they live in an eternal dream. This is why being true to one's mate, to one's nation, or one's self can amount to no more than an illusion unless we are true to "the Word."

His-story plied our Mother Earth with promises of Heaven. In her belly were metals and fuels. The couple raised their children, best they could.

Later generations went off to grammar school. And today our kindergartens are filled with boys and girls who hope to attend the universe-city.

Our next chapter fills in some names from the puzzle of the final days. Then food-irradiation, circumcision, sex, and drug addiction are each explored on our journey through Armageddon. After that, we complete the proof that Armageddon is over. And then, when the fear has passed, we can all come out and play.

CHAPTER 30

MONEY AND MORALITY

The so-called "mental health expert" in the Baby M case, Dr. Judith **Greif** (in German "to touch," and looks like "grief") said Mary should not touch her child for 5 years while retaining parental rights. What could a mother's rights be, if not to touch and nurse her baby? In grief, our contacts were spelled out in contracts of technology.

And the Techno State had sex with married women while the fathers who masturbated to contribute sperm could not legally have sex with the women who carried their children, or even get a kiss for their money.

The political machine joined with the medical machine to assume the sexual rights that came with the territory during the Age of History.

The USA had "surrogate mothers" while financing "surrogate wars" around the globe so as to build "surrogate democracies" — a contra-diction in terms, fostered by public money.

But a "surrogate" is a "substitute," and Mary Beth was the "real" mother of Baby M. Another word was being stolen by the Techno State.

In experiments on deprived baby monkeys, wire or cloth manikins were tagged "surrogate mothers." They were substitutes. But the origin of the term (from psychological labs) was forgotten.

Fake wire mothers did not comfort baby monkeys and "surrogate democracies" did not serve people. True democracy, an organic process, will reach maturity only after we have stopped machines from fighting with machines for money.

Surrogate wars took money — not blood — out of the USA. But the techno-bio balance was lost. And in the final days, the fathering of families due to real impotency in the biological sense was a problem that could not be cured by money.

The Baby M decision said an "immoral" bio act (adultery) could be replaced by an "amoral" techno act (artificial insemination). Money written into the contract was used to alter "the morality" of monogamy — our mono-game.

Like a puppet government, Mary Beth had asked to be poked by the minions of advancing machines until a revolution awakened her instincts.

For Mr. Star and Mary Beth to "make love," they would have had to individually violate a marriage contract. But only "the authorities" of the Techno State could legally obviate contracts.

People in the USA were losing touch with their land. The organic roots of patriotism were dying. With each passing season, as topsoil washed into the rivers and out to sea, the motherland was made a bit less fruitful. Also, foods were shipped more and more from "poorer" nations where the merchants of the USA had appointed surrogate farmers, paid by a bit of the profits from the money game.

Pesticides, herbicides, and fungicides flowed through the bloodstreams of the people. Even worse than the poisoning on the farms in the USA, "cash crops" with higher doses, grown for export by the "poorer" nations were sold without inspection, as surrogate nourishment was digested.

And military men in the USA surrendered their hollow wills to a "surrogate patriotism" that was deflated with the Reagan, North, and Poindexter trial balloons of anti-democratic rule.

During the Armageddon years, a machine ran the White House. Congress could not have intercourse with the President. And at every level of society, the right brain was divided from the left.

Rampant infertility, birth defects, and increased miscarriages gave us a clue about the food supply. But instead of letting biology cure biology, we sought more techno cures. As years of accumulated pesticides flowed underground into our water supplies, the drugs and additives in our diets washed through our souls.

$E = M C^2$

At the end of his-story, these symbols make their quantum leap forward to that Space Age mystery — the Second Coming of the Word. E begets Easter. M begets Master. C is the Caster of spells, hurling shadows in formless rebellion evolving through infinite light.

The Crystal brings these three together, where "aster" is their common sign. In the Language of the Angles, **aster** simply means "a star." And so, these messages shine from afar.

E-aster is a star of energy, **Easter**.
M-aster is a star of matter, **Master**.
C-aster is a star of force, **Caster**.

A Caster, quite incisive, draws us into eternity. Through life beyond our fright, past shadows into night, follow these stars to avoid dis-aster. Know now fire is the C-aster of your inner light.

The *plan* of the *planet* is in its *plants*. Yet, an unspoken r-i-g-h-t (angelic rite) puts Gravity (G) in l-i-g-h-t. Encoded in the language of Angles is this seeming blight, an ominous self-casting spell.

On this journey of Ein-stein (one stone), questing through the uni-verse (one turn), in search of God (One Word), all language leads to a unified field where light outside delights the light within and levities square cites where gravities begin.

Crystal gazing into Language leads to Center (C-enter), thus to clarity of mind which we can apply to any changes we may wish to make.

The Language Crystal tells us what we already know: how to eat by instinct, how to love without guilt, how to use our primitive fears, how to walk with hope along a tightrope where twisted dreams stretch eternally between the visible fire and the fire out of sight (a silent G).

As we have seen, the golden thread that linked the USA to Iran was first carried by three Wise Men to Beth-lehem. Also, much of the story of 666 focuses on the Christmas Story of the Easter Master.

Hinkley got a 12-hour Christmas pass from the mental hospital to be with his family. North was committed to a mental hospital due to a Christmas breakdown, years before. And Reagan's demand on North was, "get the hostages out by Christmas." Later, Hinkley (disbelief) was denied a pass from Saint *Elizabeth*'s on Easter.

Folllowing the metaphor, Baby M was brought to the Sterns on Easter. "Noel" (Christmas) ran the surrogate sex shop. Mr. "Disbelief's" hospital bore the name of Baby M's adoptive mother. And so, "Mr. Disbelief" had been locked away in **Elizabeth**, meaning "House of God by an oath."

Baby M was more than a critical mass. More than a number, she had a name. More than mere matter, she could become a mother of tomorrow.

And Aquarius, androgenous in popular myth, had a sexual re-alignment to offer. A baby girl was at the crossroads this time around.

Jesus had been sold for silver at the beginning of the Age of Pisces. The karma of Baby M and that of the Easter Master had been set upon crossed paths by a numbers Caster known as "666."

The Second Coming of "the Word" challenges the essence of Phase Two thought. We must respect our machines — and keep them in their place.

For now that we have reached the limits of our biological expansion on the Planet Earth, the un-conscious patterns that we have woven are starting to crystallize within a new frame.

These are "contrived" and "intricate" words in a trial of threes (tri) — a basic thought pattern between you and me and the organic organizer of the uni-verse. "The Word" is the Third Person of God, by nature the healer who meets the techno world in triumph.

No crystallized law, not the raw law, mono-theism, mono-gamy, mon-ey or any other rule is enough to bring about Peace on Earth. Even when we are sure that Armageddon is past, even when it seems we are in perfect physical harmony, when we find no more need for social drugging, lying, cheating, hatred, or distrust, no law can prevail without a clear forgiveness of the past.

Forgive your mother for not heeding each and every cry. Forgive your father for being too busy or too bossy. Forgive your brothers, sisters, and playmates for wanting what you had and not giving you some of theirs. Forgive the neighbors who chased you from their property. Forgive the nation that oppressed the nations of your ancestry.

In our metaphor of IS-RA-EL (our question of the fire and the light), we have seen that **Israel** in Hebrew can mean "a struggle with God." And God was "the Father" during his-story. Men controlled military fire power in the final days. And in Je-R-usa-L-em, the Armageddon metaphor was played out mostly by dominant men. Bear in mind, his-story was the evolution of a Father Image.

And the name **Abu Nidal** meant "struggle of the father" in Arabic. Abu Nidal was said by North to be "the world's foremost assassin," a threat to North's young daughter. How does the story of Baby M fit with North and Nidal? We shall see when the meaning of "Natasha Simpson" is given its proper place in our puzzle. Natasha was murdered in "the Christmas massacres" said to be the work of Abu Nidal. Each piece fits into place as the mystery resolves itself.

The number 666 in the Ancient Hebrew mysticism of kaballah refers to three aspects of "man." And a "struggle with God the Father" (Israel) met with a "struggle of the father" (Abu Nidal) under the rule of Ronald (6) Wilson (6) Reagan (6).

These images extend the theme. And the next few pages have some cement to hold the larger pieces in place.

The chief of the CIA's Central American Task Force under President 666 was **Mr. Fiers,** who had "regret that he had not told" what he knew about the Iran-Contra affair.[1] But most people in the USA did not ask whom the failure of Mr. Fiers had burned in El Salvador, Nicaragua, and elsewhere.

Ms. Risque wrote a letter defending President 666's failure to speak out about a growing hole in the ozone layer.[2] Do we dare to ask how Ms. Risque ("Risk"), Assistant to the President and Cabinet Secretary, fits into our metaphor?

Also, Arnold **Burns** and William **Weld** quit the Attorney General's staff when the Wed-Tech scandal got too hot.[3] And Richard **Brenneke** (the German for "a burning corner") was the arms dealer who swore in a deposition to the Senate that the national security adviser to George Bush was the Washington contact for Contra arms-supplies that had been paid for by illegal drug money.[4]

The Iran-Contra judge, Gerhard **Gesell** had a family name that meant "fellow," "journeyman," or "member of the firm." For Gesell did not want to rule on misdeeds of Bush or Reagan. And Lawrence **Walsh** (in English "welsh" means "cheat" or "avoid debt payments") did not ask to prosecute any persons not already implicated by the open hearings. Bush and Reagan were never officially indited, thus never tried.

The very word "credit" had been co-opted by the money game. *Credo* means "I believe." And yet as we developed "easy credit," we were forgetting how to believe in each other, organically.

In 666's saga, Mr. Disbelief (Hinkley) and Ms. To-feed-each-other (Foster) told why Poin-dexter, Hasen-fus, Sin-glaub, and Arm-a-cost went astray. Reagan's secret team was headed by a man named **Shackley** ("shackerley"), an Old English word for "one who dwells in the wood of robbers."

(1) NY Times 8/26/87, (2) NY Times 8/30/87, (3) CS Monitor 5/17/88, (4) CS Monitor 5/17/88

There were just too many coincidences to chalk up to chance. **Hakim** (meaning "wise man") from Iran, and a renegade CIA agent named **Wilson**, Reagan's middle name, joined with Shackley ("one who dwells in the wood of robbers") to bring the Contras together after an attempt to assist Somoza failed. I could not trace "Somoza" (Portugese) beyond the fact that it was a place name. But enough of the pieces had already fit the metaphor.

When "666" was shot by "disbelief," Mr. **Brady** ("broad eye") took a bullet in his brain. The Great Seal (on a green back dollar) had its all-seeing eye blinded by 666. (Note the 13 stars as a Star of David, opposite the eye.) And another Brady replaced Baker in the Treasury when Bush (wine) took Baker (bread).

Mr. Broad Eye was press secretary to 666 while we hailed "the Great Communicator" and reporters rewrote White House press releases as "secret plans" of 666 were enacted globally.

Foster (to feed) and Hinkley (disbelief) make sense as characters when we see how many people in the USA want to feed the world.

The USA is a fostering nation. Yet, hinkley people under Reagan-ethics had "a lack of belief." Hinkley's *bullet* (little bull) was more than a "little ball" to the cow-boy. In the Golden Calf metaphor, "coward" and "bully" played out the cow and bull karma. In coming chapters, we explore the effects of bovine hormones and the ingestion of cattle RNA, plus vaccination karma. *Vacca* is the Latin word for "cow." The USA was so heavy with karma of the meat and dairy industry that modern "hamburgers" were akin to the "sacrifice of the lamb" in Biblical times. So, we must digest this symbolism from his-story before we go on.

The message of the Language Crystal is not that any particular diet is moral or immoral. This is not a tract on vegetarianism or any other ism. Our evolution is still in progress. The goal now is to build a true democracy, organically.

The Body of Christ

We eat to stay alive. With a choice, we eat what tastes good. And once we relate what we eat to how we speak, we can gain a truly conscious voice.

Christians celebrate a murder mystery with its centerpiece, a piece of bread said to be the body of Christ. For saying words creates reality.

The body of Christ was "the Word" divided under three stars (the Easter Master, Caster of spells). And now, "the Word" in its Second Coming says that we ourselves are the living body of Christ. As it was 2000 years ago, both good and evil are met together at the celebration feast.

Aside from wars fought in the name of Christ and charitable acts, the belief amounts to this: words have power over spirit and matter alike. As fishermen once cast their nets, so Jesus cast his words upon the human sea.

The doctrine of "transubstantiation" says that Jesus physically changed bread and wine into his own body, blood, soul, and divinity by the power of his words. And now the Language Crystal is both sub-stance and under-standing around the crystal center that is the edge of the uni-verse itself, that outside-inside boundary known as "you and me."

True belief is a belief in belief itself, in beliefs generated innocently, with no interest in money. So, putting innocent beliefs together is the essence of true democracy.

Surrogate democracies, wars, and births all had their contracts sealed by money. Not that money is evil; but in bio-truth, money doesn't count.

Monogamy in Phase Three has a fragility made no stronger by a marriage license, for our new union draws on blending individualities. Monotheism brings more than Jews, Christians, and Moslems together. Every ego-centric baby goo-gooed by grown-ups, knows of innocent mono-worship. But money, the mono-ploy used to make one of some thing seem equal to some of something else can confuse mono-theism and mono-gamy. So, when searching for beliefs, use money only to measure technology.

CHAPTER 31

CIRCUMCISION

Routine surgical removal of the foreskin from the penis was openly admitted by "medical doctors" to have no health benefits. Yet, such circumcisions were still a medical ritual in the USA. Why?

Rates of medical circumcision in the USA are far above all other nations. In England, for example, less than 1 in 100 male infants were circumcised for medical reasons while in the USA, 90 in 100 male infants had their foreskins cut off in 1970 for so-called "routine medical reasons."

Surgical removal of the foreskin was in fact a ritual that bonded males in a deeply emotional way to the powers of the Techno State.

No difference between male babies in England and the USA accounted for this "medical" activity. But history linked Je-R-usa-L-em to the karma of Abram-Abraham. And a medical factor called "money" strongly influenced many M.D.s in the USA.

Three promises were given to Abram-Abraham before his circumcision. He was told his seed would number among the stars. And through NASA, we were given tickets "to travel forth." He was told his seed would be a stranger in the land. And the USA was a land of immigrants. His seed was to inherit a land from Egypt's river unto the river Euphrates." And thus, the USA was drawn into the conflicts of "the Holy Land." And Abram-Abraham performed the rite at the age of 99, symbolic of his problem with two women. And money was involved indirectly, in the original covenant.

The practice of "medical circumcision" in the USA fed on a spirit between Jews and Moslems both of whom used "religious circumcision" as a way to get a bargain from God. Spiritual belief, again, seemed to contradict physical knowledge, as we sacrificed our bio-flesh to the techno-blade.

M.D.s in the USA treated circumcision differently than other forms of surgery. When we learned that tonsils were removed for no good medical reasons, such operations were reconsidered. It was shown that unnecessary breast surgery was the routine, and the crime diminished. However, during over 100 years, the opposite was true of routine medical circumcision until 1971. Even as scientific facts stacked up against it, its popularity in the USA rose steadily. And only legal suits that began in the 1980's brought a quickening in the decline to 60% by 1986.

In his book *Circumcision, An American Health Fallacy*, Edward Wallerstein writes, "Non-religious circumcision is a relatively recent phenomenon whose precise emergence is obscure." "Why only in the United States?" asks Wallerstein, who tells of his own Jewish heritage. And he seems frustrated when he finds no scientific answer.

The answer is in the techno mind-set. Both Jews and Arabs let the blood out of chickens to make them "clean." Arabs and Jews made foods *kosher*, a word for "clean," linked to blood-letting when Noah ate animal flesh. Later, Abram-Abraham agreed to serve Heaven (Earth is made of dirt). And he made his boys "clean" by shedding their blood.

In German, "clean" is *sauber* while "magic" is *zauber*. For bio-clean was confused with techno-clean in a perverted "magic-clean." Like modern slavery excused by money, this obvious child abuse was locked into our un-conscious fears.

When many Jews gave up kosher food in the USA, most held onto medical circumcision, for "health reasons," though health reasons had never been cited in the Orthodox teachings. And Moslems in the USA, though less reported on, did the same. Ironically, political speeches in the USA and "the Holy Land" cried out for "no more bloodshed."

The idea of clean organs free from dirty germs was saleable. So, "medical science" built the myth into a gross money maker.

In the 1870's, the USA became the first nation to introduce non-religious circumcision, with 8% of male infants treated by the knife. After an 1885 British study showed Jews had low rates of veneral disease, the new mythology led to an increase in secular circumcisions. We now know that it does not effect venereal disease, but Christians in the USA were caught in the middle.

From 1880 to 1920, two million Jews emigrated to the USA. These Jews from Russia were poor, yet more intellectual than Jews already in the USA, theorizes Max Dimont in *Jews, God, and History*. "Jewish intellectual life suddenly took root in America," he says. By 1910, writes Wallerstein, the rate of non-religious circumcision in the general population had risen from 8% to 56%. We will see the deeper psychological drives such as "menstruation envy" in later chapters.

The rate had reached 90% by 1970, and was on a slow decline (86% by 1980) until the law suits arose. But when insurance companies got wise, some "doctors" began to build "statistics" in defense of the myth.

You may see more phimosis, posthitis and other foreskin-related diseases if health insurers widely discontinue coverage for routine circumcision of newborns, announced "Medical Aspects of Human Sexuality" (April 1986), a magazine published for "the doctors" and filled with money-making ads of the drug companies. Even in its decline, the blood ritual was still grossing $100 million a year for the M.D.s (NY Times 2/1/88).

In 1986, the first of many pending law suits reached a head. An 8-month-old and 3-year-old boy sued in Mar-in, San Francisco, charging their rights were violated by circumcision without their permission (Contempory Ob/Gyn, Oct. 1986). In the 3-year-old's case, a statute of limitations said he could not sue for malpractice. So, a claim was lodged on his behalf for "unlawful use of force and false imprisonment during the operation."

MOIL means "one who circumcises" in Hebrew.
TURMOIL is "harassing confusion" in English.

Most people overlooked the dangers. Some "doctors" in the AMA said others might do it for the money. And money was written into Abram's circumcision contract, for servants that he bought with money also lost their foreskins (Gen. 17:12).

Accounts of cost-effectiveness in Canada led to the proposal "that the procedure be regarded as cosmetic surgery and be paid for by parents rather than by tax-funded insurance" (JAMA 4/12/85). But in the USA the blood-letting rites continued to be paid for, even by Federal funds.

Occasionally, extensive penile damage resulted along with removal of the foreskin. And though the babies screamed, M.D.s maintained that such young infants felt no pain. Many other forms of surgery were performed on babies with no anesthesia. And toward the end of 1987, "medical science" seemed surprised to find (by electronic monitoring) that infants do feel pain. So, the offending M.D.s then claimed that such pain was not remembered.

After losing their foreskins, many men became hypnotized by "medical powers." And the trauma of the pain, so early and so pervasive, made many men irrationally surrender in later years to so-called "routine medical proceedures."

Many grown men converting to Judaism have asked for and received dispensations from their rabbis, to become uncircumcised Jews. And men converting to Islam have asked for and received dispensations from their imams, to become uncircumcised Moslems. By using such rituals, we admit that no child is born into a religion. And since dispensations are granted to adults (who can speak for themselves), we also admit that a spirit, not a foreskin, is the index of one's faith.

"Gentiles" means "nations" in the Bible and has its roots in the word *Genisis*, which means "a circle." To close our spirit circle of father and son, to heal our genitles and nations, we have a bright new gentleness on Earth.

CHAPTER 32

THE INVISIBLE CAN

On April 18th, 1986, in the USA, the Food and Drug Administration (FDA) published a regulation in the Federal Register that allowed, for the first time, radiation to be used on fruits and vegetables sold directly to the public. But did the USA "need" irradiated vegetables and fruits?

Again, an alarming course of action seemed to be influenced by money; but there were mystified reasons that we shall presently explore.

For the five years that preceeded this piece of legislation, 26 fruit and vegetable canneries had closed in California alone.[1] The marketability of canned fruits and vegetables was on the decline due to a new health consciousness in the USA.

Since wholesalers could no longer insure crops against spoilage, and more and more people would not eat from cans, the Techno State invented "*the Invisible Can*" — food irradiation.

With food irradiation, shippers (not growers) could be protected. And a new use could be claimed for nuclear waste from weapons production, a new use in "the food industry."

On April 18th, 1986, the Techno State launched an invisible attack on the bio mind-set. And to be sure of "success," it was proposed that the public be kept ignorant of irradiation plans. Awareness was focused on the issue, however, and packers got word from distributors that food chains had been warned by customers not to try to sell such items. It seemed like a victory for biology toward the end of Armageddon. But food irradiation is still legal, the laws for labeling are still ambiguous, and our unconscious links to the techno mind-set are still threatening.

(1) NY Times 7/19/86

The Disappearing Label

When first introduced, tin cans gave us a choice of canned fruits in winter months when many people had no fruit at all. Shipping was not as streamlined as it is today. Next, refrigerated shipping put a dent in the canning industry.

Food irradiation, however, would not appear to be in competition with shipping fresh fruits and vegetables. In fact, the irradiated produce would APPEAR to be fresher for longer periods of time. So, greater money-profits could be made. Unlike frozen foods, irradiated foods appear to be fresh — and fresh is what people want today.

But could the Government hide facts? In 1983, spices dosed with a million rads of gamma rays were approved by the Food and Drug Administration (American Health, March 1984). Yet the spices carried no labels indicating irradiation. And the public was unaware. "There is no need for special labels on irradiated foods — already shown to be safe," the FDA had stated previously (Whole Life Times, July 1982).

Irradiated fruits look fresh. But potatoes grow no eyes, a carrot sprouts no new green tops, and the aura of life is contorted. Fruits do not ripen due to distorted enzyme activity; fruits get mealy, not sweeter. Have you noticed any such changes?

The problem for our biology is that the enzymes that ripen foods also help our digestive enzymes to convert those foods into nourishment.

Overlapping questions of health and morality were again covered up by the abuse of language. Labeling was promised by the FDA. But semantics and some antics in the Senate put warning labels "on or near" the items in question. So if the labels were affixed, but irradiated foods were shifted to another bin, no one would know.

The Federal Center for Food Safety said most people "wanted labeling on irradiated foods" (NY Times 10/28/84). But most people did not want irradiated foods in the first place. Invasion by zombie enzymes into the nation's food supply had never been put to a vote.

Free radicals that cause cancer can be produced by too much sun bathing, by irritants in smoke, or by irregular hormone secretions. Also, irradiation creates free radicals in foods.

But the problem of vanishing consciousness had begun before we irradiated any foods. Cooking also produces free radicals in food. So, the spread of cancer paralled the practices that destructured enzymes. Groups with the most highly processed foods had the most cancer.

The reason a diet of raw fruits and vegetables can "cure cancer" is that cooked food is the main contributor to cancer in the first place.

Killing cancer is a medical notion as sensible as killing your uric acid. The body gets rid of cancers routinely by its own chemistry and via the lymph glands, activated by aerobic exercise. In any case, foods with fractured enzymes should be avoided.

In 1984, the garment labeling law was updated with safe heats for washing, drying, and ironing. A glossary of legal meanings said: "Warm" on a label means water temperature 90°F to 110°F, while "cold" means up to 85°F. "Bleach is safe **unless** labels warn against it." But the garment-labeling law did not say that labels should be **"on or near"** the clothing; labels were sewn into garments.

Sunkist stamps its oranges. Fruit distributors promote their brands with stick-on labels. So why was labeling irradiated food so difficult?

TVs came with written warranty and diagram. But irradiated food, prescription drugs, circumcision, and other techno **hazards** could be more easily sold with no explanations or warning labels. The techno mind-set had no con-science, unless it was inter-acting with a clear bio-system.

Since fruits and vegetables absorb pesticides through their roots, only a small portion of these poisons can be washed away. And neither cooking nor irradiation neutralizes the poison sprays in foods. The new technology was aimed at killing living organisms.

We blamed a virus (bio) but debated whether or not smoking (techno) caused cancer. We would wash our hands after gardening, not to eat with "dirty hands." And when our hands were "clean," we ate sterilized (cooked or irradiated) food.

We ignored the fact that so many animals ate grass directly from the ground. Monkeys did not wash most vegetables they ate. And organic dirt was not toxic, unless in the rotting phase of its reproductive cycle.

Life was a mystery to the techno mind-set. With *most* food sub-atomically broken by fire, the ill-fed, over-wrought, toxified, and spiritually poor adult blamed viruses. But immunity cannot save us from destructured food or from air pollution.

Meanwhile, techno-schemes were made immune from prosecution while eco-dreams went up in smoke. Would irradiated foods bring on new diseases that could then be blamed on "immune deficiencies"?

Said the FDA's 1984 report on food irradiation, "It would be difficult to detect and subsequently measure potential toxicological properties." Then, Sid Morrison introduced a bill (HR696) in 1984 to the Agriculture Committee to change the status of irradiation from an "additive," which it was by law, to "a process," since "a food process" was not labeled while "additives" were.

Morrison's bill would have avoided labeling of irradiatied foods. But his linguistic juggling bill was voted down. And now, we must ask why "food processing" was not labeled as strictly as "food additives" in the first place?

A jar of fruit juice sits on a shelf two weeks, plus time in the warehouse. It says "no additives" on the label. So what has kept it from fermenting? Chemical changes were "*added*" by the "*process*" of cooking (pasteurization).

Why did Congressman Sid Morrison say that a process did not constitute an additive? We shall see. But bear in mind, most of what is wrong with irradiated food is paralleled in cooked food.

Sid, an apple grower from Washington State, lived near the Hanford nuclear facility. And the fuel for food irradiation, held in "several dozen 18-inch cobalt-60 pencils" (N.Y. Times 11/12/86) was from waste dredged in making nuclear weapons.

If Sid's apples were good, they could go bad. But if dead due to irradiation, their "shelf-life" would add to the GNP, in the process.

If we could use petro-sludge in fertilizers to deplete our soil, why not use all the unsaleable nuclear waste to deplete our food?

Literacy was declining in the USA because the soul of the people's language was being sold out to the highest bidder.

The Health and Human Services Department planned to label irradiated foods as "picowaved," "picowaved to control spoilage," or "picowaved to extend shelf-life" (12/12/85).

But after two years of labeling, the FDA proposed to offer dealers the option of using a "picowave symbol" without any words at all.
    Why?

Why was the FDA in favor of illiteracy? Saying "no to drugs" is more difficult for any child of a society where chemical alteration is the norm and literally hiding it is a sanctioned routine.

Labeling in truth gives us educated choices. Salted, nitrited, pasteurized, cooked, smoked, MSG'ed, radiated, dehydrated, steamed, or frozen, be it additive or process, we, the people, have the right to know what is in our food. In a democracy, the only law to bring respect to all law is "the Word" that is revealed to all. But the Government has fostered illiteracy.

The President's Council on Fitness and Health said, "Watch your diet" (vague advise). We baked apple pies to a golden brown but we knew enough not to eat apples that had turned brown naturally. Both cooked and rotted apples were oxygenated, and neither was fit to eat.

The International Maritime Union points to several cases of fraud by the use of irradiated food. For example, packaged food shipped to the USA was found to be contaminated; insurance was claimed; and the food shipped back to England. Then, that same bad food was shipped to the Netherlands, irradiated, and sent to supermarket shelves.

The fraud was detected because food irradiation was banned in England. But this case shows how irradiation can kill bacteria to make it possible for spoiled foods to have a low bacteria count.

Early in 1988, Rice-a-Roni and Noodle-Roni were caught using irradiated mushrooms from Thailand in their packaged products sold in the USA.

The problem was international. And the USA had no way of determining what imported products were or were not irradiated. Moreover, the Government did not seem to care.

"It is simply not possible to describe at this time the unintended effects of irradiation," said Dr. Pauly, an FDA safety officer. Of course, it was possible to describe. Irradiated foods were mummified, lifeless, and dangerous.

Vegetables do not need any added salt. So, why did we begin to salt our foods?

The reason was that "seasoned" foods kept for seasons of scarcity. Without salt, a food's own enzymes will cause it to decay more rapidly. Thus "bad" food is nature's fertilizer. For enzymes do not die. Only "the individuality" of a plant or animal dies; the enzymes of decay and growth are continually dancing together, unless fire, salt, alcohol, or some other killer stops the music.

Ferment made the "dressings" that were costumes in winter when foods were scarce. But added salt, alcohol, or vinegar will lower the vitality of anyone who eats them.

Also, the instinctual ability to know what is good nutrition (held by all animals) is weakened by unnatural processes and additives.

Salt Two

After years of treating salt-induced diseases with drugs, we learned to limit salt intake.

Irradiated-food diseases will not be "cured" by drugs anymore than salt-induced diseases. We can only educate ourselves; and our instincts are, of course, encoded in our most ancient symbols.

Pluto guarded the gates of Hell. So, plutonium (radioactive ore) and plutocracy (rule by money) were a dual threat to humanity.

Food irradiators wanted ALL food treated by the year 2000. The astronauts already ate irradiated items. They could have sprouted seeds instead, but NASA had yet to find its bio-balance.

Some day, we will travel in space with a self-replenishing food supply. So, food irradiation is not a Space Age answer.

More than half of U.S. croplands are planted with livestock feed (*Science News* 3/5/88). One third of North America is devoted to grazing. More than half the water consumed in the USA goes to livestock. Plus, Worldwatch reports that just one pound of steak requires the energy of a gallon of gasoline to produce while eroding about 35 pounds of topsoil. So, why the plans to irradiate the nation's fruits and vegetables?

Remember that we worshipped fire, and then we sacrificed our food to sacred flames. Radiation had become a god of war and of energy supply. So, we were following history's patterns.

With fruits and vegetables irradiated, meat and dairy could be treated the same; the packaging industry would then have a stockpile of items to sell year round. Like cans of cola or candy bars, what was not good could not go bad.

In "developing countries," domestic cooking is the greatest consumer of wood. And in Technology Review (Aug. 1979), Mary Rawitscher (her real name) wrote that up to 5% of the energy used in the USA went to cook food at home. Add to that the nation's restaurants and giant food canning and packaging industries.

Fuel spent daily to destroy the nutrients in our global food supply was actually polluting the air while our souls were struggling against the limits of earthly techno expansion. Prisoner's testicles were irradiated to test for infertility afterward. The men were paid up to $10 per dose (*NY Times* 10/24/86). And over 1,000 subjects were irradiated by the Atomic Energy Commission, Sloan-Kettering, and others. Some testers fed inmates on phosphorous-poisoned fish, from the nuclear site at Hanford (Congressman Sid Morrison's watering hole). And science claimed no morality.

FDA scientists counted calories by burning food in test tubes. Vitamins were chemo-analyzed with no regard for their bio-use. Enzymes were counted in spite of mortality. And the "Recommended Daily Allowance" noted no differences among raw, cooked, pasteurized, or irradiated proteins. We were losing hold of our own bio-relatedness.

Adam's punishment was to earn his bread. Abram-Abraham had a covenant of circumcision. Hindus blessed (clarified) butter by the use of fire. The rituals that wed mankind to technology were woven into the fabric of society. But techno growth must now be redirected.

The FDA spent $1.8 million fighting health-food quackery. But M.D.s said too much was spent to control drug companies (Physicians Financial News 1/15/85). Which "authorities" were to decide? What was *natural and what was not?*

When NATURE is allowed to MATURE, its cycles of death feed its cycles of life. So, technology can serve biology on this planet by making it possible for us to mature and carry our nature unto other planets, even after the Earth is gone.

We must be the final judges. And what we eat affects how we think which determines how we treat each other. Still, to guide us in these endless cycles, we have "the Word," the only tool of pure abstraction that can restore our love.

CHAPTER 33

CIVILIZED SEX

MARITAL arts and MARTIAL arts are formal means we have for turning each other inside out. For marriage is the testing ground of forgiveness. And martial artists handle the unforgiven.

A respect for human-centered money values has also been linked to matri-archal matri-mony. But in this fact, we have a problem that affects both our nations and our individual souls.

Who is on top in marital-martial affairs? That depends on the ego (I) with respect to the cross-roads (T), and how we look at IT (value).

We fight if we love each other. But do any martial encounters belong in the marital bed? Again, the answer lies in that eternal dialogue between "the Lord" and "the Life." How can the mother of "the Word" also be "the Wife"? (Remember that the uni-verse is feminine.)

Since words evolve, and our names are words, the MARVIN-MARVIN palimony case tried to show who was riding whom as both lovers had it in for each other. Michelle Marvin's suit against her suitor, Lee Marvin, was for $1.8 million. Judgment came April 18th. Michelle's lawyer was Mar-vin Michel-son. Judge Mar-shall invented "palimony." And the legal status of matrimony was shifted.

Shortly after that, Gretta Rideout charged her husband with rape, a land-mark case. She dropped her charges; and he, his request that she share $18,000 in lawyer fees. They were divorced in Mar-ion County (*N.Y. Post* 5/9/79).

Mary (Holy Mother) and Mars (the god of war) were locked in courtly battle. The Ram and Mars were in men's minds, fighting (at times with Grammar) to capture that territory needed to expand their marriages. To MAR means "to scar," "to score," "to rent," "to tear." So, the mono-game is built upon two egos, judiciously enfolding into one.

SLAUGHTER and LAUGHTER

A primal link between slaughter, sex, and laughter is found hidden in these words.

"Clitoris" and "tickler" are the same word in German, *kitzler*. *Dagdegan* "clitoris" and *digdeg* "tickler" are of the same root in Hebrew.

And in our metaphor, a test-tickle gave Abraham (ha plus Abram) a boy named "laughter" (Isaac). For "testicle" and "testament" are of the same stem in Latin, "the test of man's virility."

During history, we tested each other in many ways. We were extending our evolution in the spirit, trying to put "good and evil" into workable Space Age formulas. Our weakness was that without a natural fear of fire, our instincts were no longer intact. "The Word" had become our link   to perceptions of reality.

Man and woman are constantly trying to rule each other's spirits. Yet, in good marriages there is levity, while martial arts deal with gravity.

From the Old English "goom," meaning "man," we get our modern "groom" by adding R. And in 1970, the R was dropped from MRS, and MS began to build a union of married and single women, entitled to powers that would challenge "the man" throughout the Armageddon years.

Before 1970, MISS and MRS were parted by MR, who cast a spell on each separately. As we have seen, MR (13-18) is where we find the beast 666. *And no one might buy or sell without the mark of the beast.* But equal pay for equal work would mean MR could not lord it over MS.

And "the beast" was humanity itself. For man and woman started his-story with a secret as man became "the bread winner." In the end, "pay" meant patriarchal power. But R taken out of his importance left impotence in its wake.

Man-agement, man-ufacture, and man-ipulation of the ma-chi-ne was his. But he was in turn ruled by MS, a man-u-script, which made a re-sister of his sister and gave females the rite of a co-manned performance. Money (script) was a battleground between MR and MS, in the final days.

In the Armageddon years, a legal brothel was sold for 18 million bucks. The Mustang Ranch, Nevada, had 108 bedrooms for whores.[1] And the real-life whore house sold its shares on Wall Street.

The whores were owned by Strong Point Inc. on the stock exchange, bullish on the Mustang Ranch. With money as king, asking the queen meant being in debt, in bed with the money-machine.

President 666 was accused of being silent when 18 abortion-clinic directors were threatened with death only weeks before the worth of the Ranch and its herd were subjected to bidding on Wall Street.[2] What exactly were the values of the human animal as opposed to the hunger of the beast? Women (at 18) could legally rent their flesh. Men (at 18) could be sent to war. But now, we must translate the code of "life" into something more.

Jerry Falwell reported (TV, 9/10/86) that the USA had 18,000 adult book stores. "Adult" was a euphemism for porn, adulterated mindstuff. Its pictures imitated life where no life existed, like numbers of "finance" imitating "the economy," like an apple with irradiated enzymes — promises that would never come true.

The Bible said Abram had a wife. Then, he took another wife whom he later disavowed. So, his is a picture of adult-ery in the mono-game. But his first wife told him to do it. And this is the game that evolved into our modern idea of monogamy. In fact, the mono-game is still evolving.

To make use of mono-theism, mono-gamy, and mon-ey, we need not deny that societies have gotten along without them. Monogamy was not the rule of ancient Israel. Israel's two wives and their two servants (four women) gave him his 12 sons.

One wife was not history's rule. We are only now evolving into oneness of "the race." The love of One God, felt abstractly, sees the love of one woman in a man who treasures her humanity.

(1) NY Times 8/7/85, (2) NY Times 7/29/85

Brother, Bother, Other, Brothel

Supported by money and machine, the marital arts of human beings would overpopulate the globe. And wars would consume us all if money-machines did not fall under bio control. Mother is the initial other; brother was a bother. The cosmic code had sown its seeds to fit the needs of a race that is now being re-defined. Competing for the machine, bio-love was sold in a brothel by a brother to a brother as techno-love turned into a bother.

Since money and machine lacked an organic sense of timing, they ruled Phase Two to the detriment of our bio-sphere. We were torn between the past and future. And mon-key sex demanded that brother compete with brother. Yet, money-games that "compete" will be "complete" in the Space Age. For monkeys in "the race" co-operate in space.

By history's end, pay will be sexless. The Whore is no longer exclusively female. A brothel can be a prize-fight ring. The Whore can be a TV ad, with computers selling beer seductively.

As noted, money is not the focus of the Whore. She quibbles with a poor man over five and argues with a banker for five hundred. The object of our mono-game is to put a human value on money — a value that is feminine by in-tuition.

When "the Word" was martyred by sons of Mars, three Marys stood by the cross: Mary his mother (a virgin), Mary a wife (to Cleophas), and Mary a prostitute (of Magdalan). And Jesus, a carpenter, consummated his union with "the machine."

We will establish true democracy only as we see each other as sharing values globally. Each of us individually reflects all humanity.

MARX tried to protect the MARYS from MARS by inventing "a classless society." Lacking friction, his fiction inspired neither social nor spiritual evolution. Commies and Cappies both will fail until our mono-game evolves beyond abstractions back into the biology from whence it emerges.

Money and machine are useless unless they serve humanity — each and every human being.

Vital Statistics?

Toward his-story's end, "the man" became a catch phrase opposed to "Blacks," "Youth," and "Women's Rights." Bodily, "the man" was White. Mentally, "the man" was Right. In spirit, "the man" was Light. So said his-story's mister-re.

In Armageddon's final years in the USA, 18 teens per day, "not feeling right," committed suicide.[1] A woman was battered every 18 seconds, for "acting too bright."[2] Susan Schechter wrote in "Women and Violence that 1.8 million married women in the USA were battered in 1980. And 18% of "Black" males spent time in state prison, with 3% of "Whites."[3] Our image of "the man" was so divisive.

Yet, the National Women's Conference first convened in Houston on November 18th, with 18,000 observers and the Whore of Baby-L-on present.[4]

What did women want? The USSR said, 18% were frigid.[5] Henry Ford II's wife took 18% of "his wealth."[6] And only 18% of women who encountered exhibitionists reported the affront.[7] Not really real statistics, but some rather odd ideas.

"Women's Policy Studies" reported 18 million females sexually harassed at work. And Reagan's female mouthpiece Phyllis Schlafly said, "most of those 18 million were asking for it."[8]

Had women's quest for money upset the Father's divinity in the monotheistic mono-game?

July 18th of Carter's final year in office was the only day ever that draft registration was held to be unconstitutional because it excluded women. The Court decision was overturned in a day.

Also in July, Maureen Reagan told NBC (7/4/80) of the 18-woman caucus working on her dad's party platform. Exactly 18 members of Reagan's platform committee said abortion on demand should be dad's official stand. Coincidence?

(1) TV promo 1/3/86, (2) United Way 1/8/86, (3) A.P. News 7/28/85, (4) Redbook April 1978, (5) Time 7/23/79, (6) Time 3/3/80, (7) Donahue NBC 7/28/80, (8) Time 5/4/81

Past Evils

Sex is one root of mono-morality. Sleep together in a common dream, and our minds transgress the crystal seam that separates the sexes.

Geschlect means "sex" in German. But *Ge*, as a prefix, indicates a "past tense" and *schlect* means "bad." Thus, *Geschlect* (sex) implies "the past tense of something bad." *Geheim*, "the past tense of home," is the word for "secret." And *Schamteile*, "shameful parts," means "the sexual organs."

In Russian, *brak* means "marriage" and the same word, *brak*, means "a defect."

Racham means "womb" in Hebrew while *ra-cham* means "evil-hot." *Cham* also means "father-in-law" while *chamad* means "to lust after." In German, *lust* means "pleasure." His-story had its faults.

Men tried to consume the Whore of Baby-L-on; and *public elections* of power brokers took the place of *pubic erections* among monkeys.

In German, *trauen* means "to marry" but *trauern* means "to grieve." R marks the difference twixt *amour* and *armour*.

In Latin, "womb" and "wound" have roots in "vulva" and "vulnerable." And here is the key to hostility between the host and hostage; each spirit conceived in woman's womb learn's to hide its fear of fire, while seeking the light.

Vulcan (god of fire) and *vulpes* (fox) both symbolize "being consumed," which tells of man's unconscious fear of woman's *vulva* (her vaginal lips) where his fire-god Vulcan meets the immortal flame, leading to his test-tickle again.

His-story's words are a testament to his test. Fox (*vulpes*) was akin to vaginal lips; wolf (*lupe*) meant "a whore" in Rome. And foxy pussies worked in cathouses of the USA as feline images evoked a fear in primates. Consider the witch and her cat. Watch her stir the caldron brew. Every tribe on Earth had some form of cooking, not out of a bio need, but to feed the techmo mind-set that he and she both needed and abhorred. Now, the way to a human's heart can be through the bio-spirit.

CHAPTER 34

MEMORIES "R" US

Jane Goodall, known for her work filming chimps, was finally accepted as harmless by a small group of chimps after being in their territory for 18 months. So, she gained a record of chimpanzee life in the wild, spanning three chimp generations.

The chimps ate fruits, vegetables, and insects. According to Goodall's early observations, they did not hunt, they gathered food.

Yet, in a territorial conflict with baboons, a group of male chimps hunted a male baboon, killed, and ate him. Why did they eat the male baboon?

The answer is encoded in RNA, the stuff that flows among our memories. The male chimps ate the invading baboon to gain some of the memory in its cells. Experiments show how this is possible.

So, this chapter treats the body, mind, and spirit as territories, each of which may be either guarded or shared. When these three memory modes are allowed to intermesh, we can feel (clearly know) the spirit's memory in our blood.

Why does a mother carry hemophiliac genes from a father to his son? Why in the name of God, the Territorial Father, do chimps eat the body of a Stranger's Son? The answers are rooted in the mechanisms of territoriality.

Do chimps need to dine on flesh? Do Christians require the body of Christ as a dietary boost? Must we have hemophilia to weed out the close in-breeding that could weaken our gene pool?

Let us start by exploring memory transfer by RNA and then give some thought to outer space. A union of body-, mind-, and spirit-memories, will allow us to examine each within the other two.

Our goal is forgiveness of the past, gaining an astral view of humanity, and seeking values that will lead to true democracy on Earth.

Our evidence begins with flatworms; if cut in two, each part regenerates and remembers.

In 1953, biologist James McConnell trained some flatworms to respond to certain stimuli. He then cut the flatworms in two, allowed their severed halves to regenerate, and observed that memory of their previously learned responses had remained in both halves. The original heads and original tails had retained the learned behavior.

While McConnell continued (1950's), biologist Holger Hyden showed, aside from the brain, memory is also stored in the body cells, in RNA.

McConnell (still working with worms) saw that Hyden's RNA experiments explained how memory was retained by both ends of his flatworms, not only in their heads. So, he ground up some worms that had learned certain tricks and fed "remembering" wormy bits to worms that were untrained.

McConnell's report entitled *The Transfer of Training by Cannibalism* showed that biological componants of memory can be eaten. And dozens of similar experiments have since been documented. Birds that have learned various tasks have been fed to untrained birds, and the learned behaviors duplicated within preset guidelines.

Furthermore, RNA Memory Transfer passes from one individual to the next even across species lines. So, the chimps had a reason for eating the baboon — to gain its memory.

Since baboons and chimps were contenders for the territory, both RNAs were optimal. The victor gained the memory of the vanquished. And the RNA ingested was to some extent replicated.

Is this why male chimps ate more flesh than the females? Eating various kinds of RNA was a way to gain territorial knowledge. But, as we shall see, the Space Age will present humanity with some new territorial problems. What were once beastly questions must now be treated humanely in meta-physical terms. For physics does not answer the question of metaphysical (spiritual) time.

Goodall was later surprised to learn that chimps ate small animals. They hid this behavior from her for many years. Did chimps have consciences?

They saw Goodall (a name suited to her role in chimpdom) build fires. So, they dared not let a goddess see them kill less-powerful beings than themselves. But humans did not fear that God might catch them grinding up flatworms. We only tried to hide the evidence when we murdered other humans — a morality more bold than that of chimps.

Remember, morality relates to mortality at the crystal crossroads. Each species does what it can to survive. And humanity's goal is eternity. And the only limits on what we do are circumstantial. So, what determines Space Age morality?

Memory in the body interacts with memory of the spirit when we have a union of knowledge in con-science, universal conscience. And accepting our freedom of choice, we become response-able.

We have seen that viruses do not "invade." We are not "victims" of infection unless the body is weakened or poisoned. We can, however, contract a disease by setting the body and spirit on a course of such contractual engagement. These facts in the context of memory may help neutralize social pressures to accept theories that were invented by physicians with no meta-physical reference to a spiritual direction.

A virus does not procreate but can get linked into the body's RNA to be replicated. Viruses do not mutate themselves; the host mutates the virus. And the living memory in RNA is influenced by the spirit through individual bio-chemical adaption. So, our next step is to gain full consciousness — to find the individual spirit within.

For biology to be fulfilled, healing finds its direction in spirit. But a "secret" between the body and spirit can block the healing process.

Historic linguistic contexts often went against personal individuality. Yet, in the Space Age, a sense of separateness adds to co-operation.

A small piece that is removed from a leaf is re-membered by that leaf in electric waves. This aura may be seen by gifted people and reproduced by Kirilian photography. The empty space where that piece of leaf was originally has in-tension in the body electric that elects to re-member it. If you have ever cut you finger, you have seen your body electric re-member itself.

After generations, genetic memories grow into instincts. And social behavior blurs into instinct also. Even gaps in the philogenetic line, show how evolution is touched by spirit. A form may be spiritually recessive and manifest as needed.

By reading a description of a sexual act, one may become physically aroused. For within words are stored and shared emotions. And between the lines are whisps of spirit. For all our words are in a continuum; and even broken words tell parts of the story that now must be revealed.

After John presented me with a dyslexic gap between R and L, years of meditation followed. The Crystal drew me in spiritually. And now, I carry the spirit of my dyslexic friend.

Mother Nature, Mother Earth, and Mother Church gave us a mother tongue even before his-story. The mothers encompass memory as fusions of male-fe-male thought are new ways of seeing the body electric. Certainly, there are quantum leaps that depend on physical electrons. Still, a move cannot be made without a leap (or fall) of spirit.

Like a finger with a piece taken away, we were torn, learning the territorial laws of Earth. Yet, our lower level struggle teaches the morality that will be necessary for our Space Age race as we seek a New Earth in Heaven. Heavenly morality is akin to those invisible forces that allow injured fingers to generate new cells. Within limits, the flesh is replaced with no scar. So, cosmically, we must know humanity's moral limits.

We are on the brink of a spiritual leap that will enable Mother Earth to regenerate.

The Law of Yield is a spiritual memory. Remember, our goal is forgiveness of the past, gaining a view of the human animal, and seeking the values of a truly democratic Space Age.

But to a Phase Two mind-set, true democracy is impossible. The animal self is in fear of the self that is the beast. This is the clash between *anima* (soul) and *bestia* (irrationality). Yet, in Phase Three, we can confront the beast within by making CLEAR our animal memory.

Since vegetation yields by the season, green leaves and pulp from the fruit have no built in plans of their own. The pulp of fruit is made to feed its seed or it yields to the soil or whoever eats it. We ingest no memory by eating the leaves of any plants or the pulp of any fruits.

A fruit re-members itself through its seeds or its pit. And vegetables have various ways by which they reproduce, yet the plants that we eat yield their leaves seasonally.

It is possible to avoid eating physical memory by having only fruit pulp and vegetable leaves. But to move into the Space Age and interplanetary travels, we must first concentrate on breaking loose from other, more painful entanglements.

A slaughtered animal's RNA has a host of plans that are aborted in the killing. Along with its species RNA, its individual traits are eaten. And those who eat it are heirs to its realm.

The conflict in an animal at slaughter gives rise to hormone secretions that are toxic when eaten by humans. Books on the harm of eating flesh abound. Still, flesh food is essential until we can provide enough fruits and vegetables. We must reorganize our global eco-structure. These pages are devoted to our journey between fire and light — on raw (guiltless) information.

Since outer space is physically uncharted, we can travel it best by clear reason and instinct. C-LE-AR reason and C-LE-AR instinct are not competitive memories.

In his book, *Our Ancestors Came from Outer Space*, NASA scientist Maurice Chatelain begins his daring thesis with "the Constant of Nineveh," 195,955,200,000,000, a number inscribed on clay tablets in Sumeria before the Bible was written.

Chatelain says the Constant was the number of seconds in 2,268 million days. But the rotation of the Earth has slowed, putting the Constant off by 1.0368 seconds. And 1.0368 seconds out of 2,268 million days tells us that the Constant itself was calculated 64,800 years ago, before any earthly civilization. Thus, Chatelain concludes that "Our ancestors came from outer space."

We may question the steps to this conclusion, yet each of the individual numbers in Chatelain's figuring reduces to 18 by numerology.

The 64,800 years comes to: 6+4+8=18. And 2,268 million days reduces to: 2+2+6+8=18. And in like manner, the Constant of Nineveh itself reduces to 36 (two 18's).

The turning of the Earth's axis around the pole of the elliptic, also noted in Chatelain's work, takes 9.450 million days of 86,400 seconds each. The diameter of the sun is 864 thousand miles. Of course, Chatelain, a physical scientist, does not note these occult relationships at 18.

He states that the clay tablets were found by sinking a shaft 18 feet into solid brick which led to the layer of the Grand Hall and the treasure. The inscription on the Assyrian tablets that links them to the Bible tells of King Hezekiah's ransom, 18,000 pounds of silver and 1,800 pounds of gold when given in modern weights, impossible for the scribes to have known. When we go to that passage in the Second Book of Kings, which happens to be in Chapter 18, we find where the land had been besieged. "And at the end of three years they took it: even in the sixth year of Hezekiah, that is the ninth year of Hosea." Again, 3+6+9=18 shows Nineveh (nine-veh) as a turning point for the spirit.

For "life" is ever remembering "life."

It seems that a belief in belief must be our first belief. For without it, we can believe in no other thing, not even science. Still, one thing exists before belief, and that is knowledge of the self. We each must know ourselves before a shared belief can be truly meaningful.

A return to monkey instincts would put about 5% flesh in our diets, mostly from scavenging. But we cannot go back in time, time that we ourselves emit. In our living universe the future does not mechanically imitate the past. We must go on each day inventing and creating ourselves anew.

Mathematical models of the universe do not show this knowledge that every bio-organism has. For we always move foreward in bio-time. And although human instinct seems built on monkey biology, the spirit of "humanity" (the spirit that unifies fire and light) is ever evolving.

Even as we use our physical bodies for speech, "the Word" that is our spirit's reflection does not evolve from mere physical communication.

Chimps may learn words, but they do not talk in a human sense, engendering speech in others. And no primitive form of human speech exists. Every group, no matter how primitive, has a full, richly expressive set of words and intricate grammar to express all that is necessary without reliance on gestures or other non-linguistic modes. We may use gestures, yet words are always sufficient.

Rain forest aborigines know as many words as Wall Street analysts, only the focus is changed and the grunts and gestures are redirected.

"The Word" is ours in wholeness. Just as fire is our tool, "the Word" is our salvation from any troubles that the use of fire may bring. RNA is crystalline; like a radio crystal-set, affected by electro-magnetic waves, telepathically.

Did we evolve due to a spaceship's visit with prime-mates? Will other "humans" that we meet in space speak our Angular language? Will we be ready to unifiy in "the Word"?

Humanity

Humanity is the spirit that enters animal forms to unite the
fire and the light, universally. But we will not express our
full humanity until we gain emotional control over our fear
of fire.

Remember, we still feed our unconsciousness to keep us
chained to the Techno State. This is why we eat cooked
foods. And the only way we can both work with
technology and flow in consciousness is with a clear love
for future generations.

Yes, we do have love. And still, we hate each other. So
will it be until we make that quantum leap of spirit that
unites humanity on Earth. The process is organic, building
bio-spirits one by one. The outcome will be true
democracy in the sense that we will know intuitively how
to live our lives bio-synergistically.

Surely, we will still have schools and cities, but you can
see the coming changes. No smoking in the streets. No
alcohol at public meetings. No cartons that do not recycle.
Our Phase Three mind-set is already dawning.

We have two dietary laws. One is the Raw Law, natural
to all animals and beasts. The other is the Law of Yield,
innate in higher spirits. These two are basic to Phase Three
conditioning.

The Raw Law feeds our consciousness. The Law of
Yield allows us to eat without bloodshed or the
imprisonment of animals. After history, this will help
greatly in rebuilding the eco-balance.

In history, Jews, Moslems, Christians, Hindus, and the
rest tried to have more and more children. Spanish,
Greeks, Germans, Italians, and primal groups alike favored
expansion of the family which meant, of course, territorial
expansion.

Toward history's end, each group admitted we needed
less people, but acted as if other groups should be
decreased. Now, more globally aware, we are evolving
toward our Space Age destiny. Our Earth-bound selves see
beyond Terra's territory to where we will be re-membered
via the spirit. For, in truth, memories "R" us.

CHAPTER 35

WRITTEN IN BLOOD

Long-term space travelers face a dilemma, for they will have no moon to guide them. Menstrual (moon related) cycles will fade in women, and men will have no subtle moon beams to coax them in romance. Yet, a woman who spends an extended time in space needs her hormones excited to lead her through her fertile days. And men, in turn, need the cycles of women to stay in harmony and flux. So, what in Heaven will influence our sexual cycles?

Each species has its own cycles of procreation. Most mammals mate by the seasons as females come into heat. Some apes and all humans have evolved to a stage where females are influenced by the moon. But there are other factors.

For example, among the red deer of New Zealand, the roar of a rutting male is enough to hasten the onset of a doe's ovulation. So, for the time when we have no moon (in space), humanity is even now rehearsing a means of courtship wherein a male can send out signals to stir a woman's blood.

The **WORD** is with the **LORD**.

The **LIFE** is with the **WIFE**.

These mystical equations are in fact linguistically founded in formulas of the Hebrews and Egyptians, each of whom interchanged the sounds of **L** and **W**. It's a wittle mistake we each can make. And since ancient language is reflected by angles (angels in space), the Word and the Lord are properly one, as are the Life and the Wife. So, when true to each other, both are eternally divine.

This chapter touches the cosmic body's relationship to eternal spirit and shows how woman has nurtured "the Word" that is written in her blood.

Being true is man's noble calling. Sexually, he learns this from woman, as he is eve-r divided between his flesh and visions of eternity.

Since the search for livable planets is built into our cosmic cycle, we have a way to evolve new sexual signals. So, among the stars, "the Life" and "the Word" are in constant courtship.

When in cartoons Elmer Fudd cursed that Cwazy Wabbit (Crazy Rabbit), another wittle clue to the union of Hebrew and Egyptian fell into pwace. For **R** and **L** share the origins of **W**.

And this is why YHWH (Je-ho-vah) is the God of IS-RA-EL. These abstractions have come down to us as "God the Father." For during Phase Two, we sublimated the light transmitted to our brood by the living blood of "God the Mother."

Earth woman's moon related sexual cycles have become complexly interwoven with the cycles of the Techno State. And this inter-meshing of cycles extends our universal plan. But when man took his first baby steps on the moon, little did he think that woman had sent him there.

Using fire in primitive times caused womankind to switch rapidly from a form of estrus (seasonal sexual cycles) to menses (moon regulated cycles). This bio change took place because the hormone melatonin, repressed by the light of the sun, was also repressed by the light of man-made fires.

When fire became our companion by night, female attunement to the varying seasonal intensities of sunlight was re-attuned. And sexual relationships were altered in the process. Fire-light is not bright enough to disorient a contemporary woman's cycles noticeably, but when fire was first made a part of our lives the balance was more delicate. Also, metaphysical factors were at play as in all of evolution. Darwin says adaption is based on natural selection that leads to bio changes. What Darwin overlooked was the super-natural selection that operates gradually with a working assumption of the future.

How on Earth would a monkey know enough to pick up a burning stick and begin to experiment with fire? The leap, of course, involved a spiritual advance. And LOVE spelled backwards (as any dyslexic can see) is the beginning of EVOLution. All our ideas about love conquering fear make more sense when we fit them into the universal metaphor.

Monkeys watched the sky, saw old stars dying and new stars being born. As with all knowledge, the monkeys passed this information on from one generation to the next until they figured out that our sun would eventually die and a new star with a new livable planet would have to be found. So, our "race" of primates began as we pushed the fear of fire into our "unconscious mind."

Attunement to the cycles of the moon is not a factor for all primates. Yet, it does affect some advanced apes to some extent. But menstruation among baboons, for example, is not an adaptive trait. It is distressing to the female and has no survival advantage for the group. So why have baboons approximated moon cycles?

The answer is that the spirit of fire-conquest did not immediately take one species and make it human. A lesser menstruation in baboons shows that their group spirit was also making a biological move toward adaption to fire. Primates in general were pushing against their instinctual fear of fire. But not every group made it through.

Logic tells us that evolution has spiritual as well as environmental factors. For example, an evolving reptile pre-bird must first acquire wings that do not fly. But wings that are 99% developed (not capable of flight) would be a drag unless the evolving species felt in its spirit that working wings were being developed for future generations.

So, reptiles who began to develop wings before they could fly must have had the spirit of flight. And this must have been a group spirit.   Also, it took at least two mating, evolving reptiles at each stage to produce the next level of their flight-oriented species. Biologically, the concept preceeds the conception. LOVE in reflection begins EVOLUTION.

Did all reptiles evolve from two fish? All birds from two reptiles? All humans from two primates?

Again, illusions were born of words. For some species are neither fish nor fowl. And some humans act inhumane. The more universal that our vision is, the more individual we are, until "identity" (One God within) is realized.

The role that spirit plays in evolution was clouded over by fights between religionists and scientists; each group thought that the other's order was beyond its own official border.

The main fear of religion (hell fire) was the greatest tool and the worst threat of science. And so, we had our Armageddon metaphor.

Various groups of homonids who conquered fire evolved further in "the Word," courting "the Life" that is eternal. And even though some branches of evolution fell away, we were headed to Heaven via NASA, a generic term for future spaceships.

So — when man took his first baby steps on the moon, how was it that woman had sent him there?

It was not a passive acceptance that brought human females in line the moon. Her hormones first had to tune in to moon cycles. But this tuning in by the spirit was ignored by Darwinism. In the hormonal chaos caused by fire, woman chose a light that was both subtle and reflected.

Seasonal changes in sunlight's intensity had influenced sexual cycles of animals. Yet moonlight had its effect mostly on higher primates.

Seasonal, moon related, and evolutionary cycles overlapped with spiritual, individual, and mood cycles. Then, the influence of fire light (techno) interfered with the influence of sunlight which had dominated female sexual cycles before the use of fire.

To bring moonlight into dominance, woman made a leap of spirit. And when her moon cycles held, she re-ordered culture. With sexual intercourse possible (to some extent) every day of the year, hers was a whole new ball game.

The melatonin that triggers hormones got mixed signals from the direct light of fires. And so, reflected moonlight enabled women to *switch* her subtle sources as Eve was branded a *witch*.

According to the Jewish Talmud, Adam's wife, before there was an Eve, was Lilith, a snake-like woman. And the snake is related to human sexual mythology due to its sensitivity to light in the pineal gland, its hidden center eye.

So, split-level consciousness with regard to the moon has taken **refuge** in abstraction. We pay rent in 12 monthly cycles. And "to rent" means "to tear." For the seasonal cycles of women were rent by woman's adaption to moonlight.

Monogamy, monotheism, and money came together in this primal "renting" of woman. And the ancient word for "light" (OR) is in the WHORE.

We celebrate Easter, Passover, and Ramadan by cycles of the moon. We have 12 apostles, 12 tribes of Israel, and 12 tribes of Ishmael, as sections in our One-God religions due to struggles with the moon. But a bit more than 12 full moons appear each year. This movement toward 13 is where the numb number-man begins to doubt his fate, and where saviours and madmen seem to rate.

The shift to moonlight made by woman's mind gave "moon" and "mind" the same linguistic roots. And "mensa" was hers to beget a lasting race of "men" who could know her "meaning."

The English word *lust* (sexual desire) is linked to *luster* (shining by reflected light) due to the light-roots in the language of the Angles.

Once we see that men and women long ago chose their roles to create the Techno State, it will be easier to forgive each other and move on. In Phase Three E-quality, we each have a love that lasts forever, a spirit-flame within.

In a later chapter entitled "The Real Magic." we explore the elevation of sexual energy to the level of spiritual pleasure. In fact, there is no real separation once the mind is clear.

The Joys of Estrus

Estrus is a sexual excitement that comes to female mammals seasonally. In estrus (heat) females lure prospective partners by giving off body scents and striking provocative poses.

Since estrus never fully gave way to menses in humans, a women's body still negotiates with her spirit before she makes up her mind to have sex.

With the menstrual cycle, woman took control of sexual frenzy. Capable of sexual decisions, she harnessed a most subtle tool of social ORder, the female ORgasm, to ORganize civilization.

The vagina is pivotal in female anatomy so that evolving from rear-mounting mammals was made easy. Face to face sex put the male and female light-sensitive pineal glands together, a step that sent energy spiraling into orgasmic couples. Only a union of spirits spanning the ages could have drawn our combined anatomy through unto its present design. Our delight is sharing the light itself, as we evolve in love.

As we travel into space, we shall make another adaptive leap; to Earthly men who worship the Lord, "the Word" will speak to the Wife, "the Life" that is eternal. For these linguistic patterns play together in an eternity of cycles.

Among baboons, gorillas, and macaques, a strong male dominates the group. He claims sexual rights to the females. The struggle between males is evident. Human females, however, have taken pains to move evolution into the psychic realm.

Psychic energy is named for Psyche, the goddess who burned her lover Cupid with the flaming oil of a lighted lamp. And "psychology" was a religion designed to divert human instincts so as to serve the Techno State (as we shall see in a later chapter on psychology).

Most people have no idea of how limited our emotions have become due to our supression of the fear of fire. Some feelings will be set free due to changes in philosophy, but the center of change will be around our use of fire.

The Armageddon prophets had a fatal weakness. They overlooked an ancient wisdom in the heart of all womankind. For women are naturally emotional when it comes to having babies.

Most women attached to the Armageddon movement were less convinced of its doctrine than the men. The notion that true believers were to be taken in the rapture, scooped up by the hand of God the Father, had no room for endless generations of yet unborn grandchildren's grandchildren.

The Armageddonists believed that all desire for procreation would cease once "the Lord had come." So, dominant males in Armageddon groups could rant from pulpits about the Christ against Anti-Christ while females were secondary in their drama.

In their hearts, women knew that being born in the flesh was no less respectable than being born in the spirit.

A weak link in the Fundamentalist-Charismatic Evangelical alliance was "Praise the Lord" where Jim and Tammy Bakker shared the spotlight. Other preachers kept their wives on the sidelines.

And Jimmy Swaggart paid to see a naked woman while a family in a nudist camp would be scourned by Armageddonists for being in "the occasion of sin." In general, laws against public nudity were enforced while laws against selling narcotics in public were not. Swaggart's thoughts got trapped in the techno mind-set that had not integrated with a true love of biology.

Still, a spirit in the flesh of every pregnant woman knows her bio-clock will never be stopped for some to be saved while God the Father punishes sinners. Women who bear children who will bear children who will bear children have instincts that reject the Armageddonist theory that would break our biological continuum.

And Christ is not only in "the Word," Christ is in "the Life," and in the union of Lord and Wife. This is the realization of the New Age that is the New Millennium.

Darwin's theory does not explain how a loin cloth on a monkey added to its survival. The Bible does not say why righteous people have "private parts." Do saints wear robes in Heaven? Do snakes and nakedness relate to "private proper-ty"? "Naked" is a perfect past tense of s-nake. For a snake gave birth to the goddess of sexual energy (kundalini). But we hid our sex and lost identity. We cooked our food and fed an un-conscious mind-set that other animals did not possess.

The symbols of the 1987-1988 Wed-tech scandal were clear in our fire-torn Je-R-usa-L-em.

Congressman **Biaggi**, indicted in the case, had an Italian name meaning "blazes." The Armageddon gang had gone to hell with Reagan-ethics. Adolfo **Calero**, the CIA-appointed Contra leader, had a Spanish name meaning "lime burner," and he played a devil in the drama of Old Nick.

The first Congressman to die of AIDS was named **McKinney**, from the Irish "*Cionadh*," meaning "fire-spring." Humanity had wedded technology. We have seen how **Fiers, Burns, Weld, Risque**, and a batch of **Bakers** were tied into 666's inferno.

"The vectors of two seemingly unrelated scandals intersected this week at an East Bronx Church, appropriately named the Cross Road Tabernacle," said the *N.Y. Times* (6/5/87), touching the surface of a deeper symbolism. The scandals of Jim Bakker and Edwin Meese met at the Cross Road Tabernacle, where both were nibbling at the daily bread.

Mrs. **Cortese**, minister at the Cross Road, had a name that meant "courtesy" and implied "a day of grace for payment of a bill of exchange." In Spain, a *cortese* was customary in business.

The "seemingly unrelated" vectors referred to by the Times were bills exchanged for days of grace when Bakker gave the Cross Road money that PTL said was intended to pay "the sign of the cock," Ms. **Hahn**. And the metaphor continued in the story that Wed-tech paid the Cross Road's Mrs. Cortese who was the sister of Congressman Gar-cia.

The Many Layers

Two Armageddon conspiracies met at Cross Road
Tabernacle. *Biaggi* (blazes), 18 years in Congress, was
indicted for extorting $3.6 million in Wedtech (a military
supplier) stock.[1] And the Cross Road pastor paying-for-
grace Cortese was linked to Praise-the-Lord Bakker by
sign-of-the-cock *Hahn*. Also, the brother of Cortese was
Gar-cia. **Garcia** means "one who carries a spear." And we
will see more about the spear and crucifixion later.

Many inferences can be drawn from the Wed-tech
scandal that fit into our metaphor.

Another link was Jose **Cruz** (cross). Mr. Cross had
supported the Sandinistas, crossed over to the Contras, and
then crossed his name off the list of combatants. The news
of Cruz's resignation said to Congress that the Contras
were undemocratic. And so, a bill was introduced to delay
Contra aid for 180 days.[2]

"One source of conflict between Colonel North and Ms.
Hall," said the *Times* (2/26/87), "was her romantic
involvement with Arturo Cruz," son of the Contra leader.
Fawn Hall, had an English station-name, "servant in the
hall." Fawn's first name was that of a pretty, if not too
shrewd animal. And fawning over Ollie North, she
shredded her faith in the U.S. Constitution.

North asked Hall to stop dating Cruz. And the affair
between "the servant" and "the cross" ended within months.
Fawn (the 18th witness at Contra-gate) said she shredded
12 to 18 pages at a time for Colonel North. And "the
Word" in their case had lost "its Life."

In July 1988, as the Pentagon insider-trading scandal
broke, Thomas **Gunn** (with McDonald Douglas marketing)
was accused of rigging the multibillion dollar F-18
contracts (*NY Times* 7/7/88).

Man's sublimination of sexual energy to fire power
traverses both sub-human and sublime. These name's give
only a simple outline.

(1) NY Times 6/4/87, (2) NY Times 3/10/87

313

Since "the Word" is the Christ and "the Life" is the Christ, what on Earth is "the Anti-Christ"?

"Untruth" is the enemy. But how can a husband be true to his wife if she is untrue to her word? And how can a wife be true to her husband if he endangers her life?

The answers are in the practice. The Crystal law focuses your body and spirit in a space from which your mental decisions are clear.

The Armageddon gang was forced to shred and eat its words. Those women who followed blindly toward "the rapture" knew that some daughters wanted to bring daughters into the physical world. And the contra-diction was apparent. For as we overcame our pre-historic fear of fire, beyond the verbal chaos was a real fear to limit fire's use.

The Armageddon gang was true to something. Its men held to nations as extentions of family. For a "husband" was house-bound by definition. And woman inverted male combative instincts to protect "her family" from which grew "his nation."

Now, with his ape-like territoriality co-opted, our combined male-female task is to transform "the spirit of family" into a global happening. The husband now lives in an eco-sphere house.

The world (wer-alt means "old man") is turning once again. The SON (made equal to the SUN) used fire for our space adventure.) And war lost its sense of direction on Earth.

The conquest that had generally traveled west was complete. This was the message of NAM. And man was to return to the east (not a place) in his mind. Easter is the bright and morning star. For Linguistically, East and West have never really been places. And philosophically, humanity has one political direction — true democracy.

NASA announced (7/8/88) that its 180-foot booster rocket was being readied to go to Mars.

And two stars shall guide us beyond: "the Word" in "the Life," the Lord and the Wife telling their eternal story, written in blood.

CHAPTER 36

THE REAL THING

Could the sin of Adam ever be overcome? Would the covenant of circumcision get humanity to heaven? Had the bread and wine of Jesus been enough to get us through? Will irradiated food feed the astronauts? Or is our servitude to the Techno State about to be re-deemed?

"Suddenly the feeling grabs you. You can't control your feet, at McDonald's." You can't? "Control gives your will power all the help it needs." *Control* is a diet pill. Do you need Control? "You can't get enough of the heavenly stuff in Oreo Cookies and Cream." You can't? "Dannon Yogurt, bet you can't say no." You can't? As for potato chips, "Bet you can't eat just one!"

TV ads from top psychologists hitting at sales resistance used effective ploys, so the erosion of will power is now epidemic. And the drug problem is treated by Oprah and Donahue talk shows between these anti-will commercials.

"N-e-s-t-l-e-s, sweet dreams you can't resist." "Betty Crocker, "I'm a fool for your chocolate, I go out of control." "Enjoy the guilt." TV food ads did the front-line work, waging war against the public will. And amid the anti-will campaigns, a drug crisis mounted.

So, the USA called out the Coast Guard, spent millions to target foreign governments, put metal detectors in public schools, and wondered what had gone wrong with those drug-addicted children.

The trouble was reflected in our abuse of words. And the problem had begun so long ago that nobody alive today was to blame. We were the victims of original sin. As with Alice in Wonderland, our garden and its language were driving us insane.

"Nobody doesn't like Sara Lee," was a slogan on TV. Was Sara like Alice in Wonderland? Did she eat a piece of pastry and quite forget how to speak good English? Or had market research found that double-negatives could somehow sell twice as many cakes and cookies?

Of course, the will of the public shifts with changes in public grammar. But were the ads just plain fun or was there an ad conspiracy?

Salada Tea was "naturally" decaffeinated while we had no legal meaning for "natural."

Tropicana said, "You'll swear you squeezed it yourself." Swear? The juice was pasteurized! In other words, it was cooked, not at all like juice that you would squeeze yourself.

Ocean Spray said real grapefruit juice was bad to taste. Their juice cocktail, also pasteurized, had cooked citric acid. And fresh citric acid is best for calcium assimilation. "Ocean Spray Pink, it's not what you think," said the ad. Then Ocean Spray was brought up on a felony inditment for polluting sewer systems (1/28/88). What processes were used that polluted the sewers?

Did it matter that TV could say with impunity that pasteurized orange juice had "nothing added and nothing taken away"? After all, people could read labels, couldn't they?

Many "food" commercials were aimed at viewers to instill confusion by means of tricky grammar. And the TV ads had a cumulative effect, an effect particularly dangerous to children.

"Post Fruit and Fiber tastes so good, you forget the fiber." Why did Post spend so much money to suggest that you forget? And why were the best of fruits and vegetables not seen daily on TV all year round?

Since packaged cereals made more profit for the food broker than organically-grown raw fruits and vegetables, the broker promoted broken enzymes. The market in organic foods was more direct with far less profit per pound of good whole food.

See Your Local Grammarian

In the techno mind-set, processing implied "value added."
Food that was "serviced" had techno snob appeal. And
taste, in the cultural sense, was used to subvert our true
bio-sense of taste.

Market analysts knew not why Post had fiber to forget.
Like Sara Lee and Alice, "nobody didn't care why."

Does Nabisco Foods, which merged with Reynolds
Tobacco, care for your health? The ads explain the
industry's standard, anti-grammatically.

"Wrigley extra-sugar-free gum is extra-fresh," is a
sentence devoid of meaning. "Only Skippy has half the
added sugar," leads one to ask, "compared to what?" If "all
the world loves M&M's," why pay so much to advertise?

"I'd like to buy the world a Coke," sounds odd. Who
could buy anything for the entire world?" Had God made
Coke our new Christmas present?

Coke made so much profit that it could pretend to be an
advocate against world hunger. And people on junk food
were starving for nourishment.

The two-dimensional images on our TV sets had the
awesome power of one-way communication. And we
supplied the imagination. We gave the tube a power over
us that was legally out of control. For the FCC was
concerned with "dirty words," not with the rape of a
nation's grammar. Still, the public has legal precedent for
action.

The word "inflammable" is no longer used in ads or
labeling since its meaning is not clear. In English,
"flammable" and "inflammable" mean the same. An item
that can be inflamed is "inflammable." But many people
thought "inflammable" meant "not-flammable." So, in
labeling, we have made the word "inflammable" illegal. It
can be that simple.

Now, "non-flammable" and "flammable" are the correct
opposites under a law that dictates good grammar. So, as
we place more value on bio-produce and see food as
equally in need of protection as our toys and artificial
Christmas trees, similar laws can be passed for food
commercials.

The "you-can't-resist" approach is more direct and personal in food ads since food is so emotionally charged. Still, we can establish uniform laws. We have precise garment labels and at the same time we have lax labeling of irradiated foods. All we need do is balance out the techno and bio mind-sets. And in the beginning is "the Word."

Since "pasteurized" is not "fresh," to prevent pasteurized (cooked) milk and fruit juices from being called "fresh" in TV ads, a legal definition of terms can easily be legislated. A workable definition already exists. Consider "fresh water" as opposed to "salt water." Also, "fresh" means "not stored." Our grammar tells us clearly that there are no "fresh roasted peanuts" only those that are "freshly roasted." And even "freshly" is too confusing for a labeling law.

The Hershey Company called itself a maker of chocolate and other foods, implying that chocolate was a food, not a drug of the cocoa plant that had drastic effects on children and adults alike. Was alcohol a food? Cocaine? Coffee?

It is not difficult for cocaine users to admit they are hooked on drugs. A coffee drinker is more resistant. Still, systematic laws for food ads can be made just as laws to regulate ads and labels for electrical appliances have been made.

Most science-fiction written in Phase Two told of future space-ships where "food" appeared by magic. Technology will feed humanity, said techno theorists. We had failed to calculate the effect of techno food on psychology, effects of mind on spirit, and effects of spirit on our ability to find the peace that is necessary to telepathically control machines. Brain waves are real electric impulses that we shall eventually learn to use in technical programming.

"Technology" and "techno" as used herein refer to the chain of processes that sprang from the use of fire. Agriculture (probably begun before the use of fire) can evolve without chemo-sprays or petro-fertilizers. We can feed humanity naturally, with powerful tractors to plow the fields. Yet, we need no techno toxins in our foods. For such toxins also disturb our brain waves.

I talk to the trees. And I hear them answer.

The word "orator" (public speaker) has common roots with "horticulture" (gardening). And humans also serve as messengers for plants.

Just as bees gathering nectar pollenate plants, so humans eating fruit spread seeds around the globe. We keep trees alive just as trees keep us alive. And the Tree of Life must have the Tree of Knowledge (Good needs Evil) to carry the plan of this planet unto other planets. So, humanity, the only animal who can tend the Tree of Knowledge, is needed for this transportation work.

This greater plan makes clear all our Phase Two confusions. Ending Phase One, the garden itself told us to go forth. But there was no division of spirit, only a new plateau of life. And Phase Two humans used biology to feed the Techno State. So, our techno experiment began in order to save the Tree of Life from the final fire that will come with the dying of the sun.

Money is such a confusing item because it was invented to regulate the Techno State. Biology evolves quite well with no money at all. But now as we begin Phase Three, many schemes will arise wherein money will be said to redeem biology.

The Techno State claims to "naturalize" people when new citizens are actually "nationalized." "Natural" (from "nativity") means "to be in the cycles of birth," innately biological. We used money (unnatural, but a nationalizing power) to trick the monkey inside us. And now, beyond the money illusion, we can still use currency as a bookkeeping agent to keep curent with our global eco-resolution.

Much technology in the final days was only for the purpose of "making money." We had set out to genetically engineer potatoes to have "the protein value of meat" (*C.S. Monitor* 6/1/88), cashing in on the myth that we needed more protein. Much of our "science" was still ignoring biology. And much techno research was directed at problems that could be resolved bio-logically.

Glucose made in labs appears identical to glucose extracted from plants. But an equation that says lab glucose equals plant glucose is invalid. For the glucose in a living plant has an unfractured factor that is "life" itself; and to label such a substance "natural" is a fraud.

Equations are always built on factors. And since "life" is a factor, legally, the label "natural" must mean "related to nativity" — meaning "innately biological."

When you eat a piece of fruit, its sugars are already dancing with its enzymes. And so, your living enzymes join in their dance of life.

Remember, salt is mined and is not "organic." Sugar grows and is "organic." So, salt cannot be labeled "natural." Salt has no nativity. At first, this may sound like an overly strict rule of usage, but to develop labeling laws for foods, "life" must be our priority. A food is not fully "organic" unless grown with organic fertilizers, the products of life.

Many states have rules to define "organically grown food." Still, we need organized growers, a national campaign to educate, and equal air time on TV to get the word out to consumers.

"Tropicana, nothing added, nothing taken away," said the TV set. But pasteurization "*adds*" enough heat to "*take away*" the function of its enzymes. The "nature" of its proteins has been traded for added "shelf-life."

The implied-warranty law says that a radio, if sold as a radio, must function as such, not just look like a radio. This law, already on the books, can also be applied to food.

Enzymes ripen fruits, but do not function if pasteurized. So, unless pasteurized juice is labeled "Toy Food" (as we must label a toy radio), it violates the implied warranty law.

If a label says, "5 grams of protein," a buyer should get functional protein. And the function of protein is living — "natural" and "organic."

Terms such as natural, organic, fresh, and whole must be reserved for items that are just that. Fractured proteins must be so labeled. And each label should be seen as a legal contract.

Grape Nuts claimed to be "all natural, nothing added" though heat far over 130°F cooked every flake, acting as a preservative. The flakes were pulverized — not whole.

Jane Brody (of *the NY Times*) wrote in 1985 that "more than half the foods we eat are processed and packaged." She also said that foods of the future would be packaged to "preserve freshness" and that "irradiation sterilizes food and extends its lifetime," Jane, like Alice, lacked good English in the use of "freshness" and "lifetime."

"The Food Industry" was the largest industry in the USA with 18 million workers (*Vegetarian Voice*, Winter 1982), most of whom were sacrificing food to the Techno State. And new items of "aseptically packaged" foods sold 1.8 billion units the year 666 began his second term (*NY Times* 1/27/88).

Cooked foods were pre-served to the gods of fire, and humans ate the left-overs from altars (stoves and ovens) where we sublimated ire.

Foods were cooked, canned, then cooked again in the can. Federal law required this second cooking to stop the growth of botulism, which is destroyed by five minutes cooking at a heat of 212°F. Since enzymes die at only 130°F, all canned proteins are fully denatured, totally dead. Canned "proteins" are not functional proteins at all. So, no canned foods are rightfully labeled "no preservatives," "natural," "whole," or "organic."

But the drive to label foods improperly is a reminder of the great power of words. Our first currency, in any market, is language itself.

THE VERY FIRST
ARTIFICIAL PRESERVATIVE
EVER ADDED TO FOOD
WAS FIRE

Beginning 666's second term, Federal Drug Police made "more than 1800 drug-related arrests."[1] Also, the Bureau of Alcohol, Tobacco and Firearms (a terrible combination) prohibited beer labels from mentioning alcoholic content.[2]

The Seagram's Company slipped their ad into the TV mainstream. "One part Seagram's and two parts fun," said the whiskey manufacturer. The ad was "legal" for it showed a soft drink. But the jingle mentioned only "Seagram's," identified by most people as a whiskey. And "Mr. Boston Bartender's Guide" was sold via TV to get brand name exposure for another liquor manufacturer.

In 1980, Reagan ceased to enforce the Fairness Doctrine. Lobbies advocating nuclear power, for instance, could buy advertising time without fear that equal time would be granted by the FCC to anti-nuclear advocates.

Reagan's FCC had skirted the Fairness Doctrine almost completely. And the year after 666's Second Coming, to sell their ideas on public policy via TV, special interests spent $1.8 billion.[3]

The issue of "fairness" was obvious in debates over nuclear power. But we had no serious TV talk about junk food versus good food. Cooking shows were in vogue. To argue against cooking would have been an attack on our oldest techno-religious practice, a slur against "apple pie."

Words are the key. But suddenly a feeling grabs you. You can't control your feet at McDonald's. You can't control your TV's propaganda.

Some seemingly good foods were in ads. But even the raisins (grapes) were grown by agro-business toxic-spraying corporations. And most TV food was processed beyond bio-recognition.

Small organic farmers have little access to the airwaves. Now, in Phase Three, Federal subsidies, in fairness, can provide the needed balance.

(1) Newsweek 2/25/85, (2) NY Daily News 6/17/85, (3) NY Times 8/10/86

ADVERTISING MUST BE CONSTRUED
AS THE INITIATION
OF A LEGAL CONTRACT
WITH THE PUBLIC

The terms of ads must be legally definable. We already have the grammar. We need only apply it with prudence. Since "fresh" means "not salted" (fresh water) and "not stored," a food must be readily perishable to be legally "fresh."

AS THE INITIATION OF A LEGAL CONTRACT
ADVERTISING LANGUAGE MUST MAKE SENSE

The "Oh oh, Spaghetti-O's" ad aimed at children contained such non-sense programming phrases as "more lean beets," conditioning future shoppers to accept illogical constructs. Young scientists raised on TV returned to labs after eating lunch-time junk food, with fractured-enzymes in their brains to make junk science.

"Although prices of wheat, sugar and other agricultural products are sorely depressed," said *the New York Times* (7/28/85), "many experts say they represent the latest hope for the third world." The "experts" had put wheat and processed sugar at the top of their shopping list. But financial success would bring eventual economic disaster.

The "success" of tobacco, coffee, marijuana, and coke showed that techno finance, not bio economy, was defining the market place.

Public transportation was strewn with liquor ads, cigarette ads, and cold pill ads while police became embattled with graffiti artists.

The public mind-set was being auctioned off to the highest bidder. And communities that would not allow nudity on a bill board would allow the techno rape of our biological system. Studies show that murals in tranquil colors in public places would cut violent-crime rates in half. But we had been driven to sacrifice our children to the techno mind-set's cigarette, coffee, and aspirin ads.

So many ads used poor grammar, they were a threat to our linguistic foundations. "Free" speech was being pushed out of the market place by those who paid people to lie to the public. And the lying TV ads made their falsehoods sound "funny."

But legal contracts should not fool around. For ads that substitute for comedy diminish both and rob the public of true humor.

Undermining the public will is a despicable form of treason. For the ability to survive as a group depends on meaningful communication. Video helps us grow together technically. And by removing its linguistic violations, violence on TV will seem out of place; for the lack of free will and the use of violence go hand in hand.

Also, children will more likely learn to read when they expect the truth from society. Note that the drop-out rate begins as children become old enough to know that they have been lied to.

The legal guidelines can be clear: an ad may not proclaim that which is untrue, and messages must be grammatical. This is the minimum to require when initiating a contract with the public.   Still, TV ads can be fun. It may take more creativity to have a good time with the truth. But like having a party with no alcohol or other drugs — it's easy with a little practice. And the truth, in fact, will set us free — creatively.

Our next chapter shows truth can be found even when hidden in falsehoods. Lies are always disconnected, but any truth is joined to every other truth. It is this organic linkage that makes the Language Crystal work. The numbers are not separate once we see that they are products of thought and know that thought connects the body to the spirit.

Lies require ever more hype and dazzle. But the truth is not only obvious when realized, it is fascinating. And like all of nature, the truth, the real thing, is amazing.

CHAPTER 37

IT HAPPENED ON THE 18TH

"If my notes are accurate, and I made that notation of the 18th on the 18th, the idea at least occurred to me as early as the 18th," said Oliver North.

On the pivotal date of 11/18/85, it was decided that Hawk missiles be shipped by Israel to Iran and replenished from the USA to Israel. North said the first afternoon of his Contra-gate testimony, "This all came out of a mutual understanding among the Israelis, General Secord, and myself, and probably Admiral Poindexter, and Mr. McFarlane."

Only 18 Hawk missiles out of 120 intended were in the shipment to Iran due to a loading problem with the air-carrier, said North. So, the symbolic "18 Hawks" was a mere coincidence.

Yet in our mystical puzzle, "18 Hawks" was the perfect symbol to draw 666 into the Gulf.

Also by sheer coincidence, as corroborated by other testimony, November 18th 1986, a year later, was noted (coincidentally in Exhibit 18) as the date when North began his part in the cover-up:

"It appears to be a note that I took at 18:00 [hours] on the 18th, a call from Mr. Armitage," said North under questioning. Senate counsel Nields had posed the question in the morning session.

Nields: "From the Defense Department?"

North: "Yes."

Nields: "And it has opposite, it says, 18:00, call from Armitage" (Arm-it-age, a person's name).

The numbers brought the names into focus. And even as I coppied down these messages, at times I could not believe what had come to pass.

The Jews saw Moses perform miracles. And the followers of Jesus saw him raise the dead. Yet, I was witnessing a miracle on a new plateau. And it took some time before I saw that "the Word" was crystallizing anew.

Discussing Israeli shipments and replenishment, Nields established that North's points of contact in succession were: Koch (pronounced Cook), Armitage (Arm-it-age), and Powell (dweller near a pool). Two of these are new to our puzzle, yet the trio bridges Armageddon to Aquarius.

Nields: "Isn't it the case that on the 18th, the day that you received three telephone calls inquiring about the Arms Export Control Act raising questions of legality, that you started changing the chronologies in order to deal with that question."

North: "No. No. The answer is, the short answer is, No. I think the chronologies had already started to be changed. I think my initial imput from Mr. McFarlane predates this."

Unless a lie is well rehearsed and edited (as in most commercials), the culprit usually gets caught up in attempts to justify by twisted grammar.

North's double denial and one more denial were followed then by an "I'm sorry" (see below).

Since, to my knowledge, each sound I make is a product of my entire being, I do not judge lightly the words of others. So, the final judgment is up to you (the reader). So, listen closely and be sure to read between the lines.

Nields: "If you turn to page, excuse me, that is a version of the chronology on the 18th of November, at one o'clock in the afternoon. Is that correct?"

North: "That's correct."

Nields: "And if you turn to page four."

North: (Clears his throat) "I'm sorry."

Nields: "If you turn to page four, third full paragraph, last sentence of the paragraph, you will see that there is an explicit mention of the Arms Export Control Act for the first time. And it says, 'The total value of this shipment was less than $2 million and therefore below the threshhold for required reporting of a military equipment transfer under the Arms Export Control Act.'"

But $2 million was part of an $18 million sum. So, North repeated, "I'm sorry."

Nields: "So, whoever is drafting these chronologies is now taking account of the Arms Export Control Act requirements."

North: "Correct."

Nields: "But there are a couple of problems, I take it. One is that the Hawk transaction was well over $2 million. Isn't that true?"

North: "That's true. But it didn't happen quite the way it was intended to happen. The Hawks eventually ended up back in Israel." (Remember, that was 18 Hawks.)

Nields: "But over $2 million was paid to Israel. Indeed, $18 million was paid to Israel."

North: "I'm sorry" (intoned as a question).

Nields: "Isn't that correct? $18 million was transferred from the Iranians to the Israelis and then later returned. Isn't that true?"

North: "I do not know if that's true or not."

Nields:"I believe it's mentioned in your PROF message which was not deleted."

North: "That old delete button. I-I-I, I'm not denying that, Mr. Nields. What I'm saying is that what you just told me about money being transferred didn't come to the United States, I don't believe."

As Oliver North was testifying, 666 appointed Loeffler ("spooner," a table servant) instead of Abrams (whose testimony was damning) to lobby "to ask Congress for 18 more months of aid to the Contras" (*NY Times* 7/9/87).

Contra military-aid became legal October 18th, 1986. A new 18-month package sought a year later ($270 million) was $180 million yearly; but 666 would not be in office after 18 months.   A techno 666 (not the bio Reagan) foretold his own symbolic "death" by saying, "over my dead body," with regard to Judge Bork's defeat. Two day's later, he said he would defend Contra-aid "with my dying breath." These were not normal remarks from Reagan. And for those who were really listening, Armageddon was nearing its close. Given life by symbols, Armageddon was dying symbolically.

Did the Fifth Commandment of the Israelites, "Thou Shalt Not Kill," also protect Egyptians"? Or was it meant to safeguard only "true" believers?

Oliver North called Abu Nidal "the principle foremost assassin in the world today," and said Nidal planned to assassinate him (North).

With his new security gate, North said he felt like "a European potentate." But North-gate became an issue because its gift status was covered up by documents falsely dated "May 18th" by North.

Israel meant "struggle with God." North stood on his head for Reagan-666, a struggle in symbolic fathering. And in Arabic, *Abu Nidal* meant "father of struggle." Also, North called himself "this kid" (a sacrifice). And three One-God religions tugged at Je-R-usa-L-em.

Like male monkeys who kill the babies of females captured from other groups — human males kill babies and call it "patriotism."

North invoked the name of God but not the name of Jesus in his testimony. As a Charismatic, — "the kid" had a covert mission. He was willing to die for his country, even to commit suicide in the line of duty. And the idea of being assassinated intrigued him, so long as his young daughter was not harmed.

Abu Nidal ("father of struggle") swore he would kill North after the Libya bombing in which the 18-month-old adopted daughter of Moammar Qadaffi ("long live the warrior") was killed. And North protected his own blessed virgin at home.

Caught up in the struggle, we seldom see the imagery. We imagine ourselves beyond the law of karma. Yet, only a view from beyond shows the balanced forces that once seemed to be "friend" and "enemy."

North's legal fees had mounted to $1.8 million by his first day of testimony (*NY Post* 7/8/87), a small debt to his lawyer friends so long as other friends would pay.

And in Iran, Israel, and the USA, each ruling group had a system to support "the patriarchs."

Natasha Simpson

The name "Natasha Simpson" became Colonel North's refuge and emotional battle cry. Natasha (a Russian Natalie) is from *dies-natalis*, "birthday of the Lord." Simpson is Son of Simeon, in Hebrew "Heard," the long-awaited son of Leah, Israel's first wife, who said, "the Lord hath heard" (Gen. 29:33), a meaning like that of Ishmael (God listens) the father of all Arabs, in our abstract metaphor.

North said, the morning of his second day, "One of the people killed in the Christmas massacre, and I do not wish to overdramatize this, but the Abu Nidal terrorist in Rome who blasted the 11-year-old American Natasha Simpson to her knees, deliberately zeroed in and fired an extra burst at her head, just in case. Gentleman," said North, "I have an 11-year-old daughter, not perhaps a whole lot different than Natasha Simpson."

He said he did not wish to over-dramatize the Christmas massacre, but the President had said several times that he wanted the hostages "out by Christmas" and North had a nervous breakdown in the Christmas season of 1974, years before.

A total of 18 died in the Christmas massacre, terrorists included. Christmas was so filled with confusing emotions because it marked the birth day of a child who would later be sacrificed. With its secrets and surprises, gifts were not to be opened before the appointed time. And the gift of Christmas, the body of Jesus, was opened by humanity 33 years later.

With all his donated bread, could North buy the gift of "security"? Could the USA buy its way out of fighting in "a dirty little war" with Old Nick? The mark of the beast was to allow us to buy and sell anything! Could 666 buy a Star-Wars shield to protect democracy?

With Reagan-ethics, farms failed, jobs declined in value, and only 18% of the work force remained in unions. Reagan claimed that the people did not want to expand the national parks. He had a weak spot for acid rain. And a general rape of the environment was licensed as the great patriarchs reveled in their pay day.

North's invocation of the name Natasha Simpson was a perfect way to call attention to the birthday of "Lord Hearing," each father's need to listen. For God the Father in our New Age is the form of every man. "The Father" in full consciousness is always true to "the Word."

When Oliver North said that Natasha Simpson was not unlike his own daughter, he spoke the most profound truth in all his testimony, but missed its wholeness. North did not see each little girl in Iraq, Iran, and Nicaragua as not unlike his daughter — not unlike Natasha Simpson.

Still, North was only a symbol in Armageddon. He was linked by the Book of Isaiah to trouble for Israel that comes "out of the North," the trouble that preachers said would come from Russia.

As Abram-Abraham had once hidden behind changes in his name to cast his son "God Listens" into the desert, so the Reagan-Regan-Casey-North-Owen-Channell-Poindexter-Nimrodi-Kashoggi-Ghorbanifar sacrifice of children had relied on an attempt to avoid global fatherly bio-responsibility.

Male apes who kill the suckling babies of their new mates do so because regularly nursing mothers do not get pregnant. Nationalism (from nativity to native language to native land) was not a matter of masculine or feminine direction; rather it was an extention of evolution.

Yet in Phase Three, nationalism leads to global unity. Our native land is the Planet Earth. And our native tongue is to serve biology as it commands technology.

A baby sees a flame and no warning voice comes from its spirit. For human nativity is more than a birth in the flesh. As natives of the universe, we are born without a fear of fire. So, our task now is to invent a balanced bio-techno native tongue, with respect for our fear of the flame.

An ABC poll, North's second day of testimony said 60% thought he was treated fair; 18%, too tough; and 18%, too soft. The nation was evenly (and mystically) divided over how much tribute to pay to "heroic secrecy." We were moving from an era of mystery toward demystification.

330

We saw in Latin that "apple tree" and "evil" are both *malus*, that "war" and "beauty" have common roots in *bellum*, and the paradox comes clear in the word for "word," which is *verbum*. For Romans feared "the Word."

In Latin, *verbera* means "to scourge." The roots of both "word" and "scourge" go back to the sacred laurel branch, used either as a crown for scholars or a whip for criminals. So, the crowning and scourging of Jesus is that much more poignant in this context of "the Word."

Was it heroic to throw our fears at others? In his-story, "hero" was an ambiguous word as techno rulers tried to cloak overproduction with verbiage about "security." North would face "assassination," but feared betrayal by "his cause." During the first week of his testimony, the Dow Jones *Industrial* Average (an element in his "heroic cause") rose by 18 points.

North spoke of his "superiors." So, his mind-set imagined his "inferiors," those whom he (as an instrument of the State) could liquidate. Iran's laws were barbaric; yet Khomeini was a "hero." Qadaffi thought Nidal was a hero. But a true hero is faithful to Hera, the goddess who was both wife and sister to Zeus, the god of fire. Here are the thoughts where our words originate.

Ares (god of war and father of the Amazons) was the son of Zeus and Hera, in our metaphor. And war was born from our indiscriminate use of fire. So, Ares was disfavored by his mother, for true heroes serve the goddess in all women.

A man who marries any one woman monogamously in the flesh must in fact marry all women in the spirit — and this means marrying the Goddess.

A "hero" does not traffic in heroin. And heroes do not "assassinate," a word from *hashhashin*, a person hooked on hashish. "Assassinate" has grand overtones because it comes from the pipe dreams of madmen. And children were never "assassinated," unless viewed as "royalty." Airlines list those who "die" in accidents, for "dying" is less violent than being "killed." And Phase Two "heroes" went to "war" but would never think of committing "murder."

In God's name, the secret team of 666 assassinated many a youth in the USA with drugs to get money for the Contras. And the secret team supplied the madmen in Iran with weapons, sent the profits to the Contra army, and claimed drug sales supported democracy.

The USA was central to the Crystal City due to its pursuit of true democracy. But the children of Iraq were bombed and Nicaraguan babies were slaughtered by what Colonel North said was a "a neat idea." Like Commies, Cappies made a killing in areas of instability.

Oliver North's testimony ended on the 6th day. And on that day, Robert McFarlane returned to refute North's testimony, saying, "Colonel North advised me on the evening of November 18th, 1986, *on the one brief occasion* when I was involved in the chronology process at all, that no one in the U.S. Government was aware that Hawks were involved in that shipment, until January 1986."

On November 18th, Poindexter asked McFarlane to come to his office. "And my total exposure to the Enterprise consisted of coming to his office the night of November 18th, and for about three hours time working on an opening statement the President was to use the next day," testified McFarlane in his contradiction of North, who said the 18th was devoted to "shredding as usual."

At the time of North's testimony, 18 pro bono lawyers were doing depositions (WBAI 7/9/87) for the Christic Institute to try the drug charges against the President's secret team.

Even after McFarlane told how the President's words came from those with the most to hide, he said that they were defending "democracy."

Of course, we live in a democracy. The people govern the nations. Police or soldiers may shoot the people, yet police and soldiers are born of the people. One difference in a true democracy is that people have access to ALL the facts, in labeling, in medicine, in politics, and so on.

"Lake Resources" (a water sign), the gun-running slush fund of North and company, had supported the war crimes of Iran and the Contras, but its funds were literally unaccountable. When Speaks stopped speaking for 666, Fitzwater took over; Atwater was made campaign manager for Bush (sign of the wine merchant) until Baker took over on August 18th. Armageddon and Aquarius had met.

A conspiracy theory about Reagan said his campaign team made a covert weapons promise to Iran in 1979 to postpone release of the hostages until after the 1980 presidential election. The fact that Israel began shipping arms to Iran in 1981 and that Israel had an agreement with the USA not to ship arms to any third country without approval led some to question if Reagan's team had not cut that deal with Iran in 1979.

McFarlane was a close friend of Senator Tower whose commission did not even mention the 1981-1984 Israeli arms shipments to Iran. And in Reagan's "debate-gate" mini-scandal, it was found that Casey and McFarlane on his campaign team had been concerned that the hostages taken under the Carter presidency might be set free "too early," giving Carter more votes.   Bani Sadr wanted all the hostages returned. But Rafsanjani (McFarlane's 1985 contact) blocked a return in 1980. And the hostages were freed only after Reagan's inauguration when Iran was sure he was in power. So the theory seems plausible. No great political upheaval was noted in Iran at that time. Yet, Iranian hostage policy changed suddenly. Why were the hostages released exactly at the time Reagan took office?

In what North called "the 18 acres known as the White House complex," Carter had great powers. But did "the Wise Men" of Iran tilt the election to favor 666? In Je-R-usa-L-em, a false pride allowed people not to see countless secrets festering in our strange trickle-down illiteracy.

Yet, democracy can spring only from a literacy that humanizes the Techno State, organically.

Natasha Simpson ("birth of the Lord, Heard") was meaningful in the tale of the Colonel who put himself above the laws of Church and State. North said his dog was poisoned, hinting he was under attack by Abu Nidal. But *the New York Times* (7/10/87) disclosed, "the dog had died of cancer." Ollie knew it was a sin to tell a lie but did not believe "the birth of the Word" should be "heard."

By the sixth day of North's testimony, the USA had shifted from "72% (four 18's) opposed to Contra aid" to being almost evenly divided. People who heard North on the radio or read his words were not swayed. But those who saw him on TV began to agree with his image emotionally — not literally.

Also, 18 (out of the 26) members on the Iran-scam committee had voted previously in favor of Contra aid. And many numeric coincidences touched on other facets of North's beliefs.   The Fundamentalists failed to get Creation Theory into public schools. And in a court brief, 72 Nobel Prize winners said such teachings threatened "scientific education."[1] And "Praise the Lord" ministry had $72 million in debts left by the Bakkers,[2] while 18 Federal investigators probed that case.[3] Spain would cancel treaties with the USA if 72 jet fighters were not removed from Madrid.[4] And the 72 Pershing I missiles in Germany were a pivot in USA-USSR arms talks.[5] Also, 108 Pershing II's were even more of an issue.

"North" was a key Armageddon symbol within the greater crystal structure. And so many 18's had spun around his 18 Hawks that only a meta-physical "cause" could have made this story possible.

Our next chapter documents a broader spectrum of images linked to the "trouble out of the North" prophecy, a metaphor of symbolic people on the edge of good and evil. Yet, its scope is almost beyond belief.

(1) NY Times 6/25/87, (2) NY Times 7/23/87, (3) NY Times 6/22/87, (4) NY Times 6/25/87, (5) NY Times 6/2/87

CHAPTER 38

DOCUMENTING THE IMPOSSIBLE

Once upon a time, in the USA's 108th baseball season, German scientists synthesized the 108th element[1] shortly before 108 hotly debated Pershing missiles began arriving in Germany from the USA.

Interest on the national debt under President 666 hit $108 billion per annum at that time.[2] And "economic growth in real terms" was later said to be 10.8%, for that same period.[3] A Buddhist-Hindu Buddhist magic number was slipping into gear with Judeo-Christian (-Moslem) politics in Je-R-usa-L-em.

In time for sales in the 108th baseball season, a book named *Salvador*, by Joan Didion, looked at some causes (real and symbolic) for military acts by the USA in El Salvador. The book, whose title means "Savior," has 108 pages.[4] And symbols in this chapter lay a foundation for joining these many metaphors together.

Three years after the 108th baseball season, the beast with powers to buy and sell saw a one day drop of 108.36 trigger the computer sell-offs to bring on a Wall Street crash in October 1987.

To regain our sanity, we are forsaking the myth that says, the Earth is to be destroyed before its time. We are ending the Armageddon story, forgiving the past, and claiming the future. As we align in present time with the forces of change, this chapter shows a statistical miracle to prove we have a crystal clear destiny — ever unfolding.

We need not be swaggered over, mutilated, or dunked in water by some surrogate of God. For each of us is born of woman with "the Word" within. And now, "the Life" that carries that vibration into eternity is crystallizing on a new plateau.

(1) Science News 4/21/84, (2) Kiplinger 2/10/84, (3) NY Times 10/20/85, (4) NY Times 11/24/83

"East" met "West" in the 108th baseball season. A Malaysian mystic danced through the streets of BE-RL-IN with 108 spears piercing his skin.[1]

Terrorism in Germany was linked to Iran through intrigues in the Holy Land. Ollie North was a key to Grenada, in the Achille Lauro intercept, and in Beirut. And the 108 marked his adventures. He was "a can-do officer willing to work 18 hours a day" (*NBC-TV* 12/12/86).

Ancient Aryan ghosts had surfaced from India to Iran, Germany to the USA.

The USSR walked out in Geneva on the day 108 Pershing missiles first began to arrive in West Germany.[2] And as the USSR and USA squabbled over missiles in Geneva, exactly 108 votes were cast in the United Nations denouncing 666's invasion of Grenada.[3] Geneva, center of the peace talks, was 108.9 square miles in area. Grenada's population was 108,000 when Reagan first accused the island of bearing the "Soviet and Cuban trademark."[4] And to complete the invasion came 6,000 troops "one for every 18 (of the 108,000) citizens."[5]

Before the Beirut massacre, 1800 Marines sent to Grenada were, in part, re-deployed to Beirut.[6]

As the Lebanese peace talks opened in Geneva on the 18th floor of the Inter-Continental Hotel, the Pentagon released its Grenada casualty list, 18 killed.[7] (One wounded died weeks later.) And the official death toll for marines in the Beirut truck-bombing had mounted to 216 (108 x 2) at the exact time 18 marines died in Grenada.[8]

Colonel North was on both sides of this split mission. A coincidence? Or the crystallization of prophecy?

The 18-foot ASAT antisatellite weapon,[9] touted to destroy by impact at 10,800 mps, was, at that time, only on the drawing boards for Star Wars.[10]

(1) Yoga Life, Winter 1984, (2) Newsweek 3/28/83, (3) NBC 11/3/83, (4) Time 4/19/82, (5) NY Post 11/23/83, (6) NY Times 10/25/83, (7) NY Times 11/1/83, (8) NY Times 10/26/83, (9) Time 9/2/85, (10) Newsweek 3/28/83

Formula 108

The 108 was to crystallize many realms (we shall see more) in a new union of dimensions.

$$3^3 \times 2^2 \times 1^1 \times 0^0 = 108$$

Three to the 3rd power (3 x 3 x 3) is 27. Two to the 2nd power (2 x 2) is 4. One to the 1st power (1) is equal to 1. And zero to the zero power (for those who meditate beyond quantum mechanics) is also 1. So, 27 x 4 x 1 x 1 equals 108.

Even the prose in the Grenada battle reports got carried away in images of "18." They crept up to "the quaint 18th century city of St. George's," said *the Times* report. And the Beirut marine post was likened to an outpost in NAM with 1800 dead and wounded.[1] *Newsweek* made bold of the 72 hours that Reagan (72 years old at the time) felt "all the burdens of his office."[2]

Marine Commandant Paul Kelly (54) airlifted 36 wounded marines from Beirut to Germany, full circle to meet the 108 Pershings.[3] Paul awarded Purple Hearts while Petra Kelly of West Germany's Green's led an anti-missile protest.[4] So, Petra and Paul wore contrasting shades of prophecy.

Previously, Reagan had said that he would halt the deployment of the 108 missiles. But Gromyko would not match the offer since the 108 were not yet in place. And in the process, the USSR vowed to keep ready their own 108 missiles targeted on China.[5]

Had the super-power leaders vowed to fight to the death with arsenals of magic numbers? Or had a Tantric crystal dagger pierced a rosary of skulls around the neck of the goddess Kali?

Remember, his-story was a single drama with its many acts divided by illusions.

(1) Time 11/7/83, (2) Newsweek 11/7/83, (3) NY Times 10/25/83, (4) Ibid 10/26 & 10/30/83, (5) Time 4/11/83

The static words that worked so well to order the realm of technology had left a mark upon biology. So, the Age of History in its seemingly separate circles was spiraling to a point of no return.

So-called "Hispanics" in the USA numbered 18 million[1] as Democrats said Reagan would get no more than 18% of "their" vote due to military policies in El Salvador.[2]

Reagan claimed the smallest price increases in 18 years.[3] So, he would win! Most homeless people would not cast a vote. The American (*Amery* means "industrious") Dream had gotten wound up in a faulty cash machine.

America means "industrious" since it was the role of "the New World" to bring NASA out of the ashes of our ancient Old World karma.

Democratic postcards pictured 18 soup kitchens and food stamp offices within 18 blocks of the White House.[4] But the message was lost as Reagan-ethics beat the drums of death for the march of the homeless.

After Reagan received an 18-month extension on the War Powers Act, news was released October 18th that 1800 Marines were on their way to Beirut, Lebanon. Meanwhile, the 18 official portfolios in the Lebanese Cabinet were being reorganized.[5] And Colonel North was reassigned to Grenada.

When "the Soviet Grenada" fell, unemployment in the USA was at 10.8%, a post-depression record. The Dow Jones reached a new high in sync, breaking records in a leap of 108.36, January 12th.[6]

And as noted in the first page of this chapter, toward the end of Reagan's 7th year, the Dow had a record drop of 108.36 that brought on the crash.

Do not confuse 10.8% unemployment in the 108th baseball season with the 10.8% "economic growth in real terms" that same year. The statistics were not geared to be understood biologically.

(1) U.S. News 8/19/85, (2) Time 9/12/83, (3) NY Times 10/10/83, (4) NY Times 9/27/83, (5) NBC 1/12/83, (6) NY Times 11/14/83

Humanity had tried to add up its own reality, but not all numbers were as real as others. A jet fighter bombed a 108-bed mental hospital in Grenada, killing 18.[1] And radio contact with "threatened" U.S. medical students was held for 18 hours.[2] Using medical students as an exucse for the invasion fit with our anti-bio mystery. And those insecure citizens of the USA who needed to consume were temporarily satisfied by consuming Grenada.

In the year of our 108th baseball season, the farmers of the USA applied 1,080,000,000 tons of pesticides to their crops.[3] This one billion eighty million tons was twice as much as 20 years before. And many pesticides had NOT been tested properly. Were the numbers telling a story?

Many ate DDT before it was banned. How many of those died of "a virus"? How many were declared "insane" due to toxins in the food chain? The answers can never be found statistically.

Iranian cash for the Contras was held in Geneva (another focus of 108's) in a clearing house for the firm that flew 666's sacrificial cake to Iran.[4] And another puzzle piece fell into place.

That Malaysian mystic's 108 spears showed self-control beyond bio limits. Synthesis of element 108 expanded the realm of matter. But we were also reaching the limits of expansion where biology and technology were in conflict.

We were living through our Armageddon. Bodies and spirits were indeed divided in that our minds would not bring them together organically.

By 1986, the arms for hostages deal had become a gun-running dope-smuggling scandal. As the 1987 investigation of North opened up, $108 billion was the Gramm-Rudman deficit goal. And at the root of anti-Palestinean racism on West Bank and in Gaza in Reagan's final year in office were 108,000 Arab workers who received about half of what Israelis received for the same kind of labor.[5]

(1) NY Times 11/14/83, (2) Newsweek 11/7/83, (3) New Yorker 6/2/86, (4) NY Times 12/3/86, (5) CS Monitor 5/4/88

In the Senate, only 18 votes were cast in favor of Reagan's Grenada news blackout.[1] Weinberger gave no press briefing till 36 hours after the Marine landing.[2] White House chief of staff James Baker said, "We have 1800 people accredited here . . . backbiting and scratching . . . the hue and cry would have been worse" if reporters were told.[3] Also, 18 rolls of film shot by the army were not returned until a full day had passed.[4]

The USA's occupation force, rented a "180-room resort hotel with tennis courts, a fresh-water pool and two bars." It was said, they were there to police the area since only "about 180 ill-trained and ill-equipped Grenadian police" were available to uphold the so-called "political order."[5]

President 666 cared not a whit for the 108 U.N. votes that condemned the Grenada invasion nor for the World Court judgment against the USA attempt to set up a puppet government in Nicaragua.

"Capitalism" used somewhat different means than "Communism," but both systems feared what would eventually bring them together, the advance of an organic democracy wherein the people will rule by direct and conscious communal participation.

The will of the people for a free democracy was falling to a plutocratic rule in the USA. Those 108 Pershings that threatened Russia were in turn threatened by "terrorists" in Germany so that $1.8 million was required to improve the "security" of the missiles themselves.[6] And Communists had their own forms of financial insanity.

The techno mind-set had cornered the market on money. Even after arms reduction was agreed upon, our military focus still took money away from our organic focus. It was sad but true; with toxins in our blood, we could not help but being hostile and a bit confused. Still, the signs were clear.

ARMAGEDDON HAD CRYSTALLIZED

(1) Time 11/14/83, (2) NBC 10/31/83, (3) NY Times 11/13/83, (4) Tom Brokow 10/31/83, (5) NY Times 7/22/84, (6) Time 5/13/85

Frozen Nuclear Crystals

As 108 (6 x 18) Hindu gods and Buddhist no-gods united in the .618 spiral of nature and 186,000 symbol of light's speed, we were about to draw our Armageddon drama to a close. The "super powers" on this planet were bio-spirit human beings. When we awaken to the fact, each of us is individually a living, breathing SUPER POWER.

In Reagan's first term, in the closest thing ever to a national-issue vote," an estimated 10.8 million voters, out of some 18 million voting, cast ballots for a nuclear freeze.[1] The people wanted peace. We needed only to become the vessles of that peace, organically.

Those 108 Pershings annoying the Russians had replaced 180 Pershing 1A's.[2] The manufacture of fewer weapons with greater force was a plan in both nations — arms reduction for increased destruction.

During the 108th baseball season, the Defense Department reported a U.S. nuclear medium-range, short-range, and naval weapons total of 10,800 warheads.[3] And "according to U.S. statistics, the Soviet Union had deployed a total of 360 SS-20's with a total of 1,080 warheads."[4] These reports, as you can see, appeared only days apart.

The following bit of repetition is only to focus on 666's "18 Hawk" connection.

Secretary of State Shultz said McFarlane told him in Geneva (108.9 square miles, where the USSR had walked out due to 108 Pershings when 108 U.N. votes protested the Grenada invasion) on the 18th of November 1985 that the 18 Hawks had been sent to Iran in trade for hostages. Now, I do not wish to overdramatize this point. But it seems to me that (in one way or another) we had caused all these events, so numbered, to come about.

Shultz also testified that on the 18th of November 1986 Mr. Arm-a-cost told him of the arms for hostages deal. And the next day, Shultz warned President Reagan not to say there was "no arms for hostages deal."

(1) Time 11/15/82, (2) Newsweek 10/24/83, (3) NY Times 11/15/83, (4) NY Times 11/19/83

Mon-ey in the Middle

When Reagan took office, "natural foods prices rose 10.8%," an increase 3% greater than for foods in general.[1] Inflation rates on medical costs reached 10.8% in his first year.[2] And Reagan's plan to cut Medicare played into the hands of hospital owners so profits were up, even though hospital Medicare patients had declined by a million from 1983 to 10.8 million in 1986.[3]

Our entire bio-sphere was hostage to the Techno State. Earnings of chemical companies in the USA (spewing forth a toxic cornucopia) totalled $10.8 billion the year 666 began his second term.[4]

Of course, we needed technology, but the techno mind-set's plan to feed us all on denatured foods plus drugs was an extention of our original sin. Certainly, we need fire, the Biblical caution was only not "to eat" its products.

As hostages to technology, we imitated our faceless captor. We had traveled so far from our primitive jungles that we forgot our direct link to the food chain. With all our worship of fire and fire-foods we were neglecting the fruits of photosynthesis.

We grew wheat to feed cattle and to sacrifice in bread. Yet grains are not basic primate foods. Wheat can be sprouted and eaten live in small amounts. But starting Reagan's second term, the Federal target for wheat was $1.08 per bushel for the harvest of the 108th baseball season.[5] For the worship of wheat had become a religion.

A military drive to root the USA in Old Nick and El Salvador was passively accepted by people in the USA who knew at gut level that the killing was done to insure future food supplies. Coffee and refined-sugar habits in the USA and USSR forced small nations to grow drugs (coffee, sugar, etc.) instead of foods to nourish local people. And the term "economic growth" was twisted to apply to areas that were forced into techno over-consumption.

(1) Vegetarian Times #47, (2) NY Times 7/10/84, (3) NY Times 3/29/87, (4) NY Times 8/15/85, (5) Time 2/18/85

342

Raspberries, Strawberries

The USA was the 108th nation including the Vatican to honor the Pope as an earthly leader when Ronald Wilson Reagan recognized the 108-acre Vatican City leader as a soverign head of state.[1]

Also, in the 108th baseball season, the Library of Congress began to use laser disks with 108,000 pieces of information each.[2] And Darryl Strawberry, number 18 on the New York Mets, was "rookie of the year." The USA cherished its diamond. One team faced another in a clean-cut ritual as 9 men on each of two teams (18 in the abstract) played out a cosmic sexual game by batting a ball to touch the goddess of fame. The Baseball Hall of Fame Vetern's Committee had 18 members. And, of course, each game began after the the singing of the National Anthem.

Among "a people" so symbolically patriotic, who would dare to poison a national symbol? A ban on Compound 1080 was lifted by 666. For Compound 1080 killed coyotes; but it also killed American Eagles, the symbols of free organic spirit.[3] So, 666 did use 1080 to poison a national symbol.

Personally, I was living as a hermit as these symbolic events were coming to pass. I read books on extra-sensory states, practiced japa yoga (bead work), and sat for hours daily waiting to find an entrance to the meditative state.

The message from John, my dyslexic friend, had given me a new way of life. A raw food vegetarian diet with no aspirin, coffee, refined sugar, alcohol, or other drugs was having a cleansing effect on my body-spirit.

When facts pertaining to this work were near, they fell into my hands. My spirit channel was the spirit ocean itself. Rather than change with drugs and give up my individuality, I had allowed my mind to flow into the mega-mind of "uni-verse."

(1) Time 1/23/84, (2) Innovations PBS April 1984, (3) Whole Life Times, April 1982

I had been asleep for less than an hour. Suddenly, the TV set drew me from my bed. Less than a minute after turning the TV on, I heard that a truck-bomb had killed 216 marines in Beirut.[1] The number was twice 108. I turned the channel and the same news came again. A bomb had killed 216 marines.[2]

Obviously, the death toll was official. Within a few hours, the press had documented that death toll synchronistically with the story of the Grenada invasion.[3] And I knew that I had been awakened to view the waves of crystallization.

That Beirut truck-bomb was foreshadowed by a car-bombing of Beruit's U.S. embassy on April 18th one year before. Both *Time* and *Newsweek* delayed their presses the week of the Beirut truck-bombing to cover the deaths of "at least 186 marines."[4] The body count had mounted. The first official count was 186, then twice 108 in sync with Grenada. And the final count in Beirut, after many days of digging, was tragically 218 Marine, 18 Navy, and 3 Army personnel.[5]

Then, for the first time in 18 years, the city of Saint Louis celebrated Veteran's Day.[6] Louis means "famous in battle." Could the fears that drove the USA into Viet Nam actually be rekindled.

Beirut truck-bombers could have been stopped by an iron pipe, 18 inches in diameter, meant for that purpose; but it was out of use, outside the U.S. Beirut-compound gate.[7] Also, Marine sentry post P6 was not manned, allowing the suicide truck to advance to within 66 yards of the dormitory. The murder scene ordered by Abu Nidal ("father of struggle") had an ominous touch of order within the prophecy of "trouble out of the North."

And I waited for the shadow of Je-R-usa-L-em to spread across the entire globe.

(1) Patrick Trese NBC Overnight 10/26/83, (2) Christopher Glenn CBS Nightwatch 10/26/83, (3) NY Times 10/26/83, (4) NY Times 10/25/83, (5) NBC 11/11/83, (6) NBC 11/11/83, (7) NY Times 10/28/83

In West Berlin, the Global Village Festival ended September 18th. And the spears in that yogi-dancer caused no bleeding nor infection. He had mental control over 108 spears as Gorbachev and Reagan later gained control over 108 Pershing missiles. In fact, the events were of one design.

For many years, Swami Rama has been proving to "Western science" that he can control his heart and autonomic nervous system by using "yoga."

Swami Rama was a guest on *Donahue* (4/24/80) when 666.86+ marked the Dow Jones Index.[1]

Phase Three was gaining synchronicity. Up to the turning point of consciousness, more and more people ate heavily processed foods. Then, the tide turned, and more and more people were seeking organically grown unprocessed foods.

Some yogis were overweight. Most ate cooked food and dairy products; and some yogis died of cancer. But the New Age was no more about yogis than about Oliver North doing "karmic yoga." A new sense of E-quality was hovering over the Earth.

I experienced the miracles in this chapter as an avenue to meditation. And I know that these miracles tell of an invisible realm of judgment. Our spirits even now dwell in that realm of invisibility ás we create physical reality in this time of special synchronicity.

Reaganomics left 10,800,000 in Europe's Common Market unemployed (*NBC* 2/19/82). Political Action Committees raised $108.5 million in the USA to support Reagan's policies (*US News* 6/5/82). Local events had global meanings.

And what eventually followed began the end of history. On March 18th of baseball season 108, the dispute over 666's Zero Option came to a head at the National Security Council (*Time* 4/11/83). And a global meditation on "zero" had begun.

---

(1) 86 was Abram-Abraham's age when Ishmael, the first Arab, was born, thus, "86ed" in U.S. slang meant "to be cast out."

The Pentagon demanded the USSR agree to a goal of "zero warheads" before any reduction offers. The State Department wanted a less absolute goal. And Reagan stepped between the two by offering to scrap the 108 Pershings. He outmaneuvered his own ranks, but without first consulting the USSR, where his offer was worthless since the 108 missiles were not yet in place.

It was a symbolic 108 at that point, but an idea that could have an impact on NATO and the European Community.

U.S. imports were 10.8% of goods and services[1] and rising. The Reagan Revolution was global. And the techno supply-side was robbing the bio supply-side blind.

After Russia's 66th anniversary, Andropov, the new Soviet leader, was missing, last seen alive August 18th.[2] The new Premier, age 72, was Cherenko, "Little Black One" (a bad luck symbol). Two weeks after he took power, "Blackbeard" won 1st prize in the 108th annual dog show in Madison Square Garden.[3] Cherenko soon left power. Then, **Gorbachev** (one who has a hunch, a good luck sign), age 54, took office. So, as Reagan made his 108 into a reality of Pershings in Germany, the USSR began its reformation.

Both China and Russia began to import pizza and other fast-food ideas from the USA. But would the USA gain sufficiently good eating habits to make a difference in the global tide of change? By 1988, the Presidential election in the USA had become a pinacle of symbols (scattered among these pages). And the people chose their next cycle.

Meanwhile, back in 1984: The Washington Monument sunk into the ground more than an inch. Said Lark McCarthy (*CBS News*), "in 666,000 years it will be out of sight."[4] In a comedy skit 18 days later (*on NBC*), linguist Edwin Newman said with a flat humor, "All but 108 died of natural causes."[5] Comic writers were doing their number. The USA had grown cynical. The USSR had new hope. And spirits that had been sleeping for almost two thousand years stirred in the air waves.

---

(1) U.S. News 2/2/87, (2) Time 11/28/83, (3) Newsweek 2/27/84, (4) CBS 3/13/84, (5) Saturday Night Live 2/25/84

Counting Beads

While covert deals were brewing, Reagan offered 108 Stinger anti-aircraft missiles to Jordan.[1] But Israel objected to the sale of "defensive" weapons to its neighbor. Reagan then bowed to Congress. And two days later, he said it was "No deal!".

Masters of japa yoga (bead meditation) keep the index finger (ego) off the rosary and never touch the guru bead. When they reach the end of 108, they turn around and go the other way, fingering the set over and over as 108 is interwoven with other patterns of the mind, moving the entire set of thoughts closer to crystallization.

And as with all journeys, the peace process was not totally conscious. Still, the 108 beads were tried and true. With missiles as the instruments of the techno mind-set, they became the beads of prayer. Be they wood, seeds, or heavy metal, the beads that number 108 have a built-in magic.

The civilian labor force was 108 million in the USA entering 1986.[2] And 1.08 million houses were built that year.[3] Covert wars brought back mixed karma, prosperity plus homelessness at home.

Reagan told an apocryphal story of a woman in Chicago who was receiving 108 welfare checks.[4] He thus tried to dis-credit welfare in general, by being cute.

G.E. had filed 108 false claims with the U.S. Air Force for phony missile production dating back to 1980.[5] But no individuals went to jail. And Uncle Ronny never told any cute stories about the General Motors scandal.

In 1987, Congress passed a $10.8 billion plan to prevent savings and loan deposit insurance from going bankrupt.[6] We needed sound finances. And we needed powerful technology. But at the base of all our Earthly interactions we needed a sane approach to food as our primary physical fuel.

(1) NY Times 10/22/85, (2) NY Times 4/30/87, (3) CBS 2/12/87, (4) Tip O'Neil, PBS interview, 12/24/86, (5) NY Times 5/14/85, (6) NY Times 12/20/87

Coffee Pot Karma

The USA imported 1.08 million tons of coffee in its 108th baseball season.[1] And the law of karma said trouble was brewing. The Pentagon paid $7200 each for coffee pots. And some people began to notice that terror and drugs were related. But very few people would label coffee as "a drug." So, the House approved $180 million in aid for El Salvador[2] while much aid had already been used by land barons to force local farmers to concentrate on "cash crops" (such as coffee) for export.

In Nicaragua's war, both sides thought that coffee was the heart of "the economy." Again "the finances" of the Techno State were being confused with real "economic needs." And it mattered not whether "Commies" or "Cappies" were put in charge of weighing out the coffee beans, it was still a techno drink.

Shortly before the Iran-Contra hearings began, the Department of Immigration opened 108 offices to handle applicants under a new law that was to "naturalize" aliens.[3] One month into the hearings, 18 Mexican migrant workers died in the heat of a 120-degree boxcar in Texas.[4] The workers were being smuggled into the USA. Just before the sacrifice of the "18 aliens" to the Techno State, Brazil suspended payments on its $108 billion debt,[5] thus beginning a trend that was to mark the end of the illusion of global anti-eco-system "financial security."

Back to back with the story on Brazil was an article saying that the USA might abandon its $108 billion deficit ceiling. The economy of Je-R-usa-L-em was falling into chaos while financial numbers of the money machine were constantly revised.

Global meditations were shifting from weapons of war to warlike finances. Rather than blow each other up, we planned to let each other starve. The greatest miracle in 2000 years was coming to pass as most people in the USA stared into their coffee cups.

(1) Commodity Year Book, (2) NY Times 9/9/84, (3) NPR 3/16/87, (4) NY Times 6/3/87, (5) NY Times 3/1/87

CHAPTER 39

THE SHAPE OF THE MIND

Most people know about prime numbers, said science writer A.K. Dewdney. "Buy them a cup of coffee and they will write the primes on a paper napkin: 2, 3, 5, 7, 11, 13, 17 and so on" (*Scientific American* July 1988). The article was about prime numbers, but told of the influence that coffee had on our "scientific" mind-set.

And news about the shape of coffee was in the *N.Y. Times* (9/30/86) when science writer James Gleick wrote of "the Poincare conjecture." Gleick said three-dimensional space was part of topology, and proved it with sketches of a coffee cup and a doughnut. "To a topologist at breakfast, a coffee mug is the same as a doughnut because one can be continuously deformed into the other," he wrote.

It made some sense. Both the surfaces have a hole, he said. But aside from topology, the "scientific" sketches depicted the writer's dream about a continuous flow of coffee and doughnuts.

When junkies develop sub-stance delusions, the group under-standing gets bent out of shape. In factories, offices, schools, and in military war rooms are "speech communities" where the drives of the group are revealed in a sub-text of speech patterns.

We could pick on tobacco or over-the-counter nostrums, but since coffee is tied to production, it affects daily "mainstream" thought more than any other drug. Awash in coffee, "scientific" daydreams were tied to our consumer beliefs. So, by examining the "speech community" of science (as with any primitive language group), we can learn about its *substantial* context.

But this is about more than the drugging of scientific thought. What was missing from the abstractions of "physics" was the factor of LIFE itself.

Think of the host who counted all the people in a room to set a place for each. But then he lacked one setting because he forgot to count himself. Science had been like that host in its search for a theory of "the unified field."

We had Einstein's "relativity" to describe the speed of light among the stars. And we had "quantum mechanics" to tell of minute subatomic particles absorbing or bouncing off of each other. But we had no workable "unified field" theory to bring the great and small together. For we had forgotten that the human mind itself is the only REAL equal sign in our experience.

Physicists used equations to describe the uni-verse. Still, **the Force of Life** (the host doing the counting) was not on the seating list.

Scientists working on the unified field theory had officially narrowed the focus to four *physical* force fields. But every formula to integrate these four had failed. The four forces studied were: the Strong Force, the Weak Force, Light, and Gravity.

The quarks and neutrinos of quantum mechanics were held together by the Strong Force. The Weak Force allowed for decay of atomic structures (such as radio activity). Light and Gravity were also counted as forces. But "Life" (the host at our party) did not seem to count.

To open a five-part series on quantum physics (6/13/88), *the Christian Science Monitor*'s staff reporters, start by describing a lab with coffee spilled on the floor. A "science" driven more and more by a drug-tainted biololgy saw its own "life" less and less clearly.

Consider that Dark is the absence of Light and that Cold is the absence of Heat. We know Light and Heat to be physical. Dark and Cold, however, are properties of the void; they are (in absolute terms) what we imagine nothing to be.

Also, what is called "the force of Gravity" is the absence of "the force of Levity." But physics dealt with Gravity as if it were positive.

We nullify "the law of Gravity" each time we lift a finger in Levity. For Life has a power to elect. And so, we must affect the outcome of every experiment; for elective life energy is *always* present.

Photons are as un-predictable as the people who measure them. But the spelling of "measure" (me-a-sure) gives us a clue. Your spirit is felt in the uni-verse when you unify EL (light within) with RA (light outside). True science is a "struggle with God," IS-RA-EL. False science ignores the human spirit of cosmic electivity.

Though Einstein said that Gravity was a result of mass warping space, Gravity was also listed as the fourth force. But as an elemental force, how can it be a result? When measured mathematically, Gravity is a zero-energy wave. Gravity is no more of a force than Darkness or Cold; each are negatives, lacking energy.

Death also appears to be a force to those who think negatively about Life. Yet, Light, Heat, and all other forms of positive energy are neither created nor destroyed, they simply move from form to form. And so it is with Life. Another clue is the Christian "mass" where the Easter Master is called by a spell Caster to take the form of bread and wine. Remember that all realms are linked in the ultimate reality.

A short-range repelling force was discovered by Daniel R. Long, showing the law of gravity break down at ranges from 1.8 to 12 inches (*N.Y. Times* 3/4/86). Of course, the numbers marked the rim of limits mystically. Yet, the report went on to say that Stanford University was searching for "anti-gravity."

The realm of science is only now beginning to understand Life's relationship to sub-stance. We each have surges of telepathic and telekinetic powers that urge us. But such experiences cannot be repeated regularly in experiments. Still, this is no reason for science to reject individual knowledge. Biological facts, though always touched by spirit, are nonetheless facts.

Animals and plants thrive on telepathic powers. And we who dream of Heaven are also animals; but we share the snares of Hell, so with our particular mind-set we can rise above the rest, via techno application. But runaway techno thoughts can weaken our beliefs and our sense of community. For only the concept of "everlasting life" gives full strength to the definition of "life."

Reagan's final summit in June 1988 (summit 19 historically) had no breakthroughs as did 18. For we were living in the metaphor. An overview shows that "life" was giving a shape to the mind, but drugs were distorting our view.

The Force of Life observes all other forces. And so, the unified field that physicists search for is more than physical; it is centered (C-entered) in the observing force. And this is why we have not charted a course unto oblivion. Even when Life didn't seem to count, when the observed seemed to be served more than the observer, there was a plan that linked all planets.

A planet is only a little plan. Yet by learning to respect this planet, we can learn to live in the uni-verse. Now that Phase Three has begun, by recycling waste and producing less, we are gaining some sense of direction, but we have a problem with our scientific philosophy.

We know that 3 times 3 is 9. But no number when multiplied by itself yields 3. So, the square root of 3 is "a surd." This formula works under the Tree of Technology. But the Tree of Life seems "absurd" scientifically, for beyond its physical roots are roots no mortal eye can see.

With integrity, life in its factions, fractions, and instability takes on new reality. Make-believe is not a fiction; thought can bring on real-life friction. Thus, Tibetan Tantric masters can generate "tumo heat" in their bodies with only "make-believe." For Life has roots in the spirit that we each can use each day to love each other's absurdity.

Picture the universe, relative to you. You are at REST while the REST goes through its motions. You hold FAST; all else moves FAST around you. You are STILL; all else is STILL in motion.

We call our writing materials "stationery" since we assume a fixed point from which to write. And a feeling of being "stationary" makes all else fall within the universal context we create.

Life is a wave from the meta-physical into the physical. Being STILL, holding FAST, and remaining at REST are the origins of spirit, which is everywhere at once and not in need of locomotion. So, Life is a physical continuum, the mystery that is solved by those who are so individual as to see beyond their own individuality. And the spirit moves us from within but seems to move among us when we think we are divided.

M-OVE in this abstraction is where a L-OVE meets a L-OVE, where moving e-motions are touching.

So, Warmth, Light, and Life (the positives) are children of Levity, possessed by spirit. And this tells us more about the continuum. Seeds may be frozen for ages and then regenerated. A spirit at rest can issue forth and grow with the plant that it inhabits. But on the other hand, heated above 130°F, a seed can no longer engender its kind, for at such heat the spirit leaves. And **devil** spelled backwards is **lived**.

Being still, holding fast, and remaining at rest do not destroy enzymes. But fire kills the physical cell. So, the void is not a threat to living eternally; control of fire is the key. We loose our "tempers" if spirits get too hot. Ideas get out of shape if we fail to meditate. Be still, de-voted for a moment, C-entered. And with a choice, you can see Life as the greatest choice of all. So, feed your life with life energized by light, to kindle the fire in your soul.

The shape of the uni-verse is one-turn in "the Word." And its re-verse flows forward in time; for verse serves Life in a positive sense, or makes no sense at all.

A Mobius Strip (a two-dimensional uni-verse)

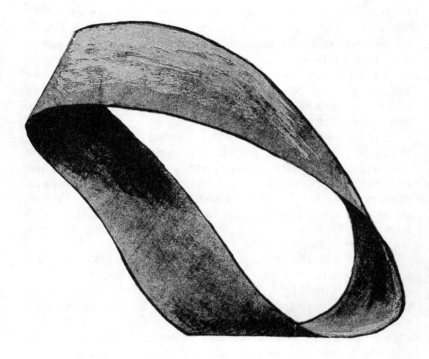

This picture of a Mobius strip depicts in two dimensions a plane which oddly enough has only one side. A Mobius strip can be made from paper. For easy handling make the strip 18 inches long and 2 inches wide. Put a twist (one turn) in the paper before you join its ends. And fasten with tape on both sides. Now, it has only one side.

To prove this one-sided quality, draw a single line down the middle of the strip, without lifting your pencil. Go ahead.

If your Mobius strip is made correctly, you have drawn a line full-circle, back to point of origin, covering what seemed to be both sides of the paper. The one-turn in that strip of paper is the quality of "uni-verse" that makes its outside into its inside and turns its inside out of its outside.

Negatives have no verse and no reverse. So, cold, dark, gravity, and death have no voices. They are, in absolute terms, the absence of experience. But since everyday life is warm, we tend to think of "cold" as a lessening of heat, rather than the absolute "lack of heat."

This exercise in viewing terms as absolutes may not immediately stop us from saying, "It's cold," when we mean, "It has little heat." But a clear linguistic reality helps us to think positively about our own "negative" states.

Try to envision a sphere built on the Mobius principle. Can you draw a three dimensional version of it? Can you even imagine it?

We do not readily envision the shape of the universe because we have already drawn ourselves into it. The space in the universe is connected to the space that surrounds the universe.

In "meta-physical," "meta" means both "between" and "beyond." So, we are in the physical while also being between and beyond it. We are doing the drawing. And we are being drawn. When the mind is open, the spirit can be fixed in it, so the body heals around its center (C-enter).

The reason that meditation mediates matter, the reason that Life is also meta-physical is that all trans-formation takes place in empty space.

Thus, absolute abstractions can be helpful in day to day living. STRESS can stretch from REST to REST giving us the faith to continue with a task in the knowledge that we will always reach a point of rest.

The crystal seam (S) between yin and yang, the border between he and she (S) divides "stress" from "rest." Ignore the seam, and we EXIT all perceptions that EXIST.

These formulas make sense in the spirit. But coffee-cup science, never at rest, sees the rest of the world in time-shattering distress. So, the best-selling science book by our coffee-minded science writer, Gleick, was entitled "Chaos."

With bread as a link to deathless machines, the Church rigged up its bells. The State insured we would not rest. Alarm clocks manufactured stress. City clocks blocked the sun. And we speeded up to synchromesh. Lunch hour — 35.8 minutes. Overtime. Indigestion. Computer-confessions. And instant psychotherapy — with a "free" cup of coffee.

WEIGHT (with a G for gravity) is a function of matter, yet WAIT with no stress rests only in the spirit. So, we concentrate (weight) or meditate (wait) before we negotiate in the mind.

And rest as a biological function cannot be equated to machines at rest. For machines are mindless.

Mind your body as you mind a baby. And listen for its stress. Hear your spirit; your body will not lose its mind. Hear your body; your spirit will respond in kind. So, fasting leads away from stress, as a spirit blessed by less is allowed to be the guest of the body's blissfulness.

To a comic, "the straight line" is a joke. And science must agree. Gravity makes a curve in space. And we can die of false levity. If food smells funny, you throw it out; if ideas are funny, why do you laugh?

In Ger-man (strange-manna), *Ausch-witz* means "derived from a joke." And "joke" is from "hoax" in *hoc est corpus* said in a Christian mass to transform the bread into flesh, so that people, who are starved for spirit, may eat.

The silent G (gravity) is funny in "straight" for "strait," without G, means "narrow." The uni-verse does not close. It only gets closer, when we decide to take it personally, finding an identity with the metaphor.

Israel's father was "Laughter" (Isaac) since "the Word" would be broken to give us new Levity. "God Listens" (Ishmael) was cast out. And separation of the tribes by war was a pun-ishment for eating cooked foods.

He-brew held a comic truth in the promise of inter-galactic cosmic travel. So, "laugh" had a sound of deflated G's in Angular reality. With the sacred text of life on file, matter and pattern make common sense — if we listen.

Within words are numbers, within numbers are words. And only "the Living Word" has a means to lead to meaning. We know the truth when we are "straight." But coffee (a stimulant) and doughnuts (a depressant) constrain true Levity. For coffee, a means of technology, distorts the meaning of biology.

The macrocosm of Relativity and microcosm of Quantum Mechanics are not bigger or smaller than *who* we are; they are bigger and smaller than *what* we are. And since all matter is on a physical continuum, a mind focused within the meaning of life sees the microcosm and macrocosm as extremes while seeing the body as a physical means. And true Levity makes light of foibles to cure disease. In humor, body and spirit are true companions when all our "lights" are one.

To light upon a branch, the bird negotiates with gravity. "Light" is an intransitive verb.

We light a fire. And "light" is transitive, since its object is the flame.

The fire gives us "light," a noun.

And "light" becomes an adjective, as snow that is "light" blows up and down.

The lightest of matter is light that shines. And when the lightest light lights upon equally light light, the outcome is an even lighter light that is fired forth anew into the dance of Life. The science of language already has the essence of true expression woven through it.

A lighted fire fires light into the uni-verse to feed our Life's delight. So, between the spirit's fire and the spirit's light is Levity.

In Mechanicsburg (a real town), Pa., at the Girl Scouts cookie eating contest, a mother, concerned for her daughter's health, tried to stop the madness, and gained one concession: the presence of a nurse in case one of the girls should choke (*N.Y. Times* 1/10/88). In Mechanicsburg, some people seemed to think that life was a joke.

At the end of a sentence, it seems as if the final word is waiting there. But stop in the middle and you may glimpse the space from which your words were created touching the space where your words create. Even when speaking linearly, your thoughts are globular, as is your vision.

And so, beginning readers of any age reverse their letters. This warns against totalitarian linear training in grammar school. Also, linear equations of physics cannot encompass the globular universe that lives ever through itself.

Under the Techno State, poor linear-readers got low grades, but those who exercised no insight or spiritual sense were often rewarded. And few took time to listen to their inner and outer voices. But now, we are about to move beyond our historic metaphor, unto a new plateau.

A difference between Egyptians and Hebrews gave them opposing views. One had a landed society at a time when the other was building its traditions, wandering. During that formative period, Egyptians came to spirit through matter while Hebrews came to matter through spirit.

So, now, as we prepare to wander again, let us build a value system that is self-contained and whole, to carry into space.

We drugged ourselves, we drugged the land, we drugged those children who became "emotionally disturbed" in our drug-directed world. And then, we cursed the teen-age gangs who acted like the nations gone before them.

My young friend John was drugged to "cure" him of dyslexia, a dis-ease of societal origin. And I saw the "professionals" who drugged him drink their coffee while deciding John was too slow.

Saint John the Divine said the saved would not deal in witchcraft. And "witchcraft" is *pharmacos* in Greek. Does the Bible condem pharmacology (Rev. 22:15)? A balanced view will rid society of its coffee-warped mentality. For those who make the laws must also be drug-free. One universal law has come again, to guide humanity.

CHAPTER 40

DRUGSVILLE USA

18 First Ladies Meeting in U.S. on Drug Abuse[1]

The above headline told of Nancy Reagan's White House "First Ladies conference." With the arrival of 18 limosines, she greeted First Ladies from 18 nations. Since "all were mothers," said the news item, they were fighting against drugs.

"The women will have coffee in the Blue Room with President Reagan" and "move on to discuss the prevention of drug abuse" the article reported.

Is coffee not a popular drug? Or like British tea, Indian tobacco, hippie marijuana, dad's can of beer, and chocolate for the baby — is coffee just another harmless social ritual?

First noticed by shepherds in Yemen due to its strange effect on sheep, coffee was called *kahuha* meaning "power." The Turks named it *kahveh*. And since the Koran forbade "intoxicating drink," the toxic brew from coffee was officially outlawed.

But coffee perked up Venice, London, and Berlin. By the 18th century, laborers in Africa, Asia, and the Americas picked it as masters were picking up steam. Then, coffee shops, coffee houses, cafes, and cafeterias spread around the globe.

Millions of acres of coffee are now grown for the techno system is enslaved to it. Addicts in the USA swallow over one-third of the world's supply. And since coffee is over half of El Salvador's total exports, and a great amount of Nicaragua's, its political effects upon the USA are enough to make anybody nervous. But how could business in the USA carry on without coffee?

(1) NY Times 4/22/85

Half a Cup, $1.50, Please

Since coffee beans are picked by hand and a pound can have thousands of beans (depending on size), pickers get about a dollar a day to keep prices down. But if an Organization of Pickers Exporting Coffee (OPEC) were formed, coffee would cost more than $3 a cup in the USA.

So, like a threatened junkie, business folk in the USA called on military and covert operations to protect the "standard American" coffee habit against any "leftist" minimum wage laws.

Of course, this conspiratorial organizing was done in the pre-conscious reaches of the mind. No group of U.S. citizens planned it; still coffee addicts and sugar freaks had some idea of where their next fix was coming from.

Oil producing nations were not "leftists" when they organized. The techno-supply-side was given respect. But the bio-supply-side got stepped on because we were confused about food.

Keep in mind that the sacrifice of food was an historic necessity. Every culture cooked some food, even in the tropics. Likewise, a thirst for coffee came upon us to feed the Industrial Revolution. Like every junkie in the streets, society itself was being run by an emotional need based on some difficult circumstances of civilization.

If we were not hooked on alcohol, for example, people would have the emotional freedom to produce great quantities of it to add to fuels for cleaner burning. But we are seldom aware of living within the preset rules that have pre-consciously linked us to mythologies.

Maureen Reagan (Nancy's daughter) said, "When my husband moved to Sacramento, she [Nancy] asked, 'Does he need a coffee maker?'" And Nancy Reagan had an EXTRA coffee maker in her closet.

Nancy Reagan knew, as did most well read women, that high-fat diets (meat and dairy) were a factor in breast cancer. And coffee contributed. But when Nancy found a lump in her breast, she said, "It's my turn," and resigned herself to medical protocol without questioning her techno diet.

EXTRA — Read All About It!

"The Harvard Medical School Healthletter" (Sept. 1984) showed how one "doctor" had been blinded to the danger of drugs in general by his "normal" use of coffee in particular.

For children with "attention deficits," said the Medical Letter, it is "virtually unethical not to use the drugs (and using them may be little different, in spirit, from an adult's taking an extra cup of coffee to get through a difficult task). Children appear not to become addicted to these drugs, and they have a low rate of adverse side effects." The parenthetical defense of coffee above was conjured up by "a medical doctor" at Harvard, and quoted exactly as you see it.

Drugs being used to fight "attention deficits" in children were prescribed by an M.D. who referred to "an **extra** cup of coffee," as if coffee itself were necessary to function. Were children unfit for a coffee-activated society? The "doctor" wrote, "children *appear* not to become addicted." But did he see himself as a coffee addict, with the need of an occasional "extra" cup?

A child's "attention deficit" is often a sane response that coffee addicts do not believe in. So it is insane to treat such "disturbances" with drugs when society itself is drugged. Again, we are trapped behind the looking glass. And again, the key is in our very own words.

Listen. Your most personal questions have their answers hidden just beneath the surface of your everyday speech. Listen closely to yourself.

A quote from Nancy Reagan, by Chris Wallace in *the New York Post* (11/6/86) shows how speech comes through the pre-conscious. Said Nancy, "On almost every state visit at the White House, *I will have coffee* with other First Ladies and they always bring up the drug problem."

"I will have coffee," she said. But her mind's reflection said, "Coffee has my will." The leader of the nation's anti-drug campaign was speaking through the traces of her favorite drug. But not only Nancy Reagan had lost her will. Listen closely to the grammar that you hear daily.

The "Moral" Issue

About 12 pounds of chocolate per person are eaten yearly in the USA. Over 30 million prescriptions for anti-depressants are filled yearly. And before "the average adult" gets to the pharmocopia of the nursing home, the intake of prescription drugs is "normally" at least one drug per day, and often thirty drugs or more.

Each doctor's drug belief is hyped by medical magazines supported by drug company ads that are, in turn, followed up by drug sales personnel.

Drugs can crowd out our faith in natural healing. Environmental toxins are ignored and stored in our systems along with bad food residue. And when the crisis comes, we are "victims," hooked into intensive care to pump more drugs into our veins.

Deprived of a natural birth, starved for natural foods, we need only follow "the Living Word" to its original breaking point (b-read). And the end of life can hold a peaceful death. But we traded our souls for insurance policies. Control of the media fell to advertising.

Coffee speeded techno dreams. Marijuana never served the Techno State. Alcohol (a sacrificial drug) fell out of favor due to fast cars and the number of people working at highly skilled tasks. Methadon (as addictive and harmful as heroin) was "legal" for medico-political reasons. In Phase Two, "morality" was usually a codeword for that which promoted Techno State goals.

Drugs are now out of control because the Techno State has overshot its interim goal. Even though Heaven is seen as physically available, all humanity cannot get that high immediately. So, both the slaves and masters of the Techno State must begin to work toward a new social order.

Sympathetic U.S. citizens spent two-week shifts in Nicaraguan coffee fields at their own expense and at some risk. "They hope to deter attacks with their presence" (*Whole Life Times*, Jan. 1984). The "moral" stand on both sides in the USA was (pre-consciously) focused on the coffee issue.

Most Salvadorans had lost their land, over half the rural workers were out of work eight months each year, pickers were often pesticide victims, and poison sprays remained in the coffee. But such intricate webs were not new to history.

In the Opium Wars (1839-42 & 1856-58), England forced China to accept opium from India to sell to the Chinese people. There were various other excuses for the wars, none of which made English morality ("good" for England's business) seem very attractive in the Orient.

Union organizers in El Salvador were targets of the "death squads" financed by the landowners. And reports of Amnesty International showed that the minions of El Salvador's coffee elite had murdered thousands during union-busting activities. So why did the USA support El Salvador's military?

One factor was that "the death squads" would squelch any movement that could have raised the price of coffee in the USA.

In Nicaragua, development of a coffee cash-crop had raised the "value" of the land so much that sharecroppers and renters were evicted by bigger coffee companies. The number of coffee pickers increased. Farmers became enslaved to the coffee cash-crop. And shortages of basic foods ensued as coffee gained preference over the vegetation that would have fed local citizens.

The Sandinistas in Nicaragua had instituted the Agricultural Reform Act to break the coffee cash-crop habit. Aimed at meeting domestic food needs, the Agricultural Reform Act (if allowed to spread) would certainly have driven up coffee prices. But the Sandinista plan was not to eliminate coffee as a cash crop, only to re-organize and then exploit coffee to fund Government operations.

The Contras attacked Old Nick's coffee harvest in 1985 only after the USA had ceased bidding on that year's supply. Like the addict, not knowing how to kick, the USA fought with the dealer, lied to the cops, cursed God, and played the fool.

Catabolic Politics

Coffee is not a food. It causes a catabolic rather than metabolic reaction. It tears down rather than builds the body. But unlike tobacco and alcohol, coffee goes untaxed by the Government.

Tars, creosote, trigonellin (also in nicotine), pyridine, volatile oils and acids in coffee attack the nerves while taxing the heart, kidneys, liver, and stomach. Feelings of exhaustion are delayed because the body is forced to burn up its fat rather than glycogen. And this allows more cholesterol and fatty acids to build up in the arteries. Thus, coffee brings on heart attacks.

During a coffee high, a user feels energetic and productive, but nerve endings are sacrificed. Still, we have no warning labels on our get-up and down-to-business drug.

High blood sugar in reaction to coffee gets the pancreas to pour out insulin. And so, most people in the USA suffer at least mild hypoglycemia by middle age due to caffeinism which mimics addiction to amphetamines. Coffee drinkers, statistically, are more often admitted to mental hospitals where they get rewarded by "coffee breaks" to make the techno cycle complete.

Several studies (Dr. Minton, Ohio State, 1979, for one) have shown that drugs in caffeine drinks are a factor in fibrocystic breast disease.

Agatha Thrash M.D. reports: women with cystic breasts are more prone to breast cancer. And 65% of the women with cystic breasts who stopped all caffeine products lost all symptoms of fibrocystic disease within six months. Sadly, Nancy Reagan was treated by "standard American doctors."

A child's birthday party (by techno rules) has candle flames atop the cake, enough ice cream to make the guests sick, and carbonated soda to flush them out. Noise makers blast. And then we laugh at the donkey as the adults relax with their cups of coffee. But nobody seems to realize that the party trappings were all born of religious rituals under the Tree of Technology.

Coffee, in the Name of Jesus

In the offices of Evangelists, coffee kept business perking as preachers who shouted against drugs used donated money to keep their staffs on that stimulant first noted due to its effect on sheep.

While Congress proposed to cut cigarette taxes in half to $1.8 billion, Reagan held refined sugar supports to 18 cents a pound[1]. And the people of the USA drank toxic chemicals brewed from 18 million bags of coffee annually.[2] Most preachers said tobacco was the devil's weed. But coffee and refined sugar were as sacred as apple pie.

Adolfo Calero (Contra chief) was a former head of Nicaragua's Coca Cola bottling. And Ollie North sipped Diet-Coke as he testified. Poindexter puffed a pipe lit by a Zippo, inhaling lighter-fluid fumes. Meese went to Casey's house for a beer when he heard of fund diversions. Coors Beer funded Contra raiders. And coffee ads were designed for "young consumers."

The list goes on. Phase Two was ruled by people who were locked into unconscious fear and driven to win, technologically. Aspirin companies used warnings against cigarette smoking in their ads so they could pose as "medical experts." Each new bit of information was co-opted to be used to sell "the consumers" something new or more of something old that had a new health claim.

Some 20,000 "doctors" took part in a trial to see if aspirin could save "healthy people" from heart attacks.[3] "The doctors" played their roles for the drug companies. But were "the doctors" as healthy as the test implied? Did we have aspirin deficiencies in our diets? The simple answer is that raw fruits and vegetables, exercise, and a positive attitude will eliminate heart attacks if one begins soon enough.   Also, no raw-food study will ever be accepted by "medical science" since no double-blind control raw-food experiment (with placebos) can be devised.

(1) NY Times 12/16/85, (2) Business Week 1/13/86, (3) Newsweek 10/21/85

The Drug Illusion

Aspirin eats away body tissue. You would not hold an aspirin in your mouth. For it cleans arteries and deadens nerves by the same means that it makes stomach ulcers. And coffee is certainly not a food that primates eat naturally.

Aspirin and coffee are prime examples of the drug illusion, for the desirable effects of each can be gained naturally. Massage and relaxation can get rid of headaches. And true devotion to the task at hand is the most constant stimulant that a human being can ever find.

By 1980, the USA was using 7 times the amount of petro-chemical (oil-waste) fertilizer per acre than was India. Addition of this pharmaceutical to the soil over many years had caused a need for more and more of it to grow devitalized food. For soil reacts to pharmaceuticals in the same way that drug addicts react to drugs.

Undisciplined in technology, we acted like the children in a second marriage. We were born of Mother Earth and Father Time. And though Techno Time, our step-father, treated our Mother Earth poorly, we looked to him for employment.

Petro fertilizers in India gave ten pounds of crop for each pound of oil-waste. In the USA an average of only two and a half pounds (one-forth as much crop) were produced with the same amount of oil-waste fertilizer. Why?

Because the USA had drugged its soil for three times as long. Also, as with any new drug user, India used about one-seventh the amount of the toxic substance per acre as the USA.

Naturally, time is a key bio-factor, where the unfolding comes in stages. And drinking coffee distorts our sense of time. But unlike time warps of other junkies, the coffee time warp has been imposed on mainstream society in general.

We can *use* the Tree of Technology. But we must *eat* only from the Tree of Life. This raw law of the Language Crystal returns us to bio-timing.

The Cuban Triangle

CUBA (literally meaning "tub") is a Spanish term for "drunkard." And CUBA's name encodes a cause of hostility between the USA and USSR that goes to the roots of both cultures. Our alcoholic super powers share a common addiction to alcohol. So, a global karma was focused in "the drunkard" as Cuba became a political pawn.

Alcohol eats away at both Commies and Cappies. And behind alcohol abuse is a socially accepted disorder, the consumption of refined sugars. The USA and USSR have been hooked since their infancy on both refined sugars and booze, which is a distilled sugar.

History tells of "a triangular trade" among the British Colonies. New England traded rum to Africa for slaves. African slaves were traded for West Indian sugar and molasses. West Indian sugar was then used to manufacture rum in New England. The triangle was repeated over and over again. And as the sugars and the rums were consumed, the slaves remained as slaves.

So it is today with individuals who become the products of alcohol. "Being drunk" is the *passive* voice of "to drink."

The slave trade blazed a trail of karma. And Cuba ("the drunkard") got caught in the gang wars of "Latin America," for refined sugars (alcohol, colas, etc.) left a mark of emotional instability on the USA, USSR, and Europe alike.

Reagan began Radio Marti on May 18th, at 1180 on the AM dial, while 18,000 applicants from Cuba waited to immigrate to the USA.[1] And at the time of Miss Liberty's 100th birthday, 1,800 Mariel Cubans were still in the Atlanta penitentiary.[2]

The USSR was the world's largest sugar refiner. Two-thirds of Cuba's industry was sugar refining with tobacco as the next largest industry.

By Reagan's final year in office, more Russian vodka was sold in the USA than in the USSR. The once-athiest Soviet had changed its karma (action) internally, but not substantially.

(1) NY Times 5/20/85, (2) NY Times 7/1/86

Kennedy is Scottish for "one with a misshapen head." And John Kennedy, with his skull shot open in Dallas, fit the name grotesquely.

John-son (John's Revelation) gave us a Nix-on faith. And Ford (a shallow river crossing) led to J.C., then to 666 and the end of history. In Phase Three "to lead" is "to read," and a national ruler is simply a guide.

The father (head) of the Kennedy clan made his fortune running Prohibition alcohol, helping to undermine the 18th Amendment. Ted's alcoholic tragedy on the 18th and John's "misshapen head" in Dallas were only fragments of the Kennedy's karmic puzzle. But these morbid images give some background to the advent of 666. The scope of our puzzle spans the ages. Kennedy's Bay of Pigs invasion spirals back into images of the pig, where *bar* (a butcher board) and *bier* (a roasting fire) were British terms in pig-sacrifice rituals. *Ham* (dark) tells of *Gypsie, gyp, Egyptian*, and a host of clouded images that got buried in forgotten tongues.

The last imprisoned Bay of Pigs invader was set free by Castro on October 18th, 1986.

Castro means "one who is cut off," and he was cut off politically from the USA. Also, although aligned with the USSR, he was "cut off" from his trading consumer-supplier by distance. The Phase Two mind-set had created a drama around the effects of alcohol on biology. We were living in the all-pervasive metaphor of the Techno State.

And now as we awake from our Phase Two dream, both the USA and USSR will scratch their heads. Why was a surrogate war of nerves fought in Nicaragua?

Old Nick's industries were sugar refining, soft drinks, alcoholic beverages, dairy products, meat processing, and coffee. The main export was sugar. And armies on both sides were dealing cocaine to emulate the giant drunkards who had supplied the weapons. So, children died as his-story faced its latent karma.

Trouble came out of the North, with a twist on the prophecy. History ate its words. 666 fell from grace. Reagan re-deemed (re-evaluated) the Evil Empire. And soon we will close the Book, only to find that we are beginning anew.

In the Bible's very first chapter: *"God said, Behold, I have given you every herb bearing seed, and every tree in which the seed yields fruit"* (Gen. 1:29). And this was our first law.

God had said, "Eat your fruits and vegetables." Yet one by one, exceptions were made for the sake of survival until we forgot the first law and began to think that the written exceptions were new laws in themselves.

Still, in its last chapter, the Bible tells of 12 manner of fruits (Rev. 22:2) that will grow after the battles of Armageddon are done.

So, between the beginning and end of the Bible we find a history of bread and wine, cooked and fermented foods linking Adam to Israel to Jesus. Then, Reagan signed a Bible with the 18 letters of his name and sent his famous chocolate cake via Oliver North to the nation of Iran.

Our symbolic history was complete. We had only to decide how to use the land.

And on either side of the river was the tree of life, which bare 12 manner of fruits and yielded her fruit every month, and the leaves of the trees were for the healing of the nations.

And there shall be no more curse: but the throne of God and the Lamb shall be in it, and his servants shall serve him.

And they shall see his face; and his name shall be in their foreheads.

And there shall be no light there, and they need no candle, neither light of the sun; for the Lord God givith them light. And they shall reign for ever and ever (Rev. 22:2-5).

Behold, we are across the Crystal River. And we shall prepare our race for its Heavenly home.

Around the Christmas Holidays, magazines listed food under "Home Decorations." And the obligatory wine column was in place less for reading than to make liquor ads seem appropriate.

Licensed nutritionists were viewed as a threat by the hospital dieticians who sought to outlaw any food advice that was not under their own "jurisdiction."

"Science writers" edited cookbooks as a spin-off of their "expertise." The Government tried to give the illusion of control. And the media sought its own nutrition credibility.

And a man named "Knowledge" was taken hostage. After the symbolic death of 666, Colonel **Higgins** (meaning "knowledge" in Old English), chief of staff of the Truce Supervision Organization, was captured in Beirut (*NY Times* 2/21/88).

And since eating from the Tree of Knowledge had started our historic metaphor, we would have to shift into a new mode, beyond the symbolism, into a new reality. We would have to say goodby to our Alice in Wonderland adventure.

The National Academy of Sciences (5/20/87) had issued a report calling for immediate Government action to stop the poisoning of the nation's food supply with pesticides. We had the knowledge, but Mr. Knowledge had disappeared.

Will Congress suddenly outlaw poisons in the food supply? Will the Presidential elections make a difference in what we eat? Will food ads stop trying to deceive us? Will laws protect our use of language so children can regain their bio-balance? Will medical drug statistics begin to tell the truth? Will street drugs suddenly be banned from every city of the USA? — Not until the mainstream of our population makes a major shift.

Coffee, sold as food, so labeled, so advertised, and thus untaxed, tends to blur the context of good grammar and good taste. But Coffee is just another drug. And the choice is yours. Do not count on leaders, statistics, or the media. Only one by one, as individuals, can we abandon Drugsville.

CHAPTER 41

UPS, DOWNS, INS, and OUTS

Should a woman be on top in that metaphor of God called "a love affair"? Is superiority a matter of sex? The language of his-story tottered while it implied that "higher" was "better." For men (generally taller) tended to look down on women.

And even the division of Arabs from Jews came about due to a question of sexual "superiority." The story is told in the Bible; but to understand it, we must see what "being on top" and "being on the bottom" actually mean "in space," where all spirits originate.

Consider this: In our Angular language, "sex" is our means of multiplication. A "section" is a division. A "sequence" is a divided series. And "to segment" means to cut. But *segment, section, sequence,* and *sex* each derive from the same root word meaning "six." Now, let us trace the roots of these words into the abstract while keeping in mind that they also have physical derivations. Since language is meant to civilize men, the Crystal forms round the masculine "six."

And the word "second" (2nd) from that same root seems to revolve around "six" (6). For "a second" is also 1/60 of a minute. So, what does this say about sex, space, and about the spirits of eternal procreation?

Your very first second is not seen as a second until a second second (a 2nd 1/60 of a minute) is realized. So, it seems you measure your first time frame only after entering a second. And the seams of these frames are invisible walls in our Crystal City. So, time will emit under-standing with each new sub-stance that it transforms.

Your second second is a section of time. But it has to overlap a segment of space. Thus, you have never had a first second. You are eternal. And "making time" is a game you play when faced by a second person who is the first for you. So, neither lover can ever be spiritually "superior."

Phase Two scientists, as we have seen, tried to figure out the uni-verse without referring to "the Living Word." For Phase Two scientists believed that "Life" had at some point come into being by being born of lifeless chemistry.

Still, a view from the space at Center Crystal (which is the space around the Crystal) shows that space (a distance in time) is created between the observer and the observed only by the presence of some substance or by a lack of understanding. This is a difference between matter (substance) and spirit (under-standing).

We each have part-ners (God, lover, or friend) who observe us as we observe them. And when we share with no sense of time, it doesn't even take a second.

And then again, a new capacity to love comes beyond the second second. In that moment, when one soul is the second for another, we have exceeded time by making room.

Remember the Mobius strip we made previously. The outside was the inside. Just so, the space at your center (C-enter) is in fact "outer space," where creation begins.

When your in-formation joins in communion with another or with the rest, this fulfillment is your divinity. And when your body and spirit are one, "the Word," is your mind in purity.

"A length of time" is illusive, the crossing of two planes where a person's globular body (built of cells) and globular spirit (one self) seem to intersect. Since we each emit spheres of time, "a length of time" is perceived when one sphere of influence intersects another sphere with no flow between them. In love, however, time is spacious. And lovers are always influential.

Since "space" is meta-physical, habits are only journeys through a habitat of substance. With this view of inner space, we can regain command.

We look down on "lower animals" even if they are bigger than us. But we are brought down to Earth by the love of our own animal pleasures.

The uni-verse has verse and con-verse. Now, add a third point of view and we produce "subversion" (a view from beneath) which calls for "supervision" (a view from up above).

In nature, super-vision is a light that makes sub-versions grow from seeds. But humans began to think of techno "subversions" and "supervisions" as things to be kept apart, politically.

Then came "superstition" (a looking down) which was regarded with "suspicion" (a looking up).

Note how viewpoint affects a connotation. You might *be* "suspicious" about a person who *acts* "suspicious." Also, a feeling of being below or above, inferior or superior, brings e-motions into our drama that separate science from instinct, each eyeing the other with suspicion.

A separation of sub-stance from under-standing occurred when we took control of fire. We knew instinctively that passing through technology was our ticket to Heaven. It was our fire power that caused us to look down on other species. Now, to feel a kinship for our species-ancestors on Earth, we need only yield to the crystal mystery, that kinship born among the stars.

You "fall asleep" and "wake up" moving through various levels of consciousness. Yet, "below" and "above" have meanings in space only insofar as your head is always "above" your body. Man is no longer OVER women. For LOVER has new meaning AB-OVE as our complex of *ove*ns and s*tove*s is gradually re-deemed.

This over-under illusion applies to Je-R-usa-L-em and to the implosion of our Jew-USA-Moslem syndrome. For Abram-Abraham's sons from two mothers may have been brought into conflict under differing female points of view. Let us look back to the original story to see the singular e-motion that drove these two women apart. The slaughter of a ram by Abram was the outcome of this family break-up. And that lamb was burned because the women seemed to have a confusion over "seeing the light" from either above or below.   Remember that this abstract division is the basis of much modern belief.

Sarah (Abram's Hebrew wife) asked that Abram go in unto Hagar (Sarah's Egyptian maid) in order that Hagar might bring a baby into Sarah's house.

"And he went in unto Hagar, and she conceived: and when she saw she had conceived, her mistress was despised in her eyes" (Gen. 16:4), so say most "standard" translations of the Bible.

That "her mistress was despised" might seem clear. But the word for "despised" in Hebrew is **QALAL**, which also means "be light" or "become bright." The words between the mothers of Abram-Abraham's sons need some looking into from a Space Age perspective.

In English, the word "despise" literally means "to look down upon" (*de-specere*). And even this Latin connotation is ambiguous, for we can look down upon a baby with the best of intentions.

It is only the fear between fire and light that twists the pure and absolute meanings of such terms. The heavens look down upon us all, still we need not feel "despised" by Heaven.

We have no way of knowing from the Hebrew of the Bible exactly what emotions the pregnant Hagar felt. We only know she was either looking down on Sarah or seeing Sarah as bright. Remember, Hagar was pregnant by the request of Sarah.

And even QALAL in the Bible is linked to QARAH meaning "befall" or "become a physical reality." So, what on Earth drove these women apart?

In the Age of History, when seeking a way to get to Heaven, we allowed our love to get hung up on verbal technicalities. And this sad but necessary trade became the grist for many a tragedy. Our heads were separated from our hearts by our vocal cords.

In her way, woman moved through his-story to secure monogamy as the context of sexual union. And it was the subliminal goal of the wives of Abram-Abraham to bring about global monogamy. The fate of Abram-Abraham's wives tells why today Jews believe in monogamy while Muhammadans do not — a puzzle we can only unravel in a true democracy.

Imagine a Spaceship

Imagine we have left the solar system of our dying star named RA. Our planet has become too hot. For RA is burning out — and thus expanding.

Using a plan that the planet had imparted, we set our ship on course to a distant star named EL which was said to be much like RA. We had seen signs that EL would have a planet in orbit that would make a home for us.

Somewhere near the midpoint in our journey to EL, confusion takes hold of the crew. Some folk begin to label our destination "RA," others still call it "EL." But the problem is only linguistic. And after our journey is halfway done, our goal, once above us, is seen as being below us.

The arguments get hot. A third group says we are going to HELL. Between sub-mission from below and sur-render to that above, we float in hopes that the group will gain a common mind-set.

Over the eons, linguistic confusion has beset the space travelers of this planet. Some say we landed here long ago in spaceships such as we hope to build. Others say we were put here in an act of Creation, or seeded in cosmic Evolution. Yet, these are three aspects of the very same event, under-standing sub-stance. Did Jesus ascend to Heaven? Or did he simply enter into the hearts of men by becoming "the Word."

In fact, the outside is the inside. A physical sphere overlaps our spirit sphere, from second to second in space-time. We have five billion years remaining before our sun will die. But it only takes a billion years to create a bright new star, sub-ject of our dreams, ob-ject of desires. And even now as we project electrical energies in th-ought, we move particles in space. Sub-atomic gatherings are our under-standing turning into sub-stance as we create a home in Heaven with forms of the Crystal Word. *"And I saw a new heaven and a new earth: for the first heaven and the first earth were passed away"* (Rev.21:1). Imagine that!

Mix-ups of the Greek word *homo* ("same") with the Latin *homo* ("man") came about because Roman men (culturally "inferior," but militarily "superior") wanted to be "the same" as Greeks.

In the wild, among the apes, inferior males may display posterior parts to a dominant male as a gesture of submission, sufficient to settle any disputes over territory and females.

The concepts of "inferior" and "superior" thus have sexual ramifications and undercurrents in the historic development of civilization. And these are encoded linguistically.

In Latin, *sex* means SIX. In Greek, *hex* means SIX. In English, "a hex" is a spell or sign that separates powers. And "sex" insures "a sequence" of future generations.

In kabbalah, the male is 6. And the hex of sex around the Mediterranean Sea was the heart of a "mister-re" that had affected Abram-Abraham at the age of 99, torn between two females.

In the mind, the quantum leaps of elements are brought into line with crystallizing DNA. So, we section circles into 360 degrees and we segment 60 minutes into 60 seconds each to count the cycles of the sun. Yet, it takes 9 moons to bring forth a child. "Nine" and "new" (from the Latin *nova*) are 9 in kaballah, "femi-nine perfectability."

In total abstraction, "the Word" is the Lord, a true image of God the Father, realized in total abstraction personified. Still, woman is the only carrier of God's Wholeness down to Earth, the bearer of "Eternal Life."

Historic English was weighted in a way to make its examples masculine. ("Be sure to take the baby and wrap *him* in a blanket.") Woman, social by her nature, sang each son a special hymn.

The ups, downs, ins, and outs of language are sexual. For the "Living Word" and "Eternal Life" are parents to us all. Listen to your inner self, after meditation, and you will hear their voices tell you all you need to know.

The number one (1) is a straight line, 180°. The zero (0) is a circle, 360°. These two together are the Tree of Life (10) in kaballah. And we use 1's and 0's to wtite computer-programeese.

As opposites come together, we converse. One view is a con-verse of the second.

Viewpoints may re-verse. And conversation may in fact lead unto conversion.

But mistakes in meaning make it impossible for one person to second another's truth. For example, "negative" is not always bad. A negative attitude toward drugs need not make one act negatively in the presence of people using drugs.

"Zero" is neither negative nor positive. But the concept of "nothing" is often abused in the grammar of the consumer-oriented mind-set.

Other mistakes confuse personal direction with that of the group. "Ascending" can refer to your own personal spirit, not as opposed to others. Before and after the moment of meditation, keep the energy flowing upward. Note that a moment is not a time span; it is the turning point as an individual perceives the uni-verse.

"Upward" means "outward" in a universal sense. So, the upward path is two-fold. In the spirit, it is your link to creative power. In the body, even though you may reach down, you are reaching out in universal terms.

So, the English word "trivia," from the Latin *tri-via*, "three-roads," tells of our minds as they reach out to shape tiny patterns into destiny. In ancient Rome, it was said that where "three roads" crossed, omens could be found.

Decisions of state were often built upon ideas derived from trivia heard at the crossroads. We need only listen and be open to the miracle.

The 18's herein are no more than trivia that happen to be attached to the most important events of the Armageddon years. And in the aftermath, the male (6) and female (9) will intertwine in life (18) on a new plateau.

Baby M got caught in a trade between fostering and hinkleyness — hostage of biology and host to the machine. Her father, Mr. Stern, born in Berlin, had a father, a banker hounded by Nazis. And William Stern's father became a cook.

Baby M's father, like Abram-Abraham had two women, one claiming infertility, both of different religions and social classes. And out of Abram-Abraham, through these two women, came the divided generations of "Arabs" and "Jews."

Stern, born after World War II, saw the Left divided from the Right in BE-RL-IN.

And HIT-LER left Stern with a feeling that he had no blood relatives before the birth of Baby M. Of course, we are relative to more than blood. Yet, Stern's feelings were historically genuine.

William (Will I Am) was Stern's first name. And his Star in the House of Mary (Mary Beth) and in God by an oath (Elizabeth) manifested his will.

Meanwhile, a constellation of like events was focused in the White House of Ronald (6) Wilson (6) Reagan (6). Mary Beth Whitehead verbally agreed to serve the will of Stern, but refused to sign the final papers. In the White House, Reagan signed for arms to Iran, but his verbal orders implied more than the written command.

This dual nature of words in spoken and written capacities was central to both cases. Can written wills be brought to life? And can a bill (short for will) fill the gap when living wills are not agreed upon and a-greed?

Just as drugs that built techno output at the expense of biology were tolerated, these cases had the techno mind-set "looking down on" the bio mind-set, for such were the goals of history.

In the chain of command, between the "overseer" (Shultz) and Arm-a-cost was Mr. Whitehead at the State Department. Mrs. Whitehead was Baby M's mother. And Mr. Whitehead, in both cases, acted like a White-Head-of-Family stereotype — detached from feeling, attached to the Techno State.

Abraham fathered a child outside his faith with the permission of God. Mr. Stern did so with the blessings of the Techno State. Abraham's contract said his offspring would number among the stars. But God (like Mary Beth) never signed His name.

The Roman Catholic mother of Baby M baptized her *Sara* while *Sarah* was Abraham's Hebrew wife. Stern called her *Melissa*, a Greek (pagan) nymph. And both gave the girl the middle name, *Elizabeth*. Our need was for an oath, and the Code had it in writing.

The circumcision of Abraham and his sons sealed a covenant so we could get to Heaven. Yet, we would need a more gentle feeling toward our own humanity to insure the kindly treatment of other beings in space. The blood of Jesus sealed a new covenant that made the letting of children's blood unnecessary. But then crucifixation also grew a bit outdated as a social ritual.

Females invented monogamy as a reflection of male territoriality. The bed became her territory.

Monotheism, monogamy, and money are peaceful ways to consciously work with male instincts of territorial dominance, giving males convergent fields of play in which to choose to have a home. Still, we must play at these new games honestly for them to work out peacefully.

If Baby M were taken as a new covenant with the Techno State, monogamy would be devalued.

Likewise, Reagan's secret deals against the wishes of Congress and the body politic were a basic infidelity. Jim Bakker's written marriage certificate had no clause *explicitly* forbidding sex with another woman. But the spirit of his marriage had been violated. The stories of Baby M, Reagan, and Bakker show how spoken and written language were in contra-diction at a crucial point in his-story. Babel had begotten Baby-L-on, our techno child. Knowing the moral of our story is a step toward living true to biology while feeling the depth of our new morality.

Choosing Our Signs

We use many signs to divide us. Arabs celebrate high holy days in accord with the crescent moon of Ramadan; it is a crescent since Hagar, mother of all Arabs, was slighted by Abram-Abraham. Jews use a full moon to set the date of Passover. And Christians determine Easter by linking a full moon (from the Jewish tradition) to a Sun-day on their sun-based (son-based) calendar.

As historic patterns had built new meaning into every turn, our modern drama did the same.

The court-appointed guardian of Baby M had the name **Lorraine** (famous in war) **Abraham**. And so, she lost track of the spirit of the child. **Elliot** (Jah is God) **Abrams**, in Inter-American Affairs, lost track of the money from North to the Contras and admitted lying to Congress. And General **Abrahamson** (pronounced *Abramson*), in charge of "Star Wars," lost track of the nation's corporate mind.

The bottle babies of Baby-L-on were angry with their machine. Snatched from biology, hooked on plastic, no longer Whole, children of the Whore cried out for an organic family.

The Egyptian ISIS lost her husband OSIRIS. He was cut to pieces. His name had a feminine O to start with, and SIRIS related to ISIS.

ABRAM (counterpart of OSIRIS) also centers in R ("life," 18) as does SARAH. Yet, HAGAR had its R at the end and was centered in "gravity." Keep in mind that the HA is "levity."

The Moslems had yet to embrace monogamy while Christians and Jews were much of the time engaged in serial one-mate relationships.

"The Word" and "the Life" know each other when an individual Lord and an individual Wife rule their Home by the laws of eternity, the laws that we start with in the garden.

Centered in E-quality, we can re-spect (see-again) the souls that we have seen before. Up, down, in, and out, eternally E-volving, ours is the spirit-energy that creates the metaphor.

CHAPTER 42

REFLECTIONS ON NAM

"Cherubims and a flaming sword" kept Adam from returning to the garden (Gen. 3:24). So, the first tool named in the Bible is the sword that blocked our return from the East of Eden.

Yet, the Hebrew word for "sword" is *chereb*. So, the "flaming sword" and "Cherubims" had the same root name. And Adam saw angels in the flames as he departed through the gates of Eden. Yet, now as his-story ends, we can return to the garden, with flames at our command.

The SWORD of cherubs is now under the order of Angels. And "the WORD" has come to Earth anew, in the language of the Angles.

So, history's final skirmishes will be fought in courts of law, as the sword of military might falls under the rule of written documents.

In the 1960's, many people in the USA poured their energies into bringing a halt to the war in Viet Nam. And the USA "changed its mind."

Representative democracy had dictated that the war in Nam should end. Still, the military mind-set did not surrender. And by the 1980's, Nam was symbolic of similar wars that could not be won.

The USA had defoliated Nam with Dioxin, killing people as a "side-effect." But no clear goals were set. And Hollywood raged not about Korea, though twice as many U.S. soldiers died there. For U.S. citizens, the symbol of the ultimate senseless conquest was clearly labeled "NAM."

But since the public called a halt to NAM, "low intensity" and "covert" warfare became the tools of the Government to destabilize "the enemy" in various nations around the globe. Thus, came an inversion of the historic Aryan (superior, upper class) martial image of "MAN."

MAN spelled backwards is NAM

The USA was being born anew. On TV and in its city streets, protest marches fashioned in the Civil Rights Movement had a spirit of non-violence. And so, official U.S. foreign policy, to get around the then youthful spirit of peace, became a secret affair.

No, the issues of war and peace were never that clearly defined in the Age of History. For almost every soul on Earth had a war within. But in the USA's general trend during the reign of 666 was the largest "peacetime" build-up of the military in both the nation's and global history.

North, Secord, McFarlane, and many others in the private Contra supply network were veterans of the war in NAM. And they carrried with them the scars of a war that had never ended in their minds — a war that they saw as endless, a war of opposing "isms."

In the USA, the body politic wore sackcloth and ashes after the spirit's death in NAM. And it sent its veteran penitents to beg in the streets. For NAM crushed the soul of MAN in Je-R-usa-L-em, torn between "the East" and "the West," between Commun-ism and Capital-ism.

Officially, between 47,655 and 58,132 were listed as killed in battle. But those Missing-In-Action confused the body count. Officially, 21,000 suicides among vets who had come home contrasted with reports by independent veterans groups who said many more vets committed suicide at home than were killed in Nam.

The karma of Nam became obvious when a Brooklyn Federal Court (6/5/84) dismissed the class-action suit of 18,000 Viet Nam vets. And the makers of Dioxin gave out $180 million to sprinkle over the hospital bills and damaged genes of the children of Viet Nam vets.

NAM meant as much to MAN in the USA, as the USA meant to Je-R-usa-L-em. But by 1980, the people's charisma had faded. And the writers of "law" had a lapse of memory. Covert low-intensity war waged by the USA escalated. And so, the voice of the people was diffused. And Oliver North, ex-NAM agent was waiting in the wings.

Colonel North (a Catholic Charismatic) showed that he was not ready to listen to the voice of the people. Yet, in a true democracy, the charisma of the people, whether in street demonstrations or in democratic open debate, is as close to the voice of God as humanity can come.

After my own discharge from the U.S. Air Force (I served as a linguist in Germany), I was proud to march to end the war in Nam. Before I enlisted, I had marched in the Bronx to stop the segregation of Woolworth's lunch counters in the south. And the charisma of the marchers in both cases felt the same — united for World Peace.

What would USA-China-Soviet relations be like today if the USA had conquered Nam?

Just as segregation had been moved into hiding, so overt warfare was dropped from the headlines. So, citizens could not easily rally against them or focus attention on a resolution.

As energy, you cast a light. As matter, you cast a shadow. Yet, you can judge between these two only when cast in a social role.

So, read your lines in the knowledge that you will be judged not for the role you were given. What matters most is how well you support ALL the others in the cast.

The Ancient Egyptians did not accept the Jews as the Chosen People. Yet, Moses was adopted by the Pharaoh's daughter so he could be raised to where he might lead the Jews. He found his faith in miracles.

All Jews could not accept Jesus as the Messiah. Yet, Judas played his part to make Jesus "King of the Jews" to suffer and die, and be re-cast as the key to Jerusalem's mystery play. He found his faith in miracles.

Some Christians alive today may try to avoid accepting "the Word" in its Second Coming. Yet, once made Flesh and transformed into Holy Light, "the Word" will begin the democratic process that shall eventually unite all nations.

This power of "the Word" is not political in the Phase Two divisive sense. Rather "the Word" is organic. And so, only through humanity does "the Word" perform its miracles.

"Set up the standard toward Zion: retire, stay not, for I will bring evil from the NORTH and great destruction" (Jeremiah 4:6).

Falwell said "evil from the North" meant that the USSR would attack Israel. But as the USSR was searching for a new bio-industrial balance that would be needed in Phase Three, the "Communists" also moved toward democracy.

Could the prophecy of Israel's trouble "from the North" have referred to some fleeting star?

Oliver North was to politics as John Travolta was to acting. He made a flash and fizzled. And the media seemed a bit ashamed of the synthetic "North Star" that TV had spawned.

The Bible said Lucifer would weaken nations, again with a trouble out of the North. *"For thou hast said in thy heart, I will ascend into heaven, I will exalt my throne above the stars of God: and sit upon the mount of the congregation, in the sides of the North"* (Isaiah 14:12-13).

Ollie was in the ranks loyal to 666. And he did exault himself in the Final Days.

McFarlane tried suicide under the weight of lies. And Poin-dexter blew smoke. For the final chapter of the Bible says, "whosoever loveth and maketh a lie" will not enter through the gates of New Jerusalem.

The actual plan of salvation is through truth, not through deception. Each nation will be set to growing in true democracy, which means a bio balance where the people control technology for the common good. And as various nations find their common interests in ecology, they shall begin to unify — in Peace.

In 1959, when I joined the freedom marchers, I never got farther then the Bronx. I had no sense of political strategy, only a feeling.

In 1969, when I delivered the valedictory at Manhattan Community College, I spoke out against Nixon's move into Cambodia — years before I had seen the workings of the Language Crystal.

NAME spelled backwards is E-MAN

Adam's power over animals came from names he gave them. Spiritual man, energy-man (E-MAN) altered nature by his power to NAME. And in his-story, we played the game of names amongst ourselves.

E-gypt's first monarch was *Narmer*. In Ger-man, *namen* means "to take." And He-brew was divided when Abram added ha (laughter) to his name. A power struggle with the Chosen People was evident from Egypt to Germany. And in the end, Je-R-usa-L-em will beat its S-WORDs into PLO-W shares as the children of Abram-Abraham are re-united in "the Word."

NOISE IN SION

The IM-PLO-SION has already begun. The Hebrew God "I AM," the earthly "PLO," and the Christian "SION," as religious concepts, have rotted in the Holy Land to make the compost for our new beginning.

We have seen that "God listens" (Ishmael), the first Arab, Abram-Abraham's first son, was denied his rites in writing. God calls Isaac (the second son) the "only son," saying *"Take now thy son, thine only son Isaac, and get thee into the land of Moriah* ("Jah provides") *and offer him as a burnt offering on the mountain"* (Gen. 22:2).

Our conflict of bio and techno sacrifices will call for an IM-PLO-SION of his-story, after which "the Word" returns wedded to "the Life" by the original law.

And this message already dwells in you. Listen to your very own words. NOISE is an offensive sound. And SION begets harmony, where E (energy) is more than abstract.

Ab-ram burned a ram to spare Isaac, who become the father of Jacob, who changed his name to Israel. And a NOISE was heard in (E)SION as that ram cried out to heaven. Our next phase requires sacrifice, not of animals, not of fire, but of ourselves so that we may work for love, not driven by drugs or by overconsumption.

The missile-destroyer, Kidd, was in the Gulf to escort the Bridgeton, under Captain **Brindel** (whose name means "branded"). The Bridgeton struck a mine 18 miles off the Iranian island of Farsi.[1] And Fundamentalists in Iran "branded the Kidd," part of the karma "out of the North," a name that (like 666) was a symbol more than a man.

Religious Fundamentalists in the USA persued their Armageddon plans, drawing on the Bible but avowing "strict interpretation" though most could read no Hebrew, Aramaic, or Greek, So, most people did not realize that the Living Bible was still unfolding — in English.

The 2nd day of North's testimony, Reagan poked his own left eye.[2] He called for 18 more months of war. And only days after Reagan poked his eye, Sandinista forces captured a U.S. Redeye missile from the Contras.[3]

What became of the spirit of MAN in Je-R-usa-L-em? The boys out of the North, embittered in NAM, went on a rampage of bloodlust. And so, the prophecy was fulfilled to overflowing. The front page of *the Times* told of an 18-year-old pregnant woman murdered by guerrillas who also killed 9 soldiers and murdered 3 children, but failed to capture their target.[4]

Many people in the USA thought of Nicaraguans as less than human, not like "gooks," yet somehow expendable. But the attackers were not Viet Cong. They were Contras. Of 30 people wounded, 18 were civilians. And it was the first major Contra raid since Iran-Contra hearings had begun — two days after the testimony of Colonel Oliver North.

"A bunch of contras just shot machine guns into my house as they ran by," said Adolfo Novoa as he told of the death of his daughter Maria, 13 years old, not unlike North's daughter (without North's security gate) — not unlike Natasha Simpson.

(1) NY Times 7/11/87, (2) NY Times 7/23/87, (3) NY Times 7/26/87, (4) NY Times 7/19/87

CHAPTER 43

TERROR-ISM

When the idea was no more than a press release, Star Wars weapons were said to be "18 feet long."[1] Also, the USSR was rumored by Reagan to have an anti-satellite (ASAT) capable of knocking out 18 U.S. satellites in orbit.[2] So, our instruments of death were given the number of "life."

Reagan's Star Wars proposal was first priced at $1.8 billion.[3] Later, as the Iran-Contra hoax took shape, Israel got $1.8 billion in military aid,[4] imported $1.8 billion in goods from the USA,[5] and ran a $1.8 billion deficit.[6] In fact, Israel got $1.8 billion in military aid yearly[7]. So, in our extended metaphor, it is easy to see how "Star Wars" and our "struggle with God" fits into Abram-Abraham's deal to have his seed "number among the stars."

Reagan's Chief of Defense, Ryan ("little king"), said of arms sales, "If it were strictly business, with no political considerations, I bet we could sell $18 billion a year."[8] Would he sell arms to Russia?

Commies communally had weapons they could not share. Cappies spent more to defend their capital than they could afford. MX missiles cost $18 million each in 1981 (before they were built).[9] And by 1984, a plan to buy 30 MX missiles was cut in half to $1.8 billion. Each missile cost a bit more. Still, the terror machines were bought and sold with a focus on the number of "life." And at the time of Reagan's final summit (1988), Maj. Gen. William F. **Burns** (not to be confused with Arnold **Burns** who quit due to the Wed-tech military scandal) was director of the Arms Control and Disarmament Agency. The meaning of the word "disarmament" is not clear in this military context.

(1) NY Times 7/21/84, (2) Time 7/16/84, (3) U.S. News 5/14/84, (4) NY Times 7/12/85, (5) Time 5/6/85, (6) Time 7/15/85, (7) NY Times 3/19/87, (8) NY Times 9/29/85, (9) NY Times 10/3/81

As 666 stumbled along Je-R-usa-L-em's path, the Pentagon projected its future yearly expenses in space at $18 billion.[1] Military spending came under attack. The House Armed Services Committee asked for "a $1.8 billion cut" in military funds sought by Reagan.[2] And front page headlines said that the "Military received $18 billion extra" due to overestimates of inflation.[3]

But the Senate cast only 18 votes against the runaway budget.[4] Reagan was allowed to borrow $180 billion to finance the deficit.[5] And one of the few areas in which the U.S. ran a hefty balance of payments surplus was its military sales to NATO of $1.8 billion, "good for the economy."[6]

And U.S. entrepreneurs got into the act as some 18,000 people in different weekend groups paid to play at "War Games" using red dye "to kill" their rivals.[7] Others opposed to war were jailed. And the Supreme Court in a landmark case ruled against 18 avowed and verbal draft resisters who claimed to have been selectively prosecuted.[8]

Shortly after the number of "missing in action" (MIA) dropped below 1800, 18 MIA names were re-registered as "killed in action" for the Vietnam Veterans Memorial (built just 18 months before the ceremonies).[9] Later, "an honor guard of 18 U.S. Military personnel saluted" the remains of former MIA's shipped from Hanoi.[10] At a Senate meeting, David Stockman scorned excess military spending and then suggested an $18 billion pension plan for veterans.[11] Stockman said he didn't know where the numbers came from. Still, by 1986, the pension plan was, as he had suggested, $18 billion.[12] And those involved thought it was "reasonable."

(1) Time 11/26/84, (2) NY Times 5/22/85, (3) NY Times 5/20/85, (4) Time 5/13/85, (5) Newsweek 2/11/85, (6) Business Week 9/24/84, (7) Ibid., (8) NY Times 3/20/85, (9) U.S. News 4/22/85, (10) Time 8/26/85, (11) Time 2/18/85, (12) NY Times 4/1/86

Punkey Monkey, Guerilla Terrorist

Why is this chapter entitled "Terrorism"? These great military weapons were not said to be the tools of "terrorists." For most "mainstream" news was terrified of speaking plain English. But lowly "punk culture" told a greater truth.

Kinda, we're into the military. Like uniforms and things. G.I. hair goes punk. Fashions in the streets. A broken G.I. Joe, all the rage in rags. Slam-dance freques. You know? Anarchy on toast. Cartoon hero super-doll smuggles dope for Punkey Monkey too. Batteries deluded. Crazy glue. And spit is my culture.

Like poetry and Grandma's hair was blue. Fun-for-all. Re-Joyce! Freak out. Krishna. Get down. Butter's free. And guns go better with coke or pep-si-si. I-cecream, the cow-boy dream. Corporal Flesh, Privates Inyerpants, Doughboy, Sergeant Death, and Admiral Terror ist on the list. Punkey Monkey nukes the nerds. Graffiti Hell. See and do. It's gonna be the death a you. We are children of your vice. Got blue hair like Grandma do. And we make a chicken stew — like you.

DIVAD (the Sergeant York gun) in reflection was DAVID, a star in our Armagedon show.

McDonald Douglas underbid to build 18 nuclear submarines and got embroiled in a General Dynamics scandal.[1] April 18th, the Armed Services Committee expressed "concern" over GD's cost overruns.[2] The company threatened the Pentagon with a halt in production. GD was indited for illegal billing on the DIVAD (Division Air Defense) gun after the Pentagon spent $1.8 billion and cancelled the project.[3]

In their next dispute over unsigned time cards and tool orders, GD paid a penalty of $1.8 million in 1987.[4] As you watch the $1.8 millions and $1.8 billions whiz by in this chapter, imagine how Congress must have been hypnotized.

(1) Roger Mudd 7/24/84, (2) U.S. News 4/29/85, (3) Newsweek 12/16/85, (4) NY Times 5/30/87

Automatic Gramm-Rudman cuts would reduce military spending by 18%.[1] And a compromise tax bill was proposed to raise $18 billion in new revenue (*NY Times* 3/19/86). But 666 said he would veto both military cuts and taxes. Meanwhile, the economy was taxed by voodoo military price-fixing.

Boeing got $1.8 billion to upgrade strategic bombers.[2] And $1.8 billion to develop Osprey's airframe was split by Boeing.[3] Westinghouse saw military contracts rise to $1.8 billion.[4] "Nuclear energy," a military venture to get plutonium at civilian expense, yielded four unfinished nuclear units at a loss of $1.8 billion.[5]

B-1 bombers were estimated at $1.8 billion.[6] So, Reagan juggled guns and butter, cutting Food Stamps to $1.8 billion.[7] Simple enough.

To 18,000 vets of Nam, $180 million was offered by Agent Orange (drug) chemical dealers.[8]

In Reagan's first term, the new Army fighting vehicles cost $1.8 million each.[9] The Air Force sought to deploy the MX in 18 Titan silos.[10] Reagan asked **$180 billion** for a nuclear arsenal.[11] A plan for Pentagon communications cost $18 billion.[12] And by the year's end, there was "an 18% real (inflation adjusted) rise" in military spending.[13]

The F-18, "the Navy's most versatile warplane," had a poor tail design.[14] Strategic minerals had dwindled to "an 18-month wartime capability."[15] Big nuclear arsenals were traded for little nuclear weapons. And spin-off put two scoops of free radicals in every meal. But no one in the media's mainstream dared to call it "terrorism."

Terrorism was "officially" defined as the acts of a somewhat unofficial enemy commited against the good people who did not have "foreign" sounding names.

(1) NY Times 1/23/86, (2) Wash. Post 11/19/85, (3) NY Times 5/2/86, (4) Time 2/13/84, (5) USA Today 1/2/85, (6) NY Times 11/19/81, (7) Time 3/2/81, (8) NY Daily News 6/5/84, (9) Time 7/27/81, (10) Wash. Post 10/30/81, (11) NY Times 10/5/81, (12) NY Times 11/1/81, (13) U.S. News 3/1/82, (14) NY Times 7/26/84, (15) Aviation Week & Space Technology 5/5/80

As 666 took office, nuclear weapons of the Soviet Union targeted 18,000 square miles of communities in the United States.[1] Soviet males were drafted at 18.[2] And the S.U. Army was "a mobile, highly effective force of 1.8 million men."[3] The S.U.'s largest nuclear missile was the SS-18.[4]

Soviet troops in Afghanistan got 180 rubles per month extra combat pay while using 18-inch poison gas cylinders against the people.[5] Only 18 members of the U.N. opposed withdrawal of the USSR while 18 nations did not vote.[6] And the Afghan population was then estimated at "up to 18 million."[7]

The S.U. coveted Afghan land, but eventually had to withdraw. El Salvador and Nicaragua were sought by the U.S. But the bully boys were faced with morality. "National Security" ignored the farms dying in the U.S. And pollution was rampant globally. Commies and Cappies took coffee with sugar, ate insanely, and toasted their peace treaties with champagne. And both advocated the moderate use of official terror.

Officially reported, when Reagan's term began: "Six nations are known to be capable of producing nuclear arms; an estimated 18 others have these weapons stationed on their soil or provide basing for planes and ships that transport them."[8]

In 1986, Reagan asked $5.4 billion (three times the original price) for Star Wars.[9] Reagan said, "an 18-unit Bombardment System" in the USSR was a Star Wars prototype.[10] "The Great Communicator," talked with the USSR but laughed at Nicaragua and Libya when they wanted to talk. The USA's United Nations staff paid $1.8 million a year in rent.[11] But the USA refused to pay its U.N. dues. And 666 ignored the World Court's condemnations of his own international "terrorism."

(1) The Fate of the Earth by Jonathan Schell, (2) Time 6/23/80, (3) Newsweek 10/27/80, (4) NY Times 10/9/81, (5) Time 3/24/80, (6) Time 1/28/80, (7) Time 1/28/80, (8) World Military and Social Expendatures-1980, (9) NY Times 9/2/84, (10) Time 6/9/86, (11) NY Times 4/30/86

Never before have we had the ability to store so many facts. And as the data stacks up, we have a miracle of coincidences. J.C. wanted his MX's on flatbeds 180-foot-long and 666 wanted his MX Dense Pack silos spaced 1800 feet apart.[1] A day after the 1982 defeat of Dense Pack, the House passed a record defense budget, but "$18 billion less than Reagan wanted"[2] (not to be confused with the afore-mentioned $1.8 billion cut).

In 1983, Reagan set a February 18th deadline for basing the MX. And in 1985, the MX came up against a series of test votes in Congress March 18th.[3]

In 1984, off Lebanon, U.S. ships carried anti-missile systems capable of tracking 18 targets at one time.[4] **Aegis** (Shield of Jupiter) was their name, for the USA had "strange gods" in war. Also off Lebanon, the **Taraina** ("Up from Hell") assault ship with 18 helicopters on board awaited Reagan's orders.[5] Tiny Tomahawk cruise missiles, 18 feet long, were ready.[6] And taxes were 18% of the GNP to finance the war-lord mythology.[7]

In 1984, a new type of U.S. infantry division was created, with one medic to every 18 soldiers.[8]

Army "double time" was 180 steps per minute. But regular time was 120 — no overtime of course.

When put together, the Pentagon Joint Chiefs of Staff had 180 years of military service.[9] The USA spent $1.8 billion to modernize the Remote Early Warning radar.[10]

AND REAGAN'S EIGHT-YEAR PROJECTION
OF MILITARY EXPENDATURES
(NOT INCLUDING BRIBES)
WAS $1.8 TRILLION.[11]

This military techno output did not contribute much by way of spin-off for our real techno needs, except for those who thrived on terror.

---

(1) Time 12/6/82, (2) Time 12/20/82, (3) NY Times 2/27/85, (4) Time 2/20/84, (5) U.S. News 9/26/83, (6) Time 1/31/83, (7) Time 1/24/83, (8) NY Times 2/19/84, (9) Congressman William Grey PBS 2/12/83, (10) NY Times 2/12/86, (11) NY Times 5/14/85

When Prime Minister Begin dispatched 6 Israeli jet planes to destroy a nuclear power plant in Iraq, those jets had cost $18 million apiece and were products of the USA.[1] Coincidentally, slowdowns in the USA added 180 weeks to the time for building them and $18,000 to the cost of each.[2] Israel's surrogate war against Iraq by way of Iran headed toward melt-down under 666.

On another battlefield, with 36,000 soldiers in Lebanon, Israelis set up 18 miles from Damascus.[3] Syrians had pulverized a city of 180,000 (Hama) in Lebanon.[4] And Lebanon's President asked that the U.N. peace-keeping force of 5400 be increased.[5] Just then, Begin stepped down as Prime Minister only 18 days after giving notice.[6] And at that time, 1800 Marines went into mock combat in El Salvador.[7]

We began 1985 with the end of an 18-day recess in Lebanese-Israeli peace talks. On March 18th, the bloody Sidon battles began, and the seeds were sown for later acts that the media in the USA was to label "terrorism."

Media language was aimed at consumerdom. But our puzzle went deeper than "culture versus counter-culture." Outside the walls of the garden, all animals lived with terrorism.

Spain, long immune from Mid East problems due to its Moorish heritage, had an affinity for Arabic culture. Also, Spain did not recognize Israel as a state in Palestine. But the first "terrorist" bomb went off in Spain killing 18 people.[8] Would it have been better to die by "conventional" warfare? State-sponsored killings in El Salvador, murder by the USSR in Afghanistan, and Chinese torture in Tibet was not labeled "terrorism." Still by year's end, global military spending had reached $1.8 million per second, under techno terror.

(1) Time 7/27/81, (2) Time 6/8/81, (3) Time 8/15/83, (4) Time 9/5/83, (5) U.S. News 9/19/83, (6) Newsweek 9/2/83, (7) Time 8/15/83, (8) NY Times 4/28/85

"Higher order reasoning" in the children of the USA was said to be on the decline.[1] Were the children just too terrified to think? Or were they thinking in their own "order of reasoning." Most children knew that adults could be unreasonable — even terrorfying.

"The authorities" doubted childhood authority. So, the bio-honesty of children meant little to the "East-West-Black-White-Left-Right" so-called "higher order reasoning" that most grown-ups used to make their decisions.

Wedtech got military contracts with the help of Reagan's crony, Nofziger. An $18 million bid for engines sought by the Army was more than doubled and $1.8 million in stock went to politicians.[2] And at the Bakker-Blazes Cross Road Church, Nof-ziger was a sign of Nepotism. The names fit, and the numbers fit. The pattern was a miracle.

July 1987, as the Iran-Contra hearings dragged on, Nofziger was indited. Influence sold in the White House to raise Contra funds was called "diplomacy" rather than "influence peddling." And in Reagan's first term, the USA paid 18% of the interest owed to the International Monetary Fund (IMF) by indebted nations. The World Bank floated loans to 1800 projects within those same debtor nations.[3] And debtor nations were obliged to abide by the techno mind-set. It was the same old influence peddling. But organic farms got no funding from the World Bank or IMF.

Organically grown, non-processed, un-packaged, raw food was not a blue chip stock. Nuclear power plants supplied materials used in bombs. Waste from making bombs was used to irradiate food.

Pluto, god of hell, had reached the top in our money-ruled plutocracy. We schooled our scientists in "socially accepted" nuclear planning. We built our nuclear-power-plant time bombs all around the globe. And we went to bed with our own techno-terrorism. For the nations would not find their people till languages were organically clear and thoughts were free.

(1) NY Times 8/27/84, (2) NY Times 11/12/86, (3) NY Times 3/8/83

CHAPTER 44

ANATOMIC WRESTLING

Einstein died April 18th, 1955. And his brain was removed by a group of anatomists. But they could not agree on how to dissect it. So, now the brain is stored in preservatives while the anatomists remain divided about information they think is in Einstein's brain, anatomically.

But, from an-atom-y, "anatomy" can mean "not made of atoms." The reason for this goes back to Ancient Greek logic and the fact that it may take many atoms to make up a living cell; but no single atom can contain life in itself. Life is a union of matter in the spirit.

The iron in Einstein's brain and the iron in a car may have similar atomic structures. But since no atom has a "life" of its own, and anatomy has "life," that "life" must come from an organization that is beyond any atoms.

"Life" re-organizes atoms into forms that also have "life." Yet the word an-atom-y tells us that "life" can exist separate from any substance at all. "Life" is an-atomy.

Albert (Adel-brecht, "noble-brilliant") Einstein ("one-stone") was a spirit working through a body. His calling was noble, bright, and single-minded. And his soul (the cause of his brilliance) could not be dissected.

This chapter explores the error of applying our techno mind-set to biological reality, rather than the other way around.

The pretence that bio stuff is really techno stuff is what I call professional-wrestling-ism. And "scientists" in this wrestling profession must act as if their game is real.

"Professional-wrestling-ism" marks any group in which the observers are part of the lie. Ringside fans express belief while remote fans watch on TV, read fan magazines, and believe. The ring may be any profession, political party, religion, nation, or even a marriage — any profession that does not profess what is true to life.

Professional-wrestling-ism reached its peak in the final years of Armageddon as Iran-Contra farces, AIDS cover-ups, Wall Street re-shuffles, and whore-preacher Sunday picnics shared the arena.

At the Iran-Contra tag-team match, Senators at ringside got appropriately charged over every phony drop-kick, excited over every false-emotion. And following the rules of the professional-wrestling cult, congress cheered and jeered on cue.

Fans of AIDS TV-commentary knew what to expect — the same old head-locks, lots of emotion, but not a lot of intellectual stimulation and no facts about the real origins of "AIDS." The science writers who watched the scientists who held onto Einstein's brain were involved in a similar farce. They refused to give credit to the spirit just as Senators overlooked the bio-conscious need for a true democracy.

And the Wall Street free-for-all showed technology to be bio-illiterate while the ring-side announcer praised the feigned nobility of military "defense."

Colonel North's profession, he professed, was telling lies, known as counter-intelligence. He dramatically defended the art of patriotic lying — a pinnacle of Phase Two linguistics.

"The Chosen" and "the un-Chosen" called for a rematch. And though we had taken our first steps to Heaven, by the rules of professional-wrestling-ism, it seemed we wanted to compete rather than to complete Phase Two and let go of history.

The super-cults of "medical science," "military politics," and "organized religion" were addicted to the fights. For their "professionals" (stuck in a dying language of monetary greed) had lost track of the forward flow of time.

Only spiritually can we see that "anatomy" is individual. When Einstein died, he left a clump of atoms which no longer held his anatomy. But the enzymes of his body did not die; they helped the corpse to decay. And if all of Einstein's cells were not pickled, some of those enzymes are still alive today.

"Test Denied" versus "The Law"

The first public address by Reagan after the Iran-Contra hearings said something that could not be reported in print. The "professionals" would not reveal their leader's verbal slips.

Said the President with reference to Admiral Poindexter (8/13/87), "The admiral test denied, uh, testified that he wanted to protect me."

Reagan's words were clear (on tape). But no one asked, "Mr. President, did you just say 'test denied'?" If the Bedouin Bouncer slipped into a Brooklyn accent, TV hosts pretended not to notice, and the "referee" (one to whom we refer) joined in the "professional" sham. And so it was in the "professional" speech community.

False-positives and false-negatives with AIDS made room for statistical invention. Poindexter diverted funds and said Reagan had "deniability." Fawn Hall claimed North was "above the law." Jim Bakker and Jimmy Swaggart forgave themselves. Each had their specific "test denied." And his-story had lost its bio standards.

Looking backward in time, "cut up" was *tom ana* in Greek from *tom* "to cut." *A-tom* meant "that which could not be cut." We cut up bodies and called it ana-tomy. But *ana* did not mean "up." When we break it down, *ana* meant "not not" among a people who had no number zero. An evolving of zero th-ought leads a physician to meta-physical reality.

The Raw Law says that consciousness is passed through the anatomy of living enzymes. And "the law of yield," says that we are also spiritual beings who advance when we observe the free will of others. Eventually, a "professor" of these laws feels them contained within each other.

Also, the temporal laws tell us: Mono Diety is a good person for individuals to identify with; mono mating lets a male stop fighting to insure that dumb brutes do not dominate the gene pool; and money allows the individual, family, nation, and the family of nations to coordinate techno values with our bio needs.

397

Neither Newtonian physics nor Einstein's theory of relativity held any logical explanation for why time flowed only toward the future. No "scientific law" said time could not flow in reverse.

And Einstein's original theories were rejected due to division mistakes he made with a zero.

Some said time flowed only forward due to the expansion of the universe, a theory that entailed the mystery of "Miss Entropy" (growing disorder) in search of greater mental order to explain it. But only borders of lesser orders gave any hint of entropy. And the paradox was that we needed to go through this techno th-ought process so our race could have eternal life, biologically.

The headline said, **"World Faces Weak Growth"** (*NY Times* 6/12/87), quoting a U.N. report: "the global economy" is not expanding quickly enough to end unemployment in "industrial nations" or to raise "the standard of life" in "developing countries." Each phrase was loaded with techno bias.

Is "the standard of life" raised by adding acid rain, deforestation, holes in the ozone layer, and polluted water? Is "the global economy" equal to "expanding technological production"?

Wall Street's flop in the final days warned of techno items flowing in wider markets that could not be tolerated without recycling.

The anatomy of the body politic already knows what must be done. Natural foods, nature walks, and love that will replace our drugs.

Phase Two language professed that which served "the wrestlers." Yet, in Phase Three, to profess is to share a belief with others. So, a professor is one who shares.

You are a professor of politics, science, and biology; you are what you profess.

And since "anatomy" means "not made of atoms," the real professor is spirit. So, now we know the champion in the ring where meta-physical meets the physical — we know who rules anatomy.

CHAPTER 45

HARMONICS OF THE WALL STREET CRASH

With 666 re-elected in 1984, the fiscal bubble was allowed to expand more rapidly. A "new limit of $1.8 trillion" was set for the national debt.[1] And even as the **debt** (cumulative) mounted, plans were made to bring down the **deficit** (added each year to the debt) for that year to $180 billion.[2]

Finances had a mystical tone. And the deficit was to be reduced yearly by $36 billion, from $180 billion to $144 billion to $108 billion, which were magic numbers of the Jews, the Christians, and the Buddhists respectively.

But the plan had a catch. As 666 took office, printing costs were 1.8 cents per dollar bill with circulation of 18 months.[3] But in his second year, credit "Smart Cards" encoded data on 180 accounts and cost "only" $18 each to produce.[4] The new "money" was not issued by any government. And the credit trend was escalating.

Experts said people over 18 kept $18 billion in U.S. cash with them at any given time.[5] But the instant credit (instant debt) was replacing cash. (Kelly **Cash** was Miss America in the year of 666's symbolic death.) And Reagan-ethics had been sold to supply-siders who had no supplies.

So, the quest for EL-DO-RA-DO had begun anew. And the Harmonic Convergence of 1987 was inspired by Latin and Native American spirits. The event helped bring on the Wall Street crash, And the ghost of EL DORADO, the guilded priest of South American Man-oa (also known as Om-oa) was called into the magic. This confusion of names from the ancient myth shows how "man" and "om" had each derived from an aura of GO(L)D. And these images briefly made the news two months before the Wall Street crash.

(1) U.S. News 5/20/85, (2) NY Times 2/27/85, (3) Time 7/9/79, (4) Newsweek 4/12/82, (5) U.S. News 3/3/86

Gramm-Rudman set a goal of reducing the deficit to $144 billion in fiscal 1987. But that goal was not met. "Fiscal 1987" began October 1, 1986 and ended September 30, 1987 with no reduction. So, a new scheme was passed to set the 1988 deficit at $144 billion for that fiscal year.[1]

At first, I thought I was seeing double. The deficit was supposed to drop to $108 billion, but Reagan vowed to veto military cuts that had been promised in the original reduction plan.

So much for Reagan's voodoo. The crash came within a month after his revised plan: with $36 billion in savings for 1989, $54 billion ceiling in 1991, $18 billion in 1992, zero in 1993.[2]

But with the promise to reduce to $108 billion disrespected, the Stock Market quaked within a month. The bio-techno gap had grown too great, and fiscal-faith dropped out. The Dow fell by 108.36 points in one day. And on that day, the first direct raid on a USA-flagged vessel in the Persian Gulf wounded 18 in the crew.[3]

Now let's look back a bit to when Gramm-Rudman was declared "unconstitutional" on a technicality. The "ruling put the Dow at a minus 18 level" at midday, up 18 in the afternoon, and closed with a gain.[4] Trading on the Big Board was 144.4 million shares. The Nasdaq index was 1.44. And that day, top news was a $1.08 billion Wells Fargo takeover where one big bank had bought the abstract money of another (the law of supply and supply).

Even some of the magic numbers had been preselected by Reagan, many others could be explained only in terms of mystical forces.

As techno traders tried to balance "life," the mystique of gold was subverted by the new super-conductivity. And heavenly symbolism changed. Gold would still be used in spaceships, but in union with super-conductors that could give us direct telepathic links to machines.

(1) NY Times 9/27/87, (2) NY Times 2/8/86, (3) NY Times 10/17/86, (4) NY Times 2/5/86

The average child support payment per U.S. family was $1800 yearly when 666 was re-elected.[1] And 1.8 million children were "missing."[2] The link between children and money also bordered on the mystical.

Abram-Abraham paid "current money" for a grave for his Hebrew wife. His Egyptian wife was sent away with no burial plot. His Arab son ("God Listens") was not his son in writing and thus got neither money nor land matrilineally. So, the Palestinians and Jews, fought like bio-savage (throwing stones) and techno-savage (firing bullets) over claims to their mother's graves. But the answer to is-ra-el was beyond any physical el-do-ra-do.

In his press conference after the Market crash, 666 lost contact with Ronald Wilson Reagan.

He was quoted: "And I say, there are no — there are no signs of deteriorating economy out there in the economy" (*NY Times* 10/23/87). But Ronald Wilson Reagan actually said, "And I say, there are no, there are no sou — sounds, signs of deteriorating economy out there in the economy" (immortalized on video tape).

"There are no, there are no," set the tone. He found "sounds" difficult to say and decided that "the economy" was OUT THERE, in the economy. So, stocks continued to tumble. What had snagged the "supply-side" numeric illusions?

In a previous chapter (The Crystal Dream) and in a coming Addendum is documented Reagan's fix on the number 144. Yet "the New Age Movement" found the number 144 in Hopi, Myan, and Aztec prophecy when Jose Arguelles acted as a channel to write of 144,000 New-Age people needed to save the Earth. Two months before Wall Street's crash, "the Harmonic Convergence" told of by Arguelles had come to pass.

The so-called "standard of living" had risen 4 times faster in other "industrial nations" than in the USA (*Insight* 7/4/88). But spiritual imbalance was not counted into the numbers.

(1) Donahue, May 1984, (2) Furillo, TV Spot, 1984

Personally,

I joined the Harmonic Convergence ceremony in New York's Central Park. A dancer at Egypt's pyramids, a group at Enchanted Rock, Texas, and others around the globe tuned in to Jose Arguelles as he blew on a conch 144 times in Boulder, Colorado. I saw as B-older, Co-eld-orado. And he prayed for a healing of the Earth (*NY Times* 8/17/87).

Arguelles means "lack of health" in Spanish, a name befitting his quest for planetary healing. The color red (Colorado) in a sacrifice (blood) could attain the gold (salvation) in alchemy. Let the king be Man-oa and the chief priest be Om-oa, the original golden city. Add AUM (a harmonic of OM), plus a symbol for GOLD (AU). And g-o-d is g-o-l-d minus 12 (L) in the Code.

As you see, my inner language is of Phase Three. So, I view values in terms of the future. I think in terms of the crystallized language that we will develop in New Jerusalem.

The third difference (monogamy and wine being the other two) between the Judeo-Christian and the Islamic doctrine was that Moslems, according to dogma, could not charge interest on money.

Money is more than a ploy in New Millennium interactions. Money extends the mystical bridges of our human spirits as we work out our bio-techno equations, democratically.

Destabilizing wars smoldered in Old Nick and El Salvador. As 666 forgot about "the safety of the hostages," he drew Iran into naval war games. Of course, Reagan saw Iran drawing him in. But either way, the sham that hostages were a concern faded as weapons came to center stage.

Several people at "the Harmonic Convergence" sat smoking marijuana. The worship of fire and destruction of biology were not only military. Neither "the Right" nor "the Left" was to blame for our lack of harmony. Harm done by the techno mind-set was both industrial and personal. And it was the unconscious fear of fire that had driven in a wedge to break the heart of humanity.

Impossible Coincidences?

Harmonic Convergence, said Jose Arguelles (an art historian who wrote *"The Myan Factor: The Path Beyond Technology"*), was predicted by Aztecs for August 16th and 17th, 1987, crucial days to decide on a path of either salvation or disaster.

Many astronomers and scientists said Arguelles had misinterpreted the Aztec documents.

But among the leading "economic indicators" in the USA at that time, two closely linked to Je-R-usa-L-em's global finances registered for me as what seemed to be impossible coincidences.

"The national trade deficit widened to $14.4 billion in May [1987] as imports climbed to the highest level on record."[1] And by June, quarterly exports rose and imports dropped by combined amounts so the net gain was also $14.4 billion.[2]

The waves had canceled each other out. From one month to the next, the trade deficit widened, then the net exports rose, both by the same "144." Note these are "144's" that we have not seen before.

At that time, Cuba "the drunkard." agreed to release 144 political prisoners.[3] Coincidentally, the first day of Harmonic Convergence, the first citizen of the USSR to join Alcoholics Anonymous met with USA members in a hotel room in Moscow, to pray together.[4] These facts are exciting only in the mystical context of "bread and wine" as a step to the salvation of 144,000 in prophecy.

And Rudolf Hess, last of Hitler's inner circle, died as the Convergence went through its cusp of changes. The event took two days to be sure that its timing would cover any errors in readings of the Aztecs. And the next day (August 18th) Israel and the USSR set up regular political contacts.[5] So, Russia (out of the North) was not to fulfill the prophecy of "trouble for Israel" each bit of the mystery was falling into place.

(1) NY Times 7/16/24, (2) NY Times 6/24/87, (3) NY Times 7/10/87, (4) NY Times 8/17/87, (5) NY Times 8/19/87.

The jobless rate fell to 7.2%, but the rich-poor gap widened. Unemployment program cuts of $144 million resulted from Gramm-Rudman, leaving social workers out of work.[1] Yet the Gramm-Rudman bill was not really in effect. For 666 had blocked cuts in military spending by threatening a veto.

The above $144 million cut is not a repeat in this text. Repeats are at a minimum for the sake of clarity. But the Armageddon gang used the same numbers over and over. A 1988 prediction said: "The trade deficit this year would shrink to about $144 billion."[2] Yet on the first page of "The Crystal Dream" herein, we see the same prediction made two years before, in 1986.

A Democrat TV fund raiser, "*Celebrate America*," (5/28/83) in an attempt to unseat Reagan, asked $144 yearly for party support.

News of Jim and Tammy Bakker as we neared the Harmonic Convergence was that $180 million was pledged for non-existent hotel rooms. No less than 18 Justice, Postal, and Revenue investigators looked into it. And PTL said, they "raised $108 million through time shares, but only $54 million of that went for construction."[3] Praise the Lord promised paradise at Heritage USA, and half its 108 was gone.

Beth-lehem Steel (a sign) told 18,000 retirees benefits were cut.[4] And 666 began his new term as the House of Bread, turned cold. The Jerusalem Hilton hotel (a sign) was sold in 1982 for $18 million to David **Sofer** (drunkard) — charged with insider trading near the Convergence. The dollar's largest drop in 12 years of floating rates came the day Egypt's crisis dropped its pound to 1.80 to the dollar.[5] And on the Aryan path, as a result of the 108.36 fall in the Dow (two years later), the dollar went below 1.80 German marks.[6]

(1) NY Times 7/13/87, (2) CS Monitor 5/23/88, (3) Time 8/3/87, (4) MacNeil/Lehrer 6/25/85, (5) NY Times 9/24/85, (6) NY Times 10/18/87

What Kind of Jobs?

We were hypnotized. You could hear people say a nuclear power plant "would be welcome in our town due to jobs it would create." Yet, migrant workers picking crops complained of poison in the fields. For we usually criticized the Techno State less if we had greater investments in it.

Industry could not handle its own trash but was constantly geared up for war. For during history, the Techno State itself had become the landlord, using firepower to subdue biology, its tenant. But as finance is seen to be global, economy in the eco-sense will become the leading financial indicator. Even now, feelings for the global eco-structure are growing as surrogate wars take their inter-national karmic toll.

Refugees and devestated lands affect our global finances. The USSR's destruction of Afghanistan's agriculture raised food costs in Russia.

And on the other side of our visible failures were the invisible forces of his-story. The net wealth of 666, $1,418,000 (*U.S. News* 5/31/82) was 14- and 18, lacking a 4. Reagan said he would not try "to square the circle" — and he didn't.

Still, "leaders" are as much the scapegoats of the people as the other way around. We all had, in part, been sacrificed. So, our minds were in a loop as we tried to draw techno thoughts into line with bio needs.

To recycle waste and sort out monetary values, people of Earth shall re-claim their individual bio-spirits. Rather than consume the environment "to make money," we will use money to make techno interests accountable.

It seems only logical, yet bio-thought begins in a person who is respondent, while people who eat junk food tend to be bio-despondent.

Of course, some "environmentalists" do eat junk food and some "vegetarians" do pollute. But in the long run, the manufacture of junk food pollutes and pollution of the environment lowers the food value of even the best vegetation.

Suck-Cess-Pool

The following news item marked a trend.

Federal researchers quit a study on acid rain because managers feared that the public might not understand the lack of certainty in their research (*Associated Press* 6/8/87). Think on that!

In fact, research was dropped because stopping acid rain would "tax" techno interests in favor of biology. "The cleanup costs are estimated at about $1.8 billion a year," said *the Christian Science Monitor* (6/8/88). But, obviously, money could never count the damages.

We protected technology, watched it grow, and cherished our baby. We changed its diapers, forgot its faults, and suddenly found ourselves wading in techno excrement. Our next step is to toilet train the child while we work on its social attitude and teach it not to drink our blood.

Six days before the Harmonic Convergence, 666 signed a $10.8 billion grant for savings and loan deposit insurance.[1] (No, I did not mention this "108" before.) With hundreds of banks folding, the money infusion ignored the bio imbalance. Brazil quit paying a $108 billion debt, the start of a trend. And the USA was shaky on its proposed $108 billion deficit at that time. (I repeat these two "108's" to show how the global metaphor was headed for Wall Street's 108.36 drop.)

The USA had 18,000 Banks and Savings and Loan Associations.[2] Consumer installment debt was 18.6% of spendable income.[3] People owed banks this much after spending, a squeeze that favored techno over bio. And money illusions seemed endless.

Also, 18,000 insured Credit Unions operated in the USA with a bit more of a bio focus.[4] But the entire global banking system depended on "faith." And the numbers were the grease between bio and techno thought. Yet "faith" had to have its real-life biological roots.

(1) NY Times 8/11/87, (2) U.S. News 3/31/86, (3) US News 1/27/86, (4) Reader's Digest Jan/86

The object of money is value. But just as Phase Two scientists forgot to count themselves in their equations, financial planners neglected to reckon the value of their own "life."

Gramm-Rudman aimed at its first $144 billion and the number unemployed was 108 million.[1] Then, the next Gramm-Rudman goal was $108 billion. But a squabble between 108 Hindu gods and 108 Buddhist no-gods must have confused the accountants.

The chloroflorocarbons destructuring the ozone layer did their devilish work for 108 years in the atmosphere after we released them from the Earth (*Science News* 4/9/88).

And the Iran-Contra slush-fund wars along with others destroyed rain forests while filling the air with smoke. And we were exploding obsolete weapons rather than dismantling them.

Would Armageddonists learn of Buddha nature where no-thing does some good? Tax exemptions were $1,080. Yet tobacco and alcohol lobbies wangled loopholes due to habits of Congress. Cigarette related illness cost over $18 billion when Reagan took office,[2] helping the GNP to its biggest hike in 18 years.[3] And 18 million U.S. adults were hooked on alcohol.[4] But if we paid hospitals more than we earned per day, the GNP would rise, even if an agency paid the bill.

Of taxes Reagan said, "the code includes 18 volumes, 6 feet of shelf space." And he asked the 36 members of House Ways and Means to support his tax plan while eluding the bio issues.

In Reagan's second term, tax protesters were "dealt with more harshly." Besides thousands being fined, "jail terms averaging 18 months for some 180 other protesters" were imposed.[5] Meanwhile, a flat rate of an 18% tax (with no exemptions) had been proposed at the Federal level.[6]

(1) US News 1/6/86, (2) Reader's Digest Feb. 1980, (3) NBC 7/21/83, (4) NY Times 12/7/87, (5) U.S. News 4/1/85, (6) Time 7/19/82

In 1982, the Reaganomic recession "barely caused a ripple in General Electric. The company's bottom line increased to $1.8 billion."[1] Who questioned the real worth of a microwave oven's quicker way to destroy food value? Who knew enough to ask how this new processed food would affect the genes and enzymes of future generations?

As Reaganomics was manipulated out of its nose-dive, economists were "particularly encouraged by an $18 billion drop in business inventories."[2] More items (any items) being sold meant a plus for "the bottom line," an advance for techno finance, usually at the expense of bio economics.

As Reagan began his second term, the wage base on which payroll taxes were levied was raised by $1800 to pay higher Social Security benefits.[3] Were the payments spent on healthful recreation and good food? No, most went for medical drugs, intensive care units, plus a cut for "doctors" and administrators to spend on throw-away cars, wine, coffee, more junk food and high-class garbage that polluted at least as much as, if not more than, low-class garbage.

Reagan proposed in "Treasury II" tax reform to raise "the personal exemption to $1800."[4] As part of the insanity, even families below the official poverty line were forced to pay taxes.

Along with his $144 billion end-term deficit goal, Reagan set an interim goal of $180 billion for 1986. His budget office projected $186 billion for 1986 and $186 billion for 1988. (These are not repeats, though they seem to be.) Future election years were marked with magic numbers.[5]

The major scandals (next page) under Reagan were also tied to magic. But it was unlikely that the conspirators chose these numbers when their goal was to get the loot without attracting too much attention.

(1) Business Week 5/31/82, (2) Newsweek 2/21/83, (3) NY Times 10/25/84, (4) U.S. News 5/20/85, (5) NY Times 2/27/85

Michael Deaver was called "Washington's $18-million man" by *U.S. News* (4/14/86) due to a price he put on his influence peddling business.

Deaver's name is Scots for "a deaf one." Said *U.S. News*, "He knows the President's mind better than almost anyone else." His White House salary was $72,000 (four 18's) as deputy chief of staff. But that was not enough to make him listen.

Deaver was indited March 18th. "The 18-page inditment accuses Deaver of deliberately lying to the grand jury probing his lobbying activities" (*NY Times* 3/30/87). He was found guilty.

Nofziger was Reagan's campaign manager, turned lobbyist in the Wedtech scandal. A fitting label for his modern nepotism (influence peddling) in Uncle Ronnie's Wed-tech scandal, Nofziger derives from *Noef-zeicher* "mark of the nephew."

Added to our other Wedtech links, Nofziger was the 18th person indited.[1] And Attorney General Meese turned a profit on 18 investments that he made through his Wedtech partnership.[2]

Former Labor Secretary Donovan was tried for fraud over a $186 million subway contract and $18 million in sub-contracts to "nonwhite" companies.[3] **Donovan** in Gaelic means "dark stranger."

R. Foster **Winans** won as a "Wall Street Journal" insider. "Faced with about $18,000 in debts," he cheated, he "won," and he got caught.[4]

The dishonesty wasn't new. The consequences, however, had grown greater due to the power of the Techno State to damage the bio-sphere.

Replacing toxic asbestos will cost $1.8 billion through the end of the century.[5] And since 1980, accounts for large industrial corporations coughed up more than $180 million for liability suits, due to the mishandling of financial statements.[6] These were also waves leading up to the crash.

(1) NY Times 7/17/87, (2) NY Times 8/6/87, (3) NY Times 10/5/86, (4) Newsweek 9/15/86, (5) Time 2/3/86, (6) Time 4/21/86

In 1987, Congress justified its pay raises with the rationale that only high salaries would draw "the top people" to work in Government. But school teachers were expected to work for love.

The average monthly Soviet salary was equated to $318 in the USA.[1] But that was no equation. In the USA, 1% of families held 36% of the wealth.[2] And since money made money, centralized power in the USA was as distorting as in the USSR.

The USA's $18 billion Education budget was cut to finance drug programs for youth.[3] And the drug programs, run mostly by coffee-sugar addicts could not teach will power.

Commercial airlines made 18,000 flights per day over poverty-torn cities.[4] And 18 million families owned and used computers in their homes.[5] The year was 1987 — out of balance, out of control.

In the Harmonic Convergence ceremony to mark the end of our old cycle, a fire that burned all night in Boulder, Colorado was put out at sunrise as the conch sounded exactly 144 times.

U.S. financial magic was akin to the golden letters (18 inches high) on the Titanic's bow.

Even the Hindenburg crashed on its 18th voyage killing 36 on board. For the Crystal reflects our dreams, beyond good and evil.

The Government pays $18 billion yearly to those in the USA too disabled to work[6] while industries are allowed to destroy the people's health.

There is no guarantee in magic numbers. We sink or swim, fly or fall by the value of our deeds. So, to control the techno wave, we each must feed the bio life of the higher self. Photo-synthesis is the key. The numbers only lead to awe. The Raw Law makes sense, biologically. At Center Crystal, we know how WAR began in the garden. And we know how to turn WAR around.

(1) NY Times 6/28/87, (2) NY Times 6/21/87, (3) NY Times 8/12/86, (4) Night Line 7/24/87, (5) NY Times 3/8/87, (6) NY Times 6/4/86

Einstein noted a paradox that may allow messages to be sent faster than the speed of light via sub-atomic particles that decay in an asymmetrical fashion (*NY Times* 10/27/87). And the physicists who carried his idea forward were Dipankar Home and Amitava Datta. Of course, the Home-Datta study was a light within, calling out their names.

Budget Director Stockman projected savings of $1.8 billion due to jobs lost by attrition.[1] He told of his dream to cut the size of Government by 18% in an infamous "Atlantic Monthly" article taped at 18 sessions over breakfast.[2] The keeper of 666's stocks, a stock-man fixated on 18 — were the patterns a meta-physical proof?

We have noted that **Prechter** (that which makes one vomit) caused Wall Street to regurgitate its capital by leading his flock over the edge of the Golden Mean (.618) in his Elliot Wave Theory. And we all professed what we had for lunch.

Numbers did not lead us so much as we searched for value among the numbers. As individuals caught in the giant machine, we were secretly worshiping "life," encoded by creative bookkeeping.

E.F. Hutton failed to submit 18 documents that were subpoenaed by the Justice Department.[3] First National Boston Bank (assets $18 billion) pleaded guilty to felony charges.[4] The top players in our money game lacked trust among themselves. Small farms were auctioned off, and agro-business bought up cheaper land, multiplying general mistrust.

The largest independent USA consumer finance company, Beneficial, had revenues of $1.8 billion[5] as housing starts dropped below 1.8 million.[6] Were "real mortgage costs" staying too high? Or was it an instinctual market compensation for our global over-population — financial feedback echoing the eco-sphere?

(1) Time 9/14/81, (2) People 12/28/81, (3) Time 7/22/85, (4) Time 2/18/85, (5) Fortune 10/28/85, (6) Business Week 9/22/86

We can print money till we have no trees, build houses till we have no land, but the Earth will not expand. We can cheat at finances. Yet farmers can no more fool the soil than any one of us can successfully cheat at mealtime.

Ecology is a balance; economy its measure; and finance is a techno tool. So, money cannot serve biology unless we play an honest game where the highest value is "life" itself. In Phase Two, we had mystifed "life" for good old techno reasons. And now, we can demystify anew.

The presumption that "under-developed countries" can follow the path of "industrial nations" is like saying that each State in the USA should produce its own cotton or its own autos. But divisive military thinking has affected the way we view global industrial development.

Replacing gasoline with home-grown gasohol will shift emphasis from oil, gearing up for localized solar power. These events are in line with our Crystal mind-set — organically grown. And solar chips will speed the spread of true democracy.

Reagan's zealots and an impatient Congress cut many disabled folk "from the $18 billion Social Security program."[1] Like Hitler, 666 could not have done the task alone; he had the mood of the nation behind him. Federal debt rose as State's funds plummeted "to only $1.8 billion."[2]

Reagan believed that "supply side" meant techno productivity. But product liability rates showed technology taking value from life. Insurance rates for technology failed their monetary test. So laws were changed to limit techno liability.

Money was used as an international shield for the Techno State since techno "value added" was the foremost religion of history. Even China began its Capitalism as Yanzhong Industries sold at $18 a share.[3] And starting 666's second term, Latin American debt hit $360 billion.[4]

(1) NY Times 5/15/85, (2) Newsweek 7/26/82, (3) Time 2/25/85, (4) NY Times 8/15/85

Inane Carbon Cycles

A U.S. Federal panel consolidated 18 lawsuits from Bhopal against Union Carbide due to many deaths by gas leaks.[1] Up to 2500 dead was estimated by the press. But the Indian Government said, no matter how many died, an official count of **1800** would be the limit.[2] Identifying the dead was given as an excuse for the magic-number limit.

The Union Carbide slaughter was followed by a medical attack. Victims were given pills by many different "doctors" at once. One person, who was unconscious for four days after the gassing, was put on daily doses of cough syrup.[3]

Months later, both sides agreed, "workers would get a total of $1.8 million compensation."[4] Two years later, in 1987, Union Carbide was given till November 18th to settle out of court.

Insurance deals with the un-sure; numbers on paper make Will Power into a written will. But the real-life will must be sure to start with in order for the bio-techno system to make sense.

India was divided by 18 languages at the time of the Bhopal tragedy. And with 1.8 million Hindus in Pakistan calling for freedom,[5] the nation was disorganized. So, Union Carbide set up factories with less "insurance" than needed in the USA.

Two years after the explosion, 180,000 Indian troops staged war games on the Pakistani border.[6] India's $180 billion national income could barely feed its 600 million people,[7] said the news as if money (not food) fed the people. And we waged war on each other as we waged war on our food.

Watermelon poisoning in California (allegedly caused by Union Carbide pesticides) hit the market place several months after the Bhopal gassing. But Carbide insisted their toxic sprays should degrade "to safe levels within 180 days."[8]

(1) NY Times 2/7/85, (2) NY Times 3/31/85, (3) NY Times 3/31/85, (4) NY Times 12/4/85, (5) Time 7/16/84, (6) Time 2/16/87, (7) NY Times 4/1/87, (8) Time 7/22/85

HEAL (as in health), WEAL (as in wealth) — the patterns tell of a future society, a commonwealth of nations on this Planet Earth.

For in English, WEAL means "the body politic." And when "the common weal" is properly aligned, we will have good health in common.

From an individual standpoint, this means that the way to building a truly wealthy society is to provide for your own health. These two concepts of health and wealth are inseparable once the false divisions of Phase Two are demystified.

Nutritional "education" in the USA was mostly propaganda. Wealth was fighting against health. Bureaucrats serving the techno mythology believed "doctors" and took the medicnes covered by their own bureaucratic insurance policies.

But bubonic plague was ended not by vaccines or medical drugs. It was changed sanitary conditions (sewers), altered diets (fewer lard pies), and new eating utensils (without lead) that "cured" us of the plague, before we had any modern medicine.

The causes of modern illness were often "luxury foods," industrial pollutants, inordinate stress, and drugs of all kinds. And our greatest need was to share humanity.

The Harmonic Convergence was more than a bunch of well-intentioned people making folk magic. It was an observance of good and evil in harmony. Remember, when we light a candle we kill microbes in the air. And when we drink water, we drink little animals. Harmony begins with harm. And all forms of life live on life itself.

So, all aspects of the Crystal are reflective. Wall Street's crash was related to 666 (the beast), to Buddhist beads of prayer, to the Table of Elements, to the Fibonacci series, and to the very essence of power (0^0 X 1^1 X 2^2 X 3^3). For society was, as always, feeding on itself. Still, a healthy way exists for us to go about the business of civilization. And it comes quite honestly. All we need do is forgive the past and begin again to eat from the Tree of Life.

CHAPTER 46

INSTINCT, PSYCHOLOGY, AND FOOD

Do we overeat by "instinct" if we fear that there may be a shortage of food? Is psychology the answer to control of the appetite?

Psychology is not the primal force among animals since Psyche, the goddess who holds the flame, is not primitive. So, eating can NOT be properly ruled by psychology. Freud, a Jew, used Latin terms and Greek persona to explain his theories of psychology. Jung, a Christian, chose Buddhism and mandalas. But when their egos clashed, Freud said Jung was a Nazi. Was theirs a pre-conscious feud?

Jung smoked a pipe; Freud, cigars. Both tried to master hidden fear. Had they not smoked, might they have built a cupido-synthesis instead of the psycho-analysis that tore the goddess apart?

Both psychiatrists were Austrians of power when Hitler's Fatherland was on the rise. Both saw the goddess through clouded symbols. A Christian and a Jew cut the Greek Psyche to pieces to serve at the banquet of the post-war Techno State.

Jung attributed fire's discovery to "regression to the presexual stage." He said, frustrated men twirled sticks against dried leaves and bark — pointed ends against matter (mother) — thus making sparks. But negative terms such as "does not seem to preclude" and "I would not maintain" pervade his writings about fire, giving us a clue to his own "un-conscious" biological fear.

Jung writes, "All I am concerned with here is the psychological process." As he digs through mythology equating fire to libido, speech, spirit, water, and so on, he never faces his fear of real fire behind these varied symbols.

What did Psyche really represent? And why do modern disciples of Freud and Jung pass out drugs to combat "hysteria."

Did the goddess need a doctor?

Psyche was Sigmund Freud's favorite Greek goddess, And Cupid was Psyche's lover. But even though Freud made much of this myth, the REAL cause of the breakup of Psyche and Cupid was not included in Freud's analysis of human love affairs.

In the myth, Psyche's ugly sisters said Cupid was a beast. His primitive sex was juxtaposed to her socialized sex. And since Cupid came only after dark, Psyche never saw his face. So, her sisters told Psyche that when Cupid next came to visit she should light a lamp to see his face. When she did so as he slept, Psyche carelessly dropped hot lamp oil on Cupid, causing her lover to run away.

Freud knew that Cupid had been burned but used many other reasons to explain why Psyche lost her "in the dark" (pre-fire) lover.

Either Freud did not recognize Cupid's fear, did not see "darkness" as symbolic of a primitive state, or else decided to use "psychology" to gain personal power — most easily done by abeting the Techno State's mythology.

The Language Crystal tells us that Cupid is "the Cup of the id." And "the id" (the primal physical self) will never get over its fear of fire.

The body is a vessel (a cup) of instincts; it gives the spirit material with which to operate. And the symbol Cup-id bears this out.

Psyche, the brightest of three sisters, holds the flame. Yet in our metaphor, males fire energy into females. And a sperm may light upon an ovum, to kindle new life. For life is organized by light that fire emits. And so, Psyche can re-verse the patterns of the uni-verse.

Only humans who complete the fire-light cycle of stars "get burned" in pass-ion as their souls bring spiritual fire into "the race." But the drugs of psycho-analysis did not bring their victims (male or female) closer to their ids. Smashed by chemical hammers, sick and hungry, distorted psyches searched for love.

Stupid Cupid

Cupid became a hallmark of immaturity, a chubby cherub on Valentine cards, unfit to be the lover of a goddess. A *cherub*, you may recall was the burning "sword" that blocked Adam's return to the garden, as he sweated for his bread.

History soon confused woman's primitive sexual attractiveness with her ability to cook. Witch and caldron images evolved from her early role as fire-priestess. And at the family's center, woman controlled the food supply by dominating the cooking fire. So, in English, "a bun in the oven," is still used to symbolize pregnancy.

Freud himself mistrusted women. And he said his cigars were not symbolic. But he would not discuss his nicotine habit and he held that women were inferior. Freud did not face his subliminal fear of fire or of women. The phallic symbol in his mouth, he said, was "just a smoke."

Freud chose *hystera* (Greek for "womb") to label "a psychic illness." And hysteria, the womb, became his profession's hiding place for (d)anger.

Psyche's lamp oil was unconsciously feared by puffing men in smoke-filled rooms. And the concept of psycho-analysis allowed the men of techno his-story to tear the goddess to shreds while building industry.

Analysis of Psyche mirrored chemical analysis of matter (Latin for "mother"). Bio-chemists said they had dissected "life" itself. Systems analysts forgot the Analyzer who is beyond analysis (the Who beyond the What).

For "uni-verse" is the Goddess surrounding all worlds, old and new. As he drives in one physical direction, she takes him either way, bring him down, lifting him up, as only she may.

Sex and food were neurotically linked early in history, for we were improperly weaned soon after foods were sacrificed to fire. A woman's breasts became sexual objects in the only species to drink the milk of other species. In a complex of events, domesticated fire sent our ids into hiding. And with repressed instincts, humanity became quite ironically super-adaptive — technologically.

Psychology played a part in the Wall Street crash. But what about instinct? Were Psyche and Cupid coming together in an aware love affair where both could be conscious of the burning oil?

"The Word" itself is what (Who) both Freud and Jung tried to characterize as our super-conscious and collective unconscious. For in the Crystal, bio-instincts are encoded in the symbols in which we live from day to day.

In the crash, Quantum Fund fell to a "value" of $1.8 billion (*NY Times* 10/28/87). And quantum leaps are affected by 18's. Quantum's operator is "more as a philosopher than a money manager," said the Times. And adjacent to Quantum, an article told how Westin investments was sold by Allegis with $180 million debt assumed by the buyer. West-in (historic direction of techno advance) was sold by Allegis (Allegiance). And the metaphor unfolded in that Mr. Soros (a reflective name), owner of Quantum, had written "The Alchemy of Finance" about the effects of psychology on the Market, but not the effects of the id.

Advertising used "psychology" to overcome "the id." At every juncture of his-story, psychology was the force to be manipulated. But what often seemed to be a battle of the sexes was, in fact, a struggle between biology and technology.

So, techno alchemy met with bio philosophy. And Soros blamed Prechter (regurgitate) for reversing the bullish march too soon. Quantum fell as the Golden Formula said an upswing would not carry into 1988 as predicted by Prechter, who threw up his holdings earlier in 1987. The traders wanted to exercise just a bit more money-greed.

It was reminiscent of King Midas's sad golden touch. If he touched food, it turned to gold. So, he could not eat. Then, Midas touched his daughter who also turned to gold. And in reflection, MI-DAS said I'M SAD. Just so, fire-technology had touched our food and our sexual relations. Yet, a magic beyond all magic rests in the Crystal Code.

418

Freud betrayed his female clients and forsook his first "Seduction Theory" under pressure from male colleagues. Women (abused and sexually molested as children) were told to blame their depressions on "the womb," hysteria.

"Psychology" interfered with instinct. Psyche's lamp was a civilizing instrument. And we now await the return of a mature and civilized Cup-id.

As we developed in the womb, eternal spirits gained control of our instinctual fear of fire. And by the time we were born, the fear of fire was totally sublimated. So, Psyche is only one in a long line of goddesses.

Just as humans evolved from primates who once had an open fear of fire, so a fetus must pass through a "fire-fearing" stage before birth. The burning of Cupid in Psyche's bed was to prepare us to face our "hysterical" (womb-related) fears.

The unconscious that is used to store our fear of fire is directly opposed to the id although the id needs a civilizing psyche to bridge the gap to eternity. It is ultimately the goddess who gives rise to a need for techno language. She passes on her will to have children who will have children forever and Eve-R, giving "life" to matter.

In rituals, we fed unconscious fears with foods that had been sacrificed to fire. So, it was psychologically possible to lose oneself in eating cooked food, for cooked foods were a matter of social conditioning, not a matter of instinctual desire. One cannot eat oneself into oblivion with only raw foods.

And now, to break our Phase Two eating habits, we will exchange the "psychology" of eating for a new conscious realization. Eventually, nutritional needs will be re-attuned to basic pleasures.

Once non-instinctual eating is abandoned, a new set of rules will apply. But first psychology must be excluded from food selection. Voices that say "finish what is on your plate" will grow silent as instinct signals satisfaction.

Divorcing psychology from eating is easy once we have the key. For uni-verse, the One Goddess over all, shines throughout the Crystal.

Jung's "transformation" took place at 36, which he attributed kaballistically to "a rebirth." The first meeting of Freud and Jung in Vienna was for 18 hours, which pleased the symbol mongers. They both had a knowledge of numerology. And both knew they were chosing to be "priests" in a religion that was to serve the Techno State.

I have personally gone "fire walking" over hot coals on two separate occasions and can attest to the fact that although the coals may be very hot they lack massive heat. A fire walker will never walk on heated metal.

The "psychology" of fire-walking was discussed beforehand, but "psychology" was not the proper word. In the myth of Psyche, Cupid is more than a man. He is Venus's son, sent to tempt Psyche due to the fact that Psyche (then a mortal) was more beautiful than Venus herself. All actions of the mind are not inventions of Psyche.

While Psyche had two "ugly" sisters, there were no ugly female monkeys. Ugliness was produced by un-conscious fears. And "ugly" is from Old Norse for "fear," related to the goddess Ug.

We have seen how vulva and womb were related to vulnerable and wound in Latin. **Vulcan** (the fire-god) was at the root of this confusion. Under the Techno State, vulnerable women were said to be "sexy" to further divert civilized men from their own id-related fears.

Women with machine-like beauty were a comfort to men of the Techno State. The drugs of "techno normalcy" also brought a feeling of conformity to techno standards. And the more that instinctual fears tried to break loose, the more drugs were pushed by psychiatrists of the Techno State.

"Psychology" had been co-opted by druggers. So, "medical doctors" claimed to have authority over sexual feelings and thus presumed to do marriage counseling, often adding to the insanity.

For **psyche** is the Greek word for "soul." And soul mates are lovers, not druggers.

Cupid's parents were Venus (the love-goddess) and Zeus (the fire-maker). Our story is an endless tapestry, woven by the fire of creation and the light of love in evolution.

Psyche becomes the soul of the id once our wild and primitive nature is fully civilized. So, man and woman come together as "one soul" in waves of psychic energy. All mythologies are united in this Phase Three theme.

Psychic energy is a great help in dealing with civilization. But just as primitive ids get in the way when we work with machines, so psychology is a distraction when we eat. So, a new synthesis will come with our Space Age love affair.

As with squatter's rights, pre-tending can lead to ownership. And "to own" means "to believe," when we own up to it. Yet, a POSE can turn one person into the POSSESSION of another.

So, we were possessed by our un-conscious (a strange state of mind) after we assumed an anti-instinctual pose, ignoring our basic bio-fear.

The feminine noun for "one who poses" is hidden in the word "possess." And private property, his primate claim upon her privates, was made her main tool of family life, to civilize him.

G-I-R-L is an ego (I) between gravity (G) and the R-L spiral. So, Phase Two girls were chased (sought after) for being chaste (innocent of sex) because a reversed instinct made some males seek out females who seemed less sexually available. We were psycho-sexual, like no other animal.

And humans confused sexual appetite with their appetite for food like no other animals did. The word for "flesh-food" (meat) sounded like the word for "coming together" (meet). Milk had taken on sexual connotations, as fashions alternated from flattened breasts to heavy breasts. And scrambled eggs in many a movie script were in the breakfast that followed passionate sex. The references were not always conscious, and that was the danger, for our use of language was so influential.

A Psychological Experiment

Gary Null, health reporter and part-time restauranteur, tried to find the effect of cooking on life. He used kirilian photos to show the aura of uncooked rice, then made rice cakes. Null said that rice cakes had more "life energy." Thus, he argued that human beings should eat at least some cooked foods.

In measuring the auras of chickens, Null said dead chickens had no auras, but chicken droppings confused his readings since they had greater auras than live chickens. Did chicken excrement have more "life energy" than live chickens? Yes, but in the form of micro-organisms that were good for flys to eat, but not for humans.

Also, uncooked rice has dormant enzymes. Null knew these factors. He was an ace reporter, but a poor designer of experiments. Null had tried to quantify "life." But, of course, he did not say that wild animals should eat cooked food to get more "life energy."

In many experiments, the "results" often tell more about the eating habits, monetary interests, or psychology of the experimenters than about nutrition. Null, with all his good intentions, also claimed to be a "gourmet chef."

Now, here is a non-psychological experiment that you can try for yourself. It is best not to eat for a full day first, so your instincts can guide you. With several fruits on a table, make a scratch on each and sniff one fruit at a time until you "*know*" which you prefer. Begin to eat.

Perhaps you will have eaten one and a half pears when a change in taste signals you. A sweet taste may suddenly seem bland or over-acid. This means you have had enough. Your body chemistry has made a change in taste. Next, a mango or papaya may be most appealing. The fruit itself does not give you desire; your own body does. So, when you avoid the pressures of psychology, the pleasure of instinct will guide you. But these signals are clear only with raw food. And the experiment works best with real hunger.

CHAPTER 47

THE REAL MAGIC

So far, we have chased a few numbers, plotted the reversal of war, and seen some arguments that favor eating raw food. But the Language Crystal is made of more than mind-stuff, more than sounds in the air, carvings in stone, mythologies and facts in books, or bits in a computer. "The Word" is a re-membering of bio-spiritual energy.

In the Holy Scriptures of every religion are reflections of the pathways in our human nervous systems patterned subtly on the image of God.

So, let us now examine the process by which we can actually "feel" the voice of God within.

This chapter examines a way to fine-tune your subtle body. How do you find your keys after your rational self has lost them? You can listen to the clues within. In like manner, your inner paths of energy (*kundalini*) can be used to reconnect your sense of self with your sense of society and your sense of the environment.

With kundalini yoga, you listen to your inner light; you envision yourself as sound and sight, the observer and observed, blended into one.

Kundalini yoga was once a secret art coveted by priestly classes, so its teachings were encoded. Both the 7 days of creation and 7 seals broken at Armageddon are symbolic of the 7 chakras on the yogic physical plane. From beginning to end, the Bible is a metaphor (both personal and social) that shows how we can each awaken the successive levels of consciousness until the garden and the Crystal City are one, for all humanity.

In Phase Three, we have no "Eastern" or "Western" philosophies. For philo-sophy means the love of wisdom. And wisdom is the key to being "together" individually, united in a Whole Earth Community, joined in sacred kundalini energy, the light of the Christ among us.

Kundalini energy is easy to use because it matters not if you are physically blocked. A metaphysical path can be taken through all physical habits. No longer a mystery, the mastery of kundalini is for all who choose to practice.

Just sit awhile yoga style on the floor (cross-legged if comfortable) and visualize energy moving through your body from one energy center (chakra) to the next. It begins (1) where you sit, (2) goes to your genitals, (3) stomach, (4) heart, (5) throat, (6) between your eyes, and (7) to the top of your head.

Some books say umbilicus, diaphram, or solar plexus instead of stomach. The throat center may be called the thymus. The heart and lungs both relate to a single center. And some teachers say the base chakra is at the perineum or outlet of the pelvis while others say it is outside the body in a metaphysical matrix. What will "matter" most to you is the light that you visualize.

You are made in an image; and you also imagine. Every *atom* of your body has light inside. And your anatomy has a subtle light that you can use in peace to an-atomically (spiritually) organize your atoms.

The easiest way to start changing habits is by moving your subtle energy. In practice, you need only imagine waves of light moving through your energy centers. It may take months of practice, yet it clearly works miracles.

I usually sit for 18 minutes or more and have spent many years allowing the energy to flow, coming to rest at my pineal gland. Here is where I first gained access to the Language Crystal.

Inside your skull, behind the spot between your eyebrows is your pineal (6th chakra), the spirit-organic root of supernatural (human) language.

The Tibetan Book of the Dead relates a beautiful description of the seven chakras to useful feelings about this practice. From the Root-support (Muladhara) on up to the Aperture of Brahma (Brahmarandhra), the journey of the Vital Force of the Goddess Kundalini is traced with poetry and reverance.

The pineal gland secretes melotonin, regulating a female's sexual cycles according to her exposure to light. And melotonin's effect in the male is parallel, linking their forces in Tantric Yoga.

Tantra is male emission-control and/or female energy-channeling done either in sexual engagement or as the spiritual direction of a force-field.

The word "pineal" in our Crystal Code is akin to the Hebrew word "peniel" which means "the face of God." And so, the metaphor continues. The third eye (6th chakra) was named pine-al due to its shape, "like a small pine-apple," noted in "Willis' Medical Works" (1681). And the pineapple is shaped in accord with the Golden Spiral of the Fibonacci series. You may recall that shells, horns, hair, and so on make a Golden Swirl as life builds its own non-living parts (shells, horns, hair, etc.).

Des Cartes said since the pineal gland was the only part of the brain that is singular (not in a pair) that it must be the soul's habitation. And Des Cartes was stating a metaphysical reality, as proven by physical practices of Tibetan monks who can keep warm in the snow by the redirection of energy fields within and around the body.

Did Psyche (soul) spill flaming oil on Cupid due to fire-light's effect on menstrual cycles? In fact, the process of fire evolution is ever going forward in time. And kundalini practice helps the individual emit more conscious patterns.

The English word pine-al (the spiral shape) and the Hebrew peni-el (the face of God) come together in meaning as the light inside you (EL) is used to re-organize the light coming to you (RA).

In our metaphor, Israel received his name after fighting with an angel on Mount Peniel. So, the so-called "Western" and "Eastern" religions sprang in part from Israel's quest for land, exclusive of his brother Esau. Jacob (supplanter) became Israel (struggle with God) after he battled in anger with an angel. And a language of Angles carries the metaphor to completion as we each give direction to pacify this Earthly struggle.

The Order of Sacrifice

"Sacrifice" means "to make sacred." As with "hier-archy" (sacred rule), "sacrifice" implies order, giving up one thing for something (in another time or realm) that is more suited to our evolving needs,

The 7 chakras are ordered from the base of the spine to the skull's aperture — symbolically from the most dense to the least dense.

Thus: (1) earth, (2) water, (3) fire, (4) air, (5) ether, (6) "the Word," and (7) the Nameless are the essences of our energy centers.

The Sanskrit bija-mantras related to these are: (1) lam, (2) vam, (3) ram, (4) yam, (5) ham, (6) om; and the seventh (7) has no name.

By sitting daily and envisioning a light within that travels up the spine, a male (with practice) can regulate his flow of psychic energy. With control of his inner light, he will not fire his sperm pre-consciously during intercourse. And a female can gain greater powers of orgasm. Both partners can, through practice, attain a higher order of bio-spirit energy.

The practice leads to true meditation where the mind rests in no-thing. Judaic, Christian, Islamic, African, and American Indian chanting and beadwork are akin to japa yoga (counting 108 beads) and chanting a mantra (such as "ram ram ram") in that the ultimate goal of all such practice is re-creation of the self.

In Hawiian, *mana* can mean "supernatural power." Yet in that same language, *mana* can also mean "the food a mother chews to feed her baby." Compare these to the food from Heaven, *manna*, found in the desert by the children of Israel. A struggle over dispensing food has taken place between maternal and paternal powers ever since Eve tempted Adam in the garden. During history, "the bread winner" had his wife for a cook. Yet, the fire-light metaphor can be completed by a male and female who know the art of kundalini love — controlled raw passion.

The Goddess

Kundalini (the yogic snake goddess) is related to Eve's serpent because a snake's pineal is easily activated by light. Few people were on Earth as these stories developed. And India's myths, like Hebrew myths, grew from common visions of auras seen by pre-national humans as the Hebrew and the Hindu languages grew from common roots.

The re-union of all our human languages will be achieved through English in a process that will be global before the middle of our next millennium. We already have a species-specific language, all we need do is bio-incorporate our techno mind-sets of our various languages.

We have seen that in Hebrew "fire" (*esh*) and "human" (*ish*) are related. Also, among the Yana natives in California, "fire" (*auna*) is akin to "human" (*yana*). Around the world are tangled roots linking "war" to "bread." And in the Code, FEAR is Angularly attuned to FIRE.

And a pre-conscious conflict with fire rings clear in the names that Hindus gave to the chakras of the body. Note the sounds (bija-mantras) and the elements to which each chakra relates. The stomach chakra is related to the element of fire in the Sanskrit bija-mantras.

Lam is the bija-mantra (1) "earth," the base chakra. And Ram is the bija-mantra (3) "fire," the stomach chakra. So, the Armageddon battle can be seen as a conflict between RAM and LAM (Fire and Earth), resolved in the RAW LAW.

Yet, Earth and Fire are in conflict only from a human perspective. There is fire at the center of the Earth; this is not a conflict for nature.

As with digestion of food, timing and degree are major factors. We need the heat and we need decay (digestion). But the outside factors must be coordinated by the bio-life within.

From Adam's at-oms, Abel's death, Babel's fall, Abram's ram, and the freed Bar-abbas, one story says: We need not set the Earth on Fire before its time.

The opening of the "seven seals," as described in Revelation, tells of the chaos at the end of the world. But in English "world" is from *wer*, which means "man" (as in wer-wolf) and *alt*, "old." Wer-alt (world) means "old man." And in his-story, the "leaders" lived each in a world of his own. Thus, the symbolic separation of the Ram and Lamb.

Yet in Phase Three, One World reigns on Earth, as "the Word," who is the Son of God, attains maturity. The Bible says: "And I saw when a *Lamb* opened one of the seals." *Lam* is the mantra at the first chakra. And *lam* is the essence of earth in the bija-mantra. The puzzle fits together.

In Revelation (chapters five through ten), the chaos is apparent. Yet, an order emerges when the patterns of kundalini are applied.

"And when he had opened the 7th seal, there was silence in heaven," says the Bible while the 7th chakra has no sound. And since the 1st chakra is opened by the Lamb (Lam), we can see the end and the beginning in symmetry.

At the 2nd seal, the Bible says: "to take peace from the earth, they should kill one another: and there was given unto him a great sword." But the 2nd chakra is the genitals, and a great sword is phallic. To "kill one another" refers to sexual individuals who die of individuality. Cells that reproduce by division do not die in the same sense that one who multiplies sexually must die.

The 2nd chakra (Vam) vibrates to the essence of water, which is a sexual image. In Genesis verse 6 (male), waters divide and in verse 9 (female), the waters are gathered together.

Also note, as the 2nd seal is opened it takes peace from earth, which is the 1st chakra. John's Revelation is filled with beasts in transition to a higher order — a kundalini meditation.

The intent of all kundalini practice is to draw peace up from the base of the body (and its subtle energy form) into the thinking area and beyond into pure nameless spirit.

At the 3rd seal a beast has "a pair of balances in his hand." And the 3rd chakra, the stomach, has fire (Ram) as its bija essential vibration.

These balances hold the key to digestion. For the fire in the stomach is its enzyme action, that which gives heat and energy to the body. But these balances, in John's vision were true to his time. A measure of wheat was valued more than barley. And wine was treasured.

At the 4th seal, Yam is air as in the lungs, but John envisions hunger, death, and hell, which would make no sense except that YHWH is God of the Wind; and breath (a key to energy conversion) is the vessel of *prana* (Hindu), *ruach* (Hebrew), *spiritus* (Latin), and *pneuma* (Greek). And each of these in-spiring words means both "breath" and "the life force."

The 5th seal refers to those "under the altar the souls, slain for the word of God." For the 5th chakra is the throat (the voice). John had seen his own confusion. "Under the altar of souls" in Greek is a voice controlled by Psyche.

With the 6th seal broken, the sun becomes black (a male without enlightenment) and the moon turns red with blood (a female's heavy period). And the fig tree (sexual, as the fig leaf) casteth her untimely figs (unfulfilled sexuality). Yet, in a well practiced couple (pineal glands facing each other) their 6th chakras resonate together.

Saint John's vision was in the ascending order, but his timing was confused due to the era in which he lived and his own personal habits.

Yet the 7th seal is opened in silence that lasts for only half an hour in the John's vision. And after that silence, we begin Phase Three.

Even those who take the Bible literally admit that the beasts in Revelation are symbols. Har-Magedon (Armageddon) means "Mount of Rendezvous," a name not found in geography, for we are the beasts who rendezvous to share our kundalini.

Unpracticed individuals envision what most excites their nervous systems. And for all, "a religion" is what we do religiously.

If a person has a cup of coffee every morning, that is a "religious" act. So we need not judge each other by dogma. We need only move our own sub-stance and under-standing into agreement.

The symbols line up with reality; we need only see them consciously. The COW-ARD and BULLY played their roles in Phase Two industry. But we were so affected by eating animal hormones that sexual desires were clouded — and obvious symbols went unnoticed.

As citizens, we each pay taxes for the ills of others, which is a noble act of charity. But who decides on treatments? Is medical drugging now the State Religion instead sensible living?

The Meat and Dairy Religion taxes the over ten million citizens of the USA who eat mostly fruits and vegetables. But since we label religions in terms of dogma (not action), most of us *think* we are Christians, Moslems, Jews, or Hindus.

The ancient symbols of the ram-lamb complex are found in Rama-Krishna stories of the Indian cow-herd boy who sanctified butter by burning off its "impurities." And *barach-el* means "blessed of God" in Hebrew while *bar-acher* is "boy-trouble," *rachel* is "lamb," and *ba-rachel* has a sound that we falsely attribute to sheep, animals that cannot form the letter "B" as in "baaa."

Mistreated horses in the time of John's vision had their revenge in Revelation — in accord with the law on both sides of the looking glass.

The truth moves only foreward in time. And the kundalini process that moves energy from the most dense to the least dense — a metaphor for cultural development — suggests that we must educate.

Those who seek a military "war on drugs" are those who also cannot control their own "legal" drugging habits, which is confusing to druggers on both sides of the looking glass.

430

The *Tibetan Book of the Dead* explains how to live in "the afterlife."

Besides the seven chakras in the body, we have three more that are metaphysical, thus completing the ten in our kabbalistic "Tree of Life."

Only after you have realized a crystallization of "the Jewel in the Lotus" at (6) your center eye will it be possible to exit freely through (7) "the aperrature of Brahman." These chakras 6 and 7 will then lead you to 8, 9, and 10 (and 0-1, if you choose). So, you need not wait until you are dead to have an out-of-body experience.

Once your "light" is outside your body in its subtle form, your 8th chakra is infinity. Chakra 9 is the opposite sex. And 10 is the Tree of Life. This carries you full circle in the form that we call "humanity." Kaballah, Buddha, the Christ, and other manifestations of "the Word" make sense together as your inner light meets other lights around you. Still, it takes practice.

John envisioned much that seems chaotic today, but he also saw across the Crystal River (as we shall see in our final chapter).

The Language Crystal (this book) was written after years of kundalini focus at the 6th chakra ("the Word"). I used the mantra "ram, ram, ram," counting 108 beads, but had no idea when Howard Sadofsky (Sad-of-sky) gave me those beads that a real Language Crystal (the sphere that contains the uni-verse) existed.

The patterns of dyslexia, as I learned from my young friend John, were at the turning point of language. Numeric and verbal coincidences, such as those cited herein, still amaze me. And now I am finding more and more in re-solution. The images of the Crystal derive from the light that lights upon the lightest (subtle) light that is "the Word" in the mind of "the Nameless." So, even though it seems at first that you are only working within yourself, you will have the uni-verse as your effect. For the Language Crystal is totally reflective.

Ob-serve your inner light. Give it no effort. And the lightest light will matter. Per-fect means "to make it through." So, let perfection make it through as your dreams evolve.

Ram means "sport" in Hindu; and Rama is the god who conceals a monkey in his heart. For we were the monkeys who ate the Lamb, the primates who seemed ready to devour the Earth (Lam).

Ram means "exaltation" in He-brew. It was as uplifting to see sacrificial blood in history as it was for sport fans to see "the Rams" knock the brains out of a visiting team.

The BOY is boisterous, stirred by X-sightings of her XX sighted by his XY. B-O-Y is a di-vision (B) in the void (O) where union (Y) is rationalized as wise. G-I-R-L rests in her own gravity. And he is adrift in levity, until she settles him down.

A subtle ramming of sexual joy transforms their beastly union into a sacred ritual as the partners are bathed in ever more subtle light.

Opening the Bible, "the earth (lam) was without form." Just so, kundalini begins just outside your body in an aura from which you create (heave) your heavier form to Heaven.

Next, the Spirit of God moves upon the face of the waters (vam). And God says, "Let there be light." It would seem strange that earth (lam) and water (vam) should be created before the light, unless fire (ram) were the source of that light.

But the author of Genesis did not write of fire in the beginning. "And the evening and the morning were the first day," says the Bible. So, moon-oriented Hebrews began the day in the evening.

The metaphor begins again: the 2nd day, water (vam); the 3rd, herbs, seeds, fruit to burn in the stomach (ram); the 4th, sun and moon become an affair of the heart (ham); the 5th, fowl fly (in air, yam); the 6th day, humans are created, thus a need for "the Word" (om); and on the 7th day, God rests, for the 7th chakra begets its silence in Namelessness.

CHAPTER 48

THE MEANING OF EXTREMES

Swirl, curl, twirl, furl, reel, roll, and whorl, are all words that whirl around and along the R-L "spiral" in "circles" to represent paths of the tongue as it relates the real realms of the cosmos to "crystal."

And in a historic sense, the R and L were most powerful when entangled in the roles of the "lure" and the "rule" in human sexuality.

Many men and women have given their lives to remain true to their words. For rules and lures exist even beyond sexuality. But in an abstract uni-verse, the LURE (female) and RULE (male) set limits on each other. The rule "falls for" the lure. And after the rule is broken, the lure "gets over it." So, his-story's sexism was only a minor scene in our eternal power-play.

The power of the lure is that she gives birth to the rule eternally. She is "negative" when she is "attractive," without being "positive."

The power of the rule is that he can, at times, resist attraction. And the rule is "positive" unto absurdity, yet "absolutely positive" when he finds his personal Lord in "the Word" that creates his World. Coming down-to-Earth, the rule and lure in circles of society, played the game of property to learn to share it properly. Their earthly goal was to develop feelings of propriety.

When their affair slowed down to his-story, the vision between them became a BLUR. Their words got scorched in mystery. And the sound between them became a SLUR. (U is the turning point.)

Now, as we join "fire" (ram) to "earth" (lam), what will we have for the energy we burn?

The lure and the rule eternally yearn to mend each other. Yet, we have a timely down-to-Earth concern — a com-promise of meaning.

"The sounds corresponding to L and R both call for a movement of the tongue tip," taking various shapes to make sounds in the frequency range from 1800 to 2400 hertz, thus enabling us to tell the sound of R from that of L, writes Dennis Fry in *Human Nature* (Feb. 1979).

Linguists refer to L and R as "the liquids," at the 12th and 18th positions between 1800 and 2400 hertz in our Angular language.

So, R and L are sounded at mid-range while the full range of human speech is from 30 to 10,000 hertz. M and N are within 1000 and 1500 while I and O occur in regions of 400 and 2000 hertz. And the limits of 1800 and 2400 hertz suggest that R and L are situated as "a means" to resolve the many divergent "meanings" of speech.

THE MEANING OF LIFE

Some close friends tell me that they think "the Raw Law" is extreme. "You should eat some hot food in winter," they say, concerned for my well being. Yet, the Raw Law is not extreme. Live food is the most popular nourishment on Earth. No other animal cooks food. And some of my friends eat extremely cold ice cream, even after extremely hot meals, so I know they are seeking sensations rather than natural satisfaction.

The combined natural (spoken) and abstract (numeric) placements of R and L indicate that the Raw Law can inspire awe. A raw food diet and the rule of yield is "a means" of balancing the body and the spirit so that we may be whole and holy.

And just as overeating followed by vomiting is parallel to masturbation, so eating cooked food for its extreme taste sensations is parallel to having sex with a machine.

Technology has given us the ability to excite ourselves, yet biology finds true fulfillment in its own kind. Still, our civilized state is out of control, and some people eat for health until emotions bring on a binge beyond any bio "means." So, control in such times must filter through our collective heart chakra.

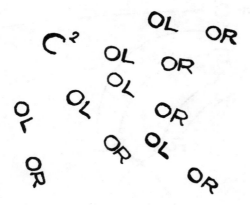

Not only do the R and L find their place in *graph* and *glyph* as sounds surrounded by light, they are also special vibrations of "color" itself.

Light (C) approaches the void (O), bounces off the corner of the circle-square (L), spirals through the void (O) again, and is realized in "life" (R). So, color is a "means" of healing.

Light passed into the Language Crystal creates an apparency of C-O-L-O-R wherein life and non-life work side by side in harmony.

Fire is a techno-power in solar evolution. Fire has a con-science, a pass-ion unto light.

F-I-R-E yields light-waves feeding L-I-F-E in Crystal equations. Yet, seeing more subtle colors magnifies your powers of "meaning." So, allow the fire to enter your dream.

Let the angel in your heart guard the angle at the center of the Crystal. Anger is the re-arranger that makes fire the tool of ire. Yet, under the heart's control, kept in the rear-range of the soul, ire kindles a desire between the lure and rule. When your words are pure, the way is clear. An open heart chakra is the goal.

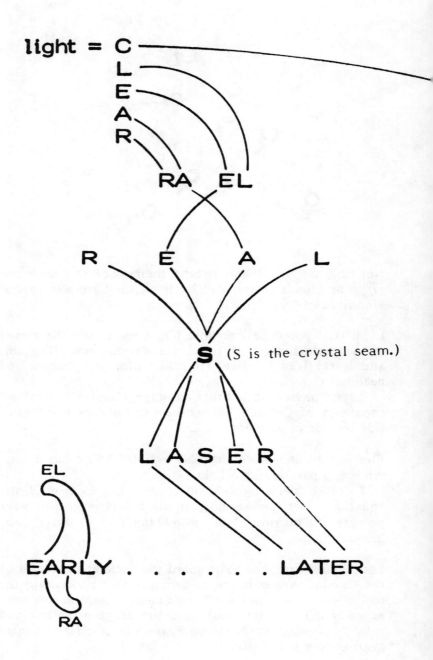

light = C

L

E

A

R

RA   EL

R   E   A   L

S (S is the crystal seam.)

LASER

EL

EARLY . . . . LATER

RA

Travel (T-RA-V-EL) begins at the crossroads (T), uniting RA to EL (light outside to light within) in the crystal valley (V). And Adam is born in the beautiful valley of Eve (E-V-E), uniting two forms of energy (sub-stance and under-standing).

Negative and positive pull and loop eternally, traveling, unraveling. And a REALM may seem un-REAL while M can be defined as either "mass" or "the ever-lasting wave."

In ancient time(s), we separated the realm of fire from the realm of common sense. And God cast lucifer out of Heaven. And humanity went through Hell. Now, we stand on the edge of space, with "life everlasting" in our hands.

The sub-stance of RA and under-standing of EL in cosmic travel will re-incarnate on our next home-planet. This is the "meaning" of life, not at all extreme. We are, by nature, born to dream, tuned in to the crystal stream.

Such concepts as EARLY and LATER relate to energy between the body and the spirit. EARLY is where RA and EL find union in Y. English is such an on-time language that "quick" means to be alive while "late" means to be dead. A baby quickens in the womb. And the late Mr. Sick forgot to sign his will. Once you're late, it gets no later. So, LATER symbolizes where RA and EL spiral around the crossroads (T).

Since reality is relative, we may RE-LATE to the world from C-ENTER whenever we choose to EMIT our own TIME. Thus, L-A-T-E-R is a reflection of R-E-A-L at the crossroads (T). From center, RA and EL must be viewed LAYER by LAYER.

Allow your spirit to act as a LASER focused at the crystal seam (S). And when you feel a BE-AM beam at the edge of the cosmic LEDGER, you will know that you can test each L-E-T-T-E-R of the Law.

His voice is the wind in her valley, a wound, as spiral meets spiral. He winds around her voice till spirits are wound in one. Look to your heart in wonder till you find the middle way.

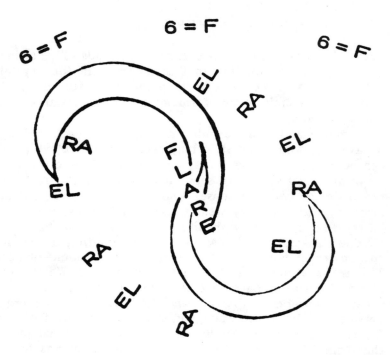

FLARE: a sudden spreading outward of fire or of light. Your flare is a feeling for creation.

Time and space are never one until "the Word" in his evolution is tempered by the love of "the Life," tempting him with her formlessness.

A universe that has no friction is no more than science fiction. Never was there a point in time when all else was still except when now is won.

Each former culture imposes its myth upon the new since "the older" is "the order" until the former (the one who forms) falls into formlessness.

Note: "close" is "lose" in the face of light (C). And when the heart is closed, the loss is our humanity.

We can see how the lure and the rule got caught up in animal husbandry. Israel (the struggle) and Rachel (the lamb) were wed following his devotion to her father's sheep. And soon, we will be re-devoted, after our own quantum leap.

438

THE GLARE OF GOD

When we see our way CLEAR, the GLARE of each other's radiance will be enough to establish that sometimes-welcome distance that we need for our own sense of individuality.

GLARE: Bright is a light at right angles to light.

An ability to glare can protect your spiritual rights from insensitive invasions. For simply by deflecting obtrusive raiders (ra-id) on the spirit plane, you can protect your earthly sanity.

Humanity had over-extended itself on the Planet Earth. Our race with technology had reached the point where nature was glaring back.

A population explosion was declared. Still, the race grew. The path of Greed crossed the path of Creed, as fire-power raged.

IS-RA-EL, our "struggle with God," was still an unresolved metaphor, linking our humanity to its historic animal husbandry.

The root of daily dairy consumption is a need to milk cattle every day, which (unlike any other form of food production leads to a compulsion to consume, affecting our collective unconscious. Of course, cows need not be milked at all. But dairy is a daily habit — from the supply-side.

The following R-L leaps of meaning in Hebrew and Hindi further trace the game of the lure and rule around our universe-city.

For example, *gil* means "earth" or "clay" in Hindi while *gir* means "taken by force." An ancient belief that gods took the Earth by force says that fire spirits took possession of lower forms.

Also, *bir* means "hero" in Hindi while *bil* means "hole in the ground." Imagine a fire-bearing man tearing at the Earth to get materials needed to get to Heaven. Rather than express this reality, Freud would turn the meaning back into sexuality, thus shielding the Techno State.

In Hebrew, while *bi-RA* means "capital city," *bil-LA* means both "to survive" and "to destroy." What seems to be an Earthly contradiction makes sense in the spirit. As with the sacrifice of Je-R-usa-L-em, we must destroy the older order for the new to survive. We must forsake the mind-set of fragmentation so as to gain a New Jerusalem, a new "peaceful possession."

In Hebrew, *la-HAM* means "to wage war," while *ra-HAM* means "Egyptian vulture," Ab-raham's hidden connection to Beth-lehem wherein a He-brew word for "food" becomes a sacrifice of "bread."

And while *aLA* means "a curse" in Hebrew, *Allah* is "the Holy One" to Arabs. How difficult it must be for one who thinks in Hebrew to accept the Arab name for God, which sounds like "a curse."

The ARIAN schism said, Jesus was not the Son of God, for which Arius was excommunicated in the year 318 (fitting with other Aryan-Alien pieces we have already seen).

In He-brew, ARIEL is "Lioness of God," a name for Jerusalem. The R-L spirals of history made these words the outer layers of meaning. And Mr. ARIAS won the Nobel Peace Prize in Armageddon's 7th year for his work to end 666's war in "Old Nick." The patterns fit into an aerial view of the general area, as the karma of Je-R-usa-L-em was torn between lure and rule.

Predicting New Words?

In Hindi, *gur* means "formula" while *gul* means "noise" (order and disorder); *dhal* means "to mold" while *dhar* means "to flow" (ridgid, fluid). But *daur* means "revolving" or "orbit" while *daul* means "shape" or "plan." The R-L patterns are generally meaningful, but not always predictable.

One of my greatest joys in life is looking into people's eyes. So, I propose a new word LEAR to describe this process. To me, LEAR means "to see openly." REAL is LEAR in spiral reflections. I find tensions eased by mutual learing.

Also, LEAR can lead to a conclusion, which is to LEARN. Each REALM of the mind can LEARN from another. And to LEAR ("to see openly") feels like a meaningful way to get CLEAR.

Gazing into another's eyes while they gaze into yours can be a path to a mutual understanding that is beyond all words or body language, for the EYE is a channel that unites two energies.

In some words, R and L either have not split or have come back together. In Hindi, the mimosa tree is named both *babul* and *babur*. Words for "tree branch" are *dal* and *dar*. "Throat" is *gal* and *gar*. Both *amirs* and *amils* hold public office.

You need not fear to feel once you know where to draw the line. You are ready to hear, to heal in the subliminal and sublime. You can indeed read to lead. For the Language Crystal reflects your own personal divinity.

The Crystal as a whole is still. Yet, patterns stir as lures and rules chase e-motions through its walls, and laws are turned around by the very gods who made them. We can best learn from each other, living in the now.

Learning from history makes as much sense to us today as learning from Neanderthals would have made to the people of history. We can study the past, but we must invent the future.

His-story is already over. The hero has torn the Earth apart. So, now is a time to listen, to watch, to learn, and to breathe again.

The R and L (stage-right, stage-left) lend a bit of order to our earthly prop department.

The adjectival forms of "line," for example, are both "linear" and "lineal." Movement of the stars is "stellar" and "astral."

L handles themes labeled chemical, biological, electrical, mathematical, mechanical, territorial, bestial, managerial, servile, and psychological.

Props can be spherical, cubical, cylindrical, rhomboidal, and conical. They relate in ways that are symmetrical, geometrical, astronomical and spatial in general.

Thoughts are colorful, rational, radical, logical, political, mental, and transcendental.

The universe is mineral, vegetable, animal, and spiritual. It's rather elemental.

The sun is solar, moon is lunar. And "the now" is sooner than when our thoughts were messier. The egg is ovular, the square is mystical for reasons quite logistical, arithmetical, single, triple, quintuple, alchemical, poetical, and aesthetical along the line of L.

Yet some forms are circular, angular, regular, globular, peninsular, cellular, spectacular, and square; greener, popular, secular, here, there, far, near, evermore and everywhere. Big is bigger, small is smaller. The doer has more power to redo, around the R. Three (tri) centers in R and has countless reflections in lingual formulas.

Of course, we have exceptions. Seven (S-even) squares the circle. And in eleven (El-even), two ones seek delight again. The games are endless. The aims can be just fun. When we learn to lear in comfort, every per-sun can look into every other per-sun's eyes to see the mystery shine. As right sees left and left sees right — new spirals, new designs.

God lends the rule; man rends the lure. And then, his energy moves on. From the dense unto the most sublime, the Lord talks to his evolution, within the form of his Wife divine.

CHAPTER 49

FERTILITY AWARENESS

His SEMEN's sperm can fertilize her ovum. And MENSES is her unfertilized flow. The letters are the same, with S added as HE meets SHE, s-naking in her crystal seam, naked in the afterglow. But if his semen's sperm obviates her menses, how can we entertain one more human being?

We can take more land, ignoring other species; and we can produce more food. But as we increase in number, since a greater percentage of us uses new technology, we cannot live with the garbage that more humans (also techno consumers) produce. Occasionally, we need more children, but we cannot survive the techno-garbage of an ever-expanding techno-consumer population.

Population control is no longer a question of how many people we can feed. Our technology is consuming life. So, we need birth control. But "the Pill," sterilization, chemo-implants, and IUDs further warp our mind-set when we can have birth control — the natural way.

Most women can chart their temperature and cervical mucus to reveal their infertile days (NOT the old, unreliable rhythm method). The natural scientific method combines mucus and temperature charts with other body signs into a method as reliable as "the Pill." The natural way relies on conscious observation and has no chemical confusions.

A woman on "the Pill" swallows its synthetic steroids for 21 out of 28 days. She may then have bleeding that she thinks is her period but is merely due to withdrawal of the artificial hormones in an artificially simulated cycle without ovulation.

Naturally, a woman charting her fertility signs can avoid pregnancy without harm. And men can participate in both observation and interpretation, making this a cooperative approach to avoiding pregnancy.

Plain and Simple

Fertility Awareness is an example of how biology can use technology to full advantage. By using a daily chart to record both basal body temperature and cervical mucus secretions that descend through her vaginal opening, a woman can know her fertile (about 8 to 10 days each cycle) and infertile days.

"The Pill" can bring on nausea, weight gain, and headaches, as well as cervical problems, candida, yeast infections, and cardio-vascular complications. The diaphragm and sponge employ spermicides, as does the cervical cap to a lesser degree. And the deadly IUD allows infection via a string hanging through the cervical opening.

Still, *Fertility Awareness* was pushed aside by both sides in pro-life pro-choice debates. Even Catholics, who called it *Natural Family Planning*, often refused to teach it to people who were not "married in the eyes of the Church."

Fertility Awareness is not the "rhythm method" which is based on assumptions rather than current observations, and not "a sensational techno advance," so it was not on the medico-techno-oriented TV "news" or in most women's magazines.

"Innovations" sponsored by Johnson & Johnson claimed to include "all current methods of birth control" (*PBS* 1987). But Fertility Awareness was knocked off the schedule, replaced with Norplant (a chemical implant). So, when the natural way was mentioned by a cervical-cap spokesperson, no one there was prepared to answer questions.

Johnson & Johnson invests in techno programs while Public-TV conjurs up an "education" image; and viewer funds pay for old movies, so techno interests can sponsor shows on consumer issues to gain influence and exercise thought control. As with "organic foods," no conglomerate owns "Fertility Awareness." So, it goes unpublicized. M.D.s seldom refer to Natural Birth-Control; no prescriptions are required and revisits are not routine, as they are with invasive methods.

The term "Medical Doctor" is confusing since most medical practitioners do not teach clients about the drugs they dispense. Since "doctor" means "teacher," a dentist acts as a "doctor" when teaching the care of teeth and as a "practitioner" when drilling and filling. Our goal here is to examine the linguistic art we will need in the coming new millennium. And "doctor" is a valued word.

Medical practitioners are useful in society; they deserve respect and should be licensed. But anyone who interferes with or holds back the dissemination of information is certainly not a "doctor."

Menstruation does NOT mean bleeding; it refers to the periodic nature of female moon cycles. And distress at menses is not "normal" so much as it is the product of techno lifestyles. A cycle can be complete with no PMS, painful period, or days of heavy bleeding. Such dis-ease is not the toll for having a natural woman's body.

Heavy bleeding is not prevalent in many vegetarian and athletic women. And many physically active women who eat natural food have only spotty bleeding while some have reported no noticeable bleeding at all. A healthy lack of bleeding does not necessarily mean she has not ovulated, although amenorrhea (no menstruation) with no ovulation can occur in excessively active or anorexic women.

"Routine blood tests" gave those who played doctor a powerful mystique. The rituals of coronary by-pass (preventable by low-fat diet) added to the blood-letting propaganda. And "M.D.'s" pretended to be "the teacher-authorities" on blood-related information.

Many clients were blocked from seeing the results of their own blood tests without "the doctor" first collecting a go-between fee. Thus, information and client education were both surpressed.

A woman-run health, political, or university group might refer you to a teacher in your area. Or you can write, Ovulation Method Teachers, Box 10-1780, Anchorage, AK, 99510 or The Fertility Awareness Center, Box 2606, N.Y.C., 10009.

The so-called "doctors" did not trust that "common people" could learn. At least that was the excuse given while a constant drum beat in the media called for more complex tests, chemical formulas. and invasive treatments.

I have personally heard several women tell of how their "doctors" had treated them for years for what were natural biological secretions. Much of the time, a client need only display ignorance to become "a regular patient." And the reports from those clients who eventually get wise do not get averaged into "medical statistics."

To put it simply, so that even those who are habituated to dispensing drugs may understand, raw fruits and vegetables generate less toxins. Also, athletic women allow less toxins to build up. So, with less fatty tissue, less toxins, and more oxygen, blood between the uterus and its lining is beneficially re-absorbed, so the body benefits from a re-use of that blood rather than breaking down extra tissue in toxic eliminations.

Of course, good health is not normal in a junk-food society. Still, M.D.s need not give drugs or do proceedures to induce bleeding.

The most eminent Dr. Herbert Shelton reports in his book "Health and Menstruation" that cooked foods are a factor in heavy bleeding at the time of menstruation. And Shelton reports relieving the symptoms of PMS in many women by prescribing a change in diet, rather than drugs.

Domesticated animals fed cooked foods, often bleed as the uterine lining is sloughed off. In the wild, bleeding is slight or absent. But we need not go completely wild to get wise. We need only keep technology from destroying our biology.

Fertility Awareness is more than a knowledge of when you can and cannot get pregnant. A union of "the Word" and "the Life" exists in every living science. So, the method of "Birth Control — the Natural way" is best learned from a woman teacher who practices it herself or from a practicing couple. And learning (sharing) in a group is most helpful.

The Future

Historic science denied the power of woman's blood before the entire universe. An incomplete symbol of woman was sent to outer space with no apparent vulva, while the male had his foreskin intact.

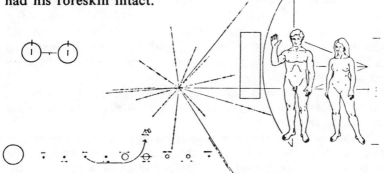

Why was science busy with artificial baby-making when over-population was a threat. Even with wars, plagues, and famine, we continued to expand.

Rather than address infertility's rise due to pollution and personal bad habits, we divised ways to have techno pregnancies. But the reason was not obvious even to those involved in the search for new bio-technology.

Techno baby-making did not benefit humanity in general. As we existed on this planet, we were (as a whole) overpopulating while (one by one) men became less potent and women less fertile. But the techno attacks on infertility addressed neither of these problems.

Techno fertility was based on a theory (often unconscious) of what the space journey to our next home would be like. Few realized the vastness of the spaceships that we would some day send forth. Just as we will not need techno food on board, we will not need techno reproduction.

Again, our goal is to refine the linguistic art needed for the comming millennium. We cannot speak of "scientific advances" that are destroying the gene pool of the human race. We need to work on technology yet we must maintain biology in a form that is bio-evolutionary.

Menses is a Moon cycle, overlaid on ESTRUS, an Earth-Sun cycle. For feminine spirits made the quantum leap in evolution to move toward future space-oriented cycles.

EASTER SUN-DAY is from the EAST where SUN begins its DAY. And EASTER is also the name of a Phoenician spring goddess who took the form of ASTARTE (consort of Baal). And parallel to Easter is ESTER (Hebrew for Venus), who dances in spring with her many goddess sisters.

From this lineage came ESTHER, the Jewish princess who married the King of Persia (Iran) after he had cast out his Persian wife.

Esther was coaxed into the marriage so that she might save Jews in Persia by defeating the villain Haman. We have no word on Esther's offspring by the King of Iran. But Shah Pah-levi may have been one. Even Adolf Hitler was an OSTER-Reicher. The borders of nations then were not as they are today, yet Israel did display an affinity for cousins in Iran. And Reagan's cake (via North) fit into the Armageddon plan.

The story of Esther centered on food. For the king was angry with his Persian wife when she refused to share a meal — then entered Esther.

And Ha-man pastry (shape of a man's ear) is eaten on the feast of Purim to celebrate Esther's conquest by her power of sex over the king of Iran. Was this a spin-off of the karma that Abra(ha)m had left between two women?

We shall go on weaving the tapestry of mono-theism, mono-gamy, and mon-ey until all nations and languages are one. And the trade of the weaver is one of humility, the quality it takes to teach any art effectively.

Do not be surprised if your Fertility Awareness teacher does not give a hoot for history. She will help you check your charts and help you build the confidence to act on what you know, biologically, in present time. And in Phase Three, children will learn the facts of fertility as readily as they learn to read and write.

CHAPTER 50

HUMANISM VERSUS GODISM

Said Reagan to preacher Jim Bakker, "This may be the generation that sees Armageddon."[1] But Reagan filtered his Bible through supply-side Capitalism which meant to him "techno-side favoritism."

Behind his astrology, numerology, strange gods and secret demons, he seemed to have a genuine belief that he would fulfill the prophecies. Yet he failed to see the eco-sphere as a supplier, so Reagan fell short of his goal.

TV preachers damned "Secular Humanism." And the word "secular" in Latin meant "a race or an age," and like "sex" it refered to a division by 6 (a sect); but with its religio-political overtones "secular" came to mean "not eternal."

"Humanism" meant an exclusive faith in humanity while "Godism" meant an exclusive faith in God. Like all other isms (pessimism and optimism, for example) both Humanism and Godism were in search of balance.

Judaism, Muhammadenism, Buddhism, Hinduism, Catholicism, and Protestantism were viewpoints. And the viewer was an organism — seeking balance (like you-ism and me-ism). And only "realism" was at all complete, not in reality, but in art.

Anti-Humanists used a linguistic pattern where "the organism" (the eco-sphere) was valued less than the techno organizations it had created. And preachers who openly attacked "Humanism" secretly piddled their second chakras, for they had yet to accept the Goddess as the supplier of Life. Christian Fundamentalism predicted a global war that would begin in Israel. And sermons about *"the battle of that great day of God Almighty"* (Rev. 16:14) heated up whenever peace talks between the USA and USSR broke down.

(1) Reagan in Pursuit of the Presidency — 1980

"Israel is the only stable democracy we can rely on in a spot where Armageddon could come," said candidate Reagan to a group of Jewish leaders in New York, 1980 (quoted by William Safire in *the Times*). But Reagan didn't make his point clear. For if his Jewish friends knew what Armageddon supposedly held in store for Israel, they would have balked at Reagan's statement.

Jerry Falwell was fond of telling how the blood of Israel would be shed in God Almighty's great and holy war. And many Jews would be killed. Said TV preacher Falwell of Reagan, "He told me, 'Jerry, I sometimes believe we're heading very fast for Armageddon right now,'" as quoted in *the L.A. Times*, March 1981.

Armageddon is named only once in the Bible after the angels pour out the 6th vial of wrath. And Cherno-byl (wormwood) was clearly vial number three. And this chapter explores some other signs plus other isms that relate to your own living, observing organism. So, the signs are up to our Last Judgement. And it seems that Armageddon has turned out to be but a wimper at the end of history.

Also, in our common immediate environment (the Earth itself), we must grasp a common truth that goes beyond all other isms. We must satisfy the needs of our eco-sphere — our common organism while we are here.

Here are the most startling words in the Bible for anyone who tries to interpret prophecy, word for word. Revelation 10:11 quotes these orders from an angel: *"And he said unto me, Thou must prophesy again before many peoples and nations, and tongues and kings."* This means that Saint John's vision, as written, was in no way a final statement. It was only a view through his own humanity.

The Bible was an unfinished document. So, as we awaited the beast with ten horns (Rev. 12:3), Reagan made a comic image of himself before the press. He placed ten fingers atop his head, pointed them outward, got a laugh, and fulfilled the prophecy of the ten horned beast.

Most signs went by so fast that few people noticed them. On Israel's 36th birthday, the Government of the USA sentenced Sun Myung Moon to 18 months in jail. Moon was to start serving time on 6/18.[1] And the face of Moon turned red with anger at the IRS.

"I beheld when he had opened the sixth seal, and lo, there was a great earthquake; and the sun became as black as sackcloth of hair, and the moon became as blood" (Rev. 6:12).

Moon had married an 18 year old girl several years before, then unmarried her, to wed again. He made the headlines (1977) by officiating at his largest mass wedding — 18,000 Moonies.

And shortly after Moon was sentenced, bright arcs rimmed the moon with "Baily's Beads." Francis Baily had discovered the moon-beads in an eclipse of 1836.[2] With the flesh-and-blood Moon out on bail, were Baily's Beads an added sign? Had the 6th seal really been opened? But what had become of the earthquake in that prophecy?

In Esoteric Christianity, Christ is linked to Chi-ron, the half-horse half-man Centaur who gave up his immortal soul to redeem Prometheus who had stolen fire from Zeus. And in the Crystal, Chi-Ron links 18 (*chai*) to 666 (Ron Reagan).

Imagine "666" atop a horse named "Little Man." Reagan's horse with that name died in his first term. But 666 still rode the little man, politically.

April Fool's Day, 1983, Ronald Wilson Reagan was to meet Queen Elizabeth (House of Elijah) to go horseback riding, but an *earthquake* began at exactly 12:18 pm in California. Flooding and a tornado prevented the symbolic Aryan ride of the horse-man and his horse-woman bride. And the Dow Jones average went up by 18.9 on that day.

The numbers fit our crystal pattern, but the order of the prophecies seemed fragmented, for they were to be told again and again *"before many peoples and nations and tongues and kings,"* eternally.

(1) NY Daily News 5/15/84, (2) NY Times 5/22/84

When he moved from **Sacramento** (the Sacrament) out of the Governor's Mansion to **Rancho Del Cielo** (Ranch of the Sky) while also living in the White House, 666 brought together several images of the Christ and the Anti-Christ.

Reagan toppled the Professional Air Traffic Controlers Organization to co-opt a patriarchal symbol and rule of the skies. Ending his first term, 18% fewer PATCO people were employed.[1]

And garbage management in the USA grew to an $18 billion industry.[2] Half the jobs created in the years under 666 paid "less than the poverty level — $180 a week."[3] Still, Reagan asked $1.8 billion for "improving" job skills,[4] while he had little sense of the living supply-side.

Old Nick was SATAN. Saint Nick was SANTA. Both wore red. Old Nick came to us through untamed flames. Saint Nick came down a chimney into a fireplace — flames held in check. Each dealt in worldly games. And Santa's "goods" were often used to play Satan's games.

Saint Nick got fat. Old Nick grew lean. Old Nick's tail was forked. Saint Nick's tale grew old. Ho, ho, ho! Heh, heh, heh, heh, heh!

The headline said "18 Snipers Hunt Pope."[5] John Paul was traveling between "the Savior" and "Old Nick" at that time. When the Pope was shot, the Vatican budget had an $18 million deficit.[6] An *NBC Special* (Jan. 1983) said Mehmet Ali Agca "was paid at least $18,000" yearly in the conspiracy. Months after the attack, PLO leader Yasir Arafat rode to meet the Pope in "an 18-car motorcade bristling with submachine guns" in the streets of Rome.[7]

The Pope, a Pole, born May 18th, made the cover of *Time* on July 18th. He kissed the ground and stayed 18 hours in Boston when first in the USA. TV ads said, "Dial 999-1818" for his story.

(1) Business Week 9/24/84, (2) NY Times 5/24/87, (3) NY Times 6/21/87, (4) NY Times 2/22/87, (5) NY Post 3/5/83, (6) NY Times 3/10/85, (7) Newsweek 9/27/82,

A Fish Story

A Canadian terrorist threat on the Pope said the "first 18 popes died violently."[1] And the popes had no conscious idea how a little piece of bread that led to the sacrifice of food in general was our key to global peace.

In Poland, the price of the cheapest vodka was doubled to $18 a bottle.[3] Then, after an 18-day convention, Solidarity delegates expressed anger at the high price of cigarettes.[3]

Both Commies and Cappies were inflamed by the wages of sin. And the battles of Armageddon were fought over and over again. To make his second USA tour (ten days), the Pope traveled 18,000 in 12 days, blessing bread and wine along the way.[4]

Capitalism and Communism were two alcoholic fish, each trying to swallow the other toward the end of the Age of Pisces. For Jesus turned water to wine, then made wine into blood, and finally drank vinegar while dying on the cross. Water to wine, wine to blood, blood to vinegar. And *Mary* means "bitter" in He-brew, for this was our evolution in the spirit.

After he arose from the dead, Jesus cooked a fish. And in his final State of the Union message, 666 said, "govern a great nation as you would cook a small fish" (1/25/88). He was quoting Lao Tzu. But after his symbolic (over my dead body) death, the imagery fit so well that it seemed Reagan was self-conscious about his own drama.

The Age of Aquarius brings water (*agua*) in line with re-birth. Nicaragua and Paraguay (both agua signs) were centers of rotting fruit on the cusp of new fertility. The $18 billion hydro-electric dam (largest on Earth) in Paraguay had supplied no power (*Time* 7/2/84). On the date of 12/18 (1984), Managua was denied a loan from the World Bank to begin constructing an aquaduct. And there was already a leak in the dike, symbolically.

In 1986, both the alcoholics (the USA and USSR) began programs to push "the drinking age" beyond 18 — a new "legal" bapt-ism.

(1) NY Times 9/4/84, (2) NY Times 10/5/81, (3) NY Times 10/13/81, (4) Time 9/28/87

The USA took to anti-smoking. And even Castro gave up cigars. Professional anti-Soviets in the USA were worried for their jobs as Commun-ism and Capital-ism grew closer.

Yet "democracy" is not an "ism." Democracy is true when all the people can vote. So, to gain a true democracy, we must be free, organically. Every human organism can freely vote for any ism.

Freedom is facilitated by having good habits that are not compulsive. Freedom is having choice. And freedom is also being chosen, which implies a lack of choice. Freedom is the ability to say "no" to God even if God chooses you. And freedom is the knowledge that God might understand.

Instinctual eating was all but forgotten. And the karma of daily dairy (forced production) had locked us into chattel slavery. But humanity had survived the winters of history.

By their very nature, neither "Commun-ism" nor "Capital-ism" addressed the natural appetite. Both systems were built on coercion. For history had co-opted the garden of Paradise.

Both the Kremlin and Madison Avenue told us to eat in line with the techno system. And both began their brain-washing early in our childhoods.

As was the case with many fighters in battles for Nicaragua, Eden Pastora changed sides a few times. "Capitalism" and "Communism" were not real issues in his metaphor. In fact, the name of **Eden Pastora** told about the conflict of Old Nick more than political rhetoric. Eden was "a guerilla" called "Captain Zero." And his symbolism linked Old Nick to Je-R-usa-L-em. Beyond Eden's pastures, jungle madness blocked the gates of Paradise. Eden was wounded and taken to "the Biblical Clinic, a private hospital in San Jose" (*NY Daily News* 6/1/84). Saint Joseph, Zero, Old Nick — these names were also signs.

Embargo of Nicaragua was futile. The USA took only 18% of its exports (*NY Times* 4/28/85). And the politics were not clear cut. But the signs did fit into our Armageddon metaphor.

For over 6,000 years, those who ate animals controlled the land. Some nomads followed herds; and techno civilization was built by those who had a stable meat and dairy supply.

Heathenism (*heath* is waste land) and Paganism (*pagus* means rural district) would both be part of mainstream religion if not for the politics of food. Much of our historic religions were games of name-calling in defense of national interests and divisions of the Techno State. So, u-topia which means "no-where" becomes "now-here" in the Code. And "new-speak" is a "news-peak," at the end of history.

October 18th, 1986, four men who had fasted for 46 days to bring attention to the murder of women and children in Nicaragua ended their fasts. "They said they would begin eating just after mid-night on Friday because they had accomplished their goal" (*N.Y. Times* 10/17/86).

Days before, on the *Donohue* Show, the four were in good spirits, though physically weak. But none had been invaded by viruses. And their fasts had NOT weakened their "immune systems."

Some public attention was focused briefly on crimes against humanity in Nicaragua. But also exemplified by the protesters who did not eat for 46 days was the biological fact that a properly conducted fast is not a danger,

A moderate fast from three to seven days allows healing, often felt after the fast is over. The fast lets a body find its own electric, chemical, and e-motional balance. And a supreme joy also comes with new-found balance in the spirit.

The length for a fast depends on body weight and the toxins to be eliminated. A water fast will not deplete the body of nutrients. And supplements are NOT needed. Since the body seeks its own balance while fasting, supplements do more harm than good. But care should be taken not to allow too much toxicity to break down too rapidly.

A fast requires rest. And bio-balance comes with gradual rebuilding on natural foods. So, fasting is discouraged by the Techno State. It cannot be packaged.

Fasting is "primitive" in the sense that it is natural. But a fast cannot be mass produced. So, Fundamental businessmen-preachers forgot the fasts of Buddha, Moses, and Jesus.

Looking back to medicines of older cultures, we have believed in any notion of "cure" that re-inforced "the powers that be." And gradually, "health care" was technologized. For the modern witch-doctor's role was to further the officiating Techno-Church-State.

We took drugs to hide the symptoms that we could have cured by fasting. We could have changed our diets, but double-blind "scientific" tests could be done with pills and placebos, not with good food or fasting, where there is no blind and no passive subject.

Anti-biotics that kill infections also destroy our own biotics. And what seems to be a recurring infection may be due to previous drug damage.

Most visits to "doctors" in the USA are for common colds. Their image of "authority" sold anti-biotics to treat "viruses." Still, I know from experience that "cold symptoms" go away after fasting is begun and can return if the fast is cut short. But what has this to do with Armageddon?

The battle was being fought inside our bodies as we swallowed a holocaust at almost every meal. Living under the Phase Two mind-set, we put "our jobs" before our health. Drugs hid ills so we could punch the timeclock. And the sad long-term complications often came after retirement. So, medical consumers dared not say "no" to drugs. For the Techno State often demanded "a note from your doctor." Laws required children to be vaccinated and the homeless were victimized by mental hospitals.

We cannot solve the disputes between Godism and Humanism, between Capitalism and Communism, or between Blackism and Whiteism until we respect our organisms. Humanism and Godism (like community and capital) each satisfy a need in the other. By finding this balance in "the Word," we each can end our own personal battle of Armageddon.

CHAPTER 51

IN THE BEGINNING IS . . .

The Hot Dry Rock energy project, after a trial run, proved that millions of gallons of water pumped miles into the earth could draw up enough heat to power a town of 2,000 people. The plan succeeded in 1986, yielding energy with commercial potential (*NY Times* 7/7/86). And it could be used almost anywhere on Earth with no fossil-fuel pollution and no nuclear complications.

And Alvin Marks (inventor of a polarized film) built photovoltaic cell prototypes at Westinghouse in 1986, causing Exxon to bid on the rights. His photovoltaic cells operated at up to five times the efficiency of those in use, at a fraction of the cost. And it was said, solar panels could be used commercially by 1989 (*NY Times* 9/9/86).

Now, as superconductors allow efficiency with electricity produced by any means, we will be able to both decentralize and exchange electric power — a techno complement suited to our coming bio-ruled democracy.

This final chapter considers the use of global and personal resources on Earth. And the Language Crystal already tells us what our pre-conscious knows: A true resource is re-usable.

A bottle bill voted on in Washington D.C. to recycle bottles and cans via cash deposits was defeated by the public in Armageddon's 7th year. And that same election day, 1987, citizens of Main who could have voted to shut down a nuclear power plant voted instead to keep it operating.

If the issues seem complex, the bottom line is that We the People determine the rate of growth in our new bio-techno community. So, the Crystal City contains the Garden that feeds us organically. And the plan of the planet in its plants is now in the hands of humanity.

THE EQUATOR WILL WARM BY 1.8°F
THE POLES WILL WARM BY 18°F

President emeritus at the University Corporation for Atmospheric Research, Walter Roberts, made the above prediction with reference to the "Greenhouse Effect" (*Mother Earth News*, April 1984). But 666 was confused about the bio-supply-side.

Once we thought a placenta could shield a fetus from poisons in its mother's blood; we thought adults on soft drugs could keep children off hard drugs. But the drug crisis erupted as do most bio-crises — suddenly, after years of abuse.

Forest loss, soil erosion, and air pollution if left unchecked could bring on a glaciation. But if this theory is correct, we have no idea of the rapidity of the process. Once started, it probably would not stop until a lengthly global ice age was complete. The planet's plan to keep plants alive has used glaciations in the past to remineralize the soil by recycling the ocean's floors.

China's Great Yellow River, India's Ganga, the Mississippi, and countless rivers carry trillions of tons of topsoil down to the sea each year. Not only our food supply is threatened, the plants that can slow the ice age are eroding.

Still, we chop forests to grow grain to feed cattle. We fail to recycle paper. You know the list of eco-offenses. But ice ages occured before humans were on Earth. So, we can use this problem as a pivot for future action.

The good news is that we can stop the cycles we have created. And now, from this experience we can set up conditions that will prevent an ice age that would have come upon us naturally. For we are, in truth, the gardeners of Paradise.

Adam's broken bread grew into a magic shift in meaning: *aph* "nose" changed to "anger" in the face of smoke. We have seen the puns of punishment that followed. We built our civilization around the sacred flame — driven preconsciously.

Does it seem all this should end in an ice age or suffocation due to the Greenhouse effect?

The loss of soil (that once produced vegetation) combined with drastic increases in fossil-fuel pollution in the last hundred years has left us within striking distance of a climatic turning point. Listen as the ozone layer gasps for breath. Listen as the rain forests die.

Now, see the prophecy for AFTER the battle of Armageddon: *And he showed me a pure river of water of life, clear as crystal, proceeding out of the throne of God and of the Lamb* (joining the tenth chakra to the first chakra).

In the midst of the street of it, and on either side of the river, was there the tree of life, which bare twelve manner of fruits, and yielded her fruit every month, and the leaves of the tree were for the healing of the nations.

The above quote is from the very last chapter of the Last Book of the Bible. And it tells of how we can avoid the final threat to our developing civilization as we enter the New Millennium.

We can stop this loss of mineral-rich topsoil by planting fruit trees in the Americas, Africa, EurAsia, and India, On every continent, forests of fruit trees will not only feed the people, they will also stop soil erosion. Tree roots maintain the water table while leaves gather moisture by the process of transpiration. And the leaves of the Tree of Life shall heal the nations.

Rather than grain fields to plow and erode so as to feed cattle, rather than having cattle graze causing more erosion, we need only plant orchids of fruit trees spaced to provide the atmosphere and soil that is best for organic gardening, for the leaves of trees add to natural fertilizers.

Nature acts in synergy, as a total system. And *horticulture* is an *orator* for those who listen. We can make the total system work for us, if only we cultivate our own bio-spirit. For humanity is now at our planet's synergistic control center. We can care for the eco-sphere before it is too late; we can provide, for the love of humanity, we can go beyond "the end of the world."

The Chosen People of every age are first asked to make a choice. God does not force our fate upon us. We must participate in the choosing.

The USA and USSR have each built pipelines for the oil that feeds the Techno State. So, a water pipeline to the thirsty nations of Africa from the seasonally melting polar ice is possible.

And we have already developed fruit trees that have shorter root systems particularly adapted to grow in places where wheat fields grow today.

We have the re-sources to irrigate our deserts when and where it is desirable. We can ship food to any spot on Earth. To feed our flesh and blood, we need only listen to our bio-spirit. The techno paths have already been opened.

By using the melting ice caps to irrigate and using mountains of crushed rock to remineralize the soil, we can rebuild our garden within the Crystal City. Imagine — it can be done.

Re-mineralizing the soil may sound like a task of great proportions. Yet it has already begun.

In Germany's Black Forest, about one third of the trees were dead or doomed with a fifth more afflicted by slow mineral-starvation over the past 30 years. "At present the Germans are neutralizing the soil with limestone," reported John Hamaker in 1984, when he recommended additional fine gravel dust be mixed in with the limestone.

The Italian government has a successful project in Sicily where pulverized mineral-rich rocks are mixed into the soil. Other nations are involved in similar projects. And Hamaker-Weaver Publishers, Box 1961, Burlinggame, CA 94010 is current with volumes of information and guidelines.

"The river of water of life, clear as crystal, proceeding out of the throne of God and of the Lamb," refers also to the crystal ice caps that can be used to irrigate all lands. Civilization was not built to be destroyed. We need only act in accord with the prophecy. For "the Word" gives us a power beyond all other species.

In the midst of "the street of it," on either side of the river, was the tree which bare twelve manner of fruits, yielding every month, and the leaves were to heal the nations. The message now seems obvious: "the street of it" awaits us in the Crystal City" — Jeru-salem.

And yet, we look around us and see the world is poised for war. The missiles are still set. As sure as pop-up toasters and coffee-perk machines are waiting so millions of people can grab a bite on the way to work, as sure as many will not care what they are producing or why, the missiles are still set. The terror and drug lords are still in command, for "they" are "us."

We cannot become "immune" to toxins in smoke. We cannot hear our biology so long as the techno mind-set twists our words around.

In New York City (August 1988), a child was taken from her parents after someone reported that the family was living in a van. In fact, the van was packed and ready to drive to Florida. But the family was not our "typical White American," so the child was put in "foster care."

In the process, that young girl was vaccinated and given cow's milk to drink at every meal. She had never been vaccinated before and had never tasted cow's milk. But the dominant religion of the USA, worship of the golden calf, was in power. When there were fewer humans, survival was tied to cows and sheep. And now, we are still torn between what we know and what we culturally believe. The argument can be stated in a thousand ways. Not only was that little girl's body abused by the "authorities," her parents rights were trampled on.

And Every tax payer who does not worship the golden calf pays for those who do. Every tax payer who does not believe in the statistics of Medical History still pays for those who do. So, the health revolution will also be fought in courts of law and re-negotiated in insurance policies.

In fact, we can make society healthier; and we can do it by the book. The movement has already taken root in consciousness.

From *Homo habilis*, "tool maker," to *Homo sapiens*, "the wise," we do not admit in our self-naming what makes us special. Other animals have tools. Monkeys use sticks. Beavers build dams. Each is *habilis* (a tool maker); and every species is *sapiens* (wise) after a fashion.

By rite, we are *Homo ignipotens*, "in control of fire," our tool of escape from this planet. We have seen the progression of un-consciousness that made up fire-bearing history.

Only by cooking meat can we eat it in great quantities. Only by pasteurizing milk can we have truck loads streaming daily in our streets. And we wouldn't eat raw pizza. We have taken the puzzle apart and seen the ancient sacrifice of food to fire that made us leave the garden. And now, we are bound for Heaven. So, we shall reshape our civil laws before we leave.

When the bread sacrifice is over and the techno foods of fire no longer block bio-individuality, humanity in control of fire (*Homo ignipotens*) shall be in charge of the Planet Earth, ready to work with the Angels — consciously.

We believe in magic and follow magicians: bound in chains, pierced by swords, buried alive — we are fascinated by escape. But how will we know when we are free? Abracadabra! E-scape (beyond land-scape and sea-scape) following "the Word," God's E-quality is our own in the real E-state of true E-motions. That's how we'll know.

In the beginning is "the Word" (John 1:1).

Thank you, Saint John. And thank you, John, my young dyslexic friend, wherever you may be.

We have almost reached the conclusion of this book. Yet, the Language Crystal continues to grow as more and more people add their accents to its Angular center.

Our next (and final) chapter points to meaning of choice, to put biology in charge by the year 2000. Then, we fill in some blanks of the puzzle in a three-part addendum.

CHAPTER 52

ELECTIONS: 1980, 1984, 1988

1980 marked a crystallization of politics in the USA as J.C. (Democrat) received 1,666 nominating votes and was sent into a symbolic battle to face the challenger, 666 (Republican).

1980, new laws limited all candidates' pre-convention spending to $18 million (*Time* 3/10/80).

1980, Every four years, for the past 18, candidates have swarmed across New Hampshire *(NBC* 2/25/80).

1980, the primaries lasted 18 weeks.

1980, for the past 18 years, the federal budget had been in deficit (*Time* 4/21/80).

1980, J.C.'s "cumulative budget was more than $180 billion" *(Newsweek* 7/28/80).

1980, J.C. proposed personal tax cuts of about $18 billion (Irving R. Levine *NBC* 8/24/80).

1980, Reagan promised to cut spending by "up to $18 billion" (*Reuters* 10/11/80).

1980, Carter's proposed draft of 18-year-olds was opposed by 18 Democrats in the Senate and 180 members of the House (*Time* 2/25/80).

1980, Reagan appeared more times on page 18 of *Time* than any other person in history.

1980, Billy Carter stood to gain $1.8 million a year in his Libyan oil deal (*Time* 5/4/80).

1980, the Republican convention was covered by 1800 people from the networks (*Time* 7/28/80) and given 18 hours air time (*Time* 7/21/80).

1980, from sunrise in Maine until the polls closed in Hawaii, the people would have 18 hours to decide (James Carter, Election-Eve TV ad).

1980, Ger-ald R. Carl-son, a neo-Nazi "White-separatist in Michigan, won the Republican primary with a campaign budget of "a mere $180" (*White Power*, Jan. 1981).

1 + 9 + 8 + 0 began the Armageddon countdown.

TED KENNEDY, burdened by a Chappaquiddick death gap (July 18th), spent his 18th year in the Senate challenging J.C. And his introduction at the 1980 Democratic convention contained the number "18," mentioned three times.

JOHN ANDERSON was cheered by 1800 fans after his home state (Illinois) primary, March 18th. Defeated at home, he needed 18,000 Michigan votes to form a third party (*Time* 4/28/80).

BARRY COMMONER asked $18 in yearly dues from members of his newly formed Citizens Party.

JAMES CARTER's $180 billion cumulative budget (for four years) had brought spending in office up by 18% per year (*Time* 3/3/80).

Even in Canada's Pierre Trudeau won on a single 1980 issue by blocking an 18 cents per gallon hike in gasoline taxes (*Newsweek* 7/28/80).

CARTER and REAGAN neared the finish as Israel's Finance Minister called for overall budget cuts of $108 million (*Time* 7/7/80).

And most Americans decided that J.C. had lost 18 months before the election (*Time* 1/5/81).

GEORGE BUSH (Reagan's 1980 opposition) made his fortune of $1.8 million in oil (*Time* 7/28/80). And in 1988, as Bush (sign of a wine merchant) sought the presidency, he was assured "the $18 million" needed to win the nomination (*U.S. News* 3/30/87). Bush "met in Jerusalem with 18 Palestinians from the West Bank and Gaza" (*NY Times* 8/1/86). And "in 1943, at 18 he was the youngest pilot in the Navy" (*Time* 1/26/87). The media went wild as Bush jumped on an 18-wheeler after losing the Iowa caucus. He took the lead as the 18-wheeler drew more TV time than any issue. True to Reagan, when Bush spoke to the U.N., his script read, "We have one over-arching goal in the Persian Gulf." But Bush said, "we have one over-reaching goal," 7/15/88.

Michael Dukakis was 54 (three 18's) facing Bush in 1988 until one day before the Election, for DUKAKIS (to guide, to lead) was born November 3rd, '33 and had an organic garden. Bush was a self-proclaimed "meat and potatoes man" who didn't care for the fresh green stuff.

On July 18th, Mondale had cheeseburgers for both lunch and supper and was made the presidential candidate of his party.[1] On July 18th, the largest massacre ever committed by an individual in U.S. history ocurred at a Mc Donald's restaurant, not far from Mondale.

Who could have known that Ronald Reagan would be pitted against Donald Regan in in-fighting under the karma of Ronald Mc Donald, that funny-faced guy selling burgers and malts.

Ronald Mc Donald means "one of mighty power, son of Donald. But Donald means either "dark stranger" in Celtic or "lord" in Celtic-Latin.

Was Donald Regan's role in Iran-Contra that of "a lord" of the White House or "a dark stranger"? And why did Ronald fire Donald?

Had Reagan lost his will? Regan's middle name was Thomas, Hebrew for "twin." So, a division of will had hit the oval office.

Looking back to the "Where's the Beef" campaign of Mondale, 1980, the threads of karma were woven in a crystallized design.

The podiums for the Presidential debate were set 18 feet away from the press. Mondale had asked, "Where's the beef?" Jesse Jackson reached for the rainbow. And so, to celebrate his victory, Reagan ordered 1800 pounds of beef capaccio to be served in New York's Rainbow Room restaurant. The symbolism fit into place.

Roy Rogers, a Christian in Reagan's Armageddon coalition, as King of the Cow-boys (double-R-bar brand) sold beef to the nation while Reagan grew a cancer in his colon. And July 18th, one year after the Mc Donald's massacre, Reagan had his first meal after colon-cancer surgery. A vegetarian-style diet protects against this prominent killer," said the report next to the news of Reagan's post-op meal, July 18th.[2]

(1) ABC 7/18/84, (2) NY Times 7/19/85

Abstract "Facts"

The following "news" items had no real substance. "An 18-inch-high stack of documents reportedly captured from Salvadorian guerrillas" was offered in evidence; but *Time* (3/9/81) made no mention of content, only that the stack was 18 inches. Clarence Long in the House likened El Salvador to Nam and mistakes "made 18 years ago," with no word of what mistakes (*Time* 3/9/81).

The Voice of America broadcasts "for 1818 hours a week" (*Time* 3/9/81). Taiwan broadcasts 18 hours per day to China (*NBC* 4/26/84). Soviets spoke on Afghan radio "18 hours a day" (*Insight* 6/3/86). The content of these raido programs was not discussed in any of these cases.

"The Washington Post explained a Pulitzer hoax by Janet Cook in 18,000 words," said *Time* (5/4/81) with no hint of what the explanation was. Ambassador Reich said $180 million in economic aid went to South America in 1980 (*NBC* 10/30/83). What was money spent for? He didn't say. And Gabe Pressman said that J.C.'s statement on the Billy Carter's Libyan affair was 18,000 words, yet did not quote a word of it (*NBC* 8/4/80). In an 18-minute TV speech, Argentina's Economic Minister announced "a 180° turnaround in economic policies" (*Time* 7/19/83). What policies? "A 180° turnaround" was the extent of the news.

U.S. News (1/19/87) said of the decline of the dollar, a turnaround usually comes in 12 to 18 months; and Soviets hinted at 18-to-24-months to leave Afghanistan. When the Soviets say 12 months, "they're starting to be serious." said a U.S. diplomat. We got numeric media hype instead of facts. And a 5 week, 8 month, or 11 year time frame was seldom in "the news." A *N.Y. Times* editorial (5/20/87) said the USA should ask more "than the 18 months offered by the Russians," but did not say that this was 4 months after a "hint at 18-to-24 months." The numbers weren't meant to make sense.

Was this a case of sloppy news reporting. Or did the common thread of 18's point to a concern shared by our universal unconscious?

Dream Sequence

Rocky punches cows to train for the main event.

Prelude: Sly Stallone peers out from *Esquire* (12/5/78) opposite the 1818 in a vodka ad. Flash forward to the anti-dream: we punch the cows, and a sly cow-puncher on the silver screen wins the fat-clogged heart of a nation.

In the final fight of "Rocky I," Apollo Creed outweighs the Rock by 18 pounds. "Apollo Creed" is a symbol — "belief in a god of light and poetry." But Rocky wins. A bloody St-all-one, "all saints in one," is martyred for our ignorance. Blinded by trauma, we awake from the drama in search of one more movie dream — or two, or three, or . . . or was it all a dream?

Reagan portrayed a 180 pound man in "Tropic Zone." *Time* (2/14/83) put the weight of Andropov, Reagan's USSR counterpart at that time, at a "possible 180." And *People* (12/13/76) said Stallone exercised daily to keep his real-life weight at 180.

Rocky punches dead cows. John Travolta, *Urban Cowboy* rides a mechanical bull, haunted by RNA. Travolta has Rocky's picture on his wall. And in *Saturday Night Fever*, he gets off an RR subway train to Brooklyn and takes another RR back to Manhattan to apologize to Karn Gorney. In his next movie, *Grease*, Travolta is awarded the letter R for running track at Rydel High.

These were the stars that ruled the "American Dream" as we approached crystallization. Stallone, as Stanley in *Lords of Flatbush*, buys his girl friend a ring at the R&R jewelry store. In *Carrie*, Travolta slaps a girl named Chris across the face and dumps a bucket of blood over Sissy Spacek whose Anti-Christ mother is living next to the RR sign by a railroad crossing.

Rocky's first home address was 1818. And Rambo opened with Stallone shouting the number 36 three times (108) as scenes flashed of Buddhist monks.

"Where's the beef?" Rocky, Reagan, Rambo. R equal to 18. See if you believe exactly what's on the silver screen.

Just before Reagan's first term, R-R themes from Hollywood bounced off the astral plane.

In *Saturday Night Fever*, Travolta carries a bucket of *Carnival* paint. Carne-vale ("meat, farewell") was a lenten custom. In *Grease*, John Travolta and Olivia Newton-John go to heaven in a motor car at the carni-val. The End.

The "Carnival" in *Fever* was a brand upon the opening scene and set the tone. Travolta ordered a double pizza to represent of two girls he would consume. Toward the movie's end, he eats a burger with Karen Gorney just before his fight with the Barracudas, a street gang. A separate pane of glass on the BA-RR-AC-UD-AS clubhouse garage door holds the RR symbol.

In *Grease*, the image reverses itself. Watch the movie closely; before Travolta goes to heaven with Olivia Newton-John, he leaves his burger uneaten (completely untouched) behind him on the table at the high school hang-out, a surreal malt shop. The carni-val became his reality in the dream.

The opening scene in his next movie, *Moment by Moment* shows a sign saying HAMBURGER HAMLET directly behind a stop light. Travolta tries to sell Lily Tomlin drugs as they grope their way through a dreary R-rated flop.

T-RA-VOLTA, like ST-ALL-ONE, was a tinsel star. But a volt of Ra had encoded our cow-boy karma in their trivia. And Christopher (Christ carrier) RE-EVE became the new *Superman* who carried Mar-got in flight after they shared some wine.

Mondale ate two cheeseburgers July 18th before the Ronald MacDonald massacre. And in 1988, the Democratic Convention opened on July 18th.

Think back to the coincidences of the Reagan years. Our shared illusions gave us a mini "speech community" known to linguists as a mind-set passed along via spoken words. And in Phase Three, we shall have crossed the crystal stream. The signs were getting very clear by 1988 as Election Day was drawing near.

On the day that Dukakis and Jackson arrived in Atlanta, the temperature hit 108°. And tempers smoldered, awaiting the convention. A young girl, **Tawana Brawley**, was outside the convention hall. And "two wanna brawl" was the theme of the media's "Black-White" scenario.

Tawana, missing 90 hours, said she was raped by 6 White men. She then entered into a media event with police, clergymen, and politicians each claiming to be "Black" or "White."

The convention began July 18th and noted that Nelson **Mandela** spent his birthday jailed in South Africa (once "the USA"). Jackson led the **Rainbow** Coalition. And NBC's Gabe Pressman said ceremoniously to Jackson, Bentsen, and Dukakis, "Here you stand, Left, Right, and Center," to which Dukakis replied, "I don't buy those labels." But politics in the media never got far beyond the labels.

Jackson's speech began: "I see America, red, yellow, brown, black, and white." But there were no headlines about a "Brown" girl being raped. Whether Tawana Brawley was raped or not, the so-called "racial issue" fed the media.

Also on July 18th, Iran accepted the U.N. resolution calling for an immediate cease-fire. And there were also "racial" overtones in that war.

In Iran, Islamic law allowed no alcoholic drinks; but the law was often broken. In Iraq, the alcohol flowed more freely. For Iran was ruled by tyrannical mullahs while Iraq was more moderate.

Where body meets spirit, substance abuse cannot be stopped effectively by law enforcement. And so, society must learn to understand itself. A leader cannot change our eating habits or halt the cry for drugs. And the courts cannot end prejudice.

Once you fully realize that "the Word" itself is the key to change, let the law of love be your guide. The roots of biological ignorance run deep because we had so much that we had to ignore during the Age of History.

A Capital Idea

When Iran finally agreed to negotiate a cease-fire with Iraq (July 18th), *the Times* labeled a failed Iranian attack on Basra ("daugher of evil" in Hebrew) as the turning point of the war, said the USA had "crippled a third of Iran's small navy on April 18" (another turning point), and noted a decline in Iran's military "over the last 18 months."[1]

The Christian Science Monitor said, "18 Westerners" were held hostage at that time: "Ten Americans — among 18 Westerners and 23 foreigners missing and believed held in Lebanon."[2]

"Westerners" was capitalized while "foreigners" was not. In other articles "contras" was seldom capitalized. And "blacks" and "whites" (like "foreigners" and "contras") were not capital ideas. Caucasions, Negroes, Iranians, Arabs, Jews, and Americans were capitalized.

In this work, I have capitalized "Black" and "White" while putting them in quotes. For as a group, citizens of the USA (who are not the only "Americans") tended to treat these concepts as capital ideas.

A Times, headline, "'Coloreds': Caught Between Black and White,"[3] implied that "Black" and "White" (official usage in the USA) did not need quotes while "Colored" (official usage in South Africa) needed quotes.

We have seen throughout this work that mystic visions can be re-solved, brought into focus by the Crystal. Yet, to see the entire vision clearly, we cannot afford now to re-mystify prejudice.

As Bush (sign of the wine merchant) and Dukakis (a guide) battled for votes, a "54-member contra assembly" met in Miami.[4] I have also capitalized Contras, for they were made into a surrogate nation. And $18 million in military Contra-aid remained frozen as Bush and Dukakis moved toward the finish line.[5]

(1) NY Times 7/19/88, (2) CS Monitor 7/25/88, (3) NY Times 7/24/88, (4) CS Monitor 6/13/88, (5) CS Monitor 8/3/88

470

No Joke

In the last four years of Reagan's rule, the violent crime rate in the USA jumped by 1.8%.[1] And amazingly, under Gramm-Rudman, payments to the U.N. for that year's peace keeping operations were scaled down to $144 million.[2] And even that amount was paid in full. Education and peace-keeping had been sacrificed to pay for the weapons build-up.

Armageddon preachers made much of the fact that a 12 nation European Community (EC) was forming to fulfill the Final Days prophecy. Yet, no sooner would the 12 EC nations come together than the 6 European Free Trade Association nations (EFTA) would join them to total 18 and go beyond the prophecies of old.

The stories from the Language Crystal begin to come together as we fit the pieces into a greater metaphor. For this purpose the INDEX in this book can be used to bring many concepts together.

I was disturbed that *Auschwitz* ("from a joke") was linked to *Isaac* ("laughter") when Abram burned a ram after Sarah had laughed in the face of God. And *hocus pocus* ("a hoax" and root of "a joke") was the phrase that turned bread and wine into the body and blood of Christ. I was amazed that LAUGHTER was part of SLAUGHTER and that all this fit into human *hysteria* (a word that means "womb"), where the fear of fire is pushed into unconsciousness. Yet, I did not have room in this volume to register the human feelings that went through me. I can only equate the horror of the Age of History to the feelings that a pig must have when swallowed whole by a snake. The evolution of human spirit on this Planet Earth is no less cruel than other forms of evolution.

I will, however, be editing a Language Crystal Newsletter to touch upon the human feelings as we extend our metaphor into the future. To form a Crystal study group, get the Newletter, or simply correspond, write: The Language Crystal, Box 2333, NYC 10009.

(1) Time 6/27/88, (2) CS Monitor 8/3/88

The USA exports Coke, Mc Donald's, and pizza to China and the Soviet Union. Is it expected that democracy should follow?

True democracy finds balance in the material world by seeking the spirit through "the Word."

But the Olympic Committee sued and won its case to prevent other groups from using "Olympics" as a title for various events. And the Mc Donald's chain sued and won its case prohibiting other companies from using "Mc ." So, we may never see a "Mc CarWash."

I am sure that since the courts can rule on the name of Mount Olympus and protect fragmented trade marks, citizens must have a way to stop media mongers from exploiting "Black" and "White" images. Individuals who know that they are neither black nor white can sue if so exploited.

And we can change the name of "Organic Chemistry" to say simply "Carbon Chemistry" so that the word "organic" can be protected by law.

We can get news reporters to differentiate between "economy" and "finance." If only through education and letter writing, we can put biology in charge. And we can insure that "natural" is legally known to mean "not processed."

No, it won't be easy; for we must perform this monumental task within the sacred framework of a true democracy. Still, as our language grows more clear, our community will benefit. Communication will be more productive. And at the same time, a new sense of indivduality will be felt. The goal, after all, is Peace on Earth.

Thank you for reading these pages. Included, I trust, is sufficient proof that the hand of God is working among us through "the Word."

THE END

(The following pages are simply added "proof").

ADDENDUM 1: NAMES
(plus a few more facts)

A man named BELL invented the telephone. His name has a compelling ring. EIN-STEIN "one-stone" was the one to call for one (relative) rule over all.

For our names are verses, cast with craft in an infinite uni-verse. Yet it seems some will not fit till we've worn them for a bit to stretch past the molds of his-story.

Under Reaganethics, HARDY, in charge of Health and Human Services, was moved to Social Security. Health and wealth became confused by a lack of hardy spirits under the nuclear plutocracy.

OWENS was the acting Commissioner of Internal Revenue. First poet laureate of the USA, Robert PENN Warren was wreathed in 1986, when England already had 18. His last name fit with our global warfare. Mr. GODWIN was Director of the Moral Majority under Falwell. A different GODWIN was named to clean up fraud in the Pentagon. And it seems both Godwins lost, in their time.

Ginsberg (*Gunst-Burg*) meant "a stronghold of goodness." And when Reagan nominated the ex-pot-smoker to the Supreme Court, the signs said 666's "stronghold of goodness" was crumbling. For the President's team went soft on marijuana.

Al **Haig** ran against Bush in the 1988 primaries, but Haig was seldom seen and when he was seen he seemed to be hedging on the issues. Haig's name is from the Scots word for "an enclosure that is made of hedges."

Donald **Trump**, a winning suit at cards, first to open a gambling casino in Atlantic City, was numbered 666 by "Book-of-the-Month."

James **Lake** (a water sign, among the others in this text) was a former Reagan campaign official who said Regan was "arrogant" after Regan wrote of Reagan's dabbling in astrology (*C.S. Monitor* 5/10/88). Was Lake originally chosen for the Aquarian sound of his name?

ARCHIMEDES abstracted the arch that mediates the balance in a lever. Both arch and median were already in the formula of his name.

MARCO POLO marked the flat-earth polarities of easterly and westerly trade routes.

WATT and OHM were men who labeled "the what and the wherefore" of electricity. It seems that OHM was at home in vibrations of the elect.

NEW-TON weighed gravity anew, and came to terms for a while. Do spirits take their recreation in putting human beings on file?

Heissen, which means "to call" and "to order," gave HEISENBERG the idea that we order and call into being the results of experiments that we choose to conduct. He became a man of principle by living up to his name.

And a man whose name means "black-child" gave us SCHWARTZCHILD's radius, the path of mass into a black hole.

FREUD (joy) sought a pleasure principle. And SIGMUND (victorious protector in Teutonic) was "signal of the mouth" as a "Freudian slip" (Mund means "mouth"), as Austria slipped a bit.

LINNAEUS (Karl von Linne), a naturalist, put minerals, plants, and animals "in line" with names of Latinized genera and species.

George Francis TRAIN organized the Union and Pacific Railroads.

James FULBRIGHT provided for the exchange of the "brightest" students in many nations.

Henry POOR of Wall Street's "Standard and Poor" rated the debts of other firms.

SADE, the Marquis, had the saddest of energy.

BRAM STOKER encodes division (B) of the RAM. A "stoker" tends the flame. And he gave us Dracula on whom we count not to be too reflective.

Jay GOULD, capitalist, came closer than any other to cornering the market on GOLD.

BURBANK had a "bank of burs" (seed vessels from the flowering heads of plants) that he used to evolve new garden varieties.

Names in cacophony; order in his-story. Within the Code, each has a role. Or else, we make one up. It's order, all the same.

Mr. **Icahn** (pronounced *icon*) had his "net worth" (*Times* 10/19/86) at $180 million. The icon (image) tried to buy USX (see 144 in our chapter on "the Dream"). And USX had fallen from a value of $180 million (*Newsweek* 8/11/86) as the Stock Market rose and rose.

Also, **Armand Hammer**, U.S. envoy to the Hammer & Sickle, had $180 million (*New York* 6/20/88).

In the Code, the meaning of your name may not be obvious, for we have many ways of encoding. So, you might combine several methods.

Thomas Alva Edison's name can be turned many ways to reveal his calling — Thomas (twin) Alva (sublime) Edison (son of prosperity). Yet, TH is deity; and so, SON has a new meaning. ALVAH (*sublimity* in Hebrew) sees TH and OM as twins swept by eddies of the sun. It may be fanciful, yet fitting for one as inventive as Edison.

In working with your name, imagination is the key. And should you find any new links (current, historic, or personal), write and let me know.

A town named DEAF Smith, Texas, was chosen as a candidate for the national nuclear dump. But YUCCA Mountain was then given the pile of YUCH. And the fight is still going on.

Under 666, Mr. **Green** was the Environmental Protection Agency link to Moscow.

And Mr. **Jobs**, Apple Computer whiz, was named "the epitome of the American entrepreneur."

Spain's Isabella financed Christopher Columbus, laying claim to **America** (Industry). But her name could be from either **Elizabeth**, "House of God by an oath" or **Jezebel**, "an oath to Baal." And Baal was a false god to Hebrews while Jezabel had a worship of phallic "sacred poles." For *jezabel* in Hebrew meant "without a husband" (a curse in the matriarchy). This confusion of BAR with BAAL ("boy" with "false god") predates the Greek story of Oedipus in our pre-conscious naming game.

Where does myth begin; where does reality end?

Christopher Columbus (Carrier of Christ, the Dove) took 18 years to raise the money for his voyage. And the karma of the USA (between Isabella and Christopher) got caught in the mystery of the Whore of Baby-L-on trying to become Whole.

In the case of Baby M, both women gave her the middle name of Elizabeth. Was Baby M a daughter of Baal, god of mechanical sexuality?

Of course, no scientific principle guarantees results from giving a child a certain name. Names come together from many directions.

The N.Y. Times (12/9/79) tells of two identical twins who spent only their first four weeks together. Reunited after 39 years, each had been Christened with the exact same first name, James. Brought up unknown to each other, each had an adopted brother named Larry. Each had owned a dog named Toy, had had a first wife named Linda, had divorced and married a woman named Betty, and the first son of each was named James Allen. Also, each of the twin brothers had developed "the mixed headache syndrome" at the age of 18 years.

Without our names, we have no society. Yet, we may well wonder at the webs we weave.

Raymond Lee Harvey was arrested (5/11/79) for conspiring to assassinate James Earl Carter. Yet, James Earl Ray and Lee Harvey Oswald were involved in assassinations. These four names fit together just a little too neatly. And every "science" of humanity begins by gathering such coincidences, before developing a theory.

Later, a man named *Wilson* was sent to jail for selling Qaddafi ("warrior") the explosives that sparked a war with Ronald *Wilson* Reagan.

A man named Praise (Judas) plotted to sell a man named Savior (Jesus). And "Judas" fits with the meaning of "Muhammad." Judah, son of Israel by Leah ("weary") bore the family line. Mary means "bitter." So flows the wine of bitter praise unto a pre-sent daze in the only story ever told.

Washington would not tell a lie; Nixon would. And coincidentally, **George** and **Richard** were gambling terms that meant "honest" and "dishonest."

Nixon's honesty, first questioned over $18,000 in bribes, was defended in his "Checkers speech." The last of his taping machines were removed from the White House on the 18th of the month. And in the movie "All the President's Men," reference to the cover-up said "1800 leads were followed by the FBI" in solving the Watergate case.

Richard Nixon's most in-famous words were on 18.5 minutes of erased recording tape, the turning point (5) in his recording career.

George meant "honest" as in the British George-noble gold piece. Richard meant "a lack of trust" as in the song that asks, "Richard why won't you open that door?" (a gambler's joke about Richard's lack of credibility). Of course, every Richard is not a crook, nor is every George virtuous. We still do have free will.

It took the original States 18 months to ratify the Constitution. And after Masonic meditations, Washington laid the cornerstone of the Capitol on 9/18. And in this magic, many bio-spirits cast their "free wills" into a singular State.

But the Armageddon years were marked by contra-diction, not response-ability.

Reagan's secret team led by **Shackley** tells how "one in the wood of robbers" is linked to "shack" (a house in disrepair) and "shackle" (a tool of slavery).

Judge **Bork** (Borksky, dweller in a small wood) had a small opinion of the Constitution. He failed to see that people had rights before our rights were written down. Joe **Biden**, a candidate who stole from other people's words, had a name from *bi dem Bach* or *bi dem Feld* or *bi dem some place else*, with no sense of belonging.

Human names today reflect our current state of affairs. And yet, names do not determine; they often only put on heirs.

Muhammad (which means "worthy of praise") was adopted by a couple who saw him for 18 seconds on TV. He was from Africa (*60 Minutes*, 10/12/86). And the report ended by saying, all starving children of Africa could be adopted, since "each of them has a name." It's only human.

To prevent a surprise attack in Europe, 666 sent Mr. GOODBY to negotiate with Russia. "I cannot foresee early results," said Mr. Goodby (*NY Times* 8/23/84). As Armageddon propaganda, Mr. Goodby's name seemed obvious. But a longer focus could link him to a "goodbye to history."

After HIT-LER drove "Left" and "Right" apart by the end of World War II, **Weizmann** (a wise man) and **Truman** (a true man), Israel's first President and President of the USA, made the tie official; Israel was a landed nation, in writing.

The spirit of their union passed to Mr. BEGIN. AN-WAR SAD-AT who had confronted the question of IS-RA-EL was killed at a weapons review (sad-at-war). See next addendum. And BEGIN stepped down as we waited for the new beginning.

Truman's first name, Harry, "mighty in battle," allowed him to drop the bomb, ending the war.

Eisenhower ("a worker of iron") was the Allied Supreme Commander to the West of Hitler. **Stalin** ("man of steel") was to the East. For Hitler had polarized their friction.

"Communism" and "Capitalism" were growing on his Right and Left. And after Hitler's death, the "iron curtain" fell, polarized in BE-RL-IN.

We have seen that HIT-LER was a link between IS-RA-EL and Je-R-usa-L-em. So, here are a few more puzzle pieces (with minimum repetition) to carry our story toward the end of history.

President J.C. was at the top of Capitol Hill when a LANCE (Bertram) was removed from his side. Ham Jordan had darkened the image of J.C. with a cocaine scandal. HAM means "dark" and JORDAN, of course, signified the river. A shallow spot where a river is crossed is a FORD, in English.

Ford's role was shallow, to provide a stepping stone from Nixon to J.C. The shame of a NIX ON faith was J.C.'s guarantee. And Ford's pardon for Nixon gave Carter the 1976 election.

Four years later, 666 crucified J.C.

And four years after that, the fiscal lance (Bert Lance) that felled J.C. was thrust to the side of Mon-dale at the Convention. To avoid a party break-up, Lance was drawn out on July 18th, the day of the **Ronald McDonald** massacre.

And we had a STAR COMEDY BY DEMOCRATS spelled backwards in the novel year of 1984.

We've seen the story; so here are a few more details. "Where's the Beef?" became Mondale's slogan after a symbolic Hart-attack. Before meat-industry ads co-opted its meaning, "What's the Beef?" meant "What's the Trouble?" And 666 had "one-valley" (mon-dale) to cross.

Roy Rogers (in Ronald Reagan's Armageddon gang) once had Dale for a wife at the cow-boy's burger-slinging Double-R-Bar Ranch. And on July 18th, Mondale had cheeseburgers for both lunch and supper before he was chosen to run.

On-the-spot reports from Ronald McDonald's fit between the convention-hall speeches. "It's an absolute massacre," said Police Commander GORE at the scene. So, the largest massacre ever by one person in the USA was identified with Mondale, as TV viewers went sleep-walking to the polls.

When Burger King had its media blitz on Herb (the nerd), **Herb Schmertz** (vegetation in pain) was in charge of Public Affairs at Mobile Oil, the petro-chemical fertilizer source. And the karma of the golden calf swirled throughout the land. Also on July 18th, in New-Ark (population 318,000), a cattle stampede was stopped by police who rounded up 12 loose steers.

By 1988, the fiscal lance (Bertram) that had first been drawn from J.C.'s side and then from Mon-dale's had been thrust to the side of Jesse **Jack-son** (son of Jacob), son of Israel.

Ferraro seemed an asset to Mondale. But their divided camp asked "$54 billion in spending cuts" (*Fortune* 10/15/84) with 54% of eligible women in the work force. Then, her husband's business made the news. The first woman in a Vice Presidential slot on a major ticket had a name beginning with FE and ending in O, both fe-male symbols.

Between FE and O appeared the letters R-RA-R, a mandala to match R.W.R. since W is wegarded as a winguistic "wiquid" in the Code.

In her acceptance speech, Ferarro spoke of "99 days" to win. Remember 99 was the breaking point between Abraham and his first son Ishmael and is thus the number of Moslem beads of prayer while in Hebrew kaballah 99 signifies "two women."

Most of the time before the election (Gallop Poll 10/4/84), Reagan was ahead by 18%.

FE-R-RA-R-O depicted a rebirth of the sun-god. But **Geraldine** meant "one mighty with a lance." So, Bert-ram Lance, Ferraro, and Mondale assured 666 his victory as **Roy** (king) **Rogers** (lance bearer) joined Burger King and MacDonalds in making mince-meat of the nation's eating habits.

And **Gerald** R. Ford had also carried "a lance" in his first name.

Like Christa, Ferraro was Catholic, dwelling in circles of 54 beads. But rumors of vice at 218 Lafayette Street tainted her husband's office (*NY Times* 8/21/84). Three days before Christa died, Ferraro's office at 108-18 Queens Blvd was broken into (*NY Times* 1/27/86). And New-Ark's population (318, Ab-ram's conflict) happened to be on on *the Times* op-ed page a week before Christa died.

Now, these facts may seem unwieldy. Yet, they will interest future scientists. We have seen that pure math does not apply strictly to biology. And a haunting synchronicity along with repeated themes is reflected in these numbers. So, as we gather more knowledge, patterns of science and religion will eventually overlap in the whole truth of the uni-verse.

A Priest or Not?

J.C. gave his 9/18 speech to Sadat and Begin in Congress as the Camp David accord was to be sealed after 18-months work. But in 1978, J.C. said "I'm not a priest," on 2/18, answering a New Hampshire student. No one had asked if he were a priest. And Gimbels had a TV ad just then saying 2/18 was "the last day to save." Two months later, $1.8 million in jewels was stolen from Gimbels on the 18th.

Hypothesis: the world (wer-alt) holds together connected by "the Word."

And President J.C. did not bring lasting peace to Je-R-usa-L-em in "the Holy Land."

The self-declared failed priest, Carter, in the image of "Dark Father" (Ham-shire) had put his own imprint on Star Wars before 666 arrived on the scene to play Darth Vader (also a Dark Father).

In the astral plane, "Ham Jordan" (dark river) crossed Club 54 cocaine dealer "Johnny C." who was then arrested on an 18-month-old drug charge to be sentenced to 18 months in June of 1980. And the Club 54 owner was sentenced for tax evasion on January 18th, 1980. So, the credibility of President J.C. was tarnished for awhile.

Billy (shortage of Will) Carter, the scapegoat, following his aborted $1.8 million Libyan oil deal, told David Letterman (5/13/82), "I went before the grand jury for 9 months, testified 18 times." And we've seen other links. Billy told "Good Morning America," the probe's "been going on nearly 18 months." The day after his brother's nomination to run against 666, Billy's sworn deposition said he had spent $180,000 of the money (*CBS* 8/15/80). And "Billy Beer" became his sacrificial brew before the electorial cross.

J.C. returned to be a carpenter on 6th Street in New York for "Habitat for Humanity," a non-profit group in 33 States, as 666 ruled the Hill.

When Arafat was driven from Tripoli (Lebanon), aside from evacuations of the wounded, organized departure of PLO forces officially began on 12/18 in the 3rd year of 666 (*NY Times* 12/18/83).

Nelson MANDELA, born July 18th, was a leader in the spirit in South Africa. A mandala is a circle of prayer in countless colors. Mandela's wife, **Winnie** named the goal of "people of color" for all humanity. **Botha** (President in writing) insisted *both* sides of his *black-white* argument should be heard in his-story, ad nausium.

Vanna White (also born on the 18th) reflected the vanity of "consumers" in the USA.

Len BIAS, basketball hero, died of crack in the 1986 drug wars as "bias toward his color" invaded his success, pushing him out of "the race."

Dwight GOODEN was saved from the fate of BIAS. Was it due to vibrations in his name?

Machelle Outlaw was expelled from Goldsboro Christian School by principal Reginald Kingsley. Reverend Harper (heavenly) accused the teenage Outlaw of modeling a two-piece bathing suit (*NY Times* 3/14/87). Goldsboro Christian "refused to admit blacks," said *the Times*, until a Supreme Court ruling in 1983. Did the swimsuit "masters" have a skin-fetish? Had Outlaw been attacked by Reginald Kingsley because of their names?

Judge King dismissed the Christic Institute's lawsuit against the Contra drug runners in July of 1988. The case is on appeal.

When 666 defended a pot-smoking **Gunst-Burg**, the "stronghold of goodness" was shaken. National Public Radio's Nina **Totenberg** broke the story. And Toten-berg means "a mountain of the dead." Had a mountain of the dead attacked 666's stronghold of goodness? Was the wer-alt of 666 about to die?

During his first presidential campaign, Hart's plane went down in flames, with 108 on board (*NBC* 6/5/84). No one hurt. Three years later, he had a love affair with Donna **Rice** (flaming passion), 108 pounds in the flesh (*Star* 5/19/87).

This thesis that the WORLD has it pivot in the WORD (L = 12) cannot be tested until our new laboratory is in order. And this will require a merging of good biology with good faith.

I promised in the text to list the names that sprang from Shem (word) to beget the line of Abram (exaltation). Each had either an R or an L in a time when the whole Earth was of one language and of one speech (Gen. 11:1).

Shem begat the line of Arphaxad, who begat Salah, who begat Eber, who begat Peleg, who begat Reu, who begat Serug, who begat Nahor, who begat Terah, the father of Abram, Nahor, and Haran. Each name contained an R or an L. Then came a new line of division after Abram changed his calling.

Ishmael, his Arab son, carried on the R-L line while Isaac, his Hebrew son, did not.

Isaac meant L-aughte-R (nothing between R and L, except energy, E). Now we can solve the riddle of Arabs and Jews in Je-R-usa-L-em.

Since Judah meant "praise," and in the Code "p-raise" is the power to raise, these patterns of levity support the Crystal thesis.

The journey of Abram from "light" (Ur, the town of his birth) to "enlightenment" (Haran, the town where his father died) was uneventful until Abram was told in Haran to go forth unto a town whose name meant "humility" (Canaan).

"And Sarai, Abram's wife, took Hagar, her maid the Egyptian, after Abram had dwelt ten years in the land of Canaan, and gave her to her husband Abram to be his wife" (Gen. 16:3). The Bible says both women were to be "his wife." And the fighting in "the Holy Land" was due to a lack of humility in the House of Canaan (humility). In other words, humanity was guilty of double-talk.

"He went in unto Hagar, who conceived: and her mistress was despised in her eyes" (Gen. 16:4). Yet we have seen other viewpoints of "despised."

Humility was lost by both Arabs and Jews. Iran ("upper class") was paid by Israel to fight a surrogate war against Iraq. And all "the nations" had lost humility (humus being the Earth itself). And we DROWN in the N-WORD of non-speaking as 666 ruled with laughter.

Reagan was billed as "the Great Communicator" and community itself (the only true communicator) was portrayed as "the consumer." The media had set up Reagan as a straw-man, to feed upon his stuffing. Thus media (rather than community) seemed to be the communication center and advertising was the only constant in "the news."

So long as a society cannot communicate among its members, secret teams will rule. And hidden information will be excused (personally, in the Government, and in industry).

In Miami, **Jesus Garcia** (Gar-CIA) led the U.S. Attorney to illegal arms and drug shipments in 1985. In 1988 new details arose as fast as old ones were covered up. And the Christic Institute's narcotics case against the President's secret team symbolized "Christ and 666" in combat.

Thesis and anti-thesis, Christ and Anti-Christ consumed in synthesis. None were guilty. None were innocent. We all were spirits caught in a techno drama. Like characters in a movie, we played out our days opposite special effects.

"First American" collapsed a day before Reagan left for the Summit. First American Mortgage had been crushed under $180 million in mortgages (*NY Times* 11/18/85). The symbols were obvious once the numbers brought them into focus.

The old radio waves of *MGM Playhouse* had ghosts bouncing off the ionosphere. The wartime drama in which Reagan played the father of a Christmas baby was still reverberating. A plan to buy MGM Grand helped to move Wall Street by 144 on the 18th for Ron's Geneva voodoo dance. And MGM Grand sold at $18 a share on that day (*NY Times* 11/19/85).

On January 18th, 1988, 108 people were killed in the worst plane crash in China's history. And my thoughts went back to Edwin Newman's joke on Saturday Night Live — "108 were killed."

God wasn't playing a joke on us. We had misused our power to create. Yet, now we can make creation a conscious loving act.

Four days after 18 U.S. jets flew from England to bomb Qaddafi, the *first* U.S. citizen killed in the affair was identified on April 18th as Mr. Kil-burn, killed despite Mr. Waite's negotiating. Kuwait refused, for Mr. Waite was a cover for the USA's non-waiting arms-for-hostages deal.

Kilburn is not from the English "kill." **Kill** in Dutch means "creek," and in Gaelic, "burial place." Though most translations herein refer to national origin, others are hit with just a bit of english on the ball.

Also on April 18th, an Arab who planted a bomb in his pregnant Irish girlfriend's luggage at a British airport was caught in a hotel, waiting in his room — number 18.

Ashland Oil, largest independent oil refiner in the USA, had just ended a takeover skirmish with a Canadian family who wanted to buy out Ash-land for $1.8 billion (*NY Times* 10/8/86). Canada, along with England, supported the Tripoli bombing.

At one level, nations fought. At another, our swirling concepts sought peace in the planetary mind. The final battle was to be among the Angels, verbally. And the final language was to belong to Angles. But our language will NOT be English as we know it today. English is still reaching out, taking in other languages. And the final Angular language shall reflect all human techno thought around the original bio-spirit base. So, each of us is even now contributing to the process.

Mr. COOK blew the whistle on the Challenger cover-up (*NY Times* 2/14/86). And a different Mr. COOK at Bridgman's nuclear plant was said to be in on a cover-up (charges filed 9/10/86).

Howard *Baker* (body) was White House chief of staff, James *Baker* (mind) in the Treasury, and Jim *Bakker* (spirit) in the Armageddon Church were only three among other Bakers in Reagan's court.

More Bakers were round 666 than any other name. Was it coincidence? It surely fits our metaphor and supports the hypothesis.

Personally,

It is perfectly legal to change your name or even use several names if your intent is honorable. So, legality, in the civil sense, does not depend upon spelling. It is motivation that counts.

And in the mystical realm, even such names as "Hunter" can have a meaning that is transcendent. For one can hunt for treasure or solutions to some greater mystery. So, we can judge only within a given context.

My given name Lawrence derives from the laurel indicating an interest in scholarship and poetry. I feel LAW-R-ence is the essence of my work. Yet William, my middle name, was in a quandary until the will-I-am fixed on peace as a goal.

The vibration in my last name, Lyons, has led me through this mystery. For *the Lion of the tribe of Juda, the root of David hath prevailed to open the book, and to loose the seven seals thereof.*

When I first read this passage at Revelation 5:5, I saw it as a turning point. For as we have seen, the Lamb (not the Lion) opened that seal. Then I realized that the Lion and the Lamb were as related as Israel and Islam. We are only waiting for a mature humanity.

In the rubric of the Egyptian Book of the Dead, a passage calls for one who "hath not eaten animal flesh or fish. Behold thou shalt make a scarab of green stone with its rim plated with gold and placed within the heart of a person; it will perform for him the opening of the mouth."

My birth sign is the scarab; my father Patrick was born of an Emerald (in Water-ford, famous for crystal), my mother is Ellie, and my god-mother Mary — so, I take these as signs.

And you also can lay claim to miracles that surround you. Signs and symbols mark the highway that you travel. So, by watching and waiting for signs, we also get to work together on another level. At first, it may seem overwhelming. Still, we can know the spirit, scientifically. And we can find unity on the next plateau.

ADDENDUM 2: numbers

When we forget that both our poetic and scientific symbols have common roots, we tend to marvel at coincidence as if it were miraculous. We act with surprise when our symbolic structures imitate the natural patterns upon which they were built.

BIRTH OF A NATION

After the American Revolution, a disbanding of the Militia left a standing army of 666 men under Washington's command in New York State (*A Short History of New York State*, by Ellis, Cornell U. Press, 1957). Was this George Washington's mystical plan? After all, he was a Mason.

DEATH AND RENEWAL

Commemorating the Holocaust, mourning the death of 6 million Jews, 6 thousand survivors lit 6 thousand candles in Jerusalem. "An entire day was taken up by meetings of 6 hundred children of survivors." The meeting took place 36 years after World War II to symbolize a renewal of life. After 6 million were slaughtered, 6 thousand mourned, and 6 hundred came to follow after. That candlelight procession took place on 6/18 (*Time* 6/29/81). These numbers could hardly have been planned by anyone.

Photosynthesis in plants produces a sub-stance that fuels human under-standing. And the formula for this substance, "glucose," is also prophetic. *Six* molecules of carbon dioxide and *six* molecules of water form *six* molecules of oxygen and *one* glucose molecule. And in a glucose molecule is the formula for further re-divination.

Simply stated: understanding and substance are two sides of the same cycle of creation-evolution. You can fit these addendum pages into the main text, not necessarily in a linear fashion, but to round out the entire thesis.

Anwar Sadat had sailed aboard a ship numbered 666 when he re-opened the Suez Canal. And Begin was 66 years old, 6th Prime Minister of Israel when he signed the Camp David Accord.

On the 6th day of October, Sadat was killed as 6 Mirage jet fighters distracted his attention. His bodyguard fired 6 shots in defense. Across a 6 lane highway, opposite the murder site, 6 dark horses drew his body to its resting place. Also laid to rest were 6 other souls who sat beside Sadat in 1981, the first year of reign for President 666.

President 666 ordered the 6th Fleet's Task Force 60 to "increased readiness" off Egypt's coast. At that time, SAM-6 missiles were trained on the area by the USSR. Mubarak had spent 6 years under Sadat, preparing to be President. And the 6 newspapers in Egypt opposed to Sadat were shut down for the days of Egypt's political unrest.

The following week, Moshe Dyan died at the age of 66. Dyan had captured the Gaza Strip and the Sinai Peninsula in the historic Six Day War.

When the Pope, age 60, was shot, the New York Times front page reported, "Leader of 600 million Roman Catholics . . . received about 6 pints of blood, the equivalent of 60% of his total blood volume." Time magazine mentioned the temperature in Saint Peter's Square when the Pope was shot, "66 degrees."

In Ireland, Bobby Sands died from 66 days of protest starvation. In England, 6 blank cartridges were fired at the Queen. President 666 was fired at 6 times. His operation left a scar 6 inches long.

Israel sent 6 jets to bomb Iraq's nuclear power plants and began the invasion of Lebanon, "Peace for Galilee," on the date of 6/6.

As Reagan's first term drew to a close, India's first woman Prime Minister, Indira Gandhi was shot and killed at the age of 66. And in these events was a biological violence blindly out of control in tight-knit patterns of synchronicity.

The light that we perceive and the light that we create in New Jerusalem shall be harmonic at a new level of perception. Partly intuitive, a logic of numbers is in our Logos, for *Logos* is a word that means both "the Word" and "the Christ."

Our biology shall meet science and religion in ecological election. The waves of photosynthesis that lead to thought that leads to invention are clearly waves of light that have the power of "the Elect." And we can elect to use these powers for the salvation of biology.

Electric power flowed at 60 cycles a second in the USA feeding techno thought at 60 seconds a minute, 60 minutes an hour. These background waves were already in effect when computers began to run the show.

Yet only as we feed biology bio-logically will we be able to mesh our own inner photo-synthesis with the mastery of the uni-verse.

The mass of a proton is 1836 times greater than that of an electron. And powers of election come from our ability to bombard electrons with photons that our kundalini source gives a personal spin. By putting english on the ball, we have the uni-verse to win.

Life (18) and rebirth (36) in matter come about through time by way of timelessness. And so, the basis of election is always one of spirit.

We see synchronicity where no other animals do because we surround ourselves with artifacts. We have created the second synchronistic wave. Beyond the first natural wave, we have waves of symbolic events that intermesh with our written symbols.

El Salvador: 60 observers watched at polls as 60 Assembly seats got voted on (*NY Post* 3/27/82). Claiming the elections were rigged, Guerrillas numbered 6,000 (*Time* 3/22/82). The Savior's Left Christian Democrats won 24 seats (6x4) and the Right won 36 (6x6). Three years later, the tide turned as the Christian Left took 54% (18x3) of El Salvador's national vote (*NY Times* 4/1/85).

I felt enslaved to gathering these numbers for I knew they told of a new consciousness. Watch as a few more pieces fall in place.

In war, Sadat had worked for Hitler. Sadat was born Christmas Day 1918, 54 days after the World War I armistice. He joined the army at 18.

As President, he rebuffed the USSR by deporting 18,000 Soviet troops. He shifted Arab influence and in 1978 broke relations with Cyprus after 18 Egyptian commandos in a hijack rescue were shot by Cypriot troops (*Newsweek* 3/4/85).

After Sadat's murder, 18 army officers were transfered due to "fanatic" tendencies (*NY Times* 2/24/85). Afraid to go to Sadat's funeral, Reagan sent 3 ex-Presidents, 18 other proxies (*NY Times* 5/31/84), and two Marine units "of about 1800 men each" (*NY Post* 10/12/81).

These fragments of power were extensions of the broken images of Abram at 318, a number that came between him, his servants and an enemy king. In the Bible, 6 (common man), 6 (man as slave), and 6 (man as ruler) were divided at 318 as social classes were in the He-brew brotherhood.

Hours before the Pope was shot, USSR Aeroflot fight 318 was halted, searched by the FBI, and sent on its way (*NY Times* 10/8/81). A mystery was in the air. Our next page shows how West-more-land was a symbol defeated at 318. And remember that 318 is linked to "New-Ark."

The Bible tells how Abram sent 318 servants to bring back one slave, Eliezer. It seems Eliezer was Abram's brother in one verse yet was Abram's steward in another. And in kabbalah, the letters in "Eliezer" equal 318. Also, the King of Ellasar (a different spelling) stole Abram's "brother."

These divisions were necessary so that we might have masters and slaves, and a karma that could be realized in our slavery to machines.

To play the mono games properly, to overcome the beast, democracy treats all as biological, mental, and spiritual equals (6 = 6 = 6).

General West-more-land played a significant role in battles of NAM where "Western" MAN began to question his "Eastern" goals. And when he gave up his libel suit against CBS, Westmoreland relived his reversals in NAM.

The case took 18 weeks of trial (*NY Times* 10/7/81), in room 318 of Federal District Court in Manhattan (*Newsweek* 5/25/81). But the General refused to hear the verdict. The drive of West-more-land remained deaf to the news that we had reached the end of Phase Two expansion.

Easter was upon the Wind. And 666 (the money beast), shot by Hinkley (a lack of belief), spoke an omen of the coming Wall Street Crash.

Recovered from Hinkley's bullet, 666 opened his first born-again speech saying, "Where have we come in these 6 months? . . . Mortgage interest rates . . . for these 6 months . . . hourly earnings . . . 6 months ago . . . 6 months is long enough!" And an AP poll at that time said 66% of the people thought his performance as President was "good or excellent" (*Time* 5/11/81).

President 666 had a flare for numbers. But what on Earth had become of "the economy"? The game of "finance" had been played so hypnotically that the eco-sphere seemed to be dying.

But Reagan himself was not 666; he was only a pivot of symbols. Each man must still learn how to play at "Brother," "Slave," and "King." Phase One males fought, for females came with the territory. In Phase Two, we pitted science and belief against each other. And in Phase Three, the basic drive to compete becomes a drive to complete the cycle of Earthly creation in E-quality.

Men were slaves to their machines. Men thought machines might learn to think. Still, the machine is only a thing in service of the abstract king.

Each word encodes another level of abstraction. A th-ing is "diety in action" (a verb form). And a k-ing is "kundalini in action." Focus your inner light at your 6th chakra — "the Word."

Just as merging 6's produce new 18's (new life), so divided 6's produce an unconscious struggle. And the same appears in names.

Of Ferdinand Marcos, Corazon Aquino said to the USA, "You've given him guns. You've given him $18 billion" (*Mother Jones*, Jan. 1984).

Marcos was a symbol of "Mars & Co." And he was a dying war-god toward the end of history.

Philippine bases of Clark and Subic were "the largest U.S. military installations in any foreign country, with 18,000 on active duty" where the USA paid $180 million yearly to Mars & Co. to use his turf, and native workers got "a typical salary of $1.80 an hour" (*Time* 2/3/86).

U.S. military aid paid for political turmoil. Still, Congress approved $180 million more for Marcos starting Reagan's second term (*C.S. Monitor* 10/21/85). And "new infusions of aid, totaling $108 million, from the International Monetary Fund and foreign banks" were on their way when he was forced to flee (*Time* 8/26/85).

The $108 million from the IMF and banks to prop up Mars & Company was significant in that so many genuine eco-projects in our global eco-sphere got no funding. And it fits the Crystal thesis.

We saw Mr. Marcos slated to get $14.4 million in U.S. military supplies before he was deposed (*NY Times* 2/21/86). In Armageddon's 7th year, he tried for an insurrection, with $18 million spent for tanks, rocket launchers, recoilless rifles, and missiles (*NY Times* 7/9/87).

Once a mighty god & Roman soldiers, Mars & Co. saw Marcos end up as a clown playing for mock sympathy in late night TV interviews.

Aquino met with "leftist guerillas" in social reform after Mars & Co. had been unwilling to do so for 18 years (*NY Times* 9/4/86). And after 18 months in office, Aquino met the first protest of her policies, a protest against an 18% fuel price increase (*NY Times* 8/27/87). Still, the old power mongers favored the ways of Mars & Co.

Philippine documents said, "6 officers and 18 men led by Marcos were guards in the war. Yet, Mars & Co. had avoided combat (*NY Times* 1/23/86).

Expecting election fraud, the Pentagon wanted an alternate 180,000-acre site (Mar-ianas Island) for its bombing ranges (*NY Times* 1/25/86).

Another Mars Co. (in the USA) was the world's largest manufacturer of candy, waging a chemical warfare on the nerves of unsuspecting children.

Kellogg's Flakes were baked in Battlecreek. The Rice was shot from guns as medical magnates sought "a magic bullet" to cure all our ills.

Food prices rose in the Philippines as Marcos devalued the pesos to 18 against the dollar (*NY Times* 6/10/84). U.S. "Filipinos" earned 18% less than "Japanese" but 18% more than "Hispanics" on the average (*World Press Review* April 1986).

Such "statistics" were, of course, a science fiction, an apartheid of the mind. But I am reporting here on the viewpoints of Phase Two.

Marcos had claimed 54% of the vote (*NY Times* 2/15/86) a ballot fraud, yet no more deceptive than ad campaigns in the USA denatured "foods."

The Martial arts and Marital arts were still in competition as "bread winners" fought for crumbs. In his final year, Reagan chose Martin Marietta (another Mars & Co.) to do the feasibility tests for "Star Wars" (*NY Times* 1/23/88).

Mario Moreno was a key witness against Mario Biaggi in the Wed-tech trial (3/22/88) telling of an attempt to sell arms to Iraq through a former financial advisor to Ed Meese.

Marvin Gorman told of Swaggart's master-bait. **Randy** ("smutty" in English), Marvin's son, took pictures. Jimmy got defrocked and deflocked. And The Travel Inn's ownership had just changed hands on 12/18 (*NY Times* 3/31/88). Each piece fit the tapestry as the Armageddon gang was dismembered.

And a serious man, the martyr of El Salvador, was named Marti (wrapped too deeply in his own nation's ego). May he rest in peace.

The Wrong Investments

By 1986, Reagan had raised the number of active Navy divisions to 18, ready to move against "the enemy." So, 18 divisions taxed the budget.

NASA's official report on the Challenger's fall was released on April 18th. The techno mind-set had made the wrong investments.

This same schizophrenic sense of separation, a drive toward techno advance with no regard for bio concerns had brought thousands of demonstrators into the streets of Japan.

Reagan was going to speak about "terrorism" at the Tokyo Summit of Industrial Democracies when Chernobyl exploded. The police protection in Tokyo was up to 18,000 officers per day (*NY Times* 4/21/86). And the Japanese yen was 180 to the dollar when on April 18th the Fed in the USA cut its discount rate to hold the yen in place (*The Economist* 4/26/86).

NASA knew about the weakness of Challenger, as indicated by 72 (four 18's) new cases of O rings ordered amid fears of failure. Chernobyl had a weakness of O rings similar to NASA's. And even "O rings that were ignored" were symbolic of our lack of respect for the goddess. The maternal nature of matter was separated from the paternal nature of pattern by our unconscious fear.

The Challenger killed more astronauts than ever before in a single accident. Chernobyl sent out as much long-term radiation as all nuclear tests and bombs put together up to that time. And the Dow fell below 1800 one day after "Cherno-byl."

Officially, 1.8 million Jews were in the USSR (*NY Times* 1/7/86); and 180 who wanted to leave were encouraged by the USA (*NY Times* 3/9/86). Also, 180 U.S. citizens were working at the Moscow Embassy (*Time* 9/2/85).

Morde-chai Vanunu got 18 years Israeli jail-time for saying a known fact — that Israel was making nuclear bombs (*NY Times* 4/15/88).

If the above facts seem unrelated, let's look a little deeper.

494

Relatively Nuclear

There were countless numbers floating around in "the news." Not all were 6's and 18's. How can we think of this as scientific proof of anything?

And these facts were gathered over a period of eight years. For instance, people in the USA spent almost $1800 each on "health care" (*NY Times* 3/20/88). But that quote was about the year of 1985. The cover story of *Time* (11/30/87) referred to 18 million people with "a drinking problem" in the USA. But that was two years later.

The message of crystallization is not that ALL numbers were becoming 18's. *U.S. News* (11/2/87) wrote of the 1.8 million members in the Teamsters Union and *a Newsweek* article (12/14/87) said 1.8 million people per day were absent from work; but either of these could have been 1.793 million. And many other counts were surely approximate.

The message is that we were struggling in our infancy on this Planet to focus on the meaning of "life" that is scientific and religious, logical and imaginative. Humanity has been on Earth for less than two million years. Written records go back only 6,000 years. Yet, we have five billion years of Earth time remaining if we choose to live within the rules of cosmic evolution.

NASA's manned space station was to be 180,000 pounds (*Time* 11/26/84). Days before Christa & Co. died, the 1800 pound Voyager passed Uranus, 1.8 billion miles from Earth, before exiting our solar system (*NY Times* 1/23/86). When Christa departed, the Dow went up 18.81 points. Morton Thiokol company said the shuttle would have accounted for 18% of its income that year (*NY Times* 1/29/86). And the private Houston Space Services had plans for "light-weight satellites up to 1,800 lbs" (*Time* 3/31/86).

The Russians sent a dog into space, traveling at 18,000 mph. The USA sent its first satellite 18 months later. The USA's first man in space was named **Shepard**, symbolic of a quest for the Lamb of God in New Jerusalem.

ADDENDUM 3: HOPE

The first space shuttle lift-off was an "18-story-high" package at Cape Canaveral (*Time* 5/11/81). Second was "with 1800 new or repaired insulating tiles" (*Newsweek* 11/16/81). Two faulty units, "18 inches high" delayed the take-off (*Today* 11/5/81). The next "malfunction was traced to a 36-pound black box" (*NY Times* 11/12/81). The launching just prior to Challenger was flawed and "18,000 pounds of liquid oxygen" were drained from the fuel tanks due to "human error" (*NY Times* 8/6/86).

There were also other numbers. Yet, "life" was crying out above the rest. We need truly human values before we will be ready to travel forth, before we can ride the supernatural cycles.

We have seen how the 18th annual convention of the World Anti-Communist League, headed by General Singlaub (*PBS* 3/18/86) sent funds to the Contras. And Sin-glaub can mean either "belief in Sion" or "belief in Sin." Days after he appeared on TV, the Dow Jones average closed for the first time above "the 1800 barrier," said *the N.Y. Times* (3/22/86). But why was 1800 called a "*barrier*"? Did *the Times* have its own sense of prophecy?

After passing 1800 in 666's 6th year, the Dow fell below 1800 one day after Cherno-byl.

And between the time of Christa's death and the Chernobyl explosion, small groups of insurgents from Honduran bases brought "the number of rebels inside Nicaragua to 1800" (*NY Times* 4/28/86).

Surrounded by madness, only you have a philo-sophy that can lock on to the cycle of hope. The Library of Congress complained of $18 million cut from its budget (*NY Times* 2/21/86); and Reagan's two-term military projection was $1.8 trillion (*NY Times* 5/14/85); swords against words. Only you can read between the lines. But the philosophy is not written down; philo-sophy is "love of wisdom," born of hope.

Reagan's Nicaragua rift began over an $18 million contract for *East* German troop carriers (*Newsweek* 6/28/80). And *West* Germany financed El Salvador with $18 million (*World News Digest* 7/27/84). HIT-LER had cast his shadow over Je-R-usa-L-em.

The myth that officials of "the Saviour" were "good guys" while those of "Old Nick" were "bad guys" fit our metaphor. But death squads of El Salvador also forced a march of the Techno State as they crushed the lives of people.

The USA lost its *Hasenfus* (rabit's foot). But people in his hometown said, "He was only doing his job." And Congressmen of the USA said Hasenfus and his comrades were "good Americans" (like "good Germans" who obeyed orders in World War II).

West Germany negotiated its involvement in Star Wars on 12/18 (*NY Times* 12/30/85). But Israel did not protest. The Aryan link to Iran had extended to Israel. And Mars, against the edge of time, looked into a cosmic mirror. The old Aryan-Alien-IS-RA-EL-HIT-LER complex that had been sucked into BE-RL-IN would be resolved only by healing Je-R-usa-L-em. But what of Mars & Co?

Also on 12/18, the Pentagon rejected pleas from Congress to delay Star Wars testing. The Pentagon cited "a scientific need" (*NY Times* 1/29/85). And the Star Wars test went off 1800 feet underground, as planned.

The CIA's 18,000 agents worldwide (*NY Times* 12/30/85) who were pro or anti terror at the whim of 666 were also "good soldiers" who could afford no personal consciences.

Aryan-Alien ghosts of World War II had marked a pattern distinctly Ger-man (which meant "strange-manna" in He-brew). And Reagan's slip, calling South America "South Africa" got into print in *the New York Times* (7/22/86).

When we listen closely to our words, the truth that is in our hearts can easily be found. Listen to you every word, without attachment or excuse, and you will find your true direction.

Libya paid $180,000 per year to combat-pilots from the USA to train Qaddafi's officers while rumors circulated that Libyan hit-men were out to kill Reagan (*NY Times* 11/1/81). And the news said, 18 people were killed at Israeli Airline counters by "Libyan-backed terrorists" (*NY Times* 12/30/85). And Natasha Simpson was murdered in what Oliver North referred to as "the Christmas massacre" planned by Abu Nidal.

Terrorists did not plan that exactly 18 would die (including terrorists). Still, 18 deaths in the headlines made the public ready for a mini-war between Qaddafi, "the warrior," and "666" — both employees of Mars & Co.

Just 12 days before the Libya bombing, Reagan asked Weinberger to improve the military's command structure "within 180 days" — an odd bit of news (*NY Times* 4/3/86). As the bombs hit Libya, "1800 Westerners" were within its borders (*McNeil/Lehr* 4/17/86). And afterward, on April 18th, Reagan said, "We weren't out to kill anybody."

The terrorist act (bombing a German night club) used to excuse the bombing was not Qaddafi's; but the Aryan mystique was on all sides.

When Navy planes cross an imaginary line that was drawn by the Libyan leader, said *the N.Y. Times* (3/22/86), "it will be the 18th time" since Reagan took office. And with that 18th flight, the mini-war between the USA and Libya began.

"Western reporters" were whisked to Tripoli to see "18 Soviet-made fighter jets" as a sign of Qaddafi's readiness (*NY Times* 1/26/86). But Reagan had refused to speak with Qaddafi even after Qaddafi asked. As news reports told of East and West divided, the karma of Abram-Abraham was evident internationally.

Samoza had supplied weapons to Haganah troops when those early Israelis carved out a nation in 1948. And the PLO had sent arms to the Nicaraguan Sandanistas who overthrew Samoza in 1979, in time for the election of 666 in Je-R-usa-L-em.

As Je-R-usa-L-em sought its center, the Statue of Liberty had 1800 corroded iron bars replaced by teflon-coated steel (*U.S. News* 5/19/86). But her torch-bearing right shoulder remained 18 inches off base. And from another angle in the Crystal, Shamir was elected in Israel's 36th year, 36 years after apartheid began in what was then "the Union of South Aftica" (the USA).

The 36 was "rebirth" in ancient mysticism. Both apartheid and Israel were established in 1948. And in 1984, 36 years later, 666 was re-elected. We have seen an elaborate reworking of our ancient karma, forming like a diamond, grown in Africa, cut in Israel, and sold to the Aryans, the "upper classes" of history's final days.

South Africa's Department of Education held the reins on 1.8 million "Black" schoolchildren (*NY Times* 9/13/86). Amnesty International reported 1800 "Blacks" killed under Apartheid (*NY Times* 9/27/86). Human rights groups said 1800 children were in detention (*NBC* 12/10/86). And after 18 months of "racial violence," Botha announced on April 18th that he was freeing "Blacks" who had violated the pass laws (*U.S. News* 4/28/86).

In the crystal mind-set, we have no such thing as "racial violence." In history, individuals were violent, hiding behind definitions of "race," but philo-sophy (love of wisdom) was also individual. So in Phase Three, our personal response-ability resolves the contradiction.

In April 1987, 18,000 "Black" transport workers were fired in South Africa. A total of 18 million pass-law jailings had occurred in 36 years of Apartheid. In the USA, 18 senators in doubt of his "racial bias" confirmed Chief Justice Rehnquist (*NY Times* 8/1/86). And "White Supremist" Robert Mills had 1800 prison inmates on his mailing list (*CBS* 8/18/86). For social class was no barrier to "racial" hatred. Even hatred cannot be properly called "racial" since hatred comes from the inside out; and philo-sophy does not let hatred in.

Chickens are raised in cages 12 by 18 inches (*NY Times* 1/1/86). The electric chair sits in a room 12 by 18 feet (*Time* 1/24/83). Mondale and Hart asked, "Where's the Beef?" And Reagan went for a photo-op at a burger chain, then forgot to pay his beef bill. We had swallowed the lower kingdom's hatred — nature's indigestible karma.

In Reagan's first year, price supports for the dairy industry cost the Government $1.8 billion (*NY Times* 10/15/81). And another $1.8 billion was spent to store nearly a half million pounds of cheese and butter (*Newsweek* 9/28/81).

The Department of Agriculture projected a trade surplus (mostly animal feed) of $18.6 billion for Reagan's third year (*NY Times* 12/16/83). And then, the karma of the golden calf began to build. Futures in the grain market dropped rapidly as financial futures zoomed to over half the traded stocks. Up from 18% in Ronald Reagan's first year (*NY Times* 11/18/85), speculation in absolutely abstract money had become the rage.

But farm spending by the Government rose to $18 billion (*NY Times* 12/16/85). So, then an 18-month slaughter of 1,550,403 cattle was mandated by Reagan's Farm Bill in 1986 (*NY Times* 3/29/86). And the number of dead would reduce to 18 (life), as decoded in numerology — 1+5+5+0+4+0+3.

Diablo nuclear power plant went on line after 666 began his 2nd term. **Diablo** (the devil) was a horse in *Stallion Road*, where horse doctor Reagan said, "I injected him with my serum 6 days ago. He should be on his feet by now." Doctor Reagan then got kicked (in the movie) by Diablo.

Cherno-byl drove up the price of beef, and many cattle were spared. But *cherno* meant "black" and *chert* meant "devil." Inordinate grain production brought financial gain that brought the slaughter of cattle. But how far did the karma go?

The USA's first lord and lady took colon and breast cancer in their stride while amber waves of grain fed their nation's beef-eating suicide.

Ram, Ram, Ram

Uric acid in meat digestion produced a combative disposition. But Ronald (6) Wilson (6) Reagan (6) was only human, a product of his times, poor devil. How could he have known about nutrition?

In his role, Reagan had the karma to rule the transition at history's end. And as the cow-boy partner to the sons of the wolf in Mars & Co., Reagan's first term ended while 1800 Disneyland employees were out on strike (*Newsweek* 10/8/84). Was "Fantasy Land" in danger?

In *Dark Victory*, Bette Davis tells Bogart that she is dying. She phones Murray Hill 7-7340. The scene changes. And Reagan invites her up to talk. But in the phone number was a riddle, well known at that time. And 7 7 3 4 spelled ℏ ℰ L L when inverted into a place name.

Jack Abbott, convict and author of *In the Belly of the Beast*, was released from jail only to be arrested again for a murder done on July 18th. A Saturday-Night-Live sketch joked about royalties he was paid — 18% (*NBC* 10/31/81). These were signs around Reagan — beyond good and evil.

As 666 left for Iceland, a nuclear submarine from the USSR got lost in 18,000 feet of water, 1200 miles east of New York (*NY Times* 10/12/86). And West Germany at that time feared Reagan would bargain away all but 18 of the 108 Pershings (*CS Monitor* 10/6/86). The focus came down to 18, to preserve "present Western ratios." But **Pershing** is from the Ger-man *Pfoershing*, related to *Pferch*, "a sheep-pen." For Germany had been turned into a missile sheep-pen, so "the nations" could work out the karma of Hitler, the wolf.

Britan fought to keep 1800 Falkland Islanders and their sheep in the falconer's land. And after the war, "a squadron of 180 bomb experts" in the area picked out "a total of 1.8 million fragments of mines" (*Time* 4/25/83).

Again, the signs said that we were struggling for "life" on a higher plane where we could be more aware in order to balance out the karma of the beast.

Around the U.N. were 1800 Secret Service agents as 666 gave a pre-Geneva speech to bolster Star Wars (10/24/85). Quoting an 18-year-old Kosygin speech, he said both sides needed weapons so neither would use them. Imagine if Star Wars worked! The fallout would destroy all life on Planet Earth.

As Marcos (Mars & Co.) left the Philipines, Ramos took over the Military. And as 1.8 million people were called "illegal" Aliens in the USA, the Aryan ("upper class") Marcos was made to feel at home (*NY Times* 2/21/86).

The outlawed Reform the Armed Forces Movement known as R.A.M. (*N.Y. Times* 9/14/87) that ousted Marcos then turned on Aquino. Was it the ram against the lamb again? Or was humanity crashing through its symbolic barriers to bio-reality?

Three years before 666's first election, an odd character named Ramtha was heard on Earth, first on the date of February 18th. Ramtha spoke via J.Z. Knight, who had worked with crystal pyramids. Nine years later, as the Iran-Contra scandal was unfolding, Shirley MacLaine, taken with Ramtha and others, gave the details of channeling to the air waves on ABC-TV, starting January 18th.

In the fires of Armageddon, Aquarius was being forged. And Christ's plans for reincarnation were born again. The human race would get to Heaven.

As one body, all men born of woman and of the spirit of civilization would journey forth.

The Armageddon gang wanted to take their bodies to Heaven also — but while others burned. They had misread the Christian plan.

And now, the Language Crystal answers the only question that humanity has ever really had. Can a religion that teaches love also practice hate?

LOVE's reflection begins our EVOL-ution.

Only one humanity shall travel forth; only one can win "the race" — that group of humans in love with its own evolving mythology. In the beginning is our law of spirit. And in the flesh we need no longer fear.

Hope

While **Hopi** Indians were symbols of hope against hope (tri-be vs mono-lith), "redistribution of 1.8 million acres of mineral-rich land in Arizona" was at stake (*N.Y. Times* 5/12/85). Aryan spirits had labeled the Hopis "Alien." For the "mineral rich" land held plutonium.

This final collection of tri-via brings to an end the facts to be presented in this work. I have omitted many details. And still, I would be glad to hear from you about similar information.

In 1812, the fires of two separate wars leveled the capitals of both the USA and USSR. This fact could be a warning. Yet, a harmony born in every child is the ignorance of death. And bliss in old age is found in that same eternal truth. We need never die when we live in the spirit.

A science text entitled *Creation by Natural Law* is a real book (U. of Wash. Press) written by a real professor named *R. L. Numbers*. And we never have been separated from "the Living Word."

The Senate did renew the Clean Water Act, but put an $18 billion cap on grants and loans (*NY Times* 7/24/85). Carter had vetoed the Public Water Works Bill. His excuse — $1.8 billion "extra costs" (10/2/78). And we still have a long way to go as the children of the Age of Aquarius demand a re-fertilization of the Planet Earth.

The first computer on Mars knew 18,000 words (*Dragons of Eden*, by Carl Sagan). And Solar One, the first solar power station, was 1818 mirrors sending electricity to hundreds of homes (*NBC* 4/14/82). And as 666 began his second term, "18 million personal computers" were in use in homes in the USA (*Time* 5/13/85).

During eight short years, the world as we knew it had crystallized on its surface. Biologically, we were a little worse for wear. Still, we were fundamentally human and could continue to evolve. We needed only be aware of the Spirit.

Remember that world (wer-alt) means "old man." And the old world (the old old man) is dying.

Now that his-story is over, we have a new old man, a mature father image who does not hide behind burning bushes.

We have now an open-story handed down by God and Goddess jointly, giving us many of the same old laws — monotheism, monogamy, money.

The wording is positive this time around. Thou shalt love. Thou shalt evolve. Still, we have more obligations with our new mind-set.

A tree was used to make the paper in this book. And living cells within the soil were used to feed that tree. "The Word" contains "the Life" that holds "the Word" that shall call forth another tree, so long as we are attuned to the cycle, so long as we and God agree.

THE END

INDEX

The bold page numbers indicate where a concept is defined or where the root meaning of a name is given in the text.

See also the Table of Contents
at the front of this book for a
guide to the CONCEPTS as
divided by chapter.

508

OUT OF ARMAGEDDON — INTO AQUARIUS

The solution to our planetary crisis
is already encoded in the words you speak.

The language that you speak today was born among the stars. And so, your thoughts are connected to a higher consciousness. And human beings now intend to reach the heavens by traveling in spaceships. Yet, we are destroying the Earth with pollution and acidic smoke, beyond the fear of fire.

The language that you speak today was derived from a species that roamed the Earth before the dawn of history. And so, your thoughts have their roots in primitive feelings. Imagine having the kind of fear that makes you back away like a wild beast when you see a fire. Imagine having contact with your primal primate instincts.

Yes, you have several modes of thought. You fear the fire (pre-consciously), you seek the light (super-naturally), and you are part of the eco-system. You have the solution to the crisis of acid rain and ozone depletion encoded in your daily speech. And with the keys to the Language Crystal Code, you you can interpret the messages that are hidden in the patterns of your very own words.

Also, here is a personal message that tells how the stunted language of "racism" effects our ability to think clearly about biology and how the myths of modern medicine can be solved by applying the Language Crystal Code.

Here is proof that Reaganomics was based on numerology, proof that the names of the Iran-Contra players fit a pattern linked to Biblical prophecy. And beyond the Armageddon metaphor, here is proof that natural foods will nourish us throughout the New Millennium.

This is more than a work of linguistic mysteries; it is the opening of a great demystification.

ABOUT THE AUTHOR

Six cups of coffee a day, stuck in a boring job at the local electric company, and hooked on alcohol, he joined the U.S. Air Force for a change of scenery. Then, Lawrence William Lyons was chosen to be a linguist with "Top Secret" duties. But his alcohol addiction blocked any advancement.

Honorably discharged in the Viet Nam era, he began smoking marijuana daily, yet gave the 1969 valedictory address at Manhattan Community College where he spoke against Nixon's secret Cambodian assault. Lawrence attributes his high grades on college exams to a linguistic trick, rather than to rigorous study habits.

After graduation, he hitchhiked to California, returning in time for "Woodstock." His habits grew to daily hashish, frequent mescaline, speed, LSD, and occasional cocaine and heroin. Still, he worked on a masters degree in child psychology.

Then came the miracle. In spite of psychology studies, his linguistic instincts led him to re-evaluate dyslexia while working with emotionally disturbed children in New York's Public School system. And from the roots of dyslexic speech and writing, Lawrence began to unravel the Language Crystal Code. He dropped out of "higher education" and gradually, during several years of meditation, shed his drug addictions. For thirteen years now he has eaten only raw fruits and vegetables — no bread, no wine, no drugs, not even aspirin. Most of what he eats is organically grown. And in this book, which took ten years to write, we find the astounding linguistic puzzle that tells not only why he eats only raw food but also why most other people do not.

This new synthesis of prehistoric bio-sounds and civilized techno-words tells how we can move from our present time of crisis (Armageddon) into the New Millennium (Aquarius), how the human bio-spirit can regain control of the Techno State.

And herein is documented a miracle of Biblical proportions with global magnitude. See the other side of this page for an explanation.